TESI GREGORIANA

Serie Teologia

84

JOY PALACHUVATTIL

«HE SAW»

The Significance of Jesus' Seeing
Denoted by the Verb εἶδεν
in the Gospel of Mark

EDITRICE PONTIFICIA UNIVERSITÀ GREGORIANA
Roma 2002

Vidimus et approbamus ad normam Statutorum Universitatis

Romae, ex Pontificia Universitate Gregoriana
die 22 mensis maii anni 2001

R.P. Prof. KLEMENS STOCK, S.J.
R.D. Prof. MARK COLERIDGE

GREGORIAN UNIVERSITY PRESS
Piazza della Pilotta, 35 - 00187 Rome, Italy

Dedicated to my parents

PREFACE

Many a student of the Gospel of Mark has been fascinated by its conciseness and its terse style. Mark the Evangelist is also famous for the preciseness of his expressions and the aptness of the words he employs in his narrative which often carry a wealth of meaning not immediately evident at first reading. One such word that is conspicuous for many reasons is the verb εἶδεν. I occupied myself with finding out what significance the Evangelist conveys when he uses the verb εἶδεν for Jesus' seeing. This book is the fruit of that research.

At the close of this academic odyssey, I raise my heart in deep gratitude to God who sustained me and gave me success throughout my studies and especially during the period of the research for this dissertation. I thank our heavenly mother, the Blessed Virgin Mary, whose intercession has been an ever powerful means for the completion of this work.

My debts to others are large, but not easy to define. I am specially indebted to Rev. Prof. Klemens Stock, SJ, who not only suggested to me the theme of this work, but also guided me towards its completion through his invaluable advice, painstaking but meticulous and accurate corrections, and above all for the much needed encouragement. To have as director of the thesis such a highly respected Markan specialist as Professor Stock was indeed a blessing. My sincere thanks is due to Professor Mark Coleridge for accepting to be the reader of this work and for the patience and competence with which he has done it.

I thank my superiors, past and present, who permitted me and encouraged me to pursue the studies here in Rome. I am grateful to Fr. General Séamus Freeman and the community at the Pallottine Generalate for the hospitality extended to me while studying for the licentiate degree at the Pontifical Biblical Institute. I owe a special debt of gratitude to the Sacred Heart Province of the Pallottines in Germany which in large part has financed my studies. My sincere thanks is due to the Provincial of the Italian Pallottine Province of the Mary Queen of Apostles Don Gaetano Ianni, the Rector Don Antonio Lotti and the Pallottine community as well as the parish community of Regina Pacis, Ostia, for their warm support and hospitality during my research. I appreciate the possibility offered there to integrate academic research with down-to-earth pastoral involvement. I acknowledge with gratitude the love and concern of the parish community of St. Agatha Pfarrei, Aschaffenburg, which welcomed me with open arms during my vacations, took good care of me and helped me to better my German.

I owe a great deal to the Pontifical Biblical Institute: its professors for their wisdom and commitment, for being a source of real inspiration, the Library for its marvellous collection, and the atmosphere at the Institute, which offered the ideal setting for serious study on the Word of God. I thank the Pontifical Gregorian University which offered me the possibility to reach my goal.

Finally, I say a big «thank you» to all my confreres and friends, especially my fellow countrymen at Ostia, who have helped me with their appreciation, encouragement and love. Special thanks to Fr. James Anchukandatil who read this work and corrected the grammar. I say a big «thank you» to my benefactors and well wishers whose huge support always accompanied my work. A big «thank you» to one and all who have contributed to bring this dissertation to a successful end.

INTRODUCTION

1. The Theme of the Study

This work examines the special nuance of Jesus' act of seeing that is expressed by the verb εἶδεν in the Gospel of Mark. The Evangelist Mark uses the verb five times to refer to Jesus' seeing. The first is the occasion of the baptism of Jesus, when Jesus *sees* the heavens being torn apart and the Spirit descending upon him like a dove (1,11). The next three uses of the verb are in the context of the call of Jesus' disciples; Jesus' call is preceded by his *seeing* them (1,16.19; 2,14). The verb is used of Jesus for the last time when he *sees* a great throng and has compassion on them (6,34). The eyes that see the heavens being torn apart, see the disciples and later see the crowd. The work will try to establish the rich concentration of meaning with regard to Jesus' seeing as denoted by the verb εἶδεν.

2. The Limits of the Study

Mark employs a variety of Greek verbs to denote the action of seeing. But he shows a marked preference for the verb ὁρᾶν. There are several occurrences of the verb and its derivatives in the Gospel. It is not our intention to do an in-depth analysis of each of the occurrences of the verb. Neither is it the purpose of the work to investigate every instance of Jesus' seeing reported in the Gospel. Our focus narrows down to the aorist, active, indicative, third person, singular, εἶδεν which is used in the Gospel of Mark exclusively to refer to the seeing of Jesus. The seeing of other characters in the Gospel are also analysed only in so far as it serves to highlight the uniqueness of Jesus' seeing by way of contrast and dissimilarity.

3. Status Quaestionis

In our investigation we have not come across any study that primarily focuses its attention on the aspect of Jesus' seeing denoted by the verb εἶδεν in the Gospel of Mark. However, we have an article of E. Bosetti[1] which illustrates the Gospel of Mark as tracing a journey of faith for the reader, proposing ultimately a new mode of seeing. E. Bosetti highlights the tension that is evident in the Gospel between, on the one hand those who are marked by their inability to see, not «knowing to see and not wanting to see, and on the other hand, Jesus' enabling the blind to see and leading the disciples as well as the readers to a new mode of seeing. The reader is called upon to undertake a journey of faith, a journey to see. In a recently published work[2] the same author develops this theme and delineates the disciples' journey of faith as a journey to see as well as a journey to follow.

It may be noted that E. Bosetti investigates the action of seeing in general terms without distinguishing between the various shades of meanings conveyed by the different Greek vocabulary. The author does not limit herself to examining any particular Greek verb nor does she concentrate on Jesus' seeing alone. All the same, E. Bosetti has noted the importance and profundity of Jesus' seeing[3]. But her interest lies in tracing a journey of faith for the disciples or for the reader that in the last analysis would be a journey to see. So the focus of E. Bosetti's studies is on seeing as human response in faith. Our work's concentration is in finding out what is implied in Jesus' seeing.

We may also allude to two more monographs that treat the theme of seeing. The first is the work of H.-J. Steichele, in which the author gives an excursus on the «theological significance of seeing in Mark's Gospel»[4]. He analyses two examples of seeing that gain importance in the Gospel: 4,11f. (βλέποντες βλέπωσιν καὶ μὴ ἴδωσιν) and 8,18 (ὀφθαλμοὺς ἔχοντες οὐ βλέπετε). However, the subject-matter of his investigation centres around the disciples' seeing. Besides, the verbs examined are also different from εἶδεν. So H.-J. Steichele's work does

---

[1] E. BOSETTI, «Un cammino per vedere», 123-145.

[2] E. BOSETTI, Marco. Il rischio di credere.

[3] For instance on Jesus' seeing the first disciples E. Bosetti writes,: «I racconti di vocazione iniziano tutti segnalando lo sguardo di Gesù che va diritto alla persona e coglie ciò che è unico e irripetibile. Coglie anzitutto l'identità personale, bene espressa dal nome [...]. Lo sguardo di Gesù raggiunge la persona nella sua unicità». Cf. E. BOSETTI, Marco. Il rischio di credere, 24.

[4] H.-J. STEICHELE, Der leidende Sohn Gottes, 219-220.

not directly pertain to our topic. The second work is of C. Hergen-röder[5]. In a lengthy study, the author investigates the vocabulary for seeing in St. John's Gospel and brings out its significance in the context of Jesus' self-revelation and human response. C. Hergenröder treats «Jesus' seeing of men» at some length[6]. However, this work too does not concern our study not only because it focuses on John's Gospel but also for the reason that seeing is here viewed once again from the human perspective. Therefore it will be the purpose of this study to try to discover what Mark has in mind when he uses the verb εἶδεν for Jesus' seeing.

4. Method

We shall employ the synchronic method in our study, since it concentrates on the finished text of the Gospel. What interests us is the message that Mark wants to communicate to us through his Gospel in its final form. The synchronic analysis sees the text as a structured, coherent quantity. The elements of the text are interrelated. Out of these relationships there emerges a unity of form[7]. However, the method also accords due importance to the individual elements of the text. As far as our study is concerned, the linguistic-syntactic, semantic and narrative analysis gains added importance since our interest is to determine the meaning of Jesus' action of seeing denoted by the verb εἶδεν. Nevertheless, in order to discover the meaning of Jesus' seeing as well as to establish the bond that links the five instances of his seeing, we need to also analyse the pericopes in which the verb occurs. The synchronic method would view these pericopes as belonging to a coherent whole, obtaining their meaning within the wider context of the Gospel of Mark.

---

[5] C. HERGENRÖDER, *Wir schauten seine Herrlichkeit*.

[6] Cf. C. HERGENRÖDER, *Wir schauten seine Herrlichkeit*, 174-175. He concludes it with the following observation: «Bei einem Blick zurück auf die Stellen, an denen Jesus Subjekt des Sehens auf Menschen ist, zeigt sich als Gemeinsamkeit: Die Formen von ἰδεῖν bezeichnen immer das einmalige, aktive Hinblicken Jesu. Jesus beherrscht mit seinem Blick die Situation. Er hat mit den Menschen, die in seinem Blick treten, etwas vor, sei es, daß er ihnen etwas sie selbst Betreffendes zeigen möchte (1,47.48.50; 19,26f), sei es, daß er an ihnen die "Werke Gottes" offenbar machen (vgl. 9,3) will (5,6; 9,1)».

[7] Cf. W. EGGER, *Methodenlehre*, 74.

5. Division of Work

This study consists of four chapters with a general conclusion. The first chapter shall examine all the occurrences of Greek words used by Mark to refer to the action of seeing and determine their exact meaning. Subsequently, the seeing of the different characters in the Gospel shall be evaluated. The inquiry will then narrow down to the verb ὁρᾶν/ἰδεῖν/εἶδεν. Before concluding the chapter, a note on God's seeing in the Old Testament shall be presented.

The second chapter shall deal with the first instance of Jesus' seeing expressed by the verb εἶδεν, that of his seeing the heavens being torn apart and the Spirit descending upon him (1,10). In analysing this event, we shall first establish Jesus' baptism as the context of his seeing and then examine the episode of his baptism. Subsequently we shall highlight Jesus' visionary experience, determine the objects of his seeing and verify the scope of his vision. The auditory experience that accompanies Jesus' seeing shall then be examined. Establishing the import of the vision and the voice is the final interest of the chapter.

The third chapter is comparatively lengthy as it occupies itself with the analysis of three instances of Jesus' seeing denoted by εἶδεν (1,16.19; 2,14). All three instances occur in the context of the call of five prospective disciples of Jesus. We shall begin the chapter by noting the common features of the three narratives that speak of Jesus' seeing them. Then, we shall treat all three narratives separately following a more or less similar procedure of making the Synoptic comparison of the narratives, analysis of Jesus' seeing: characteristics of his seeing, objects of his seeing, description of those whom he sees, the call issued to those whom he sees, their response, and by providing a summary of the analysis. Subsequently we shall establish the decisiveness of Jesus' seeing by holding it up against similar narratives of both Old and New Testaments. The chapter shall then proceed to establish the significance of Jesus' seeing as well as calling of the disciples. We argue in this chapter that Jesus' seeing implies an invitation to communion; communion with Jesus, communion with the Father as well as the Spirit, and communion with one another. We also hold that Jesus' seeing implies an invitation to share in Jesus' own mission.

The fourth chapter shall treat the fifth and the final instance of Jesus' seeing referred to by the verb εἶδεν: Jesus sees a great crowd (6,34). In studying this event we shall begin by noting the placement of 6,34 in its context and then describe the situation preceding Jesus' seeing. This shall be followed by an analysis of Jesus' seeing proper. We shall determine the crowd as object of Jesus' seeing, establish the effects of that seeing on Jesus, verify the reason for the feeling of compassion evoked in him, investigate the result of that compassion translated into a two-fold activity of teaching and feeding. We shall conclude by establishing the significance of Jesus' seeing the crowd.

The general conclusion shall sum up the significance of Jesus' seeing denoted by the verb εἶδεν, that we have established during the course of the study. We shall bring out the revelatory aspect of Jesus' seeing, highlight Jesus' seeing as an invitation to communion and establish the vocational and ecclesiological dimension of Jesus' seeing.

CHAPTER I

Mark's Vocabulary For «Seeing»

Mark's Gospel is a narrative. A narrative is made up of sentences, episodes, sequences and a general design. Sentences are the basic units of the narrative. They are words arranged according to grammatical and syntactical rules and conventions. The sentence structure is of crucial importance in determining the meaning of a text. Every individual narrator has a particular way of using words in a sentence while exhibiting preference for a few words. In describing the action of seeing of various characters in his narrative Mark employs several words. However the narrative exhibits his preference for the verb ὁρᾶν and its derivatives. This chapter shall analyse the different words that Mark uses in referring to seeing.

1. Greek Words Used by Mark to Refer to the Action of seeing

In analysing the verbs for seeing we shall pick up those verbs used by Mark that mean the physical action of seeing. The verb ὁρᾶν and its derivatives are most prominent among them. However, the verb βλέπειν and its variants are also extensively used by him. The other less occurring words are θεωρεῖν and εὑρίσκειν[1].

---

[1] Another verb that occurs in the Gospel is θεᾶσθαι. But there are only two occurrences of the verb in the Gospel of Mark and they occur in the canonical ending of the Gospel: θεασαμένοις - 16,14 (aorist middle participle) and ἐθεάθη - 16,11 (aorist passive). Θεᾶσθαι is a synonym of ὁρᾶν. It also means *to see, to visit*. In the passive *it means to be seen by someone* (cf. BAGD, 360). E. Bosetti identifies 7 verbs used in the Gospel to refer to seeing: θεωρεῖν, ὁρᾶν, βλέπειν, ἀναβλέπειν, ἐμβλέπειν, διαβλέπειν, περιβλέπεσθαι. Cf. E. BOSETTI, «Un cammino per vedere», 123, n.1. For

1.1 ὁρᾶν

The verb ὁρᾶν and its derivatives occur 59 times[2] in the Gospel of Mark. In the present tense the verb is used only thrice, twice as imperatives (ὅρα - 1,44 and ὁρᾶτε - 8,15) and once in the first person singular (ὁρῶ - 8,24). Except for three uses in the future tense (ὄψονται - 13,26; ὄψεσθε - 14,62; 16,7) all other uses of the verb are in the aorist tense. In the aorist tense itself there is only one instance of the use of the verb in the passive (ὤφθη - 9,4). The aorist active participle form of the verb is the most common use (ἰδών - 12 times: 2,5; 5,6.22; 6,48; 8,33; 9,20.25; 10,14; 11,13; 12,28.34; 15,39; ἰδόντες - 5 times: 2,16; 5,16; 6,49; 7,2; 9,15; and ἰδοῦσα - twice: 14,67.69). The aorist active indicative form is also widely used (εἶδον - 7 times: 6,33.50; 9,8.9.14; 11,20; 16,5; εἶδεν - 5 times: 1,10.16.19; 2,14; 6,34; εἴδομεν - twice: 2,12; 9,38). Another commonly used form is the aorist active imperative (ἴδε - 9 times: 2,24; 3,34; 11,21; 13,1.21[2]; 15,4.35; 16,6; ἴδετε - once: 6,38)[3]. Less frequent is the aorist active subjunctive form (ἴδωμεν - twice: 15,32.36; ἴδητε - twice: 13,14.29; ἴδωσιν - twice: 4,12; 9,1; ἴδω - once: 12,15). The aorist active infinitive ἰδεῖν is used just twice (5, 14.32).

The verb in classical Greek as well as in its normal usage means *to see, to catch sight of, to experience, to witness*. It could also further mean *to look at or upon*[4].

The subject of ὁρᾶν in the NT is usually Jesus, the disciples, the sick, the Pharisees or the crowd. There is one instance in which πνεῦμα is the subject of ὁρᾶν (Mark 9,20). In Rev 12,13 ὁρᾶν has δράκων as its subject. This anthropocentric usage has paved the way for its figurative meaning, *notice, recognise, understand* (Matt 9,2; Gal 2,14), *test*

the same list see also G.D. KILPATRICK, «Verbs of Seeing», 179-180. But since the last four are only compound verbs of βλέπειν we shall treat them together.

[2] All the statistics presented are put together with the help of HERMENEUTIKA™, *Bible Works for Windows*, Edition Version 3. 5, Serial Registration Number BWW 3526-00, 009, 876.

[3] Strictly speaking the particle ἰδού is an aorist middle imperative form of ὁρᾶν. There are 7 occurrences of them in the Gospel of Mark (1,2; 3,32; 4,3; 10,28.33; 14,41.42). However, as an imperative it would have a circumflex accent instead of the acute accent. All the instances in the Gospel of Mark are with acute accent, implying that they are almost devoid of their imperative force, and are used as explanatory particle with the meaning of see, look, behold. We shall therefore treat them as particle and not consider them as examples of the verb ὁρᾶν.

[4] BAGD, 577-578.

(Luke 2,15), *find* (Matt 2,11), *meet* (Rom 1,11) or *visit* (1Cor 16,7). In the imperative ὁρᾶν often means *take heed* (Matt 16,6; Mark 8,15), *see to it* (Acts 18,15)[5].

1.2 Βλέπειν

There are 15 occurrences of the verb βλέπειν and its derivatives in the Gospel of Mark. The present active participle as well as the present active subjunctive forms occur just once each (βλέποντες - 4,12; βλέπωσιν - 4,12). There are 5 occurrences of the present active indicative form (βλέπω - once: 8,24; βλέπεις - 4 times: 5,31; 8,23; 12,14; 13,2). The most common form is the present active imperative (βλέπετε - 8 times: 4,24; 8,15.18; 12,38; 13,5.9.23.33). There are also 17 instances of the compound forms of βλέπειν: περιβλεψάμενος - 4 times: 3,5.34; 10,23; 11,11; περιβλεψάμενοι - once: 9,8; περιεβλέπετο - once: 5,32; ἀναβλέψας - 3 times: 6,41; 7,34; 8,24; ἀναβλέψασαι - once: 16,4; ἀναβλέψω - once: 10,51; ἀνέβλεψεν - once: 10,52; ἐμβλέψας - twice: 10,21.27; ἐμβλέψασα - once: 14,67; ἐνέβλεπεν - once: 8,25; διέβλεψεν - once: 8,25.

βλέπειν is a synonym of ὁρᾶν. It also means to *see, look, view, notice, watch, comprehend*. Even before the NT times the original meaning of «seeing» had been extended to mean *look deeply into, see through, become aware of the essence*[6].

1.3 Θεωρεῖν

There are 7 instances of the verb θεωρεῖν in the Gospel of Mark. The present active indicative form has 3 examples: θεωρεῖ - 5,38; θεωροῦσιν - 5,15; 16,4. The present active participle form occurs only once: θεωροῦσαι - 15,40. The other 3 instances are all in the imperfect active indicative form: ἐθεώρουν- 3,11; 15,47; ἐθεώρει - 12,41.

The verb θεωρεῖν means *to be a spectator, look at, observe, perceive, see, notice, find*[7]. Just like βλέπειν, θεωρεῖν also is a synonym of ὁρᾶν.

1.4 Εὑρίσκειν

The verb εὑρίσκειν occurs 11 times in the Gospel of Mark. There is only one present active indicative form: εὑρίσκει - 14,37. The imperfect

---

[5] J. KREMER, «"ὁράω", see», 527.
[6] P.-G. MÜLLER, «βλέπω», 222.
[7] BAGD, 360.

form also occurs just once: ηὕρισκον - 14,55. The future active indicative form has two instances: εὑρήσει - 11,13 and εὑρήσετε - 11,2. There is one example of aorist active subjunctive form: εὕρη- 13,36. The rest of the 6 usages are all in the aorist active indicative form: εὕ ρεν - 7,30; 11,13; 14,40; εὗρον - 1,37; 11,4; 14,16.

εὑρίσκειν does not mean to see but *to find, discover, come upon*[8]. However, the verb is in some way connected to ὁράω which can also some times mean *to find*.

1.5 *Other Verbs Related to the Verb of Seeing*

A close reading of Mark's Gospel makes clear that seeing is expressed implicitly by many other verbs of sense perception which are also closely related to the verbs of seeing. We shall mention just the most prominent of these verbs. συνιέναι which occurs in Mark 5 times (4 times on the lips of Jesus: 4,12; 7,14; 8,17.21; and once used of apostles: 6,52) originally meant to *bring together*, but later it was taken to mean to *understand, comprehend, grasp, perceive*[9]. ἐπιγινώσκειν occurs 4 times in the Gospel (2,8; 5,30 - both used of Jesus; 6,33.54 - both used of the crowd) meaning to *know exactly, completely, through and through, recognise, learn, find out, perceive, notice, understand*[10]. γινώσκειν is a rather common verb in Mark, occurring 12 times (4,13; 5,29.43; 6,38; 7,24; 8,17 [the only time used of Jesus]; 9,30; 12,12; 13,28.29; 15,10.45). It means to *know, come to know, learn, ascertain, find out, understand, comprehend, perceive, notice, realise*[11]. Similar ideas are also conveyed by verbs such as εἰδέναι (occurring 18 times: 1,24; 2,10; 4,10.27; 5,33; 6,20; 10,19.38.42; 11,13; 12,14.15.24; 13,32.33.35; 14,68.71), νοεῖν (3 times: 7,18; 8,17; 13,14), ἀγνοεῖν (once: 9,32) ἐπίστασθαι(once: 14,68) μανθάνειν (once: 13, 28).

It is also worth noting that there are instances in which some of these verbs stand parallel to ὁρᾶν. For example, in 4,12 συνιῶσιν stands parallel to ἴδωσιν, thus highlighting the intrinsic connection not only between seeing (perceiving) and understanding but also between seeing and hearing (ἀκούειν). ἀκούειν occurs 44 times in Mark and 3 times it occurs in parallel to seeing (4,12; 8,18; 12,28). There is also an example of νοεῖν standing parallel to ἴδητε in 13,14.

---

[8] BAGD, 324-325.
[9] H. BALZ, «συνίημι», 307.
[10] BAGD, 290-291.
[11] BAGD, 160-161.

2. Markan Usage of the Vocabulary of Seeing

From the statistics above it is evident that Mark does not use the different vocabulary he has in his possession at random. Even though he employs synonyms in conveying his thought every selection of the verb and its form carries a specific meaning. Therefore it is important to single out the particular usage of the verb and its form in order to arrive at their meaning. This analysis, however, shall be limited only to the verbs of seeing.

2.1 Use of ὁρᾶν and its Derivatives

Mark's preference of the verb ὁρᾶν is clear from its 59 occurrences in the Gospel. He naturally uses several forms of the verb in his narrative. It is useful to treat these forms separately.

2.1.1 Aorist Active Participle Forms of ὁρᾶν

It has been noted that the verbal form of ὁρᾶν that Mark uses most commonly is the aorist active participle. Mark uses these participles mainly as *supplementary participles*[12]. Though other types of participles are well attested in the Gospel, ὁρᾶν being a word of perception, its participles are used in most cases as preparation for the main action of the sentence. The sequence almost always is: participle + the accusative noun or pronoun or as in some examples noun-clauses as object of the verb[13] + main verb.

Though participles originally had no temporal function, the aorist participle, since it expresses a notion of completion before the finite verb, has acquired to a certain degree an idea of relative past time. The same holds true for the participle coming after the verb[14]. Usually the main verb in our texts is aorist but sometimes present: Mark 2,5; 6,48; 7,5; 14,67 and sometimes imperfect: 2,16.

---

[12] BDF, § 416.

[13] Such noun-clauses are expressed by the conjunction ὅτι. It has to be noted also that in some cases there is no express mention of the object (e.g., 10,14) but it is understood from the context.

[14] BDF, § 339; J.H. MOULTON, *New Testament Greek*, 79-81. The authors further note that such an element of past time is absent from the aorist participle if its action is identical with that of an aorist finite verb: Acts 1,24 καὶ προσευξάμενοι εἶπαν and its reverse Mark 14,39 προσηύξατο [...] εἰπών.

a) ἰδών

The aorist active participle ἰδών as masculine singular in the nominative case occurs 12 times in the Gospel of Mark. Of these, 7 examples refer to an express action of Jesus: 2,5; 6,48; 8,33; 9,25; 10,14; 11,13; 12,34. The other 5 uses refer to an action of varied characters in the narrative: 5,6 - the demoniac; 5,22 - Jairus; 9,20 - the dumb spirit; 12,28 - one of the scribes; 15,39 - the Centurion.

+ ἰδών Referring to Jesus

As noted above the participle is used in the Gospel as a preparation for the main verb. Of the 7 instances of ἰδών referring to Jesus the main verb in 5 cases is aorist (8,33; 9,25; 10,14; 11,13; 12,34) and in 2 cases present (2,5; 6,48). The action of seeing expressed by ἰδών leaves different impressions on Jesus. In 5 instances the main verb expresses a verbal reaction of Jesus: forgiving sins of the paralytic as he sees the faith of the four men on the roof (2,5), rebuking Peter for his lay thinking as he turns around and sees his other disciples (8,33), rebuking the unclean spirit as he sees the crowd coming running together (9,25), encouraging the children to come to him seeing his disciples rebuking their parents (10,14), and extending a word of approval seeing that the scribe answered wisely (12,34). In the other two instances the reaction of Jesus is to approach what he sees: seeing the disciples making headway painfully in the rough sea Jesus walks up to them (6,48), seeing in the distance a fig tree in leaf he goes to see if he could find anything on it (11,13).

Forgiving sins (2,5), rebuking Peter (8,33) and rebuking the unclean spirit (9,25) all point out Jesus' superiority and the authority of Jesus' effective command. Expressing indignation at the disciples' behaviour of keeping children away from him (10,14) once again shows that he alone is in command. Even in his approval of the Scribe's answer, the initiative shifts to Jesus (12,34). He passed the test so much so that «no one dared to ask him any question» (12,34). Walking on the sea (6,48) certainly carries an emphasis on Jesus' supernatural power. Cursing the fig tree on not finding fruits on it and the resultant withering of the tree (11,12-14) shows the power of Jesus' word. Thus the subsequent actions of Jesus introduced by ἰδών highlight Jesus' authority and supernatural power.

+ ἰδών Referring to those Positively Disposed to Jesus

The first example in this regard is that of Jairus (5,22). Jairus' seeing Jesus parallels the demoniac's seeing Jesus (5,6). But unlike the demoniac who does an act of obeisance to Jesus, Jairus goes a step further, falls at his feet (πίπτει) and beseeches him (παρακαλεῖ). The present tense of the main verbs dramatises the desperation of Jairus. While «falling at his feet» (cf. 1,40; 7,25) acknowledges the authority of Jesus, «beseeching» highlights Jesus' power (cf. 1,40; 5,10; 6,56; 7,32; 8,22).

The Roman Centurion is the example *par excellence*. He sees Jesus breathing his last by letting out an extraordinarily loud cry and declares his profession of faith in Jesus, «Truly this man was the Son of God» (15,39). The Centurion's seeing is in sharp contrast to that of the chief priests who challenge Jesus to come down from the cross: ἵνα ἴδωμεν καὶ πιστεύσωμεν (15,32), and to the curiosity of the bystanders and the one who offered the sour wine who said: Ἄφετε ἴδωμεν εἰ ἔρχεται Ἠλίας καθελεῖν αὐτόν (15,36). But it is the privilege of this Roman official to see what they fail to see. The Centurion's declaration affirms the voice from heaven «Thou art my beloved Son; with thee I am well pleased» (1,11)[15] and it contrasts with the high priest's charging Jesus with blasphemy for having declared that he himself was the Son of the Blessed One (14,61-64). This outsider's seeing leads him to faith in Jesus' divinity and his identity as the Son of God.

+ ἰδών Referring to those with Ambivalent Attitude towards Jesus

The Gerasene Demoniac's reaction to «seeing Jesus from a distance» (5,6) is to run, not away from Jesus but toward him to confront him and possibly to get rid of him. Even from a distance the demoniac (unclean spirit cf. 1,23; 3,11; 5,2; 6,7; 7,25; 9,25) recognises Jesus' superior power and his «bowing» (προσεκύνησεν) is an acknowledgement of Jesus' divine majesty. The submissive obedience to Jesus' commands subsequently highlights Jesus awesome power to do the impossible.

The dumb spirit who possessed the boy, on seeing Jesus (9,20), convulses the boy in such a way probably as to intimidate Jesus. The vivid details of the unclean spirit's hold over the boy and the father's description of the boy's plight from childhood point out that only

---

[15] On the significance of the Centurion's confession see K. STOCK, «Das Bekenntnis des Centurio», 289-301.

extraordinarily superior power can liberate the boy. Once again the evil spirit can not withstand Jesus' command and it buckles under Jesus' divine majesty.

The scribe who approaches Jesus (12,28) sees him answering the Sadducees well. It is clear that the scribe too wants to dispute with Jesus with a view, perhaps, to corner him on a question that is more serious, the very commandment of God. Jesus' declaration that the scribe is «not far from the kingdom of God» (v. 34) may mean only a final turn around. The statement that «after that no one dared to ask him any question» (v. 34) speaks of the scribe's initial intention. The fact that Jesus has the upper hand shows his superiority and control over the situation.

b) ἰδόντες

Of the 5 occurrences of the aorist active masculine plural participle nominative ἰδόντες in the Gospel of Mark, the main verb in one case is present (7,2-5), once imperfect (2,16) and in 3 cases aorist (5,16; 6,49; 9,15). The participle refers twice to the Pharisees and scribes (2,16; 7,2) twice to the people or the crowd (5,16; 9,15) and once to the disciples. The object of seeing in 4 cases is either Jesus himself or some thing that he does (2,16; 5,16; 6,49; 9,15). Only once the action of Jesus' disciples becomes the object of seeing (7,2).

+ Pharisees and Scribes as Subject of ἰδόντες

The «scribes of the Pharisees» (2,16) see Jesus eating with tax collectors and sinners and are indignant. But they have no courage to confront Jesus directly and therefore question the disciples regarding this behaviour of Jesus. Their reluctance to ask Jesus point to their fear of Jesus' authority especially after the previous episode in which Jesus strongly deflected their criticism (2,1-12).

Concern for the Law and ritual purity once again brings the Pharisees and scribes in confrontation with Jesus (7,2). They see some of Jesus' disciples eat with hands defiled and this time they muster the courage to confront him directly. But Jesus counter-attacks them quoting the prophet Isaiah. Once again Jesus' superiority is on display. The Pharisees and scribes are defeated, they do not even dare to respond to him.

+ People or the Crowd as Subject of ἰδόντες

The people see what have happened to the demoniac and the swine (5,16) and they respond with fear and ask Jesus to leave their territory. There is no element of antagonism towards Jesus. It is kind of fear born out of respect and acknowledgement of Jesus' power.

The crowd see Jesus along with his chosen disciples coming down from the mountain after the transfiguration and they respond with amazement (9,15: ἐξεθαμβήθησαν). On witnessing Jesus healing the man with an unclean spirit too, the crowd react with owe (1,27: ἐθαμβήθησαν)[16]. But here the very sight of Jesus causes amazement and the compound form of the verb used accentuates their reaction[17].

+ The Disciples as Subject of ἰδόντες

The disciples see Jesus walking on the sea and they cry out thinking that it is a ghost (6,49). Though their initial reaction is one of fear, it corresponds to that of an epiphany[18]. They cry out at such an awesome sight of Jesus walking on the sea.

c) ἰδοῦσα

There are only two instances of the aorist active feminine participle nominative ἰδοῦσα in the Gospel of Mark (14,67.69). The participle in both cases is followed by a verb in the aorist. In both cases ἰδοῦσα refers to the maid of the high priest who spots Peter warming himself and obviously Peter is the object of her seeing. Peter's courage fails under pressure from a mere maid and at first he pretends not to understand her (v. 67) and when pressed further on being one of the disciples of Jesus he just denies it (v. 69).

---

[16] Amazement is a normal reaction of the crowd at Jesus' words and deeds. Mark employs other terms also to express this kind of reaction. (cf. 1,22: ἐξεπλήσσοντο; 2,12: ἐξίστασθαι; 5,42: ἐξέστησαν; 6,2: ἐξεπλήσσοντο; 6,51: ἐξίσταντο; 7,37: ἐξεπλήσσοντο).

[17] There are two more instances of the use of the compound form of the verb in the Gospel of Mark. The context of these uses suggest extreme awe: 14,33 - the prospect of imminent death; 16,6 - seeing a young man seated instead of the corpse of Jesus. The use of the same compound form to present the reaction of the crowd raises questions as to what causes such an extreme amazement. R.H. Gundry holds that the glistening white garments of his transfiguration may explain the reaction of the crowd. Cf. R.H. GUNDRY, *Mark*, 487-488.

[18] R.A. GUELICH, *Mark*, 351.

2.1.2 Aorist Active Indicative Forms of ὁρᾶν

Aorist active Indicative forms of ὁρᾶν rank second only to the aorist active participle forms in their use in the Gospel of Mark. There are only three attested forms of the aorist active indicative in the Gospel: εἶδον, εἶδεν and εἴδομεν.

a) *Εἶδον*

Of the seven occurrences of εἶδον twice Jesus is also included among those who see (9,14; 11,20). In both examples the reference is to Jesus and the disciples. In all the other instances the object of εἶδον is either Jesus (6,33: disciples also included; 6,50; 9,8) or what happens to him (9,9: transfiguration) or a heavenly being (16,5: the young man sitting in the tomb). It is of interest to note that the verb is never used to refer to anyone antagonistic to Jesus; neither the demons nor the Pharisees and scribes are subject of εἶδον. Three times the disciples are the subject, once the crowd and the last instance refers to the devout women at the tomb.

+ Jesus and the Disciples as Subject of εἶδον

From the mount of Transfiguration Jesus came down along with the chosen disciples Peter, James and John toward the remaining disciples and they saw a great crowd about them, and scribes arguing with them (9,14). The mention of the «great crowd» (cf. 5,21.24; 6,34; 8,1; 12,37) shows that Jesus is always sought after by many people. Since Jesus subsequently asks the crowd the question, why they are disputing with the disciples (v. 16), the crowd should probably be included with the scribes in disputation (v. 14). The disciples' inability to cast out a dumb spirit turns out to be the reason behind the disputation (vv. 17-19). Jesus' ability to perform the exorcism will stand out in sharp contrast to the inability of the disciples[19].

Jesus' and his disciples' seeing of the fig tree withered away to its roots (11,20) refers back to the incident of Jesus cursing the same tree (v. 14). Jesus' word is so powerful that the tree just withers. Jesus uses Peter's pointing out the withered tree to reveal the startling fact that faith can move mountains (vv. 22-26).

---

[19] R.H. GUNDRY, *Mark*, 487.

+ The Disciples as Subject of εἶδον

In two instances Jesus is the direct object of the disciples' seeing (6,50; 9,8) and in the third instance εἶδον has as its object the whole event of the transfiguration (9,9). The disciples' seeing Jesus walking on the sea (6,50) carries forward the theme of epiphany we referred to above[20]. The forward position of πάντες and αὐτόν stresses that nobody missed seeing him and that it was truly Jesus whom they saw[21].

The other two reference to the disciples' seeing is in the context of Transfiguration. However, here the word is used only of the chosen disciples Peter, James and John. After witnessing Jesus' Transfiguration and having heard the conversation between Jesus, Elijah and Moses, and having listened to the divine imperative to hear Jesus, the disciples suddenly looked around and they no longer saw anyone with them but Jesus only (9,8). Their not seeing anyone but Jesus reinforces the point that the disciples should pay attention solely to Jesus.

While descending from the mountain Jesus commands the select three not to relate to anyone what they had seen (ἃ εἶδον) till after the resurrection (9,9). The forward position of ἃ εἶδον is meant to stress all what they had experienced on the high mountain.

+ Εἶδον Used of Other People

The people saw them (Jesus and the disciples) going away in the boat (6,33). Their immediate response was to run on foot and to overtake them. The mention that people «from all the towns» show the great popularity of Jesus and his ability to attract people to himself.

Early on the first day of the week Mary Magdalene and Mary the mother of James and Salome on entering the tomb, saw a young man sitting on the right side, dressed in a white robe (16,5). The young man by implication is an angel (cf. Tob 4,5-10). He sits on the right side, the position of authority[22]. The response of the women on seeing him is extreme amazement. They see a heavenly figure and they cannot believe their eyes.

---

[20] Cf. p. 23.
[21] R.H. GUNDRY, *Mark*, 336.
[22] R.H. GUNDRY, *Mark*, 991.

b) Εἶδεν

Mark uses the verb εἶδεν five times and exclusively to refer to Jesus' seeing. The first is the occasion of the baptism of Jesus, when Jesus *saw* the heavens being torn apart and the Spirit descending upon him like a dove (1,11). The next three uses of the verb are in the context of the call of Jesus' disciples. Passing along by the sea of Galilee Jesus *saw* Simon and Andrew and he called them (1,16); going on a little further he *saw* James the son of Zebedee and John his brother and he called them also (1,19) and finally he *saw* Levi sitting at the tax office and he called him too (2,14). The verb is used of Jesus for the last time when he *saw* a great throng and had compassion on them (6,34). The focus of this study is to bring out the significance of the usage of this verb for Jesus.

c) Εἴδομεν

Of the two occurrences of εἴδομεν the first example refers to the crowd who saw the unbelievable miracle of the paralytic going out on his legs in front of them all and marvel at it (2,12). Their wonder leads them to glorify God which in turn is a recognition of Jesus' authority and power on earth (v. 10). The other instance of εἴδομεν refers to the disciples who saw a man casting out demons in Jesus' name (9,38). Even the mere use of Jesus' name is so powerful that it can effect wonders. But the disciples' response is to restrain the unauthorised exorcist. Jesus has a different point of view, if he is «not against us [he] is for us»(v. 40).

2.1.3 Aorist Active Imperative Forms

The aorist imperative ἴδε which occurs 9 times in the Gospel of Mark has been translated by the RSV as *look* 5 times (2,24; 11,21; 13,1.21[2]), as *see* twice (15,4; 16,6) as *here* in 3,34 and as *behold* in 15,35. Though an imperative, ἴδε functions more as a particle with the meanings of *see, look, here is, here* etc. Therefore in our investigation of the verb ὁρᾶν we would consider ἴδε as a particle.

The plural form ἴδετε is attested only once (6,38). Jesus commands the disciples to «go and see» what food was in their possession. The double imperative (an example of asyndeton) underscores the authority of Jesus.

2.1.4 Aorist Active Subjunctive Forms.

Of the 7 aorist active subjunctive forms of ὁράω in the Gospel, one is used to refer to Jesus (12,15). Here Jesus deftly handles the Pharisees and the Herodians who want to put him to the test by asking them to produce a coin that he «may see» (ἴδω). His masterful reply on taxation leaves his adversaries in amazement.

Three of the examples are used by Jesus to address his listeners with an eschatological nuance (ἴδητε: 13,14.29; ἴδωσιν: 9,1). In 4,12 Jesus quotes prophet Isaiah (6,9-10) to refer to the «outsiders'» (v. 11) inability to perceive (ἴδωσιν) God's redemptive activity. In this example the verb means more than to see; it means to gain insight, perceive.

The two occurrences of ἴδωμεν refer to the high priests and the scribes challenging Jesus to come down from the cross that they may see and believe (15,32) and the curiosity of the bystanders to see if Elijah would come to Jesus' aid (15,36). In these cases they demand to see in order to believe and failing to see they do not arrive at faith in Jesus.

2.1.5 The Remaining Forms of ὁρᾶν

The aorist active infinitive form ἰδεῖν is attested twice in the Gospel. It is used to explain the curiosity of the villagers who, on hearing the report of the cure of the demoniac and the loss of the swine, come to *see* what had taken place (5,14). What they see is awe inspiring and as a result they ask Jesus to leave the place out of reverential fear. The other use of ἰδεῖν is for Jesus. Jesus perceived «that power had gone forth from him» (5,30) and he looked around to *see* who benefited from his power (5,32). Seeing the woman Jesus commends her faith (5,34).

The only occurrence of aorist passive ὤφθη refers to the supernatural event of Elijah and Moses appearing to the disciples on the high mountain of Transfiguration (9,4). The verb in the passive means that the disciples do not play an active role but they are the passive recipients of an apparition that is humanly speaking impossible.

ὁρῶ (8,24) is the only instance of the present active indicative of ὁρᾶν in the Gospel. When Jesus asks the blind man after the first stage of his healing, the blind man responds: «I see [ὁρῶ] men; but they look like trees, walking». The two cases of present imperatives are used by Jesus. In the first instance (Ὅρα) Jesus calls the attention of the leper and instructs him not to publicise the healing that he received (1,44).

The second example ('Ορᾶτε) is used along with the asyndeton βλέπετε in order to warn the disciples against the leaven of Herod (8,15).

There are three instances of the future forms of ὁρᾶν in the Gospel. The ὄψονται of 13,26 and the ὄψεσθε of 14,62 have a clear eschatological sense as it refers to the seeing of the Son of Man. While in the former case the reference is to seeing the Son of Man «coming in clouds with great power and glory» (13,26) in the latter case another aspect is added to his coming. The Son of Man will be «seated at the right hand of Power» and he will be «coming with the clouds of heaven» (14,62). In 16,7 the same second person plural form ὄψεσθε is used but here the reference is to seeing the risen Jesus in Galilee. This is the last occurrence of ὁρᾶν in the gospel. The risen Lord is not said to be exercising the act of seeing. The role passes on to the disciples who after having seen the Lord will garner the courage to preach the risen Christ to the nations.

2.1.6 Synthesis

Leaving aside the 9 instances of ἴδε, there are 50 occurrences of ὁρᾶν in the Gospel of Mark. The use of the verb is as follows:

referring to an express action of Jesus:	13
referring to a saying or command of Jesus:	11
referring to Jesus and the disciples together:	2
referring to the disciples:	4
referring to the crowd or the people:	6
referring to the Pharisees and the scribes:	5
referring to the demoniac or the dumb spirit:	2
referring to the maid who spots Peter:	2
referring to Jairus:	1
referring to Elijah and Moses:	1
referring to the Centurion:	1
referring to the blind man at Bethsaida:	1
referring to the devout women at the tomb:	1

That the evangelist attaches great importance to Jesus' seeing can be seen from the fact that half the occurrences of the verb ὁρᾶν refer to an activity, a command or a saying of Jesus. 15 instances refer to persons including the crowd in general, who are favourably disposed to Jesus and who arrive at faith as a result of seeing him or seeing his actions.

Only 9 times the verb refers to persons antagonistic to Jesus. So contrary to the usual belief, in the majority of cases, Jesus is not the object of people's seeing. It is Jesus himself who is in control of the situation, it is he who sees and his seeing is effective.

2.2 Use of Βλέπειν and its Compound Forms

Of the 32 occurrences of βλέπειν and its compound forms 9 refer to the action of Jesus[23]. 12 instances refer to a command, a question or a saying of Jesus[24]. 6 examples refer to the blind men who regain sight[25]. In 2 cases the disciples are the protagonists (5,31; 9,8). The rest of the 3 occurrences refer to the Pharisees and Herodians (12,14), the devout women at the tomb (16,4), and the maid who spots Peter (14,67).

2.2.1 The Compound Forms of Βλέπειν Referring to an Action of Jesus

Only the compound forms of βλέπειν refer to an action of Jesus. Of particular importance among these is περιβλεψάμενος, the aorist participle middle nominative of περιβλέπειν which Mark uses four times exclusively for an action of Jesus (3,5.34; 10,23; 11,11). As we noted in the case of the participle forms of ὁρᾶν, being a verb of perception περιβλεψάμενος is also used as preparation for the main action of the sentence. The sequence is: participle + the accusative noun or pronoun + main verb. In one example there is no express mention of the accusative (10,23). There is only one case where the main verb is aorist (11,11). In all other three instances (3,5.34; 10,23) the main verb is always λέγει (present tense).

In the first example (3,5) περιβλεψάμενος is the first of two asyndetical phrases that precede the main verb λέγει. Jesus looks around at the Sabbath keepers with anger, grieves at their hardness of heart and says (λέγει in the historical present stresses the effectiveness of his word) that powerful word of healing «stretch out your hand», at which the man with the withered hand is cured. In the next instance too the main verb is λέγει (3,35). Looking around on those who sat about him, Jesus says, «here are my mother and my brothers!»[26]. In the subsequent verse he identifies those who do God's will as members of

---

[23] Cf. Mark 3,5.34; 5,32; 6,41; 7,34; 10,21.23.27; 11,11.

[24] Cf. Mark 4,12^2.24; 8,15.18.23; 12,38; 13,2.5.9.23.33.

[25] Cf. Mark 8,24^2.25^2; 10,51.52.

[26] For an explanation on the exploring and surveying nature of Jesus' look on those who sat around him see, E. BOSETTI, «Un cammino per vedere», 127-128.

his family. In 10,23 the object of περιβλεψάμενος is implicitly the disciples, and Jesus' pronouncement is again referred to with the historic present λέγει to bring out the force of Jesus' teaching. Jesus' remark, «how hard it will be for those who have riches to enter the kingdom of God», is surprising and the reaction of the disciples is naturally amazement at Jesus' words. περιβλεψάμενος in 11,11 has «every thing» as object. Jesus sees the commercial activity that is going on in the temple but does not react now, perhaps because it is late already. So he goes out with the twelve to Bethany.

The only other form of περιβλέπειν that is used by Mark is περιεβλέπετο (5,32) which refers to Jesus' looking around to see (ἰδεῖν) who was the recipient of the power that had gone forth from him (5,30).

There are two occurrences of the compound form ἀναβλέψας referring to Jesus' action. Both are in the context of performing a miracle: multiplication of the bread in the first instance (6,41) and healing the dumb and deaf man in the second (7,34). In both cases Jesus «looks up» to heaven before performing the miracle indicating that his power comes from God alone.

The only other compound form used to refer to Jesus' action is ἐμβλέψας occurring twice, in the narrative about the rich man (10,21) and Jesus' subsequent teaching about wealth (10,27). In the former case, looking at the man Jesus loves him and tells him what he lacks in order to inherit eternal life. In the latter case, Jesus looks at his bewildered disciples and utters the baffling teaching that wealth makes salvation humanly impossible.

2.2.2 Βλέπειν Referring to a Command, Question or Saying of Jesus

Jesus uses βλέπετε 8 times as a command (4,24; 8,15.18; 12,38; 13,5.9.23.33), meaning «take heed» (RSV), «take care»[27]. In all these instances Jesus uses the imperative as a didactic means to call attention to what he teaches. The present tense imperative «presents» the action more forcefully, more emphatically[28]. Therefore the hearers are invited to pay serious attention to what he says.

There are two examples of the use of βλέπειν as an interrogative. In 8,23 Jesus asks the blind man of Bethsaida after the first stage of healing εἴ τι βλέπεις? Jesus once again uses βλέπεις to ask the disciple

---

[27] BAGD, 143.
[28] S.E. PORTER, *Verbal Aspect*, 351-355.

who exclaimed about the «wonderful stones and the wonderful buildings», «do you see these great buildings?» (13,2).

The last two instances of βλέπειν used by Jesus is while quoting Isaiah 6,9-10 (4,12). The first use in this verse βλέποντες is a present participle which expresses the Hebrew absolute infinitive construction[29] and the next use βλέπωσιν is a present subjunctive. This verse refers to the outsiders who see but fail to perceive (ἴδωσιν) God's redemptive activity.

2.2.3 Βλέπειν and its Compound Forms Referring to the Blind Men

The two stories of the healing of blind men (8,22-26; 10,46-52) contain one occurrence of βλέπειν (8,24) and 5 occurrences of three of its compound forms (ἀναβλέψας - 8,24; ἀναβλέψω - 10,51; ἀνάβλεψεν - 10,52; διέβλεψεν - 8,25; ἐνέβλεπεν - 8,25).

ἀναβλέπειν means to *look up* (Mark 6,41; 7,34; 8,24; 16,4), *regain sight* and in the case of the one born blind to *gain sight, become able to see* (Mark 8,24; 10,51.52; John 9,11.15.18)[30]. Since ἀναβλέπειν can mean both to regain the ability to see as well as to receive sight for the first time it does not have to imply that the blind men were once able to see. However, since there is no indication that they were born blind (as in John 9,1.18) it may be better to take it as a restoration of sight[31].

In the second stage of the healing of the blind man at Bethsaida three words express the blind man's regaining of sight - διέβλεψεν καὶ ἀπεκατέστη καὶ ἐνέβλεπεν. διαβλέπειν means to *look intently, open one's eyes wide*[32]. ἐμβλέπειν means to *look at, fix one's gaze upon*, and in the case of the blind man it could mean, to *have a clear vision of everything*[33]. These two words of seeing, together with the word ἀπεκατέστη («was restored») emphasise the fact that the blind man was completely cured.

2.2.4 Βλέπειν and its Compound Forms Referring to the Disciples

There are only two attested uses of the verb βλέπω and its compound forms to refer to the disciples. In the first instance the disciples say to Jesus «you see [βλέπεις] the crowd pressing around you, and yet you

---

[29] M. ZERWICK, *Biblical Greek*, § 61.
[30] BAGD, 50-51.
[31] C.S. MANN, *Mark*, 423.
[32] BAGD, 181.
[33] BAGD, 254.

say, "Who touched me?"» (5,31). Jesus does not answer the disciples but looks around to see who was the recipient of power that went out of him. In the second instance the participle περιβλεψάμενοι is used to express the disciples' looking around but they see no one except Jesus (9,8).

2.2.5 Βλέπειν and its Compound Forms Referring to Others

The Pharisees and Herodians use βλέπεις once in putting the question to Jesus regarding paying taxes to Caesar. They tell Jesus «you do not regard [βλέπεις] the position of man, but truly teach the way of God» (12,14). The maid who spots Peter is said to have «looked at» (ἐμβλέψασα) him and told on his face «You also were with the Nazarene, Jesus» (14,67). Finally the devout women at the tomb on «looking up» (ἀναβλέψασαι) «saw that the stone was rolled back» (16,4).

2.2.6 Summary

Just like the verb ὁρᾶν, βλέπειν and its compound forms are also used predominantly for Jesus. It is Jesus who is said to be «seeing» in most cases. However, it may be noted that Mark prefers to use ὁρᾶν rather than βλέπειν in order to speak more explicitly of Jesus' seeing. The two accounts of the healing of the blind men contain several uses of βλέπειν including three of its compound forms. There are only two examples of the use of the verb for Jesus' adversaries.

2.3 *Use of* Θεωρεῖν

Of the 7 uses of θεωρεῖν in the Gospel Mark uses the verb only twice to refer to Jesus' seeing. When Jesus and those following him come to Jairus' house, Jesus sees (θεωρεῖ) a tumult and the people weeping and wailing loudly (5,38). Sitting down opposite the treasury Jesus watched (ἐθεώρει) the multitude putting money into the treasury (12,41).

The verb is used once for the unclean spirits. Whenever they beheld Jesus (ἐθεώρουν), they did obeisance to him (3,11). The people are the subject of the verb once. From the city and villages they came to Jesus and saw (θεωροῦσιν) the demoniac (5,15). The devout women are said to have been looking on (θεωροῦσαι) from afar the scene of the crucifixion (15,40). Mary Magdalene and Mary the mother of Joses saw (ἐθεώρουν) where Jesus was laid (15,47). Once again, Mary

Magdalene and Mary, the mother of James, and Salome, looking up, saw (θεωροῦσιν) that the stone was rolled back (16,4).

Mark does not seem to be attaching any special significance to the use of θεωρεῖν. It is used as a synonym for ὁρᾶν or βλέπειν. However, it is interesting to note that to refer to the devout women's seeing, the verb used is θεωρεῖν.

2.4 Use of Εὑρίσκειν

Of the 11 occurrences, only 4 times Jesus is the subject of the verb (εὑρίσκει - 14,37; εὑρήσει - 11,13; εὗρεν - 11,13; 14,40). Twice Jesus uses the verb in statements (εὑρήσετε - 11,2; εὕρῃ - 13,36). εὗρον is used three times exclusively for the disciples (1,37: Simon and those who were with him; 11,4; 14,16). Once the Syrophoenician woman is the subject of the verb (εὗρεν - 7,30). The verb is used once for the chief priests and the whole council (ηὕρισκον - 14,55). There does not appear to be any special significance to the choice of this verb, though all the instances of the verb except one (1,37) occur beginning with the narration of Jesus' entry into Jerusalem.

3. A Comparison with the Other Evangelists

Verbs of seeing are extensively used by all the evangelists. In fact Mark's Gospel account for the lowest number of occurrences, perhaps due to the fact that his is the shortest Gospel. A look at the comparative occurrences of the verbs is useful.

i) ὁρᾶν/ἰδεῖν/ ὄψεσθαι: Matt - 72, Mark - 59, Luke - 85, John - 70
ii) Βλέπειν/compound forms: Matt - 26, Mark - 32, Luke - 27, John - 24
    – Βλέπειν: Matt - 20, Mark - 15, Luke - 16, John - 17
    – ἀναβλέπειν: Matt - 3, Mark - 6, Luke - 7, John - 5
    – διαβλέπειν: Matt - 1, Mark - 1, Luke - 1, John - 0
    – ἐμβλέπειν: Matt - 2, Mark - 4, Luke - 2, John - 2
    – περιβλέπειν: Matt - 0, Mark - 6, Luke - 1, John - 0
iii) θεωρεῖν: Matt - 2, Mark - 7, Luke - 7, John - 24
iv) εὑρίσκειν: Matt - 29, Mark - 11, Luke - 45, John - 19

A detailed Synoptic comparison of the pericopes under study shall be taken up later. However, a few preliminary observations are in order. i) ὁρᾶν/ἰδεῖν are the most common verbs of seeing in the Gospels ii)

Matthew follows the terminology of Mark more faithfully in corresponding narratives. For every use of εἶδεν in Mark (1,10.16.19; 2,14; 6,34) there is a corresponding one in Matthew (3,16; 4,18.21; 9,9; 14,14) iii) Luke has a tendency to differ, there is no parallelism between Mark (also Matthew) and Luke in the use of εἶδεν iv) Mark is the only evangelist who uses εἶδεν exclusively for Jesus v) John does not use the present tense of ὁρᾶν/ἰδεῖν instead he uses θεωρεῖν.

4. Impressions on Different Characters' Seeing

In outlining the different impressions on seeing in the Gospel, along with Jesus we shall focus on two sets of characters in the Gospel, those who are positively disposed to Jesus and those with ambivalent attitude towards Jesus. So the point of reference is always Jesus. The instances of seeing in which Jesus is not involved either as subject or as object of the verbs do not seem to gain so much significance in the narrative. The only exception may be that of the seeing of the women at the tomb, but in this case their seeing of the angel (16,5) is connected to Jesus' resurrection. Where Jesus refers to a future seeing (cf. 13,26; 14,62; 16,7), once again Jesus is the protagonist, but it is yet to take place.

4.1 *Jesus' Seeing*

In the Markan narrative Jesus' seeing is generally presented as qualified. Of particular importance is the reference to Jesus' seeing denoted by the verbal forms ἰδών, εἶδεν and περιβλεψάμενος.

i) Jesus' seeing expressed by ἰδών is always a prelude to actions that manifest Jesus' authority and supernatural power (2,5; 6,48; 8,33; 9,25; 10,14; 11,13; 12,34). It is a seeing that is perceptive. This seeing thus provides the basis for the demonstration of that authority and power.

ii) When Jesus and the disciples together form the subject of the verb (εἶδον), those moments also either present an opportunity to demonstrate Jesus' power (9,14: crowd disputing) or they display the effect of Jesus' power (11,20: withered fig tree).

iii) Where Jesus is the subject of εἶδεν, his seeing is unique, the significance of which we shall establish later.

iv) In the exclusive use of περιβλεψάμενος for Jesus in Mark (also in NT; the only other occurrence outside Mark being Luke 6,10),[34] Jesus' seeing is characterised by authority and power. His seeing is prelude to

---

[34] Cf. also K. STOCK, «Gliederung», 486.

a miracle (3,5), or it is a look with love and affection (3,34; 10,23; see also ἐμβλέψας: 10,21.27), or it precedes an exercise of authority (11,11).

v) Performance of miracle is the context of the seeing of Jesus expressed by the verbs περιεβλέπτο (5,32) and ἀναβλέψας (6,41; 7,34).

Jesus' seeing is thus, perceptive, intuitive and discerning. Jesus sees clearly and accurately. His seeing evokes also concrete response from him which, in most cases, is working of a miracle, or an authoritative teaching. The five instances in which Mark uses εἶδεν to speak of the seeing of Jesus concentrate on Jesus' own personal experience which moves him to reach out to others.

4.2 Seeing of those Positively Disposed to Jesus

We have noted that the object of the seeing in most cases of those who are positively disposed to Jesus, is Jesus himself or one of his actions. The fact of mere seeing Jesus makes Jairus for instance perceive that Jesus is in possession of authority and power (5,22) and in recognition falls at his feet. The crowd are so pulled by Jesus' magnetism, that on seeing him they flock to him (6,33). Seeing the miracles that Jesus works produces in the eyewitness awe (1,27), wonder, praise (2,12), curiosity (5,14), fear (5,16), amazement (9,15). The Roman Centurion, in contrast to the seeing of the Chief Priests, does see rightly and it prompts him to express his faith in Jesus.

The disciples' reaction to seeing Jesus in extraordinary moments like walking on the sea is one of fear (6,49.50). But on the mountain of transfiguration the select disciples' seeing of Jesus alone as they come out of the cloud means that they should pay attention solely to him (9,8), keeping for the moment what they had seen there only for themselves (9,9).

Those positively disposed to Jesus thus see rightly, correctly and they grasp the power of God at work in him. Their seeing thus ultimately leads them to faith (10,52; 15,39).

4.3 Seeing of those with Ambivalent Attitude towards Jesus

Those possessed with unclean spirits or Jesus' adversaries like the Pharisees and Scribes too are said to be seeing in the Gospel. The main object of their seeing is again Jesus or his activities. They begin with accurate seeing, they sense that Jesus is in possession of power and authority (5,6; 9,20; 12,28). However, their critical mind and their concern for the Law and ritual purity (2,16; 7,2) cloud their seeing. As a result their attitude towards Jesus gradually undergoes a sea change, so much so that during Jesus' final hours they challenge him to come down from the cross «that they may see and believe» (15,32; cf. also 15,36). Their accurate seeing thus becomes futile, and unlike in the case of those who are open to Jesus, their seeing does not lead them to faith in Jesus.

5. A Note on the Verb ὁρᾶν/ἰδεῖν

Since we focus our attention on Mark's use of the aorist form εἶδεν for Jesus' seeing, a short note on the development of the verb as well as a clarification on the aorist tense are in order.

5.1 *The Development of the Verb*

The aorist root of εἶδεν is ἰδ- with an irregular augment. There is no present active of ἰδεῖν in use. So the verbal forms of ὁρᾶν are used in its place. ὁρᾶν has no aorist either, so ἰδεῖν serves as its aorist[35]. The future form ὄψεσθαι is a middle deponent. It is taken from the stem ὀπ-. The aorist passive also is derived from the same stem[36]. There are two forms of the perfect active, ἑώρακα and ἑόρακα. But there is no attested form of the perfect form in Mark's Gospel. The basic verbal forms therefore are: ὁράω, ὄψομαι, εἶδον, ἑώρακα / ἑόρακα, ὤφθην.

From the classical times onwards the verb signifies:

i) «to see», «to look» (also with εἰς, «to look at something»), and as a transitive verb with accusative means «to see or perceive something». To see is to take part in the life itself. Already in Homer the verb signifies «to experience».

ii) In the transferred sense the verb can refer to spiritual sight i.e. «to perceive», «to consider», «to see mentally»; ἰδέσθαι ἐν φρεσίν, «to see in one's minds eye».

iii) The verb can also mean «to take note», «to see to».

iv) The imperative forms can signify «to take care», «to be on the guard».

v) The passive form means «to be visible», «to appear»[37].

Mark also employs the verb with the same meaning as in ordinary Greek. However, in the five instances where the aorist εἶδεν is used for

---

[35] LSJ, 483.

[36] W. MICHAELIS, «ὁράω», 316-317.

[37] J. KREMER, «"ὁράω", see», 527; LSJ, 483; W. MICHAELIS, «ὁράω», 316-317.

Jesus' seeing, Mark seems to be implying great significance to those events. The seeing of Jesus in these instances is the decisive factor. Bereft of his seeing the events lose their weight and import.

5.2 *Meaning of the Aorist Form in General*

The aorist stem of a verb is viewed as expressing punctiliar (instantaneous) action as opposed to the present stem which expresses the durative (linear or progressive) action. These two are the most important *Aktionsarten* retained in Greek. The word *Aktionsart* has been introduced by K. Brugmann around 1885. Since then the word has been used in other languages also to express this idea. It refers to the kinds of action which the verb tenses of Greek convey. So it is possible to think of an action emphasised at the beginning or at the end of the action (ingressive and effective aorist) or to think of the action as a whole irrespective of its duration (constative or complexive aorist). For the present stem one might think of an action as durative (either as timeless or taking place in present time) or as iterative[38].

However not everyone is happy with this concept[39]. F. Stagg, after citing some of the famous scholars, who according to him «abused» the aorist to build a theology or biblical interpretation, advocates that the aorist is also suited to actions which are in themselves linear. Therefore according to Stagg the presence of the aorist does not in itself give any hint as to the nature of the action behind it. Being the oldest Greek tense the aorist simply points to the action without describing it. Other tenses were developed to stress duration or the state of completion. As a result, these later tenses are more significant for the nature of the action than is the aorist. C.E. Smith in agreement with Stagg analyses many more examples of accurate and inaccurate use of the aorist and concludes that the departure from the aorist is far more exegetically significant than its use[40].

Even without getting into this controversy regarding the aorist tense it may be stated that the aorist connotes simply the action without further determination (aorist = privative α and ὁρίζω «define, determine»), in so far as it implies nothing as to continuity or repetition (imperfect) or endurance in to the present (perfect). But if the aorist

---

[38] BDF, § 318; K. BRUGMANN, *Griechische Grammatik*, 538-541; J.H. MOULTON, *New Testament Greek*, 59-60; S.E. PORTER, *Idioms*, 27-28.

[39] See F. STAGG, «The Abused Aorist», 222-231.

[40] C.R. SMITH, «Errant Aorist Interpreters», 205-226.

does not express duration, neither does it preclude it as a fact but views the action, of whatever duration, as telescoped to a point[41].

Our analysis of the verb εἶδεν for Jesus takes into account that the verbal form used is an aorist indicative in the third person singular. Jesus' seeing is reported as an instantaneous action that took place in the past. However, what aspect the verb takes is not the focus of the study, rather what is the meaning that Mark attaches to the five instances of Jesus' seeing denoted by the verb εἶδεν. But it may be mentioned that in talking of that seeing of Jesus in the following chapters, as a matter of style in English, we shall mainly refer to it in the present tense (historical present), though the nearest English equivalent to the aorist will be the past definite or perfect. The force of the aorist is thereby not ignored. On the contrary it is our intention to stress that only the aorist indicative εἶδεν used of Jesus is replete with meaning.

6. God's Seeing in the Old Testament

The OT deals in great detail with man's desire to see God and on the consequences of seeing him. But instances and implications of God's seeing are not lacking either. We shall just refer to the main instances of God's seeing and point out the various verbs employed in describing it.

6.1 The Common Verb of Seeing

God of the Old Testament is, as Hagar calls him, a «God of seeing» (אֵל רֳאִי- Gen 16,13). God's seeing is expressed in various ways in the Old Testament. The most evident expression is רָאָה with the object marker אֵת or the preposition בְּ[42]. רָאָה אֵת occurs in: Gen 1,4.31; 6,12; 31,12.42; Exod 2,25; 3,7; 4,31; 12,23; Deut 26,7; 2Kgs 13,4; 14,26; Neh 9,9; Ps 31,8; 33,13; Isa 59,15; Jon 3,10. רָאָה with the preposition בְּ occurs in: Gen 29,32; Ps 106,44. Sometimes the conjunction כִּי occupies the place of the object marker: Gen 1,10.12.18.21.25; 6,5; 29,31; Exod 3,4; Deut 32,36; 2Chr 12,7; Ps 37,13; Isa 59,16. רָאָה is used without the object marker אֵת or the preposition בְּ in Gen 7,1; Deut 32,19; 1Chr 21,15; Job 11,11; 28,24.27; 34,21; Isa 59,15; Jer 7,11; 12,3; 23,13; Ezek 16,50; Hos 6,10. In all

---

[41] M. ZERWICK, *Biblical Greek*, § 240; ID., *A Grammatical Analysis*, xii-xiii.
[42] H. MIDDENDORF, *Gott sieht*, 22- 23.

these instances except once (Ps 37,13: προβλέπει) LXX translates רָאָה
with ὁρᾶν and in most cases the verbal form is εἶδεν[43]. God's seeing is
also expressed by the infinitive לִרְאוֹת (ἰδεῖν: Gen 11,5; Ps 14,2; 53,2).

God saw his handiwork and admired them in the creation account
(Gen 1,4.10.12.18.21.25.31). But in contrast «God saw that the
wickedness of man was great in the earth, and that every imagination of
the thoughts of his heart was only evil continually» (Gen 6,5). Again,
God was shocked when he saw the earth, «behold it was corrupt» (Gen
6,12).

God's seeing makes him act decisively in defence of the weak and
the oppressed (Gen 29,31.32 - Leah; Gen 31,12.42 - Jacob; Exod 2,25;
3,7; 4,31; 12,23; Deut 26,7; 32,36; 2Kg 13,4; 14,26; Neh 9,9; Ps 106,44
- Israel; 2Kg 20,5; Isa 38,5 - Hezekiah; Ps 31,8 - the Psalmist).

God's seeing can also provoke scorn and anger (Deut 32,19), but his
seeing can also move him to compassion. «God sent the angel to
Jerusalem to destroy it; but when he was about to destroy it, the Lord
saw and repented of the evil» (1Chr 21,15). The Lord averted his anger
on Jerusalem when he saw that «the princes of the Israel and the king
humbled themselves» (2Chr 12,7). When God saw how the people of
Nineveh turned from their evil ways, «God repented of the evil which
he had said he would do to them; and he did not do it» (Jon 3,10).

God's seeing is never casual. God sees that Noah is righteous (Gen
7,1); he goes down to see the city and the tower of Babel (Gen 11,5).
When the Lord sees that Moses turned aside to see «the burning bush»,
God calls to him out of the bush (Exod 3,4). The Lord tells Moses «I
have seen this people, and behold, it is a stiff-necked people» (Exod
32,9; Deut 9,13). God declares to Samuel «the Lord sees not as man
sees» (1Sam 16,7), his seeing is penetrating, he «looks on the heart»
(1Sam 16,7).

God's seeing is synonymous with observing; «the Lord looks down
from heaven, he sees all the sons of men» (Ps 14,2; 33,13; 53,2; Job
34,21; Jer 12,3). God sees the blood of Naboth and the blood of his
sons (2Kg 9,26); he sees the national wickedness of Israel and «it
displeased him that there was no justice» (Isa 59,15.16). God has seen
that the house of God has become a «den of robbers» (Jer 7,11); he sees

---

[43] The exceptions are ὄψεται: Exod 12,23; 1Sam 16,7; ἰδών: Gen 6,5; 29,31; Job
11,11; ἐπιδών: Gen 16,13; ἐπεῖδεν: Exod 2,25; ἑώρακα: Gen 31,12; Deut 9,13; Jer
7,11; εἶδον: Gen 7,1; Exod 3,7; 2Kgs 9,26; 20,5; Isa 38,5; Jer 23,13; Ezek 16,50; Hos
6,10; ἰδών εἶδον: Exod 3,7; ἰδεῖν: 2Chr 12,7; εἶδες: Neh 9,9; οὐδέν: Isa 34,21; εἰδώς:
Isa 28,24.

an unsavoury thing in the prophets of Samaria, «they prophesied by
Baal and led my people Israel astray» (Jer 23,13). The Lord sees the
abominable things done by Sodom and as a result removes them (Ezek
16,50). In the house of Israel he sees a horrible thing; «Ephraim's
harlotry is there, Israel is defiled» (Hos 6,10).The Lord knows deceitful
men and sees their iniquities (Job 11,11); he «laughs at the wicked for
he sees that his day is coming» (Ps 37,13). Job reflecting on God's
wisdom says that after scanning the entire earth and «seeing» (Job
28,24) all that the heaven encompasses, God «sees» wisdom (Job
28,27). God discovers her amidst the totality of all things[44].

6.2 *Other Verbs of Seeing*

Apart from רָאָה there are many other words in the Old Testament[45]
expressing God's seeing and related actions. There are instances in
which seeing stands parallel to perceiving (Ps 94,7) and hearing (Ps
5,2). בִּין expresses God's perceiving/discerning/understanding/consider-
ing, especially in the later books of the Old Testament. LXX renders it
with συνίημι (Ps 5,2; 94,7; 139,2; Job 28,23; 30,20; Isa 29,16),
γιγνώσκω (1Ch 28,29; Pro 24,12) παρόψεται(Job 11,11) and διενοήθη
(Sir 42,18).

חקר expresses God's searching and scrutinising. Ps 44,21 speaks of
God searching out (יַחֲקָר- ἐκζητήσει) when man secretly spreads forth
his hand to a strange God. Ps 139,23 prays: «search me O God, and
know my heart!» (חָקְרֵנִי - δοκίμασόν). Jer 7,10: «I the Lord search the
mind [חֹקֵר - ἐτάζων] and try the heart [בֹּחֵן - δοκιμάζων]» (cf. also Job
13,9).

Other less occurring words are חפש (Piel) meaning to search out
(Amos 9,3; Zeph 1,12; Pro 20,27), ידע meaning to know (Gen 3,5; Ps
44,22; 94,11; Hos 5,3; 8,4), חזה meaning to behold, see (Ps 11,4.7;
17,2), שׁוּר meaning to see (Ezek 31,3; Hos 13,7; Job 24,15), פלס (Piel)
meaning to watch (Pro 5,21), צפה meaning to keep watch, witness (Gen
31,49; Judg 11,10; Ps 15,3; 66,7). God's turning to someone expressed
by the verb פנה also carries the meaning of a gracious look (Lev 25,9;
Jud 6,14; 2Kg 13,23; Ezek 36,9)[46]. The psalmist repeatedly implores

---

[44] N.C. HABEL, *The Book of Job*, 400.

[45] The list of words follow the finding of Middendorf. Cf. H. MIDDENDORF, *Gott
sieht*, 25-28.

[46] F. NÖTSCHER, *«Das Angesicht Gottes sehen»*, 126-128.

the Lord: «turn thou to me, and be gracious to me» (Ps 25,16; 69,17; 86,16; 119,132).

6.3 *Summary*

From the above analysis it is clear that the Old Testament attaches great importance to God's seeing. Irrespective of the different words used to express God's seeing, his gracious look brings pardon, blessing and salvation; his angry look on the contrary means wrath and death. Man desires and seeks the former while fearing the latter. Even God hiding his face and not looking can have positive as well as negative consequences[47]. The Psalmist for instance, in 50,9 prays «hide thy face from my sins and blot out all my iniquities». But later in v. 11 he prays «cast me not away from thy presence».

Verbs of seeing also embrace a whole range of ideas of sense perception and some times it also moves away from them. Another thing to be noted is that, in order to refer to the actual «seeing» of God, the Septuagint uses only the verbs ὁρᾶν/ἰδεῖν and προβλέπειν (just once: Ps 37,13). Mark's preference also for ὁρᾶν/ἰδεῖν and to a lesser extent for βλέπειν to speak of Jesus' seeing could not be accidental.

7. Conclusion

Numerous references to seeing are reported in the Gospel of Mark. Our investigation has established that it is Jesus who is said to be exercising the faculty of «seeing» in the majority of cases. Although the fact of Jesus' seeing is denoted by several verbs, Mark's preference for the verb ὁρᾶν/ἰδεῖν is quite evident. The aorist third person singular εἶδεν stands out among all the occurrences of the verbs of seeing since it is used exclusively of Jesus. By such an exclusive usage of the verb for Jesus Mark undoubtedly wants to communicate that there is something special about that seeing. It is to discover the special significance of Jesus' seeing expressed by the verb εἶδεν that we shall now turn.

---

[47] Nötscher provides ample examples in this regard. Cf. F. NÖTSCHER, *«Das Angesicht Gottes sehen»*, 131-135.

CHAPTER II

He Saw the Heavens Being Torn Apart (Mark 1,10)

The first use of εἶδεν in the Gospel of Mark to refer to Jesus' seeing is when Jesus *saw* the heavens being torn apart and the Spirit descending upon him like a dove (Mark 1,10). Εἶδεν is the first active verb Mark uses of Jesus in his Gospel that takes a direct object. More importantly this is the only instance of a non terrestrial reality becoming the object of the verb. In all other instances (1,16.19; 2,14; 6,34) persons (disciples in three instances and the crowd in the last instance) are the object of Jesus' seeing. In treating this very important verb we shall first situate Jesus' seeing in the context of his baptism, then we shall deal with the event of the baptism proper, followed by an analysis of the visionary as well as auditory experiences of Jesus and subsequently establish the significance of these events.

1. Preliminary Observations

We shall begin by examining the context of Jesus' seeing, then look into the structure of the narrative of baptism and provide a comparison of the narrative with the other Gospel accounts.

1.1 *Baptism as the Immediate Context of Jesus' Seeing*

The setting of the seeing[1] of Jesus as presented by Mark is Jesus' baptism at the hands of John the Baptist (Mark 1,9-11). Matthew, the only other evangelist who reports the heavenly vision of Jesus, concurs

---

[1] Since the object of Jesus' seeing here is a celestial reality it is fitting to refer to it also as a vision. Therefore in this chapter the terms seeing (noun) and vision are used synonymously.

with Mark on the setting (Matt 3,13-17). As we shall see later Luke does not refer to any human agent seeing the heavenly vision. All the same Luke's account also narrates the opening of the heavens and the descent of the Spirit that follow Jesus' baptism. But he reports them as something taking place while Jesus was praying after the baptism, and independent of anyone's seeing (Luke 3,21-22). In the Gospel of John there is a report of a heavenly vision. But it is not Jesus who sees but John the Baptist who gives first person account of the vision (John 1,29-34). There is no mention as to when exactly John the Baptist sees the vision.

Mark's narrative of Jesus' baptism itself forms part of the beginning of the Gospel[2]. So the beginning of the Gospel provides the larger

---

[2] The opening verses of the Gospel of Mark are referred to by different names. It is rather common to designate them as a «Prologue», e.g., B.W. BACON, «The Prologue of Mark», 84; R. PESCH, *Markusevangelium*, 135-138; O.J.F. SEITZ, «Marcan Prologue», 201; etc. Many scholars prefer the term «introduction», e.g., L.E. KECK, «The Introduction to Mark's Gospel», 352-370; R.H. LIGHTFOOT, *The Gospel Message*, 15; V. TAYLOR, *St. Mark*, 151, etc. Yet others would call the opening section as the «beginning», e.g., C.E.B. CRANFIELD, *Saint Mark*, 33; J. GNILKA, *Markus* I, 39; R.A. GUELICH, *Mark*, 3-4; E. LOHMEYER, *Markus*, 9; E. SCHWEIZER, *Markus* I, 10-11; etc.

Closely connected to the naming is the extent of the section. To put it more concretely, does the section end at 1,13 or are 1,14-15 too included in the section? Opinions are varied. There are scholars who hold that 1,1-15 form the beginning of the Gospel, e.g., E. BEST, *The Gospel as a Story*, 129; J. GNILKA, *Markus I*, 39-40; R.A. GUELICH, *Mark*, 3-5; L.E. KECK, «The Introduction», 352-370; R. PESCH, *Markusevangelium* I, 135-138; etc. The main arguments put forward to support this view are a) the term εὐαγγέλιον forms an inclusion between 1,1 and 1,14-15 b) a number of words connect 1,14-15 with 1,1.13: κηρύσσειν (1,4.7.14) μετάνοια - μετανοεῖν (1,4.15) ἔρχομαι (1,7.9.14) Ἰησοῦς (1,1.9.14) Ἰωάννης (1,4.6.9.14) Γαλιλαία (1,9.14) c) the focus on John the Baptist in 1,2-8 provides a contrast to the appearance of Jesus in 1,9-15 d) A break between 1,15 and 1,16 would permit that the second major section of the Gospel (1,16-8,26) be divided into three sub sections, each beginning with a reference to discipleship (1,16-3,12; 3,13-6,6; 6,7-8,26).

Several other scholars with even more convincing arguments vouch for 1,1-13 as the beginning, e.g., C.E.B. CRANFIELD, *St. Mark*, 33-60; R.H. GUNDRY, *Mark*, 40-44; J.D. KINGSBURY, *Christology*, 55-71; S. KUTHIRAKKATTEL, *Beginning*, 7-20; E. LOH- MEYER, *Markus*, 9-28; E. SCHWEIZER, *Markus*, 10-19; V. TAYLOR, *St. Mark*, 151-164; etc. There are strong indications that 1,14-15 has an introductory function. The temporal designation μετὰ δέ also separates this unit from 1,1-13. The spatial designation of the previous episodes is wilderness - the river Jordan - wilderness, whereas here it is Galilee. The activity of Jesus in v. 14 also undergoes a sea change. Except for a decisive action of seeing the heavens opened, in the previous episodes Jesus is almost passive. In v. 14 Jesus begins his powerful preaching ministry and he

context for Jesus' seeing. The account of the baptism of Jesus is a literary unit by itself though not unconnected to the rest of the beginning section. The division with the preceding pericope (1,1-8)[3] is presented: a) by a twofold introduction with a temporal indication: καὶ ἐγένετο ἐν ἐκείναις ταῖς ἡμέραις; as an introduction to a pericope both the expressions are very rare in the whole Gospel (καὶ ἐγένετο: 2,23; 4,4.10; ἐν ἐκείναις ταῖς ἡμέραις: 8,1; 13,24), and they never again occur together b) by introducing the new actor Jesus who enters the scene c) by shifting the focus of the scene to a heavenly vision that follows the terrestrial event of Jesus' baptism d) by bringing in other actors apart from Jesus into the drama, the Spirit and the heavenly voice.

The subsequent pericope (1,12-13) is distinguished by a change of: a) place; the action shifts to the wilderness from the river Jordan b) the actors; the Spirit, Jesus, the Satan, the wild beasts and the angels are the actors here c) the scene; here the scene is the temptation of Jesus.

Yet, the link with the preceding and following pericopes is very strong. The introductory formula of 1,9 itself refers to what precedes: ἐν ἐκείναις ταῖς ἡμέραις speaks of the time when John the Baptist was carrying out his ministry. Jesus' baptism is thus contextualised within the time frame of the Baptist's activity. Besides, the subject matter of the preceding as well as the present pericopes is baptism. While the former deals with the baptism of «all the country of Judea and all the people of Jerusalem» (1,5) who went out to John, the latter gives an account of the baptism of Jesus and what followed. It is also evident that John the Baptist is a linking figure in both pericopes, just as the river Jordan is the location of both events. The following pericope is also well connected to the present one. καὶ εὐθύς of 1,12 connects it

---

remains the main actor in the rest of the Gospel. Another important factor that would favour the division at the end of 1,13 is the absence of the Spirit motif in 1,14-15.

In the immediate context 1,14-15 is an introduction to the Galilean ministry of Jesus. The repetition of Γαλιλαίας in v. 16 links it with the subsequent episodes in the region of Galilee. But the main themes outlined there like παραδοθῆναι, Γαλιλαία, κηρύσσειν, εὐαγγέλιον, πεπλήρωται, ἤγγικεν, μετανοεῖν, πιστεύειν apply to the whole of Jesus' message. Cf. C.D. MARSHALL, *Faith as a Theme*, 36-37. So 1,14-15 is a synthesis, a *Sammelberichte* of Jesus' message and its function in the context of the whole Gospel sets it apart from the beginning of the Gospel which is 1,1-13. The baptism of Jesus which provides the immediate context for Jesus' seeing takes place in the wider context of the beginning of the Gospel. Hence the beginning of the Gospel is also the general context of Jesus' seeing.

[3] In fact, the Westcott-Hort text even had a space between v. 8 and v. 9.

immediately with 1,11. Moreover it is the same τὸ πνεῦμα of 1,10 who drives Jesus into the wilderness in 1,12.

The account of the baptism of Jesus thus stands out at the beginning of the Gospel and provides the background for Jesus' vision. It is by analysing the essential elements of the narrative of baptism that we shall establish the significance of Jesus' seeing.

1.2 *Structure of the Narrative of Jesus' Baptism*

The narrative of Jesus' baptism (1,9-11) has two basic parts: the baptism proper (1,9) and Jesus' vision (1,10-11). The vision itself consists of two things seen by Jesus, the rending of the heavens (1,10a), and the Spirit descending upon him like a dove (1,10b), and the heavenly voice heard by him. However, it is evident that in the whole episode the focus is on what Jesus sees.

1.3 *Comparison of the Narrative of Baptism*
   with other Gospel Accounts

A short analysis of the various Gospel accounts would bring out the importance which Mark attaches to this great event of seeing in the life of Jesus.

1.3.1 Introduction and Baptism: Mark 1,9

After the rare introductory formula Mark goes on to speak very tersely of Jesus' coming from Galilee and being baptised by John.

Matt 3,13 too speaks of the coming (παραγίνεσθαι) of Jesus but adds another nuance to his coming; he came with the intention of being baptised by John. A dispute ensues as John recognises that he needs to be rather baptised by Jesus. Jesus then has to convince John of the aptness of his being baptised by him to «fulfil all righteousness» (3,14-15). Matthew too speaks of the baptism proper in a terse way. The verb used is aorist passive participle (βαπτισθείς); the active verb (ἀνέβη) refers to Jesus' going up from the water.

Luke begins the narrative (3,21-22) by his characteristic ἐγένετο δέ, but he does not speak of the coming of Jesus. Nor is information supplied on the location of the event and above all it is not said who baptises Jesus. Jesus' baptism is mentioned in a casual way and he is pictured as a certain man among many who after baptism had been praying. Luke's concentration is on the events that follow the baptism, the baptism of Jesus itself is relegated to the background.

John limits himself to mentioning the coming of Jesus and does not speak of his baptism at all. John presents the Baptist as bearing testimony to Jesus (1,29) and the whole focus is on this testimony. However, the scene of the baptism is indirectly localised through the words of John «he who sent me to baptise with water» (1,33)[4]. Besides, a reference to Jordan is already made in v. 29 («This took place in Bethany beyond the Jordan, where John was baptising»).

From the comparison made with the other evangelists it is clear that only Matthew concurs with Mark in describing the event of baptism. Luke does not pay as much attention to the details, mentions the baptism in passing. John does not even speak of it.

1.3.2 The Scene that Follows Jesus' Baptism: Mark 1,10-11

In Mark, as soon as Jesus comes out of the water after his baptism he sees the heavens being torn apart, and the Spirit descending upon him like a dove, followed by a heavenly voice. It is Jesus alone who sees and hears, and it is his seeing that is crucial.

In Matthew 3,16 the opening of the heavens is not related to Jesus' seeing. The object of seeing is the Spirit of God like a dove descending and alighting on him. Matthew specifies the Spirit as the Spirit of God. The heavenly voice unlike in Mark does not address Jesus directly. The voice speaks to others, an audience not explicitly rendered precise, confirming the identity of the Son, «This is my beloved Son, with whom I am well pleased» (3,17).

Luke 3,22 gives no reference to Jesus' seeing at all. The opening of the heavens, the Holy Spirit descending in bodily form of a dove, and the heavenly voice are presented as three facts that happen independent of Jesus and his seeing. The heavenly voice's affirmation is similar to that of Mark. It is addressed to Jesus, «Thou art my beloved Son; with thee I am well pleased» (3,22).

In John 1,32-34, it is John the Baptist who sees the Spirit descending as a dove from heaven and remaining on Jesus. Jesus is totally passive. John himself has been the recipient of an attestation: «But he who sent me to baptise with water said to me, "He on whom you see the Spirit descend and remain, this is he who baptises with the Holy Spirit"» (1,34). John's witness is similar to the one in Matthew addressed to a third party, «this is the Son of God» (1,34).

---

[4] F. LENTZEN-DEIS, *Die Taufe Jesu*, 36.

All three Synoptics speak of the opening of the heavens, John is silent about it. The descent of the Spirit is the main element of the narrative in all four Gospels. The form of the Spirit as dove is also attested to by all the evangelists. The content of the heavenly voice in the Synoptic Gospels is that Jesus is «God's Son». But only Mark and Matthew attach great importance to Jesus' seeing. The «epiphany» is presented by both as the object of Jesus' vision.

2. Jesus is Baptised by John

The analysis here will treat the presentation of Jesus and the event of Jesus being baptised by John.

2.1 *Introduction of Jesus*

The narrative of Jesus' baptism begins with a curious introduction which as we have noted is very rare in the Gospel of Mark[5]. The indication of time[6] has a clear reference to vv 4-8, to the time of the ministry of John which in turn is a time of fulfilment of OT prophecy (1,2-3).

This theme of fulfilment is further backed up when the coming of Jesus is seen as the fulfilment of John's prediction «after me comes he who is mightier than I» (1,7). In fact, it is the coming of Jesus (ἦλθεν) which is the focus of the introductory formula[7]. The coming of Jesus is also an important motif at least in the beginning part of the Gospel of Mark. ἔρχεσθαι has been employed 6 times in the first chapter to refer to Jesus' coming: ἔρχεται (1,7), ἦλθεν (1,9.14.39), ἦλθες (1,24), and ἦλθον (1,29: the first disciples included). Mark seems to be reaffirming each time that the prediction of John really finds its fulfilment in Jesus' coming. It is interesting to note that each time Jesus' mission is referred to, his coming is also explicitly mentioned (1,24; 2,17; 10,45).

---

[5] καὶ ἐγένετο followed by an indication of time with ἐν, and the finite verb is often found in LXX as a translation of the Hebrew introductory formula וַיְהִי. Cf. BDF § 4; 442,2; H.B. SWETE, *St. Mark*, 7; M. ZERWICK, *Biblical Greek*, §§ 387-390. This construction is very frequent in Luke.

[6] ἐν ἐκείναις ταῖς ἡμέραις is often found in LXX. Cf. F. LENTZEN-DEIS, *Die Taufe Jesu*, 31; H.B. SWETE, *St. Mark*, 7. Both expressions together introduce Jesus with an impressive biblical formula. In introducing John the Baptist the simpler form ἐγένετο is used (1,4) indicating already the superiority of Jesus. Cf. J. MARCUS, *Mark*, 163.

[7] Jesus' coming also contrasts sharply with the going out to John of «all the country of Judea, and all the people of Jerusalem» (1,5).

Mark's presentation of Jesus is marked by brevity and conciseness. With little information regarding his antecedents, Jesus is abruptly brought into the scene. Mark limits himself to just mentioning where he comes from. There is a general agreement that ἀπὸ Ναζαρέτ modifies the verb, that Jesus came from Nazareth rather than that Jesus from Nazareth came[8]. The important element of this presentation is that through the reference to his native place Jesus is established as a historic figure,[9] having a city of origin to talk of, firmly placed in the socio-cultural milieu of his time and practising his religion.

2.2 Jesus' Baptism

After the introductory formula and the presentation of Jesus, the main clause of 1,9 deals with the baptism of Jesus, which too is presented in a typically concise form. The passive form ἐβαπτίσθη affirms John's role as the minister of the rite he administered to Jesus in the river Jordan[10]. The use of the passive form has led some to

---

[8] E.g., R.A. GUELICH, Mark, 31; R.H. GUNDRY, Mark, 47; V. TAYLOR, Mark, 159; Cf. also W. MARXSEN, Mark, 58 (However, his argument that the original version had been Ἰησοῦς ὁ Ναζαρηνός, and that Mark then changed this to the present reading and added τῆς Γαλιλαίας is pure hypothesis). For the contrary view that «Jesus of Nazareth» came cf. W. FOERSTER, «Ἰησοῦς», 288 n. 31; G.D. KILPATRICK, «Jesus», 4-5; E. LOHMEYER, Markus, 1; N. TURNER, Grammatical Insights, 28-29. But if it modified «Jesus», a definite article would precede the phrase as in John 1,45; Acts 10,38 or in Mark 15,43 (Ἰωσὴφ [ὁ] ἀπὸ Ἀριμαθαίας). Cf. R.H. GUNDRY, Mark 47. Besides, the further qualification τῆς Γαλιλαίας would have been redundant if ἀπὸ Ναζαρέτ referred to Jesus. Cf. R.A. GUELICH, Mark, 31. In fact, Matthew (3,14) mentions only Galilee to refer to Jesus' provenience.

[9] J. ERNST, Markus, 38-39.

[10] R. Pesch has drawn attention to the fact that in many instances in the OT the «river» recurs as the place of revelation (Ezek 1,1: Chebar; Dan 8,2: Ulai; 10,4: Tigris). Cf. R. PESCH, Markusevangelium I, 90, n. 9. However, here in question is the all important river Jordan which flows not only through the promised land but also through both the Old and New Testaments. It serves as the locale for many significant events in the history of the people of God. It is on the banks of one of its tributaries called Jabbok (Gen 32,22), that Jacob is transformed into Israel (Gen 32,28). Jordan also parallels the red sea in that it is a new generation that enters the promised land in procession, passing through the river dry shod, just like their fathers returning from slavery, and entering the promised land crossing the red sea turned dry ground (Josh 3,15-16). Elijah also enters the perfect state of communion with God from the banks of the river Jordan, after he and Elisha went over it on dry ground (2Kgs 2,8.11). On purifying oneself in the waters of the river one leaves behind one's past life of sin and emerges as a new being (cf. 2Kgs 5,14: cure of the Syrian general Naaman's leprosy). So it was befitting that John administer the purificatory rite of baptism in the waters

speculate that Jesus' baptism was by immersion[11]. This view finds an added support when one wonders why Mark used εἰς τὸν Ἰορδάνην here instead of the ἐν τῷ Ἰορδάνῃ of 1,5. But for many scholars εἰς is just a substitute for ἐν[12]. For R.H. Gundry ἐν gives way to εἰς here to prepare for Jesus' coming up ἐκ τοῦ ὕδατος[13].

A few interrelated questions regarding Jesus' baptism have been posed time and again. Why did Jesus feel the need for baptism? What happened when he went down to the water, did he confess his sins? Did Jesus have sins? [14] There are no ready answers to such questions. Matthew does some explaining by way of John's protest and Jesus' reply that it was «fitting for us to fulfil all righteousness» (Matt 3,14-15)[15]. Luke and John do not care about such questions. Mark too is not

---

of the same river. It was also fitting that Jordan should be the locale for the great revelation subsequent to Jesus' reception of the baptism.

[11] R.A. GUELICH, *Mark*, 31; J. JEREMIAS, *New Testament Theology*, 51.

[12] BDF, § 205; C.H. TURNER, «Marcan Usage», 14-20.

[13] R.H. GUNDRY, *Mark*, 47.

[14] For D.F. Strauss and some others Jesus submitted himself to baptism in order to repent and find forgiveness. Cf. D.F. STRAUSS, *The Life of Jesus*, 237-239. But this calls into question the notion held by the NT that Jesus was sinless (John 8,46; Acts 3,14; 2Cor 5,21; Heb 7,26; 1Pet 1,19).

The non canonical Christian Gospels too deny that Jesus was baptised for repentance. The *Gospel of the Ebionites* report that immediately after Jesus' baptism, John asks Jesus to baptise him (Epiphanius, *Haer.* 30.13.7f) Cf. W. SCHNEEMELCHER, *New Testament Apocrypha* I, 169. In the *Gospel of the Hebrews* Jesus' mother and brothers urge him to go to John for baptism, but Jesus responds that it is not needed as he is sinless. Ignatius of Antioch is of the view that Jesus was baptised not so that the water would purify him, but so that he might «purify the water» (Ign. *Eph.* 18:2). Justin Martyr says that Jesus was baptised «solely for the sake of humanity» (Dialogue 88). V. Taylor says, «that He [Jesus] accepted baptism like other penitents is excluded by the entire absence of the consciousness of sin in His personality, as it is revealed in the Gospels» . Cf. V. TAYLOR, *St. Mark*, 618.

[15] The word δικαιοσύνη in Matthew denotes right conduct. Cf. R.H. GUNDRY, *Matthew*, 51. But there are several explanations as to what Matthew meant by «fulfilling righteousness». For a list cf. W.D. DAVIES – D.C. ALLISON, *Matthew*, 325-327.

J. Calvin takes «righteousness» to refer to the specific requirements of our Lord's own vocation. It was «that He might render full obedience to the Father» by fulfilling the mission entrusted to Him. «It was for the sake of others that He sought baptism» J. CALVIN, *A Harmony of the Gospels*, 129-130. O. Cullmann develops this theme and argues that the words of the heavenly voice echo Isa 42,1 where there is a reference to the Servant of the Lord, whose mission is further described in Isa 52,13–53,12. The righteousness that Jesus wanted to fulfil was the role of the suffering servant of the Lord. «The baptism of Jesus is related to δικαιοσύνη, not only his own but also that of

concerned about such issues, he is content to report that Jesus was baptised by John. A look at the two descriptions of baptism in v. 5 and v. 9 show that the formulations are almost identical:

Mark 1,5	Mark 1,9
καὶ ἐβαπτίζοντο ὑπ' αὐτοῦ ἐν τῷ Ἰορδάνῃ ποταμῷ ἐξομολογούμενοι τὰς ἁμαρτίας αὐτῶν	καὶ ἐβαπτίσθη εἰς τὸν Ἰορδάνην ὑπὸ Ἰωάννου

The act of confessing their sins is what distinguishes the baptism of the Jerusalem and Judean folk from that of Jesus' baptism. In all other details both the narratives concur. Jesus submits himself to John's baptism in the river Jordan just like all others. But trying to establish if he had any sins to confess or to figure out whether he confessed on behalf of the people are all attempts to uncover what motives may have led Jesus to baptism. It is impossible on the basis of evidence to reconstruct the state of mind of Jesus as he went down to Jordan[16]. However, what is conspicuous is Jesus' identification with the people in submitting himself to John's «baptism of repentance for the forgiveness of sins» (1,4)[17]. It is a moment of solidarity with his own fellowmen as he joins the crowd that flock to John. It is moreover a recognition from Jesus' part of John's role in the near approach of the Kingdom of God and seeing in his ministry the fulfilment of the OT prophecy (1,2-3).

---

the whole people». Cf. O. CULLMANN, *Baptism in the New Testament*, 16-22, especially 18. Cf. also C.E.B. CRANFIELD, «The Baptism of Our Lord», 54. But it is very much a Pauline idea that Jesus' baptism was for the «whole people» and we do not learn that from Matthew. It is also possible that Isaiah's description of the Servant of the Lord may have influenced Matthew. In simple terms «fulfilling righteousness» means, bringing about or actualising God's promise of liberation and salvation. So it may be said that «the baptism of Jesus is an *instance* of the way in which Jesus must fulfil all righteousness, and that this latter obligation perpetually rests upon him». Cf. G.R. BEASLEY-MURRAY, *Baptism in the New Testament*, 54.

[16] C.K. BARRETT, *The Holy Spirit*, 35.

[17] V. Taylor notes, «He came to be baptised as an act of self-dedication to His mission and perhaps also of self-identification with the sinful Israel in the fulfilment of righteousness». Cf. V. TAYLOR, *St. Mark*, 618.

A Christological explanation of this expression of Jesus' solidarity with sinful humanity may be found in the hymn of Phil 2,6-11[18]. Jesus emptied himself taking the form of a servant, being born in the likeness of men. He humbled himself and became obedient unto death on a cross. Therefore God bestowed on him a name, and every tongue would confess that Jesus Christ is Lord. Jesus' sharing a ritual of baptism, as an expression of solidarity is at the same time a self-emptying. But later the heavenly voice would attest to Jesus' Sonship with God. In both narratives the bestowal of a higher status directly follows Jesus' act of humbling himself[19].

The verb βαπτίζειν occurs a number of times in Mark: 1,4.5.8.9; 6,14.24; 11,30 referring to John; 7,4 referring to the Jewish purificatory rites; 10,38.39 referring to Jesus; 16,16 referring to the baptism to be received in order to be saved. In all these references, except for 10,38.39, what is implied is some sort of purificatory or initiation rite.

In 10,38-39 Jesus' query to the Zebedee brothers regarding «drinking the cup» and his subsequent comment, «to be baptised with the baptism» are formulated as synonymous parallelism and refer to his passion and death. Jesus insistently calls his sacrificial death a baptism. The verb βαπτίζειν and its noun form occur 6 times in vv 38-39. Jesus asks the Zebedee brothers if they are able to participate in the fate he is going to face. Jesus' death, which to his mind is a baptism, is the supreme expression of his identification with humanity. His baptism at Jordan provides the first occasion for a public expression to this identification. Two baptisms thus frame Jesus' life of identification with humanity as recounted by Mark. Jesus' baptism by John already points to his baptism of death as the cross is looming large on the horizon, acceptance of which is required of him in order to effect God's plan of salvation.

Thus it is the episode of the baptism of Jesus that provides the link, which connects and identifies Jesus with the sinful humanity as well as with John. That unique moment of solidarity, would also be the occasion for Jesus' seeing. The same event of baptism would be a moment of revelation which confirms Jesus' links with God and the Spirit.

---

[18] Cf. J. ERNST, *Markus*, 39. For a contrary view that the narrative of Jesus' baptism contains no hints of solidarity with the people see A. VÖGTLE, *Offenbarungsgeschehen*, 77-79.

[19] However, it has to be admitted that there is no evidence of a mutual influence of either of the texts on each other.

3. Visionary Experience of Jesus

Mark in a cryptic way in v. 10 recounts that as Jesus was coming up out of the water immediately he saw the heavens being torn apart, and the Spirit descending upon him like a dove. The whole verse calls for close analysis.

3.1 *Jesus' Coming up out of the Water*

There are two things to be established here. Firstly, what does the verb ἀναβαίνειν mean in this context, does it mean coming up out of the water (river) to the land or does it mean coming up from the water after the immersion but still remaining in the river? Secondly, should the adverb εὐθύς go with the participle ἀναβαίνων or with the finite verb εἶδεν?

ἀναβαίνειν means to *go up, ascend*[20]. Mark uses the verb 9 times. It refers to going up on the mountain (3,13), going up to Jerusalem (10,32.33), getting into the boat (6,51), coming up to Pilate (15,8), and the growing up of the seeds (4,7.8.32). The sense is always of a movement upward. However, in none of these instances is there a reference to the point of departure. Where there is a movement involved the usual reference is to the point of arrival, which is expressed by ἀναβαίνειν εἰς (3,13; 10,32.33). However, in 1,10 the point of departure is clearly specified as ἐκ τοῦ ὕδατος[21]. In Acts 8,39 a similar phrase occurs where the reference is to Philip's and the eunuch's coming out of the water: ἀνέβησαν ἐκ τοῦ ὕδατος. The plural verb here points to the coming up of both Philip and the eunuch. So the implication is that it refers to the coming up out of the water (river) to the land, not a coming up from the water while remaining in the river, in which case the verb should refer only to the eunuch, he alone would undergo an immersion.

Matthew the only other evangelist who refers to Jesus' coming out of the water, also uses the verb ἀναβαίνειν but the verbal form is finite ἀνέβη and not a participle as in Mark. He uses the preposition ἀπο instead of ἐκ to refer to the point of departure. But these differences do not indicate any change in the idea that what is more probable is a coming out of the water up on to the land. However, the idea of an

---

[20] BAGD, 50.
[21] Other examples of ἀναβαίνειν ἐκ are John 11,55; Acts 8,39; Rev 8,4; 9,2; 11,7; 13,1.11; 17,8.

immersion cannot be totally done away with either, in which case the connection between baptism and vision would be very close. Whereas in the coming up out of the water on to the shore and in the ensuing vision such connection is not as close as in the former case[22].

The adverb εὐθύς is quite frequent in Mark occurring 41 times[23] (Matt 5, Luke 1, John 3, Acts 1). It means *immediately, at once*[24]. The question that concerns us is should the adverb εὐθύς in 1,10 go with the participle ἀναβαίνων or should it be taken together with the finite verb εἶδεν. In other words, after the baptism did Jesus immediately come up out of the water (εὐθύς go with ἀναβαίνων) or did Jesus have the vision immediately on coming up out of the water (εὐθύς go with εἶδεν)?

Mark uses εὐθύς to connect both the participle as well as the finite verb. So in v. 10 too it could go with either ἀναβαίνων or εἶδεν . In the parallel passage Matthew understands that Jesus immediately came out

---

[22] D. Daube sees in Jesus' coming up a connection with Josh 4,15-24, where the priests bearing the ark of the covenant as well as the people come out of Jordan turned dry ground. So Jesus' coming up is a new coming into the promised land. Daube also argues that coming up is the decisive moment in proselyte baptism. Cf. D. DAUBE, *Rabbinic Judaism*, 111-112, 243. For A. Poppi Jesus' coming up is a sign that «Gesù è il nuovo Mosè che sale dalle acque (cfr. *Es.* 2,1-10), è il nuovo Israele, vero figlio primogenito di Dio (cfr. *Es.* 4,22), che corrisponde pienamente all'amore del Padre, riparando l'infedeltà dell'antico popolo». Cf. A POPPI, *L'inizio del Vangelo*, 104. H.J. Klauck sees in Jesus' going down to the water for baptism a prelude to his sinking into death and his coming means resurrection. He says, «Jesu Getauftwerden im Wasser des Jordans, in den er - vermutlich: tiefhinabsteigt, deutet auf sein Versinken in den Fluten des Todes, sein Hinaufsteigen aus dem Wasser vielleicht auf seine Auferstehung». Cf. H.J. KLAUCK, *Vorspiel im Himmel*, 91.

[23] εὐθύς which sometimes appears as εὐθέως in various manuscripts appear only once in Mark (7,35; see also Matt 13, Luke 6, John 3, Acts 9). Even in this instance (7,35) it is not certain if Mark intended really to use εὐθέως. The *Novum Testamentum Graece* 27th Edition and *The Greek New Testament* 4th Revised Edition, enclose εὐθέως within square brackets. The Editorial Committee of the United Bible Societies Greek New Testament, has chosen to retain εὐθέως considering that the external support for εὐθέως before ἐλύθη is strong whereas for εὐθύς is extremely weak. But the witnesses that lack εὐθέως is also quite impressive (א B D L Δ al) cf. B.M. METZGER, *A Textual Commentary*, 82-83.

In Mark's Gospel εὐθύς connects finite verbs 24 times and participles 17 times. Of these 4 finite verbs (1,20.43; 6,45.50) and 6 participles (1,10.21.29; 2,8; 5,30; 8,10) refer to an activity of Jesus. εὐθύς is attributed to the disciples only twice: 1,18 and 1,30. All other instances are used to refer to various characters in the narrative.

[24] BAGD, 321. P. DSCHULNIGG, *Sprache*, 84-86. J. MARCUS, *Mark*, 159: «The adverb imparts vividness to the narrative and leaves readers with the impression that the divinely willed series of events is unfolding at great speed».

of the water: Ἰησοῦς εὐθύς ἀνέβη ἀπὸ τοῦ ὕδατος (3,16). Here εὐθύς refers to an aorist finite verb ἀνέβη. In Mark 1,10 the participle is present (ἀναβαίνων) and not aorist as one would have expected. εὐθύς in Mark, except once (11,2), always connects an aorist participle[25]. Even in the case of 11,2 the meaning is that on entering the village immediately they will find the colt. So εὐθύς is connected to the finite verb εὑρήσετε and not to the present participle εἰσπορευόμενοι. In the same way in v. 10 too εὐθύς could be taken together with the finite verb εἶδεν[26] and may be translated as, «as he was coming up out of the water, immediately he saw»[27].

Jesus' seeing is also closely connected to his coming up. This would mean that Jesus' baptism is not connected to the confession of sins as in v. 5. Instead his baptism is connected to the vision that follows. The indeterminate temporal connection between the baptism and the vision would also signify that it is not the baptism which effects the vision. So Mark's interest is to show that the baptism of John is the occasion of something greater that follows[28] which is not the result of the rite administered by him.

3.2 *Jesus' Seeing*

The seeing of Jesus is expressed by the verb εἶδεν[29]. The use of the verb is of particular interest to us. As seen in the analysis of the

---

[25] Mark 1,18.21.29; 2,8.12; 5,30; 6,27.54; 7,25; 8,10; 9,15.24; 14,45; 15,1.

[26] Besides, if εὐθύς should go with ἀναβαίνων, the likely reference would be to a baptism by immersion. But in the case of immersion there is no need to specify that Jesus immediately came out of the water while still remaining in the river. It is clear that otherwise it would be tantamount to drowning. Cf. R.H. GUNDRY, *Mark* 47.

[27] J. MARCUS, *Mark*, 159. See also W.D. DAVIES – D.C. ALLISON, *Matthew*, 328.

[28] R. Pesch wants to establish a possible connection between the coming up and the vision in general (cf. Mark 9,2; Acts 10,9-11; Rev 4,1). Cf. R. PESCH, *Markusevangelium* I, 90, n. 9. In Mark 9,2 the verb used is ἀναφέρειν and not ἀναβαίνειν. However, Pesch has a point in Acts 10,9-11 and Rev 4,1 where the verb ἀναβαίνειν does appear and the narratives do present accounts of vision.

[29] There is some ambiguity regarding the subject of the verb since Mark does not name Jesus explicitly but only employs the third person singular verb to refer to the action of seeing. The proximity of the name John to the verb is no indication that John is the subject of the verb. We have seen that v. 9 focuses on the main actor of the scene, Jesus. The name of John is mentioned only as the agent of the baptism that Jesus receives. The verb ἀναβαίνων has to necessarily refer to Jesus and the following finite verb εἶδεν has to also refer to Jesus' action of seeing. Moreover, in Mark the heavenly voice addresses Jesus directly, «Thou art my beloved son [...]» (1,11). It does not make sense to imagine that John sees and Jesus hears; Jesus is the recipient

previous chapter Mark is fond of using the different verbal forms of
ὁρᾶν. But he employs the aorist indicative εἶδεν to denote events that
have special significance and v. 10 contains the first of such events (for
other occurrences cf. 1,16.19; 2,14; 6,34).

3.2.1 Centrality of Jesus' Seeing

Taking into consideration the main events in the episode of the
baptism of Jesus it is interesting to note that Jesus' seeing is the central
element:

a   – the baptism
b   – Jesus' seeing
c   – the heavenly voice

This focus on the seeing of Jesus is also apparent when the use of the
finite verbs for Jesus are considered:

v. 9 a in those days
    b Jesus came (ἦλθεν) from Nazareth of Galilee
    c and was baptised by John in the river Jordan

    v. 10a and on coming up, immediately
        b he saw (εἶδεν)
      c the heavens being torn apart and the Spirit descending
        upon him like a dove

    v. 11a and a voice came from heaven
      b «Thou art (εἶ) my beloved Son
      c with thee I am well pleased»

---

of both the vision and the audition. In Matt 3,16 too it is Jesus who is the subject of
εἶδεν, though the text is a bit more ambiguous than that of Mark since the heavenly
voice in the following verse (3,17) speaks to an indeterminate audience.

Nowhere in the NT is John the Baptist the subject of the verb εἶδεν. It is true that in
John 1,32f. John the Baptist bears testimony by referring to his seeing, but the verbal
form used is always different (1,32: τεθέαμαι; 1,33: ἴδῃς; 1,34: ἑώρακα). In Mark only
Jesus is ever described as the subject of εἶδεν. Given the special significance of the
verb and the quality of the seeing involved there can be no doubt that in 1,10 too
Jesus is the subject of εἶδεν.

The three finite verbs used of Jesus take the position «b» in our schema, thus occupying the central position in every verse. Among these only εἶδεν takes an object. Jesus' coming and being baptised (v. 9) were in preparation of the vision. The sentence pictures Jesus as the passive recipient of a purificatory rite. The only action of Jesus, apart from his coming (intransitive), narrated in the whole scene is his seeing (v. 10). The voice that ensues (v. 11) confirms what Jesus sees and experiences and authenticates his being. Once again Jesus is characterised by his passivity, receiving the divine communication. So the only explicit, principal action of Jesus is εἶδεν. Only in his seeing Mark presents an otherwise passive Jesus as actively involved.

The centrality of Jesus' seeing can be further verified when looking at the voice that comes from heaven. Of the voice it is stated: καὶ φωνὴ ἐγένετο ἐκ τῶν οὐρανῶν (1,11). The aorist ἐγένετο implies that the voice comes about or happens independent of hearing. At the same time Mark does not say that the voice is ever heard. He does not say that Jesus ἤκουσεν the voice. Jesus is characterised again by his passivity. So it is logical to suppose that hearing of the voice is already inserted into the only active verb in the account, that of his seeing (cf. also 9,7 where the experience of being overshadowed by the cloud precedes the voice from the cloud). Hearing is already contained in his seeing. It is in his seeing that Jesus also hears the voice and comes to know its content.

We have also alluded to the fact that in v. 10 the object of Jesus' seeing is an extra-terrestrial reality. It is rather common in the NT to use the aorist forms of the verb ὁρᾶν to report experiences of vision. In the book of Revelation 53 times the verb[30] occurs in the aorist indicative referring to the celestial vision of John[31]. The Acts of the Apostles also contains numerous examples of vision, all referred to by the verb εἶδεν[32]. The use of εἶδεν to refer to Stephen's seeing (Acts

---

[30] There is extensive use of the verb ὁρᾶν in the book of Revelation occurring some 56 times. εἶδεν occurs twice (1,2: John; 12,13: dragon), εἶδες occurs 7 times (1,19.20; 17,8.12.15.16.18 all referring to John), εἶδον occurs 45 times (all referring to John giving a first person account of what he saw). The two non-aorist occurrences of the verb are: 17,6b (ἰδών) and 18,7 (ἴδω).

[31] For reference to a similar seeing cf. Amos 1,1: «the words of Amos [...] which he saw», and Hab 1,1: «the oracle of God which Habakkuk the prophet saw».

[32] Acts 9,12.27: referring to Paul's vision at his conversion; 16,10: Paul gets instruction in a vision to go to Macedonia; 10,3; 11,13: Cornelius; 10,17: Peter. εἶδεν occurs all together 12 times in Acts; Apart from the above 6 instances 3 times it is used to say that «he whom God raised up *saw* no corruption» (2,31; 13,37), whereas

7,55) is of particular importance as it could be considered a close parallel to the seeing of Jesus.

Parallelism	Mark 1,10	Acts 7,55
– participle in preparation for seeing	καὶ εὐθὺς ἀναβαίνων ἐκ τοῦ ὕδατος	ὑπάρχων δὲ πλήρης πνεύματος ἁγίου ἀτενίσας εἰς τὸν οὐρανὸν
– verb of seeing	εἶδεν	εἶδεν
– the first of the two objects of seeing	σχιζομένους τοὺς οὐρανοὺς	δόξαν θεοῦ
– the second object of seeing	καὶ τὸ πνεῦμα ὡς περιστερὰν καταβαῖνον εἰς αὐτόν	καὶ Ἰησοῦν ἑστῶτα ἐκ δεξιῶν τοῦ θεοῦ

The construction of the sentence is identical: εἶδεν is preceded by a participle (in Acts 7,55 ἀτενίσας is aorist); but no movement of Stephen is referred to by the participle, the only possible movement is the shifting of his gaze to heaven (ἀτενίσας εἰς τὸν οὐρανὸν). Stephen like Jesus is said to have literally seen an extra-terrestrial reality. Stephen does not see a vision in a dream or in a similar trance-like state, as may be suggested by the contexts of other occurrences of the verb εἶδεν in Acts. The object of his seeing is also two-fold: the glory of God and Jesus standing at the right hand of God. However, the revelation of what he sees contributes to his lapidation. What distinguishes Jesus' seeing from that of Stephen is quite evident. The rending of the heavens, the Spirit descending, the heavenly voice that issues forth and the effect this event has on Jesus' consciousness, they all set Jesus' seeing apart from any other NT instance of a vision.

David did *see* corruption (13,37); once it is used of the people who *saw* the miracle of the lame beggar walking (3,9); as they came out of the water the eunuch is said to have *seen* Philip no more (8,39); and the seeing of Stephen (7,55) is the only one that has as object a celestial reality.

Mark refers to another case of seeing which takes a double object in 14,62:

τὸν υἱὸν τοῦ ἀνθρώπου ἐκ δεξιῶν καθήμενον τῆς δυνάμεως ὄψεσθε

καὶ ἐρχόμενον μετὰ τῶν νεφελῶν τοῦ οὐρανοῦ.

Here Jesus is responding to the challenge of the high priest, proclaiming himself as the Christ, the Son of the Blessed (14,61). In doing so he predicts his own destiny which would become a public manifestation and object of a single literal seeing of the Son of Man at the last day. The construction of the sentence in 14,62 has similarities with 1,10: a verb in the indicative taking two participial objects, the elevated position of the Son of Man as well as his coming with the clouds of heaven. The allusion here also is to an extra-terrestrial phenomenon. The verb ὄψεσθε in the plural form indicates that those who see it will not be the high priest alone, but the whole Sanhedrin who prosecute him. However, the future form of the main verb projects the event as yet to take place. Instead, Mark presents Jesus' seeing at his baptism as a definitive, instantaneous action that has already taken place and as having tremendous effects on his personality.

In John 1,32-34, John the Baptist is the recipient of the vision of the Spirit descending and remaining on Jesus[33]. The vocabulary that expresses his seeing is rich and varied:[34]

1, 32: Τεθέαμαι τὸ πνεῦμα καταβαῖνον
1, 33: Ἐφ᾽ ὃν ἂν ἴδῃς τὸ πνεῦμα καταβαῖνον
1, 34: κἀγὼ ἑώρακα

It is curious to note that the verb εἶδεν is never employed to refer to the seeing of John the Baptist, in spite of a very vivid description of his seeing. In bearing witness John the Baptist insistently refers to his

---

[33] It is from the Johannine account that we come to know that the Spirit remained (ἔμεινεν) on Jesus. The variant reading of Mark 1,10 in ℵ has exactly this clause, καὶ μένον, which is probably an assimilation to John 1,33.

[34] F. Lentzen-Deis points out that the seeing is decisive for one who gives witness. The testimony by eye witness is often expressed by the perfect of θεᾶσθαι and ὁρᾶν. These verbs express seeing something supernatural and extraordinary. All the same the object of such seeing is some external event that the one who gives witness saw, in the example here it is the coming down of the Spirit. Seeing such events is never expressed by βλέπειν and θεωρεῖν. Cf. F. LENTZEN-DEIS, *Die Taufe Jesu*, 42.

having seen a very singular event taking place. That seeing leads him to understand who Jesus is, and to perceive his role and to bear witness to him. The evangelist John however, gives no information on whether Jesus saw the descent of the Spirit, nor on the effect that event has had on Jesus' consciousness. Mark instead focuses wholly on Jesus, his experience of the whole event and its effects on his consciousness[35]. So in the Markan narrative everything that surrounds the episode of Jesus' baptism hinges on Jesus' seeing.

3.2.2 Jesus' Seeing and Deute-Vision

F. Lentzen-Deis in his study proposes as literary *Gattung* for the narrative of the baptism of Jesus and particularly for the vision, the contemporary Targumic parallels of the «Deutevisionen» of the Patriarchs[36]. He refers to two visions: first, the vision of Abraham and particularly of Isaac in the context of the Aqeda (Tg Gen 22,10 f.) and second, the vision (dream) of Jacob (Tg Gen 28,10-12). The MT in the first instance does not have any account of the vision. It is added by the Targums. Isaac «sees» the angels appearing on high and watching him and his father. The angels then say to each other «Come, see two unique righteous ones who are in the world. The one slaughters and the other is being slaughtered. The one who slaughters does not hesitate and the one who is being slaughtered stretches out his neck»[37]. After analysing the vision of Isaac, Lentzen-Deis concludes that it had an interpretative function of the figure of Isaac and that of Abraham as «the two unique righteous ones». In the second instance, the MT contains an account of a vision, but the Targums have other details to add. Jacob in his dream sees a ladder fixed on the earth and its head

---

[35] P. Vielhauer argues that in the Markan account there is an element of secrecy involved in the fact that only Jesus sees. He says, «Die wunderbaren Ereignisse bei der Taufe werden von Jesus allein wahrgenommen, dem Täufer bleibt das Geschehen verborgen; [...] Der Offenbarung von Jesu Würde korrespondiert die Verborgenheit [...]». Cf. P. VIELHAUER, «Erwägungen», 213-214. But it is doubtful if there is any motif of secrecy involved here, if at all such a motif exists in Mark's Gospel!

[36] F. LENTZEN-DEIS, *Die Taufe Jesu*, 195-289. We shall treat this work in some detail as it has particular interest in the vision.

[37] *The Aramaic Bible* 1 A, *Targum Neofiti 1: Genesis*, 117-118 , apparatus, *n.* Targum Pseudo-Jonathan has a different version: «Come, see two unique ones who are in the world; one is slaughtering, and one is being slaughtered; the one who slaughters does not hesitate, and the one who is being slaughtered stretches forth his neck». Cf. *The Aramaic Bible* 1 B, *Targum Pseudo-Jonathan: Genesis*, 80.

reaching to the height of the heavens, and the angels that had accompanied him from the house of his father ascending to bear good tidings to the angels on high, saying, «Come and see the pious man whose image is engraved in the throne of Glory, whom you desired to see»[38]. Then the angels from before the Lord ascended and descended and observed him. Here too the vision has the function of interpreting the figure of Jacob as the «pious man».

Lentzen-Deis identifies a schema of «Deute-vision» and applies this schema to Jesus' baptism and the events that follow:[39]

The Schema	Mark's account
i) the starting point in the context:	the baptism of Jesus by John
ii) the actual «Deute-Vision» – the introduction:	the expression «and he saw» as well as the heavens opening,
– the content of the Vision:	the «Deute-Vorgang», the descent of the Spirit,
iii) – the introduction to the audition:	no angels present, no conversation between them, so the voice is present right from the beginning,
– the content of the audition:	the «Deute-Wort», «Thou art my beloved Son; with thee I am well pleased».

One basic point to be mentioned is that the «Deute-Vision» and the «Deute-Wort» are always additions to the events narrated in the Bible, as proposed by the Targums and the Haggadah. How far these additions could be verified as historical is a legitimate question. The historicity of the event of the baptism of Jesus and the close connection of the

---

[38] *The Aramaic Bible* 1 A, *Targum Neofiti 1: Genesis*, 140. Targum Jonathan has: «Come and see Jacob the pious, whose image is fixed in the throne of glory». Cf. *The Aramaic Bible* 1 B, *Targum Pseudo-Jonathan: Genesis*, 100.

[39] F. LENTZEN-DEIS, *Die Taufe Jesu*, 249-252.

ensuing events to the baptism are beyond doubt[40]. The events of Jesus'
seeing, the opening of the heavens and what the voice proclaims are not
additions like in the Targums. The narrative of Mark is a single unit.

---

[40] A number of sources have the account of Jesus' baptism by John. Mark is our
most important witness (1,9-11). Matthew (Matt 3,13-17) and Luke (3,21-22) also
present the narrative and in John (1,31-34) it is assumed. The *Gospel of the Hebrews*
(*GHeb* § 2) too makes references to the baptism of Jesus. Besides, the attempts by the
evangelists to play down the embarrassing fact of Jesus having been baptised by John
is a proof that the event did take place. In Mark the baptism of Jesus is balanced by
the subsequent events (1,9-11). Luke makes only a casual mention of Jesus' baptism
and concentrates on the epiphany (3,21-22). Matthew inserts in the account the
contention of John that he need to be baptised by Jesus (3,14). In the Gospel of John,
the purpose of John's baptism was in order that Jesus «might be revealed to Israel»
(1,31). The historicity of the event is also supported by a good majority of the
scholarly opinion. For instance, J. ERNST, *Johnnes der Täufer*, 337-39; F. LENTZEN-
DEIS, *Die Taufe Jesu*, 56; C.H.H. SCOBIE, *John the Baptist*, 146-48; R.L. WEBB,
«John the Baptist», 214-216; etc.
On the other hand the Gospel of the Nazarenes explicitly denies that Jesus was
baptised by John (*Gnaz* §2, from Jerom, *Adv. Pelag.* 3. 2). The Gospel of Thomas
does not speak of Jesus' baptism although it talks of John (*GThom* § 46). The
Protoevangelium of James makes no mention of the baptism of Jesus. There are also
scholars who doubt the historicity of the event, e.g., R. Bultmann calls the narrative of
the baptism of Jesus a legend. Cf. R. BULTMANN, *Synoptic Tradition*, 247-53. For
Dibelius it is a myth. Cf. M. DIBELIUS, *Die Formgeschichte*, 271-72. E. Haenchen too
doubts its historicity. Cf. E. HAENCHEN, *Der Weg Jesu*, 58-63. M.S. Enslin argues
that the paths of John and Jesus did not cross, and that the early church invented the
story of Jesus being baptised by John for two reasons: a) the disciples of John proved
a very real hindrance to the rise of Christianity. The followers of Jesus and John
continued to follow in the steps of the respective masters and there was open rivalry
between them. The rivalry led to nowhere, so it was decided to incorporate John in the
Christian story. As a result of this Christian take-over Johnnine rite of baptism gained
prominence in Christian practice b) it was intended to satisfy the Jewish claim that the
Messiah must be preceded by Elijah (Mal 4,5) so the need to present John the Baptist
as the Elijah, the forerunner of Jesus who is the Messiah (p. 10-12). Cf. M.S. ENSLIN,
«John and Jesus», 1-18.
Enslin claims that the universal practice of baptism in the Church helped create the
story of Jesus being baptised by John. In fact it is the patristic period, not the NT, that
forges such a connection. One would also wonder why the Church should create the
only story in the Bible that subordinates Jesus to John by undergoing a baptism at
John's hands in order to explain this incorporation of two rival sects. Even though
Enslin contends that the path of Jesus and John did not cross, yet he suggests that it
was the shock of the execution of John that forced Jesus to begin his own ministry.
Such emotional reaction from Jesus' part regarding John whom he did not bother to
hear nor receive his baptism is totally unexpected (so J.P. MEIER, *A Marginal Jew* 2,
182-183, n. 3). For a further critique of Enslin, see R.L. WEBB, «John the Baptist»,
216-218.

Jesus' seeing can never be compared to the seeing of Isaac (for MT it never took place) nor the seeing of Jacob in a dream. There is no immediate comparison to the descent of the Holy Spirit at baptism; the angels appearing or their ascending and descending have only an observatory function. The «Deute-Wort» is a conversation between the angels in the Targums; what Jesus receives is a direct communication from God.

However, it has to be acknowledged that the event has an interpretative function as in the Targums and as proposed by Lentzen-Deis to the extent that the voice proclaims the identity of Jesus. But the basic question is whether this comparison with the «Deute-Vision» was really necessary[41]. The «Deute-Vision» of the Targums in fact suffers from the late date of the Targums as well as from the uncertain date of the traditions in them[42].

---

[41] Cf. E. RUCKSTUHL, «Jesus als Gottessohn», 196-197.

[42] R.H. GUNDRY, *Mark*, 53. Cf. A. VÖGTLE, *Offenbarungsgeschehen*, 77-78 for further criticism of F. Lentzen-Deis' theory.

J. Marcus has another explanation as to what constituted Jesus' baptismal vision. The key lies according to him tucked away in an unexpected corner of the tradition - in a saying found in Luke 10,18, «I saw Satan fall like a lightning from heaven». Following Bultmann he argues that this is the only saying in the Synoptic Tradition that can be classed as a report of a vision. For Marcus the narrative of Mark 1,10-11 is inauthentic. However, a baptism is an appropriate occasion for a vision. Luke 10,18 is a vision without a setting. So he argues for linking the vision that lacks a setting with the visionary setting that lacks a plausible vision. He also argues that the baptism is the appropriate occasion for an eschatological vision of Satan's downfall. Such a vision would explain Jesus' subsequent break with John the Baptist and the beginning of his independent ministry. Satan's fall marks the advent of the royal rule of God. Finally Marcus goes a step further and suggests that the present narrative of Jesus' baptism could have grown out of Jesus' account of a baptismal vision about Satan's fall. Even though the evidence to support it is not «overwhelming», Marcus is convinced that originally Luke 10,18 was part of Jesus' baptismal vision. The church eventually excluded the vision of Satan's fall because the vision locates Satan's overthrow at the beginning of Jesus' ministry, so that his death and resurrection become, in a way, superfluous. Cf. J. MARCUS, «Jesus' Baptismal Vision», 512-521.

The fallacy of Marcus' basic point that Mark's narrative of Jesus' baptism is inauthentic itself calls into question the rest of the argument he so painfully constructs. Luke 10,18 is a text that has given rise to lively discussion. In addition to the commentaries see S.R. GARRETT, *the Demise of the Devil*, 46-57; J.V. HILLS, «Luke 10.18», 25-40; S. VOLLENWEIDER, «Ich sah den Satan», 187-202. Linking this text with the narrative of Jesus' baptism is an easy solution to explain the text. But it remains a mere conjecture.

3.3 Objects of Jesus' Seeing

Mark presents a twofold object of the verb εἶδεν: rending of the heavens and the coming down of the Holy Spirit.

3.3.1 Rending of the Heavens

The verb that Mark uses to express the rending of the heavens is the present participle of σχίζεσθαι. Matt 3,16 and Luke 3,21 use the aorist passive forms of ἀνοίγειν. σχιζομένους of Mark shows in graphic detail the extraordinary action in progress[43] and Jesus as the recipient of its unfolding. In Matt 3,16 and Luke 3,21 the opening of the heavens is described as something of a normal phenomenon (cf. John 1,51; Acts 10,11; Rev 19,11) which seems to be in preparation for a subsequent event. In Mark the very opening of the heavens is an event which is significant by itself[44]. Mark's emphasis on the event of the rending of the heavens is evident in the chiastic structure he uses to refer to the objects of Jesus' vision in v. 10:

σχιζομένους τοὺς οὐρανοὺς
καὶ τὸ πνεῦμα ὡς περιστερὰν καταβαῖνον εἰς αὐτόν

---

[43] V. TAYLOR, St. Mark, 160.

[44] For a discussion on the motives of the opening of the heavens in the literary milieu of the NT, see F. LENTZEN-DEIS, «Das Motive der "Himmelsöffnung"», 301-327.

The rending of the heavens is considered to be a common feature of apocalyptic thought. Cf. S. LÉGASSE, Marc I, 87; F. LENTZEN-DEIS, Die Taufe Jesu, 109-126; V. TAYLOR, St. Mark, 16. Cf. also Apoc. Bar. 22,1: «And it came to pass after these things that lo! the heavens were opened [...]». Cf. R.H. CHARLES, The Apocrypha, 495; Test. Levi 2,6: «And behold the heavens were opened [ἀνεῴχθησαν], and an angel of God said to me, Levi, enter»; Test. Levi 18,6: «The heavens shall be opened [ἀνοιγήσονται], and from the temple of glory shall come upon him sanctification [...]»; Test. Jud. 24,2: «And the heavens shall be opened[ἀνοιγήσονται] unto him, to pour out the spirit [...]». Cf. R.H. CHARLES, The Testaments, 27.63.96. The apocalyptic visions represented in some of these passages either post-date Mark's Gospel or their dates are uncertain. Besides, the opening of the heavens is not limited to apocalyptic or eschatologic thoughts. It is also found in Jewish-Hellenistic legends and miracle stories (3Macc 6,18) Cf. R.H. GUNDRY, Mark 50; H.-J. STEICHELE, Der leidende Sohn Gottes, 119, n. 36.

The plural τοὺς οὐρανοὺς is no proof for Palestinian origin of the narrative (Against L.E. KECK, «The Spirit and the Dove», 60). There are also several examples of the plural οἱ οὐρανοι in the Hellenistic Christian writings (cf. 2Cor 5,1; Eph 1,10; 3,15; 4,10; 6,9; Phil 3,20; Col 1,5.16.20; Heb 4,14; 1Pet 1,4). Even LXX also has the plural (so G. SELLIN, «Das Leben des Gottessohnes», 249, n. 22).

The forward placing of the verb σχιζομένους in the first instance and the noun τὸ πνεῦμα in the second shows clearly where Mark's interests lie. His concentration is obviously on the action of the rending and the person of the Spirit.

a) OT Echo of the Tearing of the Heavens (Isa 63,19)

Scholars have seen a clue to the action of rending in the prayer of Isa 63,19:[45]

MT: לוּא־קָרַעְתָּ	LXX: ἐὰν ἀνοίξῃς τὸν	Mark 1,10: εἶδεν
שָׁמַיִם יָרַדְתָּ	οὐρανόν τρόμος	σχιζομένους τοὺς
מִפָּנֶיךָ הָרִים נָזֹלּוּ	λήμψεται ἀπὸ σοῦ ὄρη	οὐρανοὺς
	καὶ τακήσονται.	

That heaven is the abode of God (Ps 123,1; 80,14; Tob 5,16; Ecc 5,2; Lam 3,41), a closed place (2Kgs 7,2.19) which is opened only for extraordinary divine interventions (Exod 9,23; Ps 78,24; John 6,31) is a popular conception. A constant cry to God that echoes in the Old Testament is to «look down from heaven» (Deut 26,15; Ps 80,14; Isa 63,15). The idea underlying this cry is that heaven is a kind of barrier that has to be crossed if there has to be a communication between God and men. The cry in Isa 63,19 goes a step further and asks to intervene on behalf of Israel by rending the heavens and coming down. God's presence itself is sufficient for Israel to feel safe. The rending of the heavens would imply that God would be again accessible.

Mark's use of the verb σχίζειν[46] provides the verse a connection with Isa 63,19. The verb σχίζειν is an exact translation of קרע (MT Isa 63,19). The LXX however, translates it with ἀνοίγειν (which means to open). The same verb ἀνοίγειν is used by both Matthew 3,16 as well as Luke 3,21[47]. D.H. Juel notes that Mark with his use of the verb σχίζειν implies an irreversible cosmic change. «What is opened may be closed; what is torn apart cannot easily return to its former state»[48]. Jesus not

---

[45] E.g., I. BUSE, «Baptism of Jesus», 74-75; C.E.B. CRANFIELD, Saint Mark, 53; W.L. LANE, Mark, 55; E. SCHWEIZER, Markus, 15.

[46] σχίζειν is a rare verb in the Gospels (Matt - 2; Mark - 2; Luke - 3; John - 1) R. Pesch points out that σχίζειν generally indicates the tearing of robes or clothe. Cf. R. PESCH, Markusevangelium, 91.

[47] Mark uses the verb ἀνοίγειν only once (7,35) referring to the opening of the deaf man's ears (Matt - 12; Luke - 6; John - 9).

[48] D.H. JUEL, Mark, 33.

only sees the preparation but also the fulfilment of the deep longing of the people, «O that thou wouldst rend the heavens and come down» (Isa 63,19).

In Mark, God is pictured as tearing apart the heavens at Jesus' baptism, never to shut it again. The distance between God and man is bridged and communication is established in an irrevocable way. Jesus is the recipient of this momentous event. His seeing of the event taking place sets him apart as the perfect human representative in whom God is made accessible to man and man in turn is made accessible to God.

But there are great misgivings on the part of some scholars to see a connection between v. 10 and Isa 63,19[49]. For Lentzen-Deis the opening of the heavens indicates only the place of origin of the dove and makes the apparition possible[50]. Lightfoot suggests that the rending of the heavens is Mark's «description of the incarnation, in and by which heaven and earth were joined in an irrevocable, unbreakable union»[51]. For C.E.B. Cranfield the opening of the heavens is «the natural prelude to a divine communication»[52].

---

[49] F. Lentzen-Deis in his work investigates in great detail on «the opening of the heavens», in the literary genre of theophany, and concludes that even though the passage of Isa 63,19 contains all the elements of theophany like, a) place of origin (here heaven) b) coming down c) effect of the coming, they do not correspond to Mark 1,10. Firstly, the LXX translation of קרע with ἀνοίγειν and the use of the same verb by Matthew and Luke is a sign that it is the normal translation. Secondly in 63,19 the prayer is: ἐὰν ἀνοίξῃς τὸν οὐρανόν τρόμος λήμψεται ἀπὸ σοῦ ὄρη καὶ τακήσονται. The prayer is addressed to God and not to the Holy Spirit. Whereas in Mark 1,10 it is the Holy Spirit who descends. Thirdly the effect of God's coming as described in Isa 64,1 in no way correspond to the effect of the descent of the Holy Spirit in Mark 1,10. Cf. F. LENTZEN-DEIS, *Die Taufe Jesu*, 100-103. Cf. also R. PESCH, *Markusevangelium*, 91-92. But we may reiterate that it is possible to view the event at baptism as fulfilment of the aspirations of the people expressed in Isa 63,19. Mark seems to have grasped the exact meaning of קרע in his description of the tearing open of the heavens (σχιζομένους). It is much more vivid and suits the atmosphere of God's intervention than the mere opening (ἀνοίγειν) of the heavens. The eminent presence of God is verified through His voice. The descent of the Holy Spirit and Jesus' seeing it all taking place imply that God is made accessible in a concrete person. It is evident that the effect of God's coming surpasses human expectations.

[50] F. LENTZEN-DEIS, *Die Taufe Jesu*, 280: «Es bezeichnet den Herkunftsort der Taube und ermöglicht ihr Erscheinen». Cf. R. PESCH, *Markusevangelium*, 91-92.

[51] R.H. LIGHTFOOT, *The Gospel of Mark*, 56.

[52] C.E.B. CRANFILED, «The Baptism of Our Lord», 57.

b) *Mark's Use of* σχίζειν *at 15,38*

The verb σχίζειν occurs only once more in Mark. It is used to speak of the rending of the veil in the temple at the time of the death of Jesus in Mark 15,38 (ἐσχίσθη). A number of scholars have tried to establish a link between the rending of the heavens (1,9) and the rending of the veil in the temple (15,38)[53]. As usual there are also those who hold for no connection at all between the two events[54].

S. Motyer points out that there are actually several motifs that occur at both the baptism and the death of Jesus: i) at both of these moments something is torn, and in both cases the rending involves a theophany ii) at both moments there occurs a declaration of the identity of Jesus as the Son of God – at the baptism it is the voice of God, and at the death it is the voice of the Centurion iii) at both moments something is said to descend – at the baptism it is the Spirit-dove and at the death it is the tear in the curtain iv) at both moments the Elijah-symbolism is present – at the baptism in the figure of John the Baptist, and at the death the onlookers think that Jesus is calling out to Elijah v) the Spirit which descends at baptism is recalled at his death by Mark's repeated use of the verb ἐκπνέω, a cognate of πνεῦμα to describe Jesus' death. So the repetition of these motives in both the incidents constitutes a symbolic *inclusio*[55].

---

[53] E.g., I. BUSE, «The Markan Account», 75; A. FEUILLET, «Le baptême de Jésus», 468-490; R.H. GUNDRY, *The Use of the Old Testament*, 28-29; D.H. JUEL, *A Master of Surprise*, 34-36; S. MOTYER, «The Rending of the Veil», 155-157; V. TAYLOR, *St. Mark*, 596.

[54] F. LENTZEN-DEIS, *Die Taufe Jesu*, 280-282: F. Lentzen-Deis rejects any link between these two events and argues that the veil that is torn is the inner one and this way the holy of holies is made open to all. But no one comes out from there (opposite to the baptism where the Spirit descends) and no one steps in either.

[55] Cf. S. MOTYER, «The Rending of the Veil», 155-157. H. Jackson also argues for a link between the tearing of the heavens and the rending of the temple veil and sees also a parallel between Jesus and the Centurion: just as Jesus saw the rending of the heavens, so the Centurion also saw the tearing of the temple veil which in Jackson's opinion was the outer veil as the inner veil was hidden. Jackson also goes on to argue that the Spirit-wind which had entered into Jesus at the rending of the heavens at his baptism, left him with such force that it was this Spirit-wind that was responsible for the tearing of the veil. Cf. H. JACKSON, «The death of Jesus», 23-24.
D. Ulansey agrees with S. Motyer that the two events are located at two pivotal moments, the precise beginning (the baptism) and the precise end (the death), of the earthly life of Jesus and that the placement of the two instances of the motif of tearing suggests a symbolic *inclusio*. He also accepts the argument of Jackson and holds that it is the outer veil of the temple that was torn. In order to support this argument he

Even if seeing a symbolic *inclusio* as proposed by Motyer meets with scepticism, his presentation of the several parallel motifs present in both the episodes cannot be ignored. First and foremost Mark's use of the verb only in these two instances itself points to some intrinsic connection between them. Secondly, the declaration in both instances concern the identity of Jesus. Just as Jesus' entry into the public scene at baptism is marked by a divine confirmation of his real identity, so also his exit from the public scene is characterised by a proclamation of his identity, this time from the part of a human representative who finally begins to see ('Ιδὼν δὲ ὁ κεντυρίων [...] εἶπεν, 'Αληθῶς οὗτος ὁ ἄνθρωπος υἱὸς θεοῦ ἦν) and gains courage to profess it[56]. At baptism this declaration is preceded by an act of Jesus' identification with the sinful humanity. This self-identification finds its supreme expression in his death which Jesus willingly accepts in obedience to the Father. Thirdly, it is not lost on the readers to see a connection between τὸ πνεῦμα which descends at baptism and Mark's repeated use of the verb ἐκπνέω, a cognate of πνεῦμα to describe Jesus' death.

3.3.2 Descent of the Spirit as Dove

The descent of the Spirit is the second object of the seeing of Jesus. Every word and every phrase in the statement καὶ τὸ πνεῦμα ὡς περιστερὰν καταβαῖνον εἰς αὐτόν is rich in meaning. Therefore we shall undertake a detailed analysis of it.

a) *The Spirit*

Mark here uses the absolute form τὸ πνεῦμα for the Spirit, (also in 1,12; cf. John 1,32). R. Bultmann holds that the absolute use of the

---

quotes Josephus (J. W. 5.5.4 § 212-214) and says that the outer veil of the temple portrayed a panorama of the entire heavens. So when Mark says that the «veil of the temple was torn in two from top to bottom», his readers would have an image of the heavens being torn and would immediately have been reminded of Mark's earlier description of the heavens being torn at baptism. Cf. D. ULANSEY, «The Heavenly Veil Torn», 123-125.

Though some of the parallels drawn from both events are significant, it has to be acknowledged that in the arguments the authors have given a free reign to their imagination resulting in exaggeration.

[56] Cf. E.S. JOHNSON, «Mark 15,39», 406-413, for the view that the Centurion's exclamation cannot be understood as a full confession of Jesus as the Son of God in Mark's Gospel.

term τὸ πνεῦμα is a decisive pointer to its Hellenistic origin[57]. That may be true, but examples of such usage is not lacking elsewhere. Num 11,26 for instance, does speak of «the Spirit» resting on Eldad and Medad and 1QS 4,6 also contains a reference to «the Spirit of the Sons of truth»[58].

It is quite obvious that Mark here speaks of the «Holy Spirit» he referred to in 1,8. Matthew and Luke specify what Spirit they are talking about: Matt, 3,16: [τὸ] πνεῦμα [τοῦ] θεοῦ; Luke 3,22: τὸ πνεῦμα τὸ ἅγιον. Mark instead, makes it abundantly clear from the immediate context that he intends the Holy Spirit with which the mightier one will baptise (1,8)[59]. It is the same Spirit that would immediately after the baptism drive Jesus out into the wilderness (1,12). As Jesus would indicate later, the denial of the presence, and liberating deeds of the selfsame Holy Spirit in him would amount to blasphemy (3,29). In Jesus' view it is the Holy Spirit who is the source of inspiration to a scriptural statement by David (12,36). It is the same Holy Spirit who would be speaking in Jesus' followers when they have to confess boldly before the authorities (13,11). The seeing of that Holy Spirit descending into him at his baptism is a decisive experience for Jesus and it affects his whole being and life.

b) *The Act of Descending*

The verb that Mark uses is the participle form καταβαῖνον. The Spirit's καταβαίνειν in fact contrasts sharply with Jesus' ἀναβαίνειν. Matthew (3,16) and John (1,32) also have the same form, Luke (3,22)

---

[57] Cf. R. BULTMANN, *Synoptic Tradition*, 251.

[58] J. GNILKA, *Markus* I, 50; J. MARCUS, *Mark*, 159. H.-J. Steichele argues against an absolute use of the Spirit outside the Hellenistic circles and says that 1QS 4,6 is only an abbreviated form of «the Spirit of truth». For him the τὸ πνεῦμα of 1,10 probably is the abbreviated form of πνεύματι ἁγίῳ of 1,8. He acknowledges that there is a break between 1,8 and 1,9 whereas the Qumran text is unitary. The point he wants to arrive at is that the narrative of baptism has a Hellenistic origin. Cf. H.-J. STEICHELE, *Der leidende Sohn Gottes*, 110-112.

L.E. Keck has successfully shown that the absolute use of the term appears in Palestinian literature, especially Qumran. Cf. L.E. KECK, «The Spirit and the Dove», 59. E. Ruckstuhl rejects the evidence of Qumran Literature because «dort hrwḥ durch einen Attributsatz als Gabe Gottes bestimmt wird [...]». Cf. E. RUCKSTUHL, «Jesus als Gottessohn», 198.

[59] A similar usage can be noticed in 9,20 where Mark employs τὸ πνεῦμα recalling the πνεῦμα ἄλαλον of 9,17 (cf. 9,25). In 14,38 by juxtaposing τὸ πνεῦμα with ἡ σάρξ, it is made evident that Jesus is referring to the spirit as part of the human personality.

alone uses an aorist infinitive καταβῆναι. Even in other passages that speak of the vision of a descent from heaven the tense used is present participle of καταβαίνειν (John 1,51; Acts 10,11; 11,5; Rev 21,2). If another tense is used the reference to the vision also is absent (John 3,13; 6,38.41.42.51.58; Eph 4,10). It is characteristic of such vision to see the course of the descent itself, to see the things that come down in their connection to heaven and God (cf. Rev. 21,2 «And I saw the holy city, new Jerusalem, coming down out of heaven from God»).

c) *The Use* ὡς

Mark narrates that Jesus εἶδεν [...] τὸ πνεῦμα ὡς περιστερὰν καταβαῖνον εἰς αὐτόν . ὡς[60] περιστερά could modify either the noun that precedes it (τὸ πνεῦμα) or the participle that follows (καταβαῖνον). If it is taken to qualify the noun the use is adjectival but if it qualifies the verb the use is adverbial. L.E. Keck holds for the adverbial use of ὡς περιστερά and argues that it referred to the manner of the Spirit's descent[61]. Mark very explicitly states, and that is the most significant element of the narrative, that Jesus saw (εἶδεν) the descent of the Spirit. It is essential therefore to have some visible form for the Spirit which descends, to have been seen by someone[62]. It is difficult to imagine

---

[60] W.D. Davies – D.C Allison explain that ὡς points toward the world of apocalyptic symbolism. So it is no surprise that it occurs some 70 times in Revelation, more often than in any other NT book. Its frequency reflects the visionary character and symbolic content of apocalyptic literature. Cf. W.D. DAVIES – D.C ALLISON, *Matthew* I, 331; see also E. LOHMEYER, *Markus*, 21-22.

[61] L.E. KECK, «The Spirit and the Dove», 41-67. L.E. Keck's is a very detailed study in which he deals with the previous attempts to understand the descent of the dove, investigates the origin of the dove story in Jewish, Hellenistic and Hellenistic Christian traditions, and proposes that the story belongs to the old Palestinian Jewish Aramaic Christian tradition. For him «the point is not a dove-like descending but the Spirit coming with dove-like descent» (p. 63). It is surprising that he should reach such a conclusion after such an erudite study.

L.E. Keck's view had been already proposed by B. Weiss (*Das Matthäus-Evangelium*, 72-73); J. Jeremias: «ὡς περιστερὰν did not originally mean that the spirit became a dove or appeared in the form of a dove, but that it descended with a gentle sound "like a dove"». Cf. J. GNILKA, *Markus* I, 52; J. JEREMIAS, *New Testament Theology*, 52.

[62] A good number of scholars therefore rightly take ὡς περιστερά as having an adjectival force; e.g., H. GREEVEN, «περιστερά», 68; R.A. GUELICH, *Mark*, 32-33; R.H. GUNDRY, *Mark*, 49; S. GERO, «The Spirit as a dove», 17-35; E. LOHMEYER, *Markus*, 23; R. PESCH, *Markusevangelium* I, 91; G. RICHTER, «Zu den Tauferzählungen», 43-45; etc.

how one can just see a manner of descent irrespective of whether it has a bodily form. It is here that Luke's precision is valuable (3,22): «and the Holy Spirit descended upon him in bodily form, as a dove» (σωματικῷ εἴδει ὡς περιστεράν). Matthew's account is similar to that of Mark but he uses the phrase ὡσεὶ περιστεράν (Matt 3,16)[63]. In John's Gospel, John the Baptist bears witness to having seen τὸ πνεῦμα καταβαῖνον ὡς περιστεράν (John 1,32).

d) *The Spirit as Dove*

The Markan account identifies the Spirit as a dove. Various proposals have been advanced to understand the dove symbolism[64]. We shall enumerate the prominent ones and establish the Markan position.

+ Attempts to Explain the Provenance of Dove Concept

The basic question is why does the Spirit take the form of a dove and not some other birds?

i) Various suggestions have been put forward according to which περιστερά is a scribal or translational error[65]. A close reading shows that they are mere conjectures.

---

[63] The Gospel of Hebrews does not make a reference to the dove. The Gospel of the Ebionites has ἐν εἴδει περιστερᾶς, but the Ebionite narrative is believed to be dependent on the canonical Gospels. Justin has both ὡς περιστερὰν τὸ ἅγιον πνεῦμα ἐπιπτῆναι ἐπ αὐτόν and ἐν εἴδει περιστερά (Dialogue 88, 3. 4). Matthew's ὡς is translated in the Sinaitic Syriac version as ܟܝܘܢܐ ܒܕܡܘܬܐ (the Curetonian version has ܟܝܘܐ ܐܝܟ). Cf. A.S. LEWIS (ed.), *The Old Syriac Gospels*, 6. Luke's σωματικῷ εἴδει ὡς περιστεράν is translated in Sinaitic Syriac as ܒܕܡܘܬܐ ܓܘܫܡܢܐܝܬ ܕܝܘܢܐ. The literal translation of ܒܕܡܘܬܐ ܕܝܘܢܐ would be ἐν εἴδει. So the variation between ὡς and ἐν εἴδει may be just stylistic (so S. GERO, «The Spirit as Dove», 20, n.2). It may also be noted that a comparison of the Markan rendering is not possible as the Syriac versions do not contain Mark 1,1-11; these verses are considered lost.

[64] At the same time many scholars reject any association of the Spirit with the dove. Cf. A. FEUILLET, «Le symbolisme de la colombe», 533; H. GREEVEN, «περιστερά», 69, n. 65; L.E. KECK, «The Spirit and the Dove», 49.

[65] E.A. Abbott suggests an emendation of יוֹנָה (dove) to יָנוּחַ (will rest) probably with an appeal to Isa 11,2: וְנָחָה עָלָיו רוּחַ יְהוָה. Abbott also cites other instances of possible mistaken reading: e.g., הָעִיר הַיּוֹנָה of Zeph 3,1: speaks of the «oppressing city» (RSV) but LXX has ἡ πόλις ἡ περιστερά Cf. E.A. ABBOTT, *From Letter to Spirit*, 115. Cf. also S. GERO, «The Spirit as a Dove», 22, n. 8; L.E. KECK, «The Spirit and the Dove», 44, n. 1.

S. Hirsch argues that the narrative of baptism, temptation and transfiguration was originally an integrated unit. The transfiguration in fact reports the giving of God's *Kabod* to Jesus. This is *shekinah*. She also appeals to the idea that the proselytes are

ii) It is quite reasonable to look for evidence of the dove as symbol for the Spirit in contemporary Judaism. E. Lohmeyer, for instance holds for an apocalyptic nature of the whole account in which any creature is an apocalyptic entity and the dove is chosen because of the comparison of the Spirit with a dove in Jewish literature[66]. E. Lohmeyer's argument may be logical, but there is not sufficient evidence to suggest that in Jewish literature there was any clear reference to the form of the Spirit as a dove nor was there any instance of anyone having seen the Spirit in the form of a dove[67].

iii) There have been attempts to appeal to *Hellenized Judaism* and look to Philo and the Wisdom tradition to explain the provenance of the dove concept[68]. Although Philo commenting on Gen 15,9f. sees a similarity between the birds, he appears to be more interested in their differences[69]. Philo distinguishes between τρυγών and περιστερά. While the former, according to him, is fond of lonely places and loves solitude, and therefore represents the divine Word or wisdom, the latter is quiet and tame, and gregarious, haunting the cities of men; it therefore stands for human reason. In fact for Philo the dove is a bird which is inappropriate as a symbol of the divine[70].

---

said to come under the wings of the shekinah (Mekil. Exod xviii. 27) and שְׁכִינָה easily became שְׁכִּינָה (that which is like a dove). Cf. S. HIRSCH, *Taufe*, 43-59. Cf. also L.E. Keck who points out that there is no attested instance of שְׁכִּינָה. L.E. KECK, «The Spirit and the Dove», 45-46. H. Greeven sees a possible connection between John's ἔμεινεν ἐπ' αὐτόν and shekinah (μένειν = שׁכן). Cf. H. GREEVEN, «περιστερά», 68, n. 56.

[66] E. LOHMEYER, *Markus*, 21-22. E. Lohmeyer understands the ὡς as the apocalyptic ὡς in Rev. 5,6: ἀρνίον [...] ὡς ἐσφαγμένον. He points out that Ezekiel speaks of the cherubim at the throne of God; Daniel refers to the great beasts in his dreams; the book of Revelation has references to the many creatures who are apocalyptic beings and above all Christ himself appears in the book of Revelation as the «lamb of God» or the «Lion of Judah». He continues that, «es sind mehr als bloße Gleichnisse und weniger als klare Bezeichnungen himmlischer Gestalten, sie halten zwischen Bild und Realität eine schwebende Mitte wie sie apokalyptischen Größen und apokalyptischem Denken gemäß ist. Wenn darum Christus als das Lamm erscheinen kann, so auch der Geist als eine Taube [...]».

[67] See also L.E. KECK, «The Spirit and the Dove», 46-47.

[68] F.C. CONYBEARE, «New Testament Notes. (1) The Holy Spirit as a Dove», 451-458; E. NESTLE, «Zur Taube als Symbol des Geistes», 358-359; G. SELLIN, «Das Leben Des Gottessohnes», 243.

[69] PHILO, *«Quis Rerum Divinarum Heres»*, § 126f. 234; ID., *«Quaestiones et Solutiones in Genesin, III»*, § 3.

[70] C.K. BARRETT, *The Holy Spirit*, 38; A. FEUILLET, «Le symbolisme de la colombe», 532, n. 22; L.E. KECK, «The Spirit and the Dove», 47-48; G.W.H. LAMPE,

iv) Appeal to Noah's dove has been made by some scholars to explain the descending of the Spirit as dove[71]. It is argued that just as Noah's dove was the harbinger of the first covenant so also the dove at Jesus' baptism opens the way toward the new covenant in which all Israel «will know the Lord» through the indwelling presence of the Spirit. The basic problem is that Noah's dove does not descend from heaven; it is one among the birds saved.

v) The dove has been considered the symbol of all kinds of virtues. Particularly its gentleness and innocence has been proposed by some as the rationale behind the association of the Spirit with the dove[72].

vi) Others going further, argue that the dove is a symbol for Israel. Especially basing on the Midrash on the Song of Songs which compares the qualities of a dove to a faithful Jew, it is argued that the symbol of Israel takes up residence in Jesus, and Jesus is thereby transformed into embodied Israel[73].

vii) Another tendency among scholars is to trace the association of the dove with Spirit in the rabbinic literature[74]. Some important texts may be referred to:

– The most important of such texts is Gen 1,2: וְרוּחַ אֱלֹהִים מְרַחֶפֶת עַל־פְּנֵי הַמָּיִם . Rashi on Gen 1, 2 says: «The Spirit of God was moving: the Throne of glory was standing in the air and moving on

---

The Seal of the Spirit, 36. F. Hahn thinks that the Diaspora Judaism might provide the ground for equating the dove and the Spirit. Cf. F. HAHN, *Hoheitstitel*, 342-343, n. 3.

[71] C.W.H. LAMPE, «The Seal of the Spirit», 46, n. 3; A. RICHARDSON, *The New Testament*, 181. For further links between Noah's dove and the Spirit cf. P. GARNET, «The Baptism of Jesus», 52-55.

[72] BAGD, 651-52; W. HENDRIKSEN, *Mark*, 43-44; W. TELFER, «The Form of a Dove», 241.

[73] E. LOHMEYER, *Markus*, 21; Str-B I, 123. Cf. A. EDERSHEIM, *The Life*, 287: «If, therefore, Rabbinic illustration of the descent of the Holy Spirit with the visible appearance of a dove must be sought for, it would lie in the acknowledgement of Jesus as the ideal typical Israelite, the Representative of His people»; A. PLUMMER, *S. Luke*, 99: «It is not true that the dove was an ancient Jewish symbol for the Spirit. In Jewish symbolism the dove is Israel»; Cf. also F. LENTZEN-DEIS, *Die Taufe Jesu*, 170-183.265-270.

Against this interpretation see G. Richter, «Zu den Tauferzählungen», 46. Richter holds that «die Taube ein im Judentum und Judenchristentum (zumindest in manchen jüdischen und judenchristlichen Kreisen) geläufiges Symbol des Geistes gewesen ist». See also R. PESCH, *Markusevangelium*, 91; A. VÖGTLE, *Offenbarungsgeschehen*, 77-78.

[74] I. ABRAHAMS, *Studies*, 47-50; C.K. BARRETT, *The Holy Spirit* 38-39; Str-B I, 123.

the face of the waters by the Spirit of the mouth of the Holy One, blessed be he, and by his Word like a dove that broods on the nest [...]»[75].

– Midrash Rabbah records a conversation between R. Simeon ben Zoma and R. Joshua in which ben Zoma narrates: «"I was contemplating the Creation [and have come to the conclusion] that between the upper and the nether waters there is but two or three fingerbreadths", [...] "For it is not written here, And the spirit of God blew, but hovered, like a bird flying and flapping with its wings, its wings barely touching [the nest over which it hovers]"»[76]. The ben Zoma story is repeated in the Talmud (Hagiga 15a). Here ben Zoma says that the Spirit is «like a dove which hovers over her young without touching them».

The ben Zoma analogue has important parallels to the Synoptic account. There is first and foremost a comparison of the Spirit to the dove. Secondly the Spirit's appearance «on the face of the waters» fits in well with the baptismal scene at the Jordan.

viii) Among all the different possibilities, the most plausible suggestion may be that the dove symbolism echoes Gen 1,2, where the Spirit broods, birdlike, over the waters. But the main problem is that here it does not imply that the Holy Spirit appeared visibly as a dove, but that the motion and action of the Spirit were comparable to the motion of a dove over her young. Neither is there a reference to the descent of the dove here. It has to be acknowledged that in any case, there is in the older literature no passage in which the dove is plainly and clearly a symbol of the Holy Spirit[77].

+ Mark's Position

The canonical Gospel accounts unanimously[78] and explicitly speak of the Spirit descending at Jesus' baptism in the form of a dove[79]. The

---

[75] I. ABRAHAMS, *Studies*, 49, quotes the saying of Rashi as it is considered to be representing the more orthodox view as against the Talmund which in general is thought of as presenting Ben Zoma's idea.

[76] H. FREEDMAN – M. SIMON, ed., *Midrash Rabbah, Genesis*, 18.

[77] Str-B I, 125: «Jedenfalls gibt es in der älteren Literatur keine Stelle, in der die Taube klar u. deutlich ein Symbol des heiligen Geistes wäre».

[78] The Sinaitic version of John 1,32 omits the mention of the dove. The Baptist talks of only the «Holy Spirit» (ܪܘܚܐ) descending form heaven. But the Curetonian version has «Spirit like a dove» (ܪܘܚܐ ܐܝܟ ܝܘܢܐ). Cf. A. S. LEWIS, *The Old Syriac Gospels*, 210.

independence of the canonical accounts is much more credible than attributing to them any dependence on extra biblical sources[80]. Mark's interest in v. 10 is to present the presence of the Spirit. The Spirit had to take some form as well to manifest itself. That the Spirit took the form of a dove is beyond doubt for him[81]. But why precisely the form of a dove was of no interest to him, nor to other evangelists, neither have they attempted to explain it.

3.3.3 The Scope of the Descent of the Spirit

Mark narrates that the Spirit descended εἰς αὐτόν. Matthew, Luke and John have ἐπ᾽αὐτόν. εἰς is used for ἐπί in koiné and it does not imply a penetration of the Spirit. Scholars however, understand this phrase differently. For those who especially advocate a divine-man Christology in Mark, it is here that the divine Spirit penetrates (εἰς = into) Jesus so that he ceases to be mere human being and is transformed into a divine man[82]. Quite a good number of scholars understand that Jesus has been endued with the Spirit[83]. Following E. Lohmeyer's assertion that here the Spirit is «not a gift, but a form»[84], many other scholars have argued that Mark does not «speak of endowment with the Spirit, but of the Spirit coming down to Jesus»[85]. In fact, the great event seen by Jesus is the descent of the Spirit. If it was the endowment with the Spirit that merited attention, emphasis would have been laid on Jesus' experience as the recipient of a supernatural power taking hold

---

[79] But the non canonical versions are not as unanimous. Gospel of Hebrews does not have a comparison of the Spirit to a dove. The gospel account reads: «And it came to pass when the Lord was come up out of the water, the whole fount of the Holy Spirit descended upon him and rested on him [...]». Cf. W. SCHNEEMELCHER, *The New Testament Apocrypha* I, 177. The Gospel of the Ebionites however, does mention that Jesus «saw the Holy Spirit in the form of a dove [...]». Cf. *Ibid.*, 169.

[80] S. Gero («The Spirit as a Dove», 18-19) argues that possibly Mark had recourse to a pre-Markan tradition about the baptism of Jesus. Gero takes the 24 th Ode of Solomon as providing the link with the narrative of Mark. In the opening lines of the poem a reference is made to the dove that «fluttered over the head of our Lord Messiah». However, the main problem here too is that there is no indication that the dove is the symbol for the Spirit.

[81] The fact that the dove is considered innocent and pure (Matt 10,16), and that it is the bird fit for sacrifice (Lev 1,14) makes it an appropriate candidate.

[82] R. BULTMANN, *The Synoptic Tradition*, 252; F. HAHN, *Hoheitstitel*, 342-45; etc.

[83] R.H. GUNDRY, *Mark*, 51; G. SELLIN, «Das Leben des Gottessohnes», 242.

[84] E. LOHMEYER, *Markus*, 23: «Denn er ist hier nicht Gabe, sondern Gestalt [...]».

[85] H.B. SWETE, *St. Mark*, 9; V. TAYLOR, *St. Mark*, 160.

of him. But the narrative wants to focus on what Jesus sees and by necessity the form of the Spirit and its descending upon him are the points of interest.

A comparison with another seeing of a descent may provide an explanation to the significance of the Spirit's descent at the Baptism of Jesus. In John 1,51, Jesus tells Nathanael, «you will see (ὄψεσθε) the heavens opened, and the angels of God ascending and descending upon the Son of Man». There are common elements with the narrative of Mark 1,10f.: there is a seeing, an opening of the heavens, and the descent of the divine beings. The only thing that is lacking is heavenly voice.

The image of the angels ascending and descending is probably taken from Jacob's dream of the ladder and the angels ascending and descending on it (Gen 28,12). This awesome experience leads Jacob to exclaim «This is none other than the house of God, and this is the gate of heaven» (Gen 28,17). The house of God or temple is the place where the people meet God. According to John 1,51, the disciples of Jesus would recognise in the person of Jesus the embodiment of the presence of God; Jesus is the temple of God and in Jesus the possibility is offered for all men to meet God. In John 1,51, the scope of the angels ascending and descending is not in order to confer anything on Jesus but to show the mystery of his being.

Having seen that in Mark 1,10 the Spirit is not a gift but a form and reading it in the light of John 1,51 the conclusion that may be drawn is that the scope of the descent of the Spirit is not to endow Jesus with gifts but to manifest the mystery of Jesus. It signifies that the Spirit of God is present in Jesus. For Jesus seeing the descent of the Spirit is all too important because it reinforces his insight into the mystery of his being which the ensuing voice confirms eloquently. There is also another dimension to this event. Just as the presence of God in the temple is for the people, the powerful presence of the Spirit in Jesus is at the service of the people. God is made accessible to the people in Jesus. The «mightier one» foretold by John the Baptist is thus ready to baptise with the Holy Spirit.

4. Auditory Experience of Jesus

A voice from heaven (φωνὴ ἐγένετο ἐκ τῶν οὐρανῶν) follows the vision. As we have noted earlier it is not said that Jesus heard the voice, but the fact of the voice issuing out of heaven is reported. It is evident that Mark wants to put the emphasis on Jesus' seeing. It will not be illogical to say that Jesus' hearing is already contained in his seeing.

It is not an uncommon feature of a vision to be succeeded by a voice (cf. Acts 10,10-16 and Rev 21,2-4). Scholars in the past have argued that the notion which is conveyed by the words φωνὴ ἐκ τῶν οὐρανῶν is similar to that which is frequently described in the Rabbinical literature as קוֹל בַּת[86]. The expression bath-qol (Aramaic בְּרַת קָלָא or קָל בְּרַת) means «daughter of the voice» and signifies an echo of a heavenly voice. After the destruction of the second temple and the death of the last prophets in Israel, Haggai, Zachariah and Malachi, there developed among the Rabbis the idea that the Holy Spirit ceased out of Israel, and in His place God caused the voice from heaven (bath qol) to come forth. So the usual notion of the bath qol is that of an inferior substitute to the voice of God communicated through the Holy Spirit[87].

For Mark there is no doubt that the voice from heaven is the voice of God (cf. Gen 15,4; Deut 4,36; Dan 4,31). He clearly speaks of a voice, and not a «daughter of the voice» (bath qol). So there is no reason to turn to the bath qol to understand the significance of the voice that issues out of heaven[88]. In Mark 1,11 the voice from heaven says: «Σὺ εἶ ὁ υἱός μου ὁ ἀγαπητός, ἐν σοὶ εὐδόκησα»[89]. Scholars generally turn to the OT for a key to understand the statement from heaven. A closer look at the statement makes clear that several OT motifs are fused in this expression.

---

[86] I. ABRAHAMS, Studies, 47-49; C.K. BARRETT, The Holy Spirit, 39-40; O. BETZ, «φωνή», 288-290.298-299; C.E.B. CRANFIELD, «The Baptism of our Lord», 58; E.S. JOHNSON, «Mark 15,39», 407.411; Str-B, I, 125-134.

[87] See Str-B I, 125-28 for numerous evidences. See also O. BETZ, «φωνή», 288-290. I. ABRAHAMS, Studies, 47-49: notes that the sound of a bath qol is sometimes compared to the chirping of a bird. Abrahams thus argues that this association of the bird (dove-symbolism) and the heavenly voice underlie the Gospel narrative of the baptism.

[88] R. PESCH, Markusevangelium, 92. R.H. Gundry adds that never was a bath qol accompanied by an epiphany as the voice in Mark is accompanied by one. Cf. R.H. GUNDRY, Mark, 51-52.

[89] The evangelists report the voice from heaven variously: Matt 3,24: «This is my beloved Son, with whom I am well pleased». Luke 3,22: «Thou art my beloved Son; with thee I am well pleased». John 1,34: «This is the Son of God». As we have already noted Luke's rendering is same as that of Mark. In Matthew the voice addresses an indeterminate audience. In John the voice speaks to John the Baptist. But unlike the Synoptics John notes only the basic theme that Jesus is the Son of God.

4.1 *«You Are My Son»*

The reference to Jesus as Son, is commonly viewed as a rendering of Ps 2,7: (υἱός μου εἶ σύ ἐγὼ σήμερον γεγέννηκά σε)[90]. Psalm 2 is a *royal psalm* and more specifically a *coronation psalm*. It celebrates the setting of a crown upon a new Davidic king, and his proclamation and anointing. An important part of the ceremony is the king's declaration of his mandate by reading the «covenant document» which contains the quotation from the words of God which are written in the «Lord's decree» (2,7). At the heart of the covenant is the concept of *Sonship*. The human partner in the covenant is thus made *son* of the covenant of God, who is *father*[91]. The early Christian community used the psalm particularly with reference to Jesus' resurrection from the dead (cf. Acts 13,33; Heb 1,5; 5,5)[92].

The most important concept that both Mark 1,11 and Ps 2,7 have in common is that of υἱός . Both Jesus and the Davidic king are addressed as Son. The voice speaks directly to the Son using the second person «you». But there are important differences between these two texts. In Mark there is no coronation, no enthronement, no adoption[93]. Mark 1,11 is a declaration of who Jesus is. Ps 2,7 (both MT: בְּנִי אַתָּה אֲנִי הַיּוֹם יְלִדְתִּיךָ as well as LXX: υἱός μου εἶ σύ ἐγὼ σήμερον γεγέννηκά σε) puts the «my son» first and lacks the definite article before «son». So it could read «a son of mine are you». Mark instead puts Σὺ in the first position; places the definite article ὁ before υἱός μου and adds the qualifying adjective ὁ ἀγαπητός[94]. Thus the word order[95] is different in Mark and more importantly the second part of the quotation from Ps 2,7 (ἐγὼ σήμερον γεγέννηκά σε) is lacking in Mark.

---

[90] In Luke 3,22 some western texts (D it; Justin, Clement etc.) read the exact quotation from Ps 2,7. But it is considered secondary. Cf. B.M. METZGER, *A Textual Commentary*, 112-113.

[91] P.C. CRAIGIE, *Psalms 1-50*, 64.67.

[92] C.R. KAZMIERSKI, *Jesus, the Son of God*, 37.

[93] Such an idea of an adoption theology in Christianity is understood to be a later development. Cf. E. HAENCHEN, *Der Weg Jesu*, 54; E. LOHMEYER, *Markus*, 23.

[94] It has been argued that in a Targum to Ps 2,7 the designation חביב is found perhaps helped by the ἀγαπητός motif in the Messianic expectation. Cf. R.H. GUNDRY, *The Use of the Old Testament*, 30-31; E. SCHWEIZER, «"υἱός"», 37-68.

[95] These changes in word order have been pointed out by many authors, e.g., R.A. GUELICH, *Mark*, 33; R.H. GUNDRY, *Mark*, 49.52; C.R. KAZMIERSKI, *Jesus, the Son of God*, 38-39. But F. Hahn argues that Mark's word order was in keeping with the current style of preaching! Cf. F. HAHN, *Hoheitstitel*, 343, n.2.

Moreover, in every other instance Ps 2,7 is quoted in the NT, its word order is strictly maintained[96].

4.2 The Adjective ἀγαπητός

Gen 22,2 (also 22,12.16) is thought of as providing a reference to the adjective ἀγαπητός[97]. In Gen 22,2 God commands Abraham to take his

---

[96] A view that was first propounded by W. Bousset is that the original form of the voice from heaven contained the designation ὁ παῖς μου instead of ὁ υἱός μου and that it was based on Isa 42,1. Cf. W. BOUSSET, Kyrios Christos, 57 n. 2. It gained wide support and was developed by O. Cullmann (Baptism in the New Testament, 16-18) and J. Jeremias («παῖς θεοῦ», 700-709; also New Testament Theology, 53-55). Jeremias' main arguments are: a) the descent of the Spirit upon Jesus at his baptism finds its parallel in Isa 42,1(Isa 42,1: I have put my Spirit upon him) b) παῖς is ambiguous and can mean «servant» or «son» c) The בְּחִירִי of MT in Isa 42,1 is translated by LXX as ὁ ἐκλεκτός μου (Jeremias takes the reading ὁ ἐκλεκτός τοῦ θεοῦ as the oldest text of John 1,34 even though poorly attested, because according to him its witnesses are very early [$p^{5\ vid}$ sa ℵ*] if not the earliest [a b e ff.^{2} sy $^{sin\ cur}$] in Egypt, in Syria and in the west. See also ἐκλελεγμένος of Luke 9,35), but some versions translate it as ἀγαπητός μου (see the version quoted in Matt 12,18), so the indication is that ἀγαπητός too comes from Isa 42,1 d) since the designation of Jesus as ὁ παῖς θεοῦ was avoided in a Hellenistic milieu from an early date, it is reasonable to suppose that ὁ υἱός μου in the voice at the baptism represents the Christological development of an original ὁ παῖς μου. As a further clue to the reference in Isa 42,1, C. Mauer notes that especially in the Markan passion narrative, the concept of Jesus as Servant of Yahweh is often emphasised, therefore it makes it probable that a Servant Christology can be detected in the baptismal narrative as well. Cf. C. MAUER, «Knecht Gottes», 1-38, especially 31.

The main problem that Jeremias' argument faces is that there is little indication that a change from παῖς to υἱός took place within the narrative. Cf. A. FEUILLET, «Le Baptême de Jésus», 481; R.H. GUNDRY, Mark, 52; I.H. MARSHALL, «Son of God», 328-330. The texts in Luke 9,35 and the variant version of John 1,34 which Jeremias points out have the variants for ἀγαπητός and not for υἱός. Cf. I.H. MARSHALL, «Son of God», 328. Besides, only the version quoted by Matthew in 12,18 has this expression. It reads: Ἰδοὺ ὁ παῖς μου ὃν ᾑρέτισα, ὁ ἀγαπητός μου εἰς ὃν εὐδόκησεν ἡ ψυχή μου. The problem is that Matthew's rendering is nowhere else attested. The LXX, Theodotion and Symachus (Aquila does not have it) all render the Hebrew בחיר by the Greek word ἐκλεκτός. Cf. C.R. KAZMIERSKI, Jesus the Son of God, 50. R.H. Gundry is of the view that Matthew has assimilated the designation ἀγαπητός into his citation of Isa 42,1 under the influence of the baptismal narrative. Cf. R.H. GUNDRY, The Use of the Old Testament, 112; For J. Grindel Matthew's version is an exegetical reading of בְּחִירִי prompted by early Christian vocabulary. Cf. J. GRINDEL, «Matthew 12.18-21», 110-115.

[97] R.A. GUELICH, Mark, 34; R.H. GUNDRY, Mark, 52; C.R. KAZMIERSKI, Jesus, the Son of God, 53-60.

son Isaac (τὸν υἱόν σου τὸν ἀγαπητόν) and offer him as a burnt offering. The term ἀγαπητός is a derivative of ἀγαπᾶν which means to love and is mainly used for the affection of persons[98]. C.H. Turner[99] has pointed out that in the classical period, when used with such terms as υἱός, θυγάτηρ, or παῖς, ἀγαπητός often referred to an *only child*. Though ἀγαπητός is used in LXX to translate ידיד (Ps 44[45],1; 59,5 [60,7]), יקיר (Jer 38, 20[31,20]), אהב (Zech 13,6), and יחיד (Gen 22,2.12.16; Amos 8,10 etc.), the sense of the only child according to Turner, is reflected only where LXX uses ἀγαπητός to translate the Hebrew word יחיד[100]. Thus the term designates Isaac as Abraham's only son. The heavenly voice too identifies Jesus as God's beloved one, his «only» son.

The Isaac typology[101] has probably influenced the early Christian Christology (Rom 8,32 and perhaps Mark 12,6)[102]. But it is not certain if this typological association has given rise to the firmly established tradition of the voice from heaven[103]. Moreover, what permeates the

---

[98] BAGD, 4-5.

[99] C.H. TURNER, «ὁ υἱὸς μου ὁ ἀγαπητός», 113-129.

[100] P.R. DAVIES – B.D. CHILTON, «The Aqedah», 531; C.R. KAZMIERSKI, *Jesus, the Son of God*, 54-55; F. LENTZEN-DEIS, *Die Taufe Jesu*, 187f.; C.H. TURNER, «ὁ υἱὸς μου ὁ ἀγαπητός», 113-129.

[101] C.R. Kazmierski following other authors have argued that such Isaac - Jesus comparison is present not only in the NT, but also among the Fathers of the church. He sees the sources of such tradition in Palestinian and Hellenistic Judaism, later Targumic and Midrashic collections, the Book of Jubilees, Josephus, IV Maccabees, Pseudo Philo and Philo of Alexandria. He draws out two main themes from an examination of the texts: a) Isaac's complete acceptance and willingness to be the sacrificial victim b) the atoning nature of his action. Cf. C.R. KAZMIERSKI, *Jesus the Son of God*, 56-75; see also A.R.C. LEANEY, «The Gospels», 28-34; G. VERMES, *Scripture and Tradition*, 206-223, especially 222.

The details in the Targums especially Isaac's consenting to be sacrificed, his asking to be bound lest by struggling he make the sacrifice unfit and be cast into eternal punishment, his seeing the «angels of the height» and the glory of the «Lord's Shekinah» as he lies bound on the altar, and his hearing a voice that says, «Come, see two unique righteous ones in the world» have nothing to do with the narrative of Mark. There is no mention in Mark of sacrifice, consent, binding, eternal punishment, angels, or Shekinah. Moreover, in Mark the voice speaks directly to Jesus unlike in the Targums. Cf. R.H. GUNDRY, *Mark*, 52. See also I.H. MARSHALL, «Son of God», 334.

[102] It is not sure either if the rest of the NT alludes to Gen 22. See P.R. DAVIES – B.D. CHILTON, «The Aqedah», 514-546.

[103] P.G. Bretscher suggests that on the other hand if the tradition of the voice already existed, together with the account of Jesus' passion, it is easier to conceive of

narrative of Gen 22 is the pathos of losing the only son. On the contrary it is pleasure not pathos that permeates the present text[104]. However, the force of the adjective ἀγαπητός in both texts cannot be ignored, nor the fact that the identification of Jesus as one destined to die does seem crucial for Mark's understanding of Jesus[105].

4.3 «With Thee I Am Well Pleased»

This phrase most likely is a rendering of Isa 42,1. εὐδοκεῖν means to *be well pleased, take delight*[106]. εὐδόκησα seems to translate רָצְתָה (MT has, «נַפְשִׁי רָצְתָה», «my soul is well pleased» and LXX reads, «προσεδέξατο αὐτὸν ἡ ψυχή μου»)[107]. Mark and the version of the Isaian verse quoted by Matthew 12,18 use the aorist form of εὐδοκεῖν. According to G. Schrenk the use of εὐδοκεῖν in the baptismal declaration means God's decree of election of the Son, which includes his mission and his appointment to the kingly office of Messiah[108]. Though the words associate Jesus with the unidentified and mysterious servant in Isaiah who has a very important role to play in God's plan, it is doubtful if an idea of election is involved. The Markan «εὐδόκησα» corresponds with the «ἀγαπητός», which also implies affection, delight and pleasure expressed by the verb εὐδοκεῖν. What is emphasised here is Jesus' relationship to God. For God, Jesus is «my Son», the «beloved Son», «with whom I am well pleased».

The heavenly statement in Mark does not refer to any election or appointment of Jesus on the part of God, it rather expresses the pleasure that God takes in him. The aorist does not also carry a temporal reference either[109]. God takes constant pleasure in Jesus, the primary reason for which is because Jesus is his «only son». There is however, a juxtaposition of role and relationship in the words of the voice from heaven. The role of Jesus as «Son» is combined with the filial

---

a possible typological application of the account in Gen 22. Cf. P.G. BRETSCHER, «Voice from Heaven», 305.

[104] R.H. GUNDRY, *Mark*, 53.

[105] J. SWETNAM, «On the Identity of Jesus», 414. Swetnam argues that the repetition of the same words υἱός and ἀγαπητός at the transfiguration (9,7) and in the parable of the vineyard and the wicked tenants (12,6) is a further proof for such an understanding.

[106] BAGD, 319.

[107] F. LENTZEN-DEIS, *Die Taufe Jesu*, 191-192.

[108] G. SCHRENK, «εὐδοκέω», 740.

[109] R.H. GUNDRY, *Mark*, 53; S.E. PORTER, *Verbal Aspect*, 126-129.

relationship, that embraces the sphere of affection and intimacy, so he is the beloved Son, in whom God is well pleased[110].

4.4 *The Meaning of the Voice*

The investigation of the OT texts as references to the voice from heaven shows that no single text (Ps 2,7; Isa 42,1; Gen 22,2) by itself

---

[110] There are other proposals too regarding the origin of the heavenly voice. For instance, it is argued that the heavenly voice addresses Jesus in virtue of his Messianic office. The Testaments of the Twelve Patriarchs give evidence of an expectation of two messianic figures, a kingly messiah of the tribe of Judah as well as a priestly messiah of the house of Levi. In Test. Levi 4,2 the priest Levi himself is called God's son. In 17,2 Levi speaks to God as a father. Levi 18,6-7 resembles Markan baptismal narrative:

The heavens shall be opened,
And from the temple of glory shall come upon him sanctification,
With the Father's voice as from Abraham to Isaac.
And the glory of the Most High shall be uttered over him,
And the Spirit of understanding and sanctification shall rest upon him (in the water).

Cf. R.H. CHARLES, *The Testaments*, 63-64. So the Markan Baptismal narrative is thought to be presenting Jesus in terms of this messianic figure. Cf. C.K. BARRETT, *The Holy Spirit*, 42-44. See also G. FRIEDRICH, «Beobachtungen», 265-311.

Christian influence on the Testaments of the Twelve Patriarchs is generally accepted. Cf. M.D. JONGE, «Christian Influence», 182-235; C.R. KAZMIERSKI, *Jesus the Son of God*, 43-45. So the idea of Jesus as a Messianic High Priest may have been taken from Christian circles.

P. Bretscher relying heavily on the OT theme of Israel as God's son, and the sonship of Jesus, proposes Exod 4,22-23 as the source of the baptismal saying. The important clause is MT: בְּנִי בְכֹרִי יִשְׂרָאֵל, LXX: υἱὸς πρωτότοκός μου Ἰσραήλ. Bretscher argues for a literal, precise translation of the Hebrew text. For MT בְכֹרִי is a noun, but LXX translates it as an adjective: πρωτότοκός. So Bretscher suggests to translate the phrase as ὁ υἱὸς μου ὁ πρωτότοκός μου Ισραηλ (ἐστιν). This comes close to the Matthean version of the voice from heaven. οὗτός supplants Ισραηλ in Matthew. The link with Exod 4,22 becomes even stronger according to Bretscher when the version of the heavenly voice in 2Pet 1,17 is considered: Ὁ υἱός μου ὁ ἀγαπητός μου οὗτός ἐστιν. For Bretscher whether Jesus as Son of God is called ἀγαπητός, or μονογενής, or ἐκλεκτός, the root term which seems to stand behind all these is πρωτότοκός referring to the בְכֹרִי of Exod 4,22 (cf. Jer 31,9 and 31,20; 4Es 6,58). Cf. P. BRETSCHER, «Exodus 4,22-23», 305-311; Other scholars also have argued in similar terms; see also B. BYRNE, *Sons of God*, 13-16.23-28; F. LENTZEN-DEIS, *Die Taufe Jesu*, 184-185.

It is an impressive argument. The fact that Jesus as «Son» embodies the relationship between God and Israel and vice versa is well taken. The difficulty in accepting the argument lies mainly in the alterations to the text which Bretscher suggests as well as his proposal to consider that πρωτότοκός stands behind ἀγαπητός.

underlies the utterance of the heavenly voice. But these texts cannot be easily dismissed as having little influence on the baptismal saying. Important motifs from these texts are fused in the statement from heaven and they provide the background for the interpretation of Mark 1,11.

The heavenly voice cannot also be interpreted without reference to the vision. In explaining Jesus' seeing the Spirit descending upon him we have established that its importance lies in proclaiming the mystery of Jesus. The voice too does not confer any title on Jesus, but expresses who Jesus is: «Thou art my beloved Son; with thee I am well pleased». So the proclamation of the identity of Jesus is the function of the voice from heaven[111]. Evidently in Jesus not only the hopes of a Messiah-king are converged, but also that of the Messiah-servant presented by Isaiah (Isa 11,2; 42,1). But Jesus is much more than that, he is the Son, the beloved, of the same reality of God himself. The fact that the heavenly voice reiterates the same at the transfiguration of Jesus (9,7) is further proof that it does not imply any bestowal of a title, adoption,[112] commissioning[113] or enthronement[114]. Even the other similar texts in Mark 3,11; 15,39 (also 12,6) have the same function, that of proclaiming the identity of Jesus, his relationship with God and the Spirit.

4.5 *Summary*

Jesus sees both the tearing open of the heavens as prelude to the direct intervention of God and the progression of the descent of the Spirit upon him. The voice that accompanies these events confirms what Jesus experiences in his seeing. It reveals his identity and his role. Jesus is the only Son of God, the beloved son whose relationship to

---

[111] R.H. GUNDRY, *Mark*, 50: «The question whether Jesus was God's Son before his baptism does not come into view. As an omniscient narrator Mark is simply telling his audience of Jesus' true identity, as already indicated by Mark in v 1 but now as acknowledged by none other than God, and is setting the stage for Jesus' exercise of divine power». D.H. JUEL, *Mark*, 33: «It could be said that the words of the heavenly voice contain in summary form a preview of Jesus' career: he is the Christ, God's Son, the servant on whom God pours out the Spirit so that he may bring forth justice among the nations-God's beloved Son who is destined to be offered as a sacrifice. There are hints that the story of Jesus has "been written"».

[112] Against P. VIELHAUER, *Erwägungen*, 213.

[113] The voice communicates no commission to fulfil. So R.H. GUNDRY, *Mark*, 53.

[114] Against P. VIELHAUER, *Erwägungen*, 212-214.

God is completely unique, who is the object of the immense love of the Father. The heavenly voice will once again proclaim the same identity at Jesus' transfiguration. But the voice at that instance is accessible to the select three disciples too, who are commanded to listen to Jesus (9,7). It is precisely Jesus' relationship to God that obliges the disciples to listen to him.

5. The Import of the Vision and the Voice from Heaven

The event of Jesus' seeing at his baptism and what follows as Mark presents them, are of utmost importance for Jesus. We shall establish that Jesus' seeing was a great moment of communion with God and try to indicate Jesus' consciousness at the beginning of his ministry and find out the significance of the events at Jesus' baptism for salvation history.

5.1 *Seeing as an Extraordinary Moment of Communion*

It is our view that the verb εἶδεν which expresses Jesus' seeing the heavens being torn apart and the Spirit descending upon him carries with it the added weight of the idea of interaction and communion. It clarifies that Jesus' experience is more than a vision; the Spirit's activity is eminently superior to what is witnessed to by the OT; God's voice is supremely greater than what is alluded to in the call-narratives and other divine interventions of the OT. Here is God speaking to his Son; the Son experiencing the love of God in the Spirit; the Spirit, by His powerful presence, moving Jesus to undertake the ministry entrusted to him by God. Jesus thus is involved in a state of sharing or exchanging the same thoughts or feelings, and aligning his will to the will of God. His seeing at his baptism was thus a moment of extraordinary actualisation of his communion with God and the Spirit. The rest of the Gospel is an account of the interaction of God, the Spirit and Jesus himself in his ministry.

At the same time, Mark portrays Jesus throughout his narrative as actively involved in an ongoing communion with God. Since all of Jesus' actions are guided by the Spirit, Jesus' life is characterised by a sure and constant communion with the Spirit. But communion with God is also maintained by time exclusively dedicated to that purpose. It was Jesus' habit to seek communion with God in prayer either at the beginning of the day's ministry (1,35) or especially after a heavy day's strenuous activity (3,13; 6,32.46) or during moments of intense communication with God (9,2; 14,32-42).

When seeking moments of communion Jesus withdraws himself from the public all by himself (1,35; 6,46; 14,32-42), or in the company of his disciples (3,13; 6,32; 9,2). Jesus also seeks out a place conducive for prayer and solitude. He goes to a «lonely place» (1,35.32), or goes up on the mountain (3,13; 6,46; 9,2), or as in those moments before his arrest, proceeds to the garden of Gathsemene (14,32-42). Mark seldom reports what transpires during these intense moments of communion, nor are the contents of his prayer narrated[115]. Mark's interest is exactly to point to the fact of Jesus' ongoing communion with God, rather than presenting the mode of communion. Any attempt from the part of the Evangelist to describe what happens during those moments would be a limitation. So he does not attempt it. All the same in a rare instance Jesus alludes to his relationship to God by calling him Abba, Father and pleads that he may be spared of «the cup» (14, 36). But he hastens to choose God's will rather than to succumb to the momentary inner urging. In doing so Jesus was aligning his will wholly to the will of God entering thus, into a perfect communion with God.

5.2 The Consciousness of Jesus at the Beginning of his Ministry

Mark presents Jesus as one who sees (εἶδεν) the heavens being torn apart and the Spirit descending upon him, accompanied by the declaration of the heavenly voice regarding his status. It implies that Jesus begins his public ministry fully conscious of his relationship to God and to the Spirit.

5.2.1 Jesus is Aware of His Status in Relation to God

Jesus sees the Spirit descending upon him like a dove and then hears the voice from heaven. There is no doubt that the voice belongs to God. The voice confirms what Jesus experiences in his seeing and strengthens his insight into the mystery of his being. It cannot but be a

---

[115] R.H. Gundry speculates on why Mark omits the content of the prayer. It could be either: a) to underline the closeness of Jesus as Son to God as Father b) or to present in Jesus' praying evidence of godliness, as opposed to dying a criminal's death by crucifixion c) or to show Jesus' prayer as evidence of Jesus' piety to forestall suspicion that Jesus is a magician. Cf. R.H. GUNDRY, *Mark*, 93-94. The first reason Gundry provides looks reasonable. The other two points could be defended even by providing the content of the prayer.

decisive moment in which God proclaims the identity of Jesus. Jesus is the Son[116]. The fact that it is narrated solely as a private experience of Jesus implies that the account wants to concentrate solely on Jesus' experience of his relationship with God. Jesus is thus fully aware of his position as Son in relation to God.

Jesus' consciousness of being the «Son», will be evident in his preaching and activity in the rest of the Gospel. It is demonstrated in Jesus' successfully resisting Satan (1,12-13), in the authority with which he teaches (1,21; 4,2; 6,2.34; 11,17; 12,35), in the power of his «I say to you» (2,19; 3,28; 5,41; 812; 9,1.4; 10,15.29; 11,23; 12,43; 13,30.37; 14,9.18.25.30), in his claim to be the Lord of the Sabbath (2,28), in the numerous miracles he performs, in his own reference to himself as the Son (12,1-9; 14,62), and in foretelling and accepting his own death and resurrection (8,31-33; 9,30-32; 10,32-34) as carrying out the divine imperative as ransom for many (10,45) in fulfilment of the scriptures (14,21). This mystery of the divine Sonship is also proclaimed by others in the Gospel. Apart from the heavenly voice's reiteration at the transfiguration which the select three disciples also hear (9,7) it is also acknowledged in the Gospel by the demons (3,11; 5,7), by Peter, though in an imprecise way (8,29), by Bartimaeus in an implicit way (10,47.48) and by the Centurion in the most eminent way (15,39).

5.2.2 Jesus is Aware of His Relationship to the Spirit

The extraordinary event of Jesus' seeing the Spirit descending upon him (1,10) confirms his relationship to the Spirit. As we have noted above the Spirit's descent had the scope of manifesting the mystery of Jesus. That awareness moves him to assume his role as Messiah and Saviour. As a result, all his actions are going to be determined by the Spirit; the Spirit would be the moving principle of his ministry (cf. Acts 10,38). So there are good reasons to suspect that John the Baptist's announcement of the mightier one baptising with the Holy Spirit becomes a reality (1,8)[117].

---

[116] One is inclined to suppose that the baptismal scene substitutes for an account of the epiphany of Jesus (Matt 2,1-12) which is lacking in Mark.

[117] An important scope of the narrative on Jesus' baptism is to introduce Jesus as greater than John. John compares the expected figure to himself «Ἔρχεται ὁ ἰσχυρότερός μου ὀπίσω μου» (1,7). The key to this comparison is expressed by the word ἰσχυρότερός. The only other two occurrence of the adjective in the Gospel of

The Spirit's driving him out into the wilderness immediately after (1,12) is proof that from now on the presence of the Spirit is so powerful in him that all his actions are guided by the Spirit. In the next reference to the Holy Spirit in the Gospel of Mark (3,29),[118] Jesus says «whoever blasphemes against the Holy Spirit never has forgiveness, but is guilty of an eternal sin – for they had said, "He has an unclean spirit"». In fact the scribes did not blaspheme against the Holy Spirit, they spoke ill of Jesus and his actions only: «He is possessed by Beelzebul, and by the prince of demons he casts out demons» (3,22). But Jesus takes the blasphemy against him as an attack directed against the Holy Spirit. The logical conclusion implicit in this discussion regarding casting out impure spirits (3,22-30), is that the Holy Spirit is eminently present in Jesus and that Jesus acts by virtue of the Holy Spirit.

It is evident that Mark does not refer to any explicit baptismal activity on the part of Jesus, in spite of the fact that John had predicted

---

Mark is in the context of Jesus' defence of his power over the demons (3,27). Here ἰσχυροῦ and ἰσχυρὸν are used to describe the strong man who has to be bound up before his house can be plundered. By implication Jesus has the power to overpower the demons (ἰσχυρὸν) and so he must be stronger. Therefore John's reference to ἰσχυρότερός may be understood as a reference to Jesus' superior power over the demons which John did not have.

It is precisely the difference in their activity that would confirm the expected one as greater. In 1,8 John says:

ἐγὼ   ἐβάπτισα ὑμᾶς ὕδατι,
αὐτὸς δὲ βαπτίσει ὑμᾶς ἐν πνεύματι ἁγίῳ

There is a perfect parallelism here. As far as the activity and the recipients of the activity are concerned there is agreement, but the subjects of the action and the means used are substantially different. John uses water for baptism, the expected figure will give a baptism with the Holy Spirit. John proclaimed and administered a baptism of repentance the result of which was the forgiveness of sins (1,4). In the case of the baptism given by the expected one, John does not say what effect it will have. The very means used for baptism itself is sufficient to portray its unequaled excellence. Water is a terrestrial reality, the Holy Spirit belongs to the Spiritual realm; He is the life of God.

[118] In fact these are the four references to the Holy Spirit that pertain to Jesus. There are only two more instances of the references to the Holy Spirit in the Gospel of Mark: 12,36 referring to David speaking in the Holy Spirit and 13,11 which is a promise to the disciples that when they are delivered up to the tribunals it will not be they who speak but Holy Spirit.

it[119]. For Mark it seems that the whole of Jesus' ministry is an administration of the baptism in the Spirit. Casting out impure spirit is a purificatory act which is akin to the cleansing brought about by baptism. Even the other miracles of healing that Jesus performs have a nuance of purification and liberation. In fact the whole of Jesus ministry assumes the purificatory role as it promises liberation and salvation. Jesus does not dispense the Holy Spirit; the Holy Spirit is the medium of the activity of Jesus (Isa 4,4 «spirit of judgement and a spirit of burning»; cf. also the Cornelius story in Acts 10–11, where too the Spirit is the agent). Just as water was not a gift but the medium of John's baptism, so too the Spirit is not a gift but the medium of the activity of Jesus; he is present in Jesus and acts through him. Anyone who is disposed to be open to the message of Jesus and welcomes the liberation he offers, is capable of being baptised in the Holy Spirit, to be placed under the powerful cleansing action of the Spirit[120].

---

[119] Neither Mark nor the other Synoptics have any reference to Jesus' baptising activity. The data from John's Gospel (John 3,22.26; 4,1) affirm Jesus' practice of baptising during his ministry after he struck out on his own. John 4,2 which states «although Jesus himself did not baptise, but only his disciples» is generally considered to be the fruit of editorial activity. Cf. R.E. BROWN, *John* I, 164; R. SCHNACKENBURG, *St John*, I, 422 n. 4. The historical reliability of the traditions concerning Jesus and John in the Gospel of John is widely accepted. Cf. J. ERNST, *Johannes der Täufer*, 206-210; J. JEREMIAS, *New Testament Theology*, 45-46; B.F. MEYER, *Aims of Jesus*, 122.

The witness of the Fourth Gospel is considered important mainly because the Gospel contains traces of polemic directed against the «Baptist sectarians». Cf. R.E. BROWN, *The Community*, 69-71. John is presented throughout the Gospel as subordinate to Jesus; John is only the «voice» (1,23), his role is to reveal Jesus to Israel (1,33) and his life's desire in his own words is that «he [Jesus] must increase, but I must decrease» (3,30). So if it was not a historical fact the Fourth Evangelist would have avoided presenting Jesus as gathering some of the Baptist's disciples (1,35-37.40.43-44), and using the rite of baptism in his ministry. Cf. J.P. MEIER, *A Marginal Jew*, 116-130; especially 122. Meier calls this argument based on the «criterion of embarrassment». Those who support the notion that Jesus did baptise include J. GNILKA, *Jesus of Nazareth*, 77; M. GOGUEL, *Jean-Baptiste*, 235-274; B.F. MEYER, *Aims of Jesus*, 122; J.P. MEIER, *A Marginal Jew*, 116-130; C.H.H. SCOBIE, *John the Baptist*, 153-156; R.L. WEBB, «John the Baptist», 219-223; W. WINK, *John the Baptist*, 55.94. However, the lack of multiple attestation regarding Jesus' baptising ministry grants it only a high probability.

[120] R.H. GUNDRY, *Mark*, 38-39; E. LOHEMYER, *Markus*, 19; J.E. YATES, «The Form of Mk 1.8B», 334-338.

5.3 *Importance of the Events for Salvation History*

Jesus' consciousness of his identity and his relationship to God and the Spirit implies that Jesus is also fully conscious of his relationship to humanity and inevitably, of his mission. That makes him embrace the role of the Son, which combines the role of the messianic king (Ps 2,7) and that of God's chosen servant (Isa 42,1), already implicit in the statement from heaven. Hence, «the descent of the Spirit effects not so much a change in Jesus, his person or his status, as the beginning of a new age in salvation-history»[121].

As seen above it marks the fulfilment, first of all, of John's prediction of the mightier one who would baptise with the Holy Spirit (1,7). We have established that the scope of the descent of the Spirit was not to endow Jesus with gifts, but to manifest his being. The powerful presence of the Spirit in Jesus is present to all the people. In fact it is in view of their salvation that God decides to reach out to them in the person of Jesus. The fact that even during the ministry of Jesus, the disciples succeeded in casting out the impure spirits and performing miracles (6,13) is proof enough to suggest that the Holy Spirit was active in them through Jesus.

The advent of this fulfilled time could also be seen as the realisation of the aspirations of the people articulated in Isa 63,7–64,11. This is commonly identified as a psalm of communal Lamentation[122]. The setting for the scene (63,1-7) is a call for continuous prayer of the people after the destruction of Jerusalem and the temple. The scene presents the prayer of the people with complaints, claims, demands as well as aspirations. The people nostalgically recall God's gracious deeds in the past for the house of Israel and remind Him that He is their Father (63,16): «For thou art our Father, though Abraham does not know us and Israel does not acknowledge us; thou, O Lord art our Father, our redeemer from of old is thy name». They express their fervent plea for God's intervention: «O that thou wouldst rend the heavens and come down» (63,19). The people pray God to literally tear down the heavens, the barrier that separates God from the people, and establish His powerful, spectacular presence in their midst to save them from the disaster that has engulfed them. They also acknowledge that

---

[121] J.D.G. DUNN, *Baptism in the Holy Spirit*, 28.

[122] C. WESTERMANN, *Isaiah 40-66*, 392. But some others call it the «sermon-prayer». Cf. J.D. WATTS, *Isaiah 34-66*, 329.

they have wronged against him (64,5-6), but they have confidence that God will act in their favour (64,11)[123].

The account of the baptism of Jesus is the literal fulfilment of the prayer of the people. The people who longed for a rending of the heavens were not fortunate to see it happening. Jesus instead sees the heavens being torn apart. He also sees the Spirit descending upon him; henceforth, the powerful presence of God's Spirit is present in him, thus fulfilling the deep yearning of the people for God's presence amidst them. God the Father himself acknowledges and proclaims that Jesus is His Son. So all that the people longed for is realised in Jesus.

Jesus' seeing takes place at a very important moment of his life. We have already noted that Jesus, in submitting himself to John's «baptism of repentance for the forgiveness of sins» (1,4), was identifying himself with the people flocking to John. This moment of solidarity established Jesus' links with the sinful humanity who alienated themselves from God. The same moment also provides the occasion for the supreme revelation of his identity and for establishing his links with God. Jesus' intimate and continuing union with God is the basis for God's intervention in human history. In Jesus both the humanity and Godhead meet in a supreme expression of reaching out; God reaching out to the people and people reaching out to God. The events at baptism usher in a new era for humanity.

6. Conclusion

The evangelist Mark presenting the vision (εἶδεν) of Jesus indicates with what consciousness Jesus begins his ministry. Jesus is fully aware of the tearing open of the heavens, of the presence of the Spirit and of his relationship to God the Father. At the same time, Jesus is equally aware of his relationship to humanity and the work of salvation he has to undertake on their behalf.

The events at his baptism already point to Jesus' inevitable destiny that includes death on the cross. We have noted that Jesus' final moments are already evoked by the use of the verb σχίζειν for the tearing open of the heavens as well as for the image of the torn veil in the temple (15, 39). The declarations at both instances confirming Jesus' identity link them together. At baptism the statement from heaven associate Jesus with Isaac (in so far as he is destined to die) and

---

[123] C. WESTERMANN, *Isaiah 40-66*, 392-398; E.J. YOUNG, *Isaiah* III, 490-491.

the mysterious servant in Isaiah whose destiny is irrevocably bound up with the plan of God. Thus a hint as to the destiny of the beloved Son of God is already in sight at baptism. Furthermore, in response to the Zebedee brothers' craving for privileged positions, Jesus refers to the cup he himself has to drink as undergoing a baptism (10,38). The cup and baptism stand in close parallelism and refer to the suffering and death Jesus has to undergo. For Jesus thus, his baptism is a baptism unto death. The events at his baptism already give him a glimpse into what is in store for him.

The narrative presents Jesus as the only one who sees and experiences what transpires at his baptism. John the Baptist who administered the baptism is not described as being party to the events that surround Jesus' baptism (cf. John 1,32f.). An obvious contrast between Jesus and John is intended here. John belongs to the time of prophecy (1,2-3), he is the messenger, the forerunner, the servant who is unworthy to untie the sandal of the expected one (1,7). Jesus belongs to the time of fulfilment (1,15), he is the greater one, the expected figure, one who would baptise with the Holy Spirit (1,8). John is distinguished from the time of Jesus in terms of anticipation. With Jesus, the time of fulfilment becomes a tangible reality. The events at baptism mark the turning point. Jesus sees and comes to know of his identity and role. John does not see, his role is to indicate the mightier one and fade away into the background, God's beloved Son takes the centre stage.

CHAPTER III

Jesus' Seeing the Prospective Disciples (Mark 1,16.19; 2,14)

The most eminent use of the verb εἶδεν for Jesus' seeing is in the context of the three narratives that speak of the call of the first of Jesus' disciples. They all have Jesus' seeing them as the most crucial element. The call of Simon and Andrew (1,16-18), the Zebedee brothers James and John (1,17-20) and that of Levi (2,14) is preceded by Jesus' seeing (εἶδεν) them. In the following analysis we shall examine the common features of the three narratives that speak of Jesus seeing them, which will be followed by a detailed analysis of each of the three narratives. Then we shall establish the importance of Jesus' seeing in these narratives, holding them against other similar call narratives both in the OT and in the Gospels.

1. Common Features of the Three Narratives

i) All three narratives begin with information on Jesus' movement: 1,16: Καὶ παράγων παρὰ τὴν θάλασσαν τῆς Γαλιλαίας; 1,19: καὶ προβὰς ὀλίγον; 2,14: καὶ παράγων . More importantly these episodes are reported as taking place on the sea-shore. The verb of movement used is a participle which in itself is a preparation for the main verb. In these instances Jesus' movement comes to a halt when he sees those whom he wants to call. Nevertheless, the details of Jesus' movement are quite different in all three accounts.

ii) The main action of Jesus is expressed by the aorist indicative εἶδεν. It is not a casual look[1] or a glance, rather it is an attentive,

---

[1] Against J. MATEOS – F. CAMACHO, *Marco*, 132: «La vista di quei [...] uomini sconosciuti, i primi nei quali si imbatte Gesù, dà l'occasione per la chiamata; poiché

intuitive, selective and penetrating seeing; a seeing that is loaded with meaning.

iii) The narrative then goes on to give the names of the ones seen: Simon and Andrew (1,16); James and John (1,19); and Levi (2,14). However, all three accounts differ in supplying the exact information regarding these men.

iv) A present participle in the accusative form indicates what they are engaged in as part of their daily occupation (1,16: ἀμφιβάλλοντας ἐν τῇ θαλάσσῃ; 1,19: καταρτίζοντας τὰ δίκτυα; 2,14: καθήμενον ἐπὶ τὸ τελώνιον).

v) The call from Jesus follows. Whereas in the call of Simon and Andrew and Levi the words used by Jesus are reported (1,17: Δεῦτε ὀπίσω μου; 2,14: Ἀκολούθει μοι), the account on James and John merely states that Jesus called them (1,20).

vi) In the first episode, the call is accompanied by a promise in the future tense (1,17: καὶ ποιήσω ὑμᾶς γενέσθαι ἁλιεῖς ἀνθρώπων).

vii) The reaction of those called is stated next. Although all three narratives have differing accounts, an aorist participle refers to their leaving their work (1,18: καὶ εὐθὺς ἀφέντες τὰ δίκτυα; 1,20: καὶ ἀφέντες τὸν πατέρα αὐτῶν [...] μετὰ τῶν μισθωτῶν ; 2,14: καὶ ἀναστάς).

viii) An aorist indicative which notes the unconditional following of the first disciples concludes the narrative (1,18: ἠκολούθησαν αὐτῷ; 1,20: ἀπῆλθον ὀπίσω αὐτοῦ; 2,14: ἠκολούθησεν αὐτῷ).

It may also be pointed out that the narrative on Jesus' seeing the first disciples and calling them is preceded by a notice about Jesus' preaching or teaching activity (1,14-15; 2,13). A sentence with a historical present that follows the narrative proper of the call, talks about the connection between Jesus and those called: they go to Capernaum (1,21), they enter the house (2,15). So Jesus' proclamation of the Gospel is portrayed as being linked to the appearance of the disciples.

---

l'incontro è casuale, questa non risponde ad alcuna qualità particolare che Gesù ha scoperto in loro né ha un carattere selettivo. Li invita senza prima aver intavolato un dialogo. L'unica cosa che ha visto in loro è l'attività di pescatori, che è figura del loro malcontento per la situazione».

2. He saw Simon and Andrew

The story of Simon and Andrew is the first of the three narratives that speak of Jesus' seeing his prospective followers. It sets the tone for the other narratives, with the simplicity and power similar to that of a medieval woodcut[2].

2.1 *Synoptic Comparison*

2.1.1 Mark 1,16-18 and Matt 4,18-20

For the most part Matthew is faithful to the Markan narrative. More importantly Matthew employs the same verb εἶδεν for Jesus' seeing. The differences between Mark and Matthew are slight and they arise mainly from certain vocabulary and style. Thus in the first scene (Mark 1,16-18 // Matt 4,18-20), Matthew has περιπατῶν for Mark's παράγων to refer to Jesus' movement. Matthew attaches importance to Jesus' seeing two[3] brothers (δύο ἀδελφούς) Simon and Andrew. Moreover, Matthew also informs that Simon is called Peter[4]. Mark instead speaks of Jesus seeing Simon and Andrew the brother of Simon. Even though both attach primary position to Simon, in Mark it is more obvious. Matthew uses a verb plus a noun (βάλλοντας ἀμφίβληστρον) to speak of casting net, Mark instead uses the verbal form ἀμφιβάλλοντας to refer to the activity of the brothers. Matthew has the historical present λέγει αὐτοῖς for Mark's εἶπεν αὐτοῖς ὁ Ἰησοῦς;; «I will make you fishers of men» (ποιήσω ὑμᾶς ἁλιεῖς ἀνθρώπων) for Mark's «I will make you *become* fishers of men» (ποιήσω ὑμᾶς γενέσθαι ἁλιεῖς ἀνθρώπων); and the more archaic εὐθέως for Mark's εὐθύς. The stylistic οἱ δέ of Matthew (vv 18 and 22) is an elegant construction that avoids repetition of the names of the pair of brothers.

---

[2] S. KUTHIRAKKATTEL, *Beginning*, 114.

[3] Matthean preference for two is well-known: Matt 8,28: two demoniacs; 9,27: two blind men; 10,29: two sparrows; 14,14: two fish; 18,16: two witnesses; 18,19.20: two or three gathering in Jesus' name; 20,21: mother of Zebedee brothers saying, «Command that *these two sons* of mine may sit, one at your right hand and one at your left, in your kingdom»; 20,24: two brothers; 20,30: two blind men; 21,1: Jesus sending two disciples; 21,28.31: the parable of the man having two sons; 24,40.41: the story of the two on the judgement day; 27,38: two robbers.

[4] This way Matthew harmonises the mention of Simon in the list of the Twelve in 10,2.

2.1.2 Mark 1,16-20 and Luke 5,1-11

Luke presents the story of Simon and the Zebedee brothers in a single scene as happening together. Therefore the two different scenes in the Markan account shall be considered together. The Lukan parallel to the Markan narrative of the call of the first disciples of Jesus has a number of differences that they almost eclipse the similarity between them. The main points of difference are:

i) The Lukan account of the call is framed in the context of the miraculous catch of fish.

ii) The call of the first disciples is not the first activity of Jesus. Jesus has been presented as fully engaged in his missionary activity prior to winning the disciples (4,14-44).

iii) Simon, who is the leading figure in the scene apart from Jesus, has already been introduced in 4,38. Jesus is known to him, and it can be presumed to the others, who also decide to follow Jesus, so that the invitation does not surprise them as they might have had reflected on the question beforehand. Mark's narrative is characterised by the unexpected invitation of Jesus and the more dynamic, mysterious as well as immediate following of the disciples.

iv) The dominance of Simon dwarfs the other disciples in the scene. Actually Andrew is not mentioned at all. That others are also involved in the story is brought out only by the use of the verbs in plural (vv. 5.6.7.11) and by the phrase «and all that were with him» (v. 9). The Zebedee brothers are introduced as «partners with Simon» (v. 10). So it is not certain how many disciples respond to follow Jesus on this occasion. Besides, the promise/mission is addressed only to Simon (v. 10).

v) From our point of view what is of utmost importance is that Jesus does not «see» any of these disciples. The verb εἶδεν is used in v. 2 to speak of Jesus seeing two boats. In fact Luke does not attach any special significance to the use of the verb ὁρᾶν/εἶδεν for Jesus. Even though 3 of the 4 occurrences (5,2; 15,20; 21,1.2) are used of Jesus' seeing, none of these instances indicate a particular use of the verb. They signify normal seeing of Jesus (5,2: Jesus seeing two boats; 21,1: Jesus seeing the rich putting their gifts into the treasury; 21,2: Jesus seeing a poor widow put in two copper coins; the other occurrence refers to the father seeing the prodigal son returning: 15,20)[5].

---

[5] Interestingly Luke's use of εἶδον (plural) is noteworthy. It is used in Luke to refer to seeing something marvellous and supernatural. Thus, shepherds glorify and praise

vi) Jesus does not even call anyone. The miraculous haul of fish moves Simon to realise his sinfulness. Peter's confession makes Jesus to issue a metaphorical saying. Nothing in the statement «Do not be afraid[6]; henceforth you will be catching men» (v. 10) implies that there is a call to follow the person of Jesus.

All the same there are similarities between the accounts of Mark and Luke. Both deal with the following of the first of Jesus' disciples; both the narratives are preceded by a reference to the teaching (preaching) of Jesus (Mark 1,14-15 and Luke 4,14-44; 5,3) and followed by accounts of his working miracles (Mark 1,21f. and Luke 5,12f.); primary position in both narratives are given to Simon whom Luke also calls Simon Peter (5,8 // Matt 4,18); both deal with a pair of brothers (even when Luke does not explicitly mention Andrew); the promise/mission (Mark 1,17: ποιήσω ὑμᾶς γενέσθαι ἁλιεῖς ἀνθρώπων and Luke 1,10: ἀνθρώπους ἔσῃ ζωγρῶν[7]) has to do with men; the narratives conclude with the disciples' renunciation of everything and unconditional following of Jesus.

2.2 Preliminary Observations

In the Markan narrative after the summary report of 1,14-15 a new scene (1,16-18) opens. The fact that it is a new scene is evident from the change in place, change of activity and the appearance of new characters. Mark 1,14 has a general reference to Galilee without being definite about the location; in 1,16 the sea shore of Galilee is specifically referred to. Even though Jesus remains the main actor new characters appear on the scene, namely Simon and Andrew. Moreover,

---

God for what they had *seen* (2,20); Simeon exclaims, «mine eyes have *seen* thy salvation» (2,30); Peter and those who were with him *saw* his (Jesus') glory and the two men who stood with him (9,32); the whole multitude of the disciples rejoice and praise God with a loud voice for the mighty works they had *seen* (19,37). In keeping with the Lukan theme of joy, all these seeings are an occasion for joy and praise. The only negative use of the verb is to say that the disciples did not *see* the risen Lord at the tomb (24,24). However, the fact of resurrection is so faith-compelling that the report of the women is sufficient motif for joy.

[6] «Μὴ φοβοῦ»is a common phrase in Luke especially familiar in epiphany scenes (cf. 1,13.30; 2,10; cf. also 8,50; 12,32). Cf. W. DIETRICH, *Das Petrusbild*, 46-47; R. PESCH, *Fischfang*, 139.

[7] ζωγρῶν means catching alive and is so used in the LXX. Cf. J. NOLLAND, *Luke 1–9: 20*, 223.

unlike the previous account which refers to Jesus' preaching, the activity of Jesus here is of making disciples.

Although 1,16-20 could be taken as a unit,[8] it is possible to distinguish 1,16-18 as a separate scene because: i) a word of movement again indicates (1,19) Jesus shifting to a new location ii) there is a change of actors in the new scene (1,19-20) iii) The narrative reaches a conclusion when the first disciples accept an unconditional following of Jesus (1,18).

However, the scene has also links with 1,14-15 as well as the subsequent scene (1,18-20). 1,14-15 serve also as an introduction to the Galilean ministry of Jesus. Γαλιλαίας of v. 16 takes up the Γαλιλαίαν of v. 14. The themes outlined in v. 14 form the basis for the ministry of Jesus in Galilee and beyond. It would be reasonable to think that the disciples who are called upon to a specific mission would have to participate in the programme delineated there. The subsequent scene deals with the call of a new pair of disciples. So the activity of Jesus continues in the next scene too providing a link with the present scene.

2.3 Jesus' Seeing

In the previous chapter we have noted that Jesus is characterised in the beginning section of the Gospel of Mark by his passivity. Apart from the summary report of 1,14-15, the only transitive verb used of Jesus is the verb εἶδεν employed to refer to his seeing the heavens being torn apart. The other verbs used for Jesus are either intransitive or passive. Now even in this subsequent pericope (1,16-20) the next transitive verb used of Jesus is again εἶδεν, the importance of which can not be lost on the readers.

---

[8] The pericope 1,16-20 could be set between two movements, that of Jesus passing along by the sea of Galilee (1,16), and that of Jesus and his new companions going into Capernaum (1,21). Change of place is thus quite evident between 1,16-20 and the pericope that follows (1,21-28). From the shore of the sea of Galilee the action shifts to the synagogue of Capernaum. The actors too are different. Jesus the main actor is accompanied by the four new disciples in his journey to Capernaum, but once there so many new figures appear on the scene. The man with the unclean spirit and the congregation at the synagogue together with Jesus form the characters in the scene. While the activity of Jesus in 1,16-20 was calling the first disciples what transpires at the synagogue is entirely different. Jesus both teaches as well as performs an exorcism. Chronologically, 1,21-28 supposes a different day. Apart from the time spent for the journey to Capernaum, the visit to the synagogue itself takes place only on the Sabbath.

Whereas in its first occurrence εἶδεν was used to refer to Jesus' seeing an extraterrestrial reality, here the object of seeing is very much this worldly; to be precise two men engaged in their daily occupation. Suddenly Jesus becomes active, inviting those whom he sees to follow him. Those called are now instead characterised by their passivity, captivated by the towering personality of Jesus and his powerful look; meekly and unconditionally responding to the call.

Many scholars have noted that the key event of the narrative of Jesus' calling his first disciples is his seeing. For some the use of the word is purely technical and it just means «finding» the first pair of brothers at work[9]. Our investigation has the scope of establishing that Jesus' seeing is much more than that.

2.3.1 Jesus' Movement Precedes his Seeing

The seeing of Jesus is preceded by a movement. Mark refers to Jesus' movement with the phrase παράγων παρὰ τὴν θάλασσαν[10]. This phrase is unusual as it is overloaded with two παρά. It is Mark's style to use παρά with accusative (2,13; 4,1.4.15; 5,21; 10,46). However, the repetition of παρά in the same phrase does not occur anywhere else in the Gospel. Many consider it an addition of Mark[11]. Matthew has a neat phrase «περιπατῶν δὲ παρὰ τὴν θάλασσαν» (Matt 4,18). Getting rid of any indication of the place E. Lohmeyer interprets the phrase as an «Epiphany of the divine master»[12]. But his position has invited wide criticism. The context of Jesus «passing by» here is so different from an epiphany. Neither are other indications provided to suggest one. The narrative structure of the phrase itself clearly favours taking the phrase as a description of the situation. Jesus as already mentioned in v. 14 is in Galilee. Passing along by the sea of Galilee portrays Jesus in motion in the region of Galilee.

Only the participial form of the verb παράγειν is used by Mark in the Gospel. παράγειν indicating motion on the part of Jesus is used twice,

---

[9] J. ERNST, *Markus*, 56-57.

[10] That Mark uses a paratactic καί to link a scene with what precedes is widely noted. Cf. J.C. HAWKINS, *Horae Synopticae*, 150-153. So the use of καί in v. 16 is his characteristic way of connecting the scene with the summary report of 1,14-15.

[11] E. BEST, *Following Jesus*, 167; J. GNILKA, *Markus* I, 78; R.A. GUELICH, *Mark*, 49-50; V. TAYLOR, *St. Mark*, 168.

[12] E. LOHMEYER, *Markus*, 32: «eine Epiphanie des göttlichen Meisters».

both dealing with discipleship (1,16; 2,14)[13]. Jesus is pictured in the Gospel as being continually on the move[14]. It is a theme that is very important to Mark, because it is closely connected to Jesus' mission. From the very start, Jesus' forward movement into the lives of human beings is emphasised[15].

The sea of Galilee (θάλασσα τῆς Γαλιλαίας) is mentioned for the first time in v. 16. There is only one more reference to the sea of Galilee (7,31) and that happens to be the last reference to the sea in the Gospel[16]. The Sea of Galilee is the centre of Jesus' movement largely in the first half of the Gospel of Mark (cf. 2,13; 3,7; 4,1.35.37f.; 5,1.18.21; 6,53-54; 8,10.13). The sea was known by different names at the time of Jesus: Sea of Galilee; Sea of Tiberias (John 6,1; 21,1); Sea of Gennesaret (Josephus, War 3.10.7); Lake of Gennesaret (Luke

---

[13] In fact a word of movement on the part of Jesus regularly appears in the discipleship sections in Mark. Besides 1,16 and 2,14 see also 10,17 and the use of ὁδός in Mark. Cf. E. BEST, *Following Jesus*, 167.

An allusion could be made to the Lord's passing by before Moses on Mount Sinai (Exod 33,19; but the verb used by LXX is different: παρελεύσεται- עָבַר) and before Elijah on Mount Horeb (1Kgs 19,11: παρελεύσομαι - אֱבִיר). See also the reference to Elijah's passing by Elisha before commissioning him (1Kgs 19,19). Seen in this context the apparent casualness of Jesus' passing by takes on a different meaning. The fact that the decisive seeing and election of the disciples follow such movement indicates that it is more than chance. It is part of divine plan. It may be possible that Jesus is portrayed «not only as Elijah-like but also as godlike [...]». Cf. J. MARCUS, *Mark*, 179.

[14] A look at the first two chapters suffices to make the point:
1,9: Jesus came from Nazareth
1,12: The Spirit immediately drove him out into the wilderness
1,14: Jesus came into Galilee
1,16: And passing along by the Sea of Galilee
1,19: And going on a little farther
1,21: And they went into Capernaum
1,29: And immediately he left the synagogue
1,35: He rose and went out to a lonely place
1,39: And he went throughout all Galilee
2,1: He returned to Capernaum after some days
2,13: He went out again beside the sea
2,14: And he passed on
2,23: On the Sabbath he was going through the grain fields
[15] J. MARCUS, *Mark*, 183.
[16] For A. Stock these references to the sea frame Jesus' activities around the sea of Galilee. Cf. A. STOCK, *The Method and Message*, 66-67. But that is not true. Even after 7,31 the narrative talks of Jesus' movement between the shores of the sea: 8,10.13.

5,1)[17]. םי could mean both sea and lake. Among the evangelists only Luke calls it lake (5,1). Although this mass of water is an inland, fresh-water lake, which is twelve miles in length and six miles across its widest point,[18] we shall take the more common English translation «sea».

2.3.2 Characteristics of Jesus' Seeing

i) Jesus' seeing is not casual. In our analysis of Mark's vocabulary to refer to Jesus' seeing we have established that in order to express a casual look of Jesus, he does not employ the verb ὁρᾶν and never the aorist indicative εἶδεν. Its use has been reserved for events of particular importance. Jesus' passing along by the Sea of Galilee was a preparation for the next action of seeing. It is not that he just happens to pass by; nor does he happen to see the two brothers. His seeing them is not accidental but done on purpose.

ii) Right from the beginning the initiative rests solely with Jesus[19]. An up until now passive Jesus seizes the initiative and acts. Within the episode the first important word is a verb with Jesus as subject and the last a personal pronoun relating to him. The whole focus is therefore on Jesus' action. In fact the whole scene is dominated by Jesus. It is he who is on the move, sees and calls. He alone decides whom he is seeing and whom he is wanting to call. The disciples just respond to his call.

iii) Jesus' seeing is intuitive. He knows whom he is seeing; he knows what they are. There is nothing hidden from him. It is with a perceptive knowledge of the persons whom he sees that he is reaching out to them and calling them[20].

---

[17] Some like to replace «sea» with «lake». Cf. for example B.M.F. VAN IERSEL, *Mark*, 129 n. 5. For retaining «sea» rather than «lake» see E.S. MALBON, «The Jesus of Mark», 363-364. Cf. also R.A. GUELICH, *Mark*, 50.

[18] W.L. LANE, *Mark*, 67.

[19] K. Barth, by means of a minor change in the Descartian phrase «Cogito ergo sum», «I think therefore I am» converts it into a biblical truth: «Cogitor ergo sum». I am thought of by God, therefore I am, exist, live, believe. It is God who takes the initiative and reaches out to man. Man can only in all humility respond to God's kindness.

[20] Cf. Mark 12,34 for an explicit instance of the perceptive knowledge of Jesus expressed by the verb ἰδών.

iv) It is a seeing that chooses[21]. The vocation of the disciples has its beginning in this seeing of Jesus[22]. Unlike in the case of rabbis, the disciples are not the ones choosing their master after having listened to him, it is Jesus himself who selects them (cf. Matt 8,18-22 // Luke 9,57-62)[23]. The disciples are not prepared for the kind of seeing of Jesus and the ensuing call. Nor does Jesus meet them in the context of the study of Torah or any other religious activities[24].

v) Jesus' seeing flows out of his authority. Fully conscious of his links to God as well as to humanity at his baptism (1,10), and after withstanding Satan (1,12-13), Jesus comes into Galilee preaching, on his own authority (1,14-15). The seeing and calling of disciples which follows also is a demonstration of his authority. Jesus can in his own right see and choose whom he desires.

vi) Jesus' seeing is effective. It can be said that the call that follows Jesus' seeing is already contained in the fact of seeing. In other words, the call issues forth from the seeing and it meets with positive response from the disciples.

vii) Jesus' seeing is personal. Jesus directs his gaze on these two men not because they belong to the same family. Jesus sees them as two individuals, as two persons[25]. It is to emphasise this fact that both men are named in the narrative.

viii) Jesus' seeing is not just business-like, but he also loves whom he sees (cf. Mark 10,21: «And Jesus looking upon him loved him»).

Thus it can be concluded that Jesus' seeing is more than human, it is supernatural, absorbing and discipleship-creating.

2.3.3 Description of those whom Jesus Sees

The narrative hastens to furnish the names of those whom Jesus sees. Simon is a Greek name. It has a Hebrew equivalent: שִׁמְעוֹן (Gen 29,33; Simeon in Luke 2,25.34; 3,30; Acts 13,1; 15,14). Andrew (᾽Ανδρέας) on

---

[21] J. MARCUS, *Mark*, 183: «This seeing is not to be interpreted as passive observation but as an active "possessive gaze" by means of which Jesus lays claim to something through a inspection of it (cf. 11:11) - though this claim can sometimes be refused [...]».

[22] R. PESCH, «Berufung», 14; E. SCHWEIZER, *Markus*, 21; A. STOCK, *The Method and Message*, 67.

[23] J. DONALDSON, «Called to Follow», 68; R.H. GUNDRY, *Mark*, 66.70; M. HENGEL, *The Charismatic Leader*, 51; E. SCHWEIZER, *Markus*, 22.

[24] E. SCHWEIZER, *Markus*, 21.

[25] E. BOSETTI, «Un cammino per vedere», 126-127.

the other hand is a relatively unknown but strictly Greek name[26]. The name Simon is used 7 times in the Gospel. But it is the name Peter that is widely used: 19 times. However, both names never occur together[27]. The fact that Mark refers to Simon first and that also twice in v. 16 itself points to his prominence and his position of leadership in the early church. Andrew on the other hand is a relatively minor figure in the Gospel. Apart from the list of the Twelve (3,18), his name is mentioned only once more together with Peter, James and John, as recipient of Jesus' eschatological teaching (13,3). Very little is known about him in the Gospel except that he is the brother of Simon (ὁ ἀδελφός Σίμωνος). The need to identify him by his relationship to Simon reflects his relative obscurity.

ἀμφιβάλλοντας explains the occupation of the brothers Simon and Andrew. The verb ἀμφιβάλλοντας does not occur elsewhere in the NT and it denotes casting of a round net by one person to catch fish[28]. The explanatory phrase ἦσαν γὰρ ἁλιεῖς is precisely necessitated by the ambiguity of the verb itself. However, it is typically Markan style to add explanatory phrases with an imperfect indicative of εἰμί followed by γάρ (cf. ἦσαν γάρ: 1,16; 2,15; 6,31; 14,40; ἦν γάρ: 1,22; 5,42; 6,48; 10,22; 16,4)[29]. Nevertheless, this addition has its significance. It means that Jesus sees these men in the midst of everyday life and work[30].

---

[26] R.A. GUELICH, *Mark*, 50; S. LÉGASSE, *Marc*, 113, n. 5.

[27] V. TAYLOR, *St. Mark*, 168. V. Taylor adds that Jesus addresses the apostle as Simon notably when his weakness is apparent (14,37; Luke 22,31). Simon (Peter) is the first (1,16) and the last (16,7) disciple mentioned in the Gospel of Mark thus forming an inclusion around his name.

[28] R.A. GUELICH, *Mark*, 50; For a further explanation of fishing with a round net see W.H. WUELLNER, *Fishers of Men*, 39.

[29] Scholars consider this γάρ clause to be a clue that Mark is relying on pre-Markan tradition for the call narrative, because Mark has the tendency to use a γάρ clause in order to comment on existing material. Cf. E. BEST, *Following Jesus*, 166; J. MARCUS, *Mark*, 182; E.J. PRYKE, *Redactional Style*, 126.

[30] E. SCHWEIZER, *Markus*, 21-22: «Jesus begegnet dem Menschen nicht in einer besonderen religiösen Sphäre, sondern dort, wo er wirklich lebt, mitten in seinem Alltag».

2.4 *Jesus Calls those whom he Sees*

Jesus' seeing these two men impels him to address them. His seeing that is selective and the ensuing call constitute a homogeneous unit[31]. It could be said the call is contained in the seeing. What Jesus perceives in his seeing issues forth in a call to whom he sees. The formula «καὶ εἶπεν αὐτοῖς ὁ Ἰησοῦς» gives to what Jesus says an aura of solemnity. Jesus speaks just as God in the OT (καὶ εἶπεν ὁ θεός). What Jesus says consists of a call and a promise.

The call is expressed by the words Δεῦτε ὀπίσω μου which means «come, follow me»[32]. Δεῦτε is the plural of Δεῦρο regarded as an imperative (Here!, Come!)[33]. There are several other expressions used by Mark that imply following Jesus (cf. ἀκολουθεῖν - 1,18; 2,14.15; 8,34; ἔρχεσθαι ὀπίσω - 8,34; ἀπέρχεσθαι ὀπίσω - 1,20). «The imagery graphically depicts the pupil's role and relationship to the master illustrated by the disciples' following the teacher who leads the way»[34]. But this does not mean that Jesus and his disciples looked like the rabbinical schools of his day[35]. Neither is «following after» to be considered as deriving from the model of rabbinical scribes. In the opinion of M. Hengel «following after» was never used to describe becoming a student of the Law[36]. The expression «Δεῦτε ὀπίσω μου»

---

[31] R. PESCH, «Berufung», 14: «sein Blick dürfte als erwählender Blick verstanden sein, mit dem die Berufung der Jünger schon anhebt, sofern Jesu erwählender Blick und sein Ruf zusammengehören».

[32] BAGD, 575.

[33] V. TAYLOR, *St. Mark*, 169. cf. also Δεῦτε: 6, 31; 12,7; δεῦρο: 10,21. Δεῦτε originally was an adverb meaning «hither», but here it takes the force of an imperative in hortatory sense. Cf. M. ZERWICK, *A Grammatical Analysis*, 102.123. R. Pesch thinks that the expression «Δεῦτε ὀπίσω μου» could be a citation from 2 Kg 6,19 where Elisha with this invitation tells the Syrian army, which was struck with blindness by the Lord in answer to Elisha's prayer, to follow him. The army follows him, but is taken captive. Cf. R. PESCH, *Markusevangelium* I, 111. But here there is no notion of a call nor that of following in the sense of discipleship. So it is not a citation from 2Kgs 6,19. There is only a mere verbal similarity there.

[34] R.A. GUELICH, *Mark*, 50-51.

[35] Against A. SCHULZ, *Nachfolgen*, 7-32.

[36] M. HENGEL, *The Charismatic Leader*, 51. This makes R.A. Guelich to affirm that the term «follower», the familiar synonym for «disciple,» has its roots in the Christian rather than Jewish usage. Cf. R.A. GUELICH, *Mark*, 51. It has to be said that the OT itself refers to following in the sense of discipleship. For instance 1Kgs 18,21: And Elijah came near to all the people, and said, «How long will you go limping with two different opinions? If the LORD is God, *follow* him; but if Baal, then *follow* him»

therefore is a call to discipleship, the meaning of which is articulated by Mark in the course of the Gospel narrative[37].

The command to follow has its point of convergence on the person of Jesus: «follow me». The disciples are not called to carry out a programme. Jesus alone is the point of reference, they are called to a personal relationship with him. Jesus is the leader and they are followers. Jesus goes before them and shows them the way because he knows both the destination as well as how to reach it. The disciples are called to go behind him and to entrust themselves to him[38].

The call comes from a Jesus who is in motion, who seems to be relentlessly moving somewhere, pressed on by some urgent sense of mission[39]. When the disciples are called within this context to follow after him or to walk behind him, the call also acquires a missionary dimension.

2.5 *Jesus' Promise to those whom he Sees*

The call is reinforced by a promise which implies a mission as well, «καὶ ποιήσω ὑμᾶς γενέσθαι ἁλιεῖς ἀνθρώπων». The verbal form ποιήσω occurs 5 times in the Gospel of Mark (1,17; 10,17.36.51; 15,12). But the first person singular of ποιεῖν in the future as well as in the subjunctive forms are the same. Among all these references 1,17 alone has the verb ποιήσω in the future tense. The other uses are all in the subjunctive form[40]. However, the formulation, verb with the accusative followed by the infinitive (ποιήσω ὑμᾶς γενέσθαι: I will make you become), is seldom found in the Bible.

(εἰ ἔστιν κύριος ὁ θεός πορεύεσθε ὀπίσω αὐτοῦ εἰ δὲ ὁ Βααλ αὐτός πορεύεσθε ὀπίσω αὐτοῦ). Cf. also Prov 7,22.

[37] For the parallelism that exists between Mark 1,16-20 and the narrative of the calling of Elisha by Elijah (1Kgs 19,19-21) see below, p. 133f.

[38] K. STOCK, «I discepoli», 19: «I discepoli non sono obbligati a un compito o a un programma, ma alla persona stessa di Gesù. Il comando fonda la loro comunione di vita con Gesù e al contempo determina un rapporto fondamentale e immutabile. Gesù è la guida ed essi sono i suoi seguaci. Gesù precede e indica il cammino perché egli conosce la meta e sa come raggiungerla. I discepoli vanno dietro a lui e si affidano a lui, benché talvolta la via non piaccia loro e si sentano tentati di fare essi stessi la guida e di mostrare la via giusta a Gesù».

[39] F.J. MOLONEY, «The Vocation», 498.

[40] ποιήσω in these instances generally form part of the usage Τί θέλετέ [με] ποιήσω ὑμῖν (10,36.51 - Jesus; 15,12 - Pilate). In 10,17 the rich man puts a question to Jesus using the verb preceded by the interrogative alone: τί ποιήσω.

The verb ποιεῖν (Mark 40, Matt 65, Luke 74, John 85) is a frequently used verb in the Bible. In the creation account the verb that describes God's creating the world is ποιεῖν: ἐν ἀρχῇ ἐποίησεν ὁ θεὸς τὸν οὐρανὸν καὶ τὴν γῆν (Gen 1,1). The Hebrew equivalent בָּרָא, introduced by the Priestly tradition,[41] has always God, the God of Israel as its subject. בָּרָא in the OT never states what God creates out of. Neither is the verb בָּרָא (also ποιεῖν) exclusively reserved for creation out of nothing. Rather it denotes «God's effortless, totally free and unbound creating, his sovereignty»[42]. By exercising that sovereign power God brings something into being[43].

Though it cannot be exaggerated, Mark's use of the verb ποιεῖν here has some allusion to the great event of God's creative activity by which every thing comes into existence[44]. Jesus' promise to *make* them become fishers of men implies effecting a new creation, an efficacious, free and unconditional act that only God can perform[45]. Jesus promises them that they would be created anew, enabling them to become something that they were not before; by exercising his sovereign power

---

[41] The earlier tradition used instead עָשָׂה. Cf. K.-H. BERNHARDT, «בָּרָא», 246.

[42] W.H. SCHMIDT, *Die Schöpfungsgeschichte*, 166: «es meint gerade [...] das mühelos, völlig freie, ungebundene Schaffen, Gottes Souveränität».

[43] The most frequently named products of creation referred to by the verb בָּרָא are heaven and/or earth (Gen 1,1; 2,4 etc.), wonders and novelties (Num 16,30; Isa 65,17 etc.), man in general (Gen 1,27; 5,1; 6,7; Isa 45,12), and the people of Israel (Isa 43,1). In all these references LXX translates בָּרָא with ποιεῖν. Cf. G.J. WENHAM, *Genesis 1–15*, 14.

[44] The same verb ποιεῖν is used by Mark to refer to the appointment of the Twelve (3,14). Many scholars would also see a connection between the use of ποιεῖν in 3,14 and Genesis 1,1. Naturally the understanding is that in 3,14 there is an allusion to the creation of the new tribes of Israel, the new people of God. Cf. L. CERFAUX, «La mission de Galilée», 388; J. ERNST, *Markus*, 113; E. LOHMEYER, *Markus*, 74; K.H. SCHELKLE, *Discipleship and Priesthood*, 10; G. SCHMAHL, *Zwölf*, 55.

[45] Creation of man is particularly important to the author of Genesis. He uses בָּרָא/ποιεῖν three times in 1,27 alone to refer to the fact of God's creation of man. Isa 42,5 and 45,18 too celebrate, using the same verbs, the creation of man as the most important work of creation. In Deutero-Isaiah there is a further development, he connects his theology of creation with the theology of election. Though mankind as a whole is the creation of God (Isa 45,12), Israel alone is said to have been created by Yahweh (43,1). Thus בָּרָא/ποιεῖν in Deutero-Isaiah takes on a soteriological character. Cf. K.-H. BERNHARDT, «בָּרָא», 247. The notion of election is also not lacking in Jesus' seeing of these disciples.

he would transform their old nature and occupation, empowering them to embrace the demands of this specific task[46].

The same verb ποιεῖν is used in Exod 18,25 for the appointment of leaders over divisions of people. Moses, following Jethro's advice, chose able men out of all Israel and made (ἐποίησεν) them heads over the people[47]. Jethro's two-fold counsel leaves no doubt that God is the source and centre of what he advocates. Moses, first of all, is to remain the representative of the people to God. On the other hand he has to delegate some responsibility in the matter of hearing the people's problems[48]. Moses as representative of God would choose men who are able, trustworthy, and having reverence for God (Exod 18,21) and make them leaders over divisions of people, specified on a numerical basis. These leaders would have delegated authority from God.

Jesus' promise of making the fishermen «fishers of men» obviously has similarities with Moses' action. The verb used in both instances is ποιεῖν. It goes without saying that Jesus knows those whom he sees to be having basic reverence for God. Those whom he sees too would be leaders of people, they would be «fishers of men». They too would have delegated authority. However, Jesus' action surpasses that of Moses. He does not need to have recourse to counsel from a third party; God does not communicate with Jesus through an intermediary; Jesus is also more than a representative of God. Jesus on his own authority and power would act to make those whom he sees «fishers of men». If there is anything wanting in them, if they are not able or trustworthy, Jesus himself would make up for that. He would give them power and authority to fulfil their task. Mark can point to Jesus' authority this way because he has made it clear right at the outset that Jesus is the Son of God (1,1; cf. also Jesus' own self-references to divine Sonship in 2,10-11; 13,32; 14,62 with 14,61, as well as others' references to it in 1,11; 3,11; 5,7; 9,7; 14,61; 15,39).

Though Jesus' promise is given in the future tense, commentators argue that the gnomic future allows no time distinction between discipleship in the present (before Easter) and the missionary assignment after Easter. Discipleship and the missionary assignment

---

[46] St. Paul in 2Cor 3,5f. puts it beautifully: «our competence is from God, who has made us competent to be ministers of a new covenant».

[47] L. CERFAUX, «La mission de Galilée», 385-389; S. FREYNE, *The Twelve*, 84; F.J. MOLONEY, «The Vocation», 500; R. PESCH, *Markusevangelium* I, 204, n. 4; V. TAYLOR, *St. Mark*, 230.

[48] J.I. DURHAM, *Exodus*, 250.

are two sides of the same coin. The promise of missionary engagement grows out of the call to discipleship[49]. However, we see that the disciples undertake the missionary activity on their own only later in the narrative when Jesus sends them out two by two on the mission (6,7-13; Cf. also 3,14-15). So the future tense used is not out of place.

The expression «fishers of men» (ἁλιεῖς ἀνθρώπων) is ambiguous. Scholars have looked for clues in the OT to understand this phrase. Jer 16,16 has been widely quoted as providing a link with the expression («Behold, I am sending for many fishers, says the LORD, and they shall catch them»: ἰδοὺ ἐγὼ ἀποστέλλω τοὺς ἁλεεῖς τοὺς πολλούς λέγει κύριος καὶ ἁλιεύσουσιν αὐτούς)[50]. There is in fact no metaphor «fishers of men» in the text from Jeremiah. The only similarity is in the word ἁλιεῖς which occurs in both texts. But in Jeremiah the «fishers» are agents of judgement. Even the other plausible references from the OT too convey the sense of judgement carried out by God himself with «hooks» (Ezek 29,4-5; Amos 4,2; Hab 1,14-17)[51].

---

[49] J. ERNST, *Markus*, 57; A. STOCK, *The Method and Message*, 68; R. PESCH, «Berufung», 16.

[50] R. FABRIS, *Gesù di Nazareth*, 154; R. PESCH, *Markusevangelium* I, 111; V. TAYLOR, *St. Mark*, 169. C.W.F. Smith argues that Jesus' call is an eschatological call, i.e. he is summoning the men in question to serve as agents of the Kingdom of God now announced to be at hand, that they are to gather a people for judgement. Smith takes the parable of the net (Matt 13,47-50) to support his view where the function of the net is to gather fish indiscriminately. But the purpose of the gathering is sorting and disposition. Angels, not fishermen, are the ones doing the sorting. That itself is the main problem with this argument. There is absolutely no reference to the disciples in the parable of the net. They have no role of gathering people for judgement. Jesus clearly indicates that angels are the ones whom the Son of man will send forth at the close of the age to gather (13,27) and presumably separate for the judgement of fire. Cf. C.W.F. SMITH, «Fishers of Men», 188-203.

[51] Cf. W. WUELLNER, *Fishers of Men*, 88-133. Wuellner mentions a number of references having both negative (judgement) and even some positive (salvation) connotations. Cf. also M. HENGEL, *The Charismatic Leader*, 76-78. Hengel and many other scholars refer to the Qumran literature as well (1QH 3,26: 1QH 5,8).
   J.D.M. Derrett, in his article, «Jesus' Fishermen», 108-137, argues that Ezek 47,8-10 would provide an explanation for the metaphor. In these verses reference is made to the water which contains many types of fish, but the fish are living souls healed by that water. In short the fish are the saved souls. The fishermen represent God's agents bringing about that salvation.
   J. Mánek takes this Markan expression to refer to the mythical understanding of the sea as representing chaos and evil, and those called by Jesus are to rescue human beings from the underworld of sin and death. Cf. J. MÁNEK, «Fishers of Men», 138-

The OT does not help to understand the Markan metaphor. One has to look at the gospel itself to understand how Jesus makes them fishers of men. We shall deal with this aspect later. For the moment it suffices to say that Jesus' call to a mission that has to do with the salvation of men finds its resemblance in the disciples' current trade[52]. Jesus is calling them to be his fellow workers.

> The immediate function of those called to be fishers of men is to accompany Jesus as witnesses to the proclamation of the nearness of the kingdom and the necessity for men to turn to God through radical repentance. Their ultimate function will be to confront men with God's decisive action, which to faith has the character of salvation, but to unbelief has the character of judgement[53].

2.6 *The Response of those whom Jesus Sees*

The immediate effect that Jesus' words have on those whom he called is made clear by the favourite Markan adverb εὐθύς. We have already noted in the previous chapter Mark's frequent use of εὐθύς (41 times and the more archaic εὐθέως just once). By the use of εὐθύς Mark wants to say that the response of Simon and Andrew to the call of Jesus is immediate and without delay.

The participle ἀφέντες together with the object τὰ δίκτυα express what it costs them to respond to Jesus' call. The sense of the aorist participle ἀφέντες in our text is one of leaving or abandoning with an indication of the object left behind. Leaving the nets (τὰ δίκτυα) which is the gear of their occupation amounts to quitting their present job referred to in 1,16 and accepting the offer made by Jesus in 1,17.

The disciples' action has puzzled many a reader. It is also pointed out that it would be more intelligible if Simon and Andrew have had contact with Jesus previously[54]. Mark's account does not allude to any

---

141. Cosmic myth forms the background of several biblical narratives. But if it provides the background for the metaphor used by Jesus is very doubtful.

[52] J. GNILKA, *Jesus of Nazareth*, 163: Jesus «demonstrates his uniqueness by adapting to the current occupation of these men, whereby they were able to realise that they were to be «fishers» in a different realm from now on».

[53] W.L. LANE, *Mark*, 68.

[54] V. TAYLOR, *St. Mark*, 169. Some scholars speculate that the story of Jesus' seeing and calling the disciples perhaps followed the healings and exorcisms in 1,21-34. It would mean that the disciples have had some contact with Jesus before deciding to leave everything to follow him. It would also alleviate the difficulty that in the present narrative Peter and Andrew seem to abandon everything to follow Jesus in

such acquaintance. Nor is the Gospel interested in giving the psychological state of the disciples[55]. The narrative rather stresses the overwhelming nature of Jesus' seeing and the compelling power of his call[56]. The emphasis also falls on the disciples' renunciation. It is this abandonment, immediate and wholehearted, unconditional and unquestioning, that would prompt Simon to say later in the Gospel: «Lo, we have left everything and followed you» (10,28).

ἠκολούθησαν αὐτῷ expresses in a very cryptic manner how the disciples respond to Jesus' call. While the aorist participle ἀφέντες expresses the preparation that is required for the definitive action, the finite verb ἠκολούθησαν denotes that concrete action itself which the disciples undertake in response to Jesus' proposal in v. 17.

Of the 18 occurrences of the verb ἀκολουθεῖν in the Gospel of Mark (NT 90; Matt 25; Luke 17; John 19; Acts 4; 1Cor 1; Rev 4) in 17 instances it refers to following Jesus. The syntax of the phrase itself is noteworthy. ἀκολουθεῖν occurs in most cases with the associative (comitative) dative[57] referring to Jesus (Mark 9,38: ἡμῖν referring to Jesus and his company together) who is the goal of following. Some times ἀκολουθεῖν ὀπίσω τινός, the LXX translation of the Hebrew phrase הָלַךְ אַחֲרֵי[58] is also found (Mark 8,34; cf. Matt 10,38). Although

---

1,18, yet are back in their house in Capernaum in 1,29. Cf. J. MARCUS, *Mark*, 178. This is a guess-work. It could also be argued that the pericope fits better still later in the narrative. The present setting of the pericope is apt for two reasons. First, by placing the seeing and call of the disciples at the outset of Jesus' ministry, Mark attests that the disciples were present at the beginning and therefore are legitimate bearers of tradition (cf. Luke 1,1-2; Acts 1,21-22; 10,37-39). Second, by opening each of the sections of Jesus' ministry (1,16-3,12; 3,13-6,6; 6,7-8,26) culminating in Peter's profession of faith in the messiahip of Jesus, with pericopes that concern the disciples (1,16-20; 3,13-19; 6,7-13) Mark also stresses the integral relationship between Christology and discipleship. Cf. R.A. GUELICH, *Mark*, 49.

[55] W.T. Shiner has shown that the absence of psychological motivation in the case of those whom Jesus sees and calls is unusual for an ancient call narrative. W.T. SHINER, *Follow me*, 183-186.

[56] J. MARCUS, *Mark*, 185: «all human reticence has been instantaneously washed away because *God* has arrived on the scene in the person of Jesus, and it is *his* compelling voice that speaks through Jesus' summons [...]».

[57] BDF, § 193,1.

[58] הָלַךְ אַחֲרֵי has different meanings in the OT. i) It is used to speak of somebody following a respected person: warriors following a leader (1Sam 17,13f. 25,13; Judg 9,4.49), wife following the husband (Ruth 3,10; Jer 2,2) and disciple following the master (1Kgs 19,20-21) ii) It is used especially in Hosea, Jeremiah and the Deutronomic writings as a technical term for apostasy into heathenism (Judg 2,12;

the verb in Mark can also refer to external following in the sense of accompanying (Mark 3,7); going behind (11,9), and walking at a distance (14,54), what stands out is the notion of following in the sense of discipleship so much so that it is almost a technical term for following Jesus[59].

Simon and Andrew are the first of several people who are reported to be following Jesus (1,18: ἠκολούθησαν); James and John come after him (1,20: ἀπῆλθον ὀπίσω); the disciples (μαθηταί) as a group follow him (6,1: ἀκολουθοῦσιν); Peter later points out this fact of their following him (10,28: ἠκολουθήκαμεν). The crowd or multitude are also expressly referred to as following Jesus (3,7: ἠκολούθησεν; 5,24: ἠκολούθει; 10,32; 11,9: ἀκολουθοῦντες; 2,15: ἠκολούθουν). In other cases, individual followers are identified by name. Levi stands out among these followers (2,14: ἠκολούθησεν); Bartimaeus, the blind beggar is the only man healed by Jesus who follows him (10,52: ἠκολούθει); Mary Magdalene and Mary the mother of James are the other individual followers of Jesus referred to in the Gospel (15,41: ἠκολούθουν). A certain man is successful in casting out demons in Jesus' name but he does not follow Jesus and his company (9,38). The rich man on the other hand is described as failing to follow Jesus (10,21). So, following, while central to discipleship, however, is not limited to the close circle of disciples. However, the disciples' following stands out from the following of the others in the Gospel because their following has its origin in Jesus' initiative of seeing and command, their following is exclusive and personal and they follow Jesus to be «fishers of men», to share in his mission. The emphasis also falls on the disciples' prompt obedience to the call of Jesus. No questions asked, no objections raised,[60] no delaying tactics employed (cf. 1Kgs 19,20; Luke 9,59.61). The disciples readily and uncondi-

---

Deut 4,3; 6,14; 1Kgs 21,26; Jer 11,10; Hos 1,2; 2,7.13 etc.) iii) The idea of following Yahweh though less prominent occurs in a Deuteronomic context (Deut 1,36; 13,5; 1Kgs 14,8; 18,21). Cf. G. KITTEL, «ἀκολουθέω», 211-213.

[59] In the whole of NT the special use of ἀκολουθεῖν in the sense of discipleship is strictly limited to discipleship of Christ. The only exception outside the gospels is Rev 14,4 which refers to the following of the lamb. This obviously formed the starting-point for the concept of *imitatio Agni*. cf. G. KITTEL, «ἀκολουθέω», 214 n. 32.

[60] It is very unlike in the case of those whom God calls in the OT. e.g., Moses: Exod 3,11; Gideon: Judg 6,15; Jeremiah: Jer 1,6; etc.

tionally accept the call of Jesus (Δεῦτε ὀπίσω μου) and follow him (ἠκολούθησαν αὐτῷ)[61].

2.7. *Summary*

The discipleship of Simon who is given pride of place not only in this pericope but throughout the Gospel and that of his brother Andrew, has its origin in the selective seeing of Jesus. Jesus with his perceptive seeing, knows them, and invites them to follow him. The presence of the Spirit in him, whom Jesus saw descending upon him at baptism, could be understood as enabling Jesus to see rightly and pick out his disciples who would assist him in carrying out his mission. The immediateness of the unconditional response of Simon and Andrew to the call of Jesus implies that Jesus indeed rightly saw and that his summons did not fall on deaf ears. The brothers place their whole trust in the person of Jesus and follow him on an as yet unknown journey, to be collaborators with Jesus, to form the first Christian community!

3. He Saw James and John

The second narrative of Jesus' seeing another pair of brothers is thought to be modelled after the narrative on Simon and Andrew. But it adds a few significant details and omits some others. However, it is Jesus' seeing that forms the crucial element even in this story.

3.1 *Synoptic Comparison*

The difference between Mark and Matthew (Mark 1,19-20 // Matt 4,21-22) is still more marginal in this second scene: Matthew has προβὰς ἐκεῖθεν instead of Mark's προβὰς ὀλίγον; Matthew continues to stress the point that Jesus sees two brothers (ἄλλους δύο ἀδελφούς), Mark just names them as individuals and the blood relation is alluded to only as a secondary information. Matthew does not employ the epexegetic καί with the object which in Mark complements the verb

---

[61] M. ADINOLFI, *L'apostolato dei Dodici*, 84: «Il sì della loro docile risposta non è facoltativo, pur nel pieno rispetto della libertà umana. Non è la conclusione di un ragionamento basato su motivi più o meno validi. È un salto di fede nel buio luminoso di una semplice parola di invito. È un affidarsi incondizionato, per quanto riguarda Simone e Andrea, alla promessa di venire iniziati e formati giorno dopo giorno alla missione di evangelizzatori: "Vi farò diventare pescatori di uomini". Una nuova professione che è prolungamento organico, a livello spirituale, del loro antico mestiere».

εἶδεν. Matthew unlike Mark mentions explicitly that Zebedee their father too was present in the boat, but while referring to the Zebedee brothers' leaving, Matthew mentions the boat first where Mark gives primary importance to their leaving their father. Matthew does not also make any mention of the hired employees at all. εὐθέως is used by Matthew to speak of the brothers immediate leaving, unlike in Mark where it refers to Jesus call. Finally Matthew repeats the term ἠκολούθησαν for the second pair of brothers' following of Jesus[62].

3.2 *Jesus' Seeing*

In Mark' account this second scene has the same location, theme and the main actor. «Going on a little further» (προβὰς ὀλίγον) indicates that the scene takes place still «by the sea of Galilee» (1,16). Once again Jesus is the main character in the scene and the subject matter of the scene again is Jesus' seeing and call of his disciples.

3.2.1 A Reference to Jesus' Movement

As is his wont Mark refers to the movement of Jesus by means of a participle (προβὰς) before talking of his seeing. προβαίνειν means to *go ahead, go on, advance*[63] in years as in Luke 1,7. προβαίνειν in the sense of going forward occurs only twice in the NT both in the same context of Jesus' choosing his disciples (Mark 1,19 and Matt 4,21: προβὰς ἐκεῖθεν). ὀλίγον is used as an adverb of both space and time (see 6,31)[64]. προβὰς ὀλίγον indicates proximity between the two pairs of brothers and may even explain the Lukan suggestion that they «were partners with Simon» (Luke 5,10; cf. also Mark 1,29)[65]. But the focus here is on Jesus and his movement which comes to a halt only when something decisive takes place.

3.2.2 Jesus' Seeing is most Decisive

The participle προβὰς prepares for the action of Jesus' seeing (εἶδεν). The construction of the sentence is typical as in 1,16: participle

---

[62] As noted above Luke mentions the Zebedee brothers only in passing as «partners with Simon» (5,10) while treating the miraculous catch of fish and the vocation of Simon (5,1-11). See p. 96 above.

[63] BAGD, 702.

[64] V. TAYLOR, *St. Mark*, 169.

[65] R.A. GUELICH, *Mark*, 51.

followed by the aorist indicative with the accusative indicating the persons whom Jesus sees and a present participle supplying information on what they are engaged in. Everything hinges on Jesus' seeing. The initiative rests wholly with him. When he sees these men his movement ceases and he reaches out to them. Jesus' seeing is once again not casual or by accident. It is active, attentive, elective, and personal.

3.2.3 Information on those whom Jesus Sees

In this case too Jesus sees a pair of brothers, «James the son of Zebedee and John his brother». Unlike Simon and Andrew these two brothers have Semitic names. James appears to be the more important of the two. The name of their father Zebedee (also in 3,17 and 10,35) is mentioned in order to distinguish James the son of Zebedee from James the brother of Jesus (6,3), James the younger (15,40) and James the son of Alphaeus (3,18).

James and his brother John together with Peter form the inner circle of Jesus' disciples. They are allowed to be present at important events in the life of Jesus like raising of the daughter of Jairus (5,37), the transfiguration (9,2), on the Mount of olives (13,3 with Andrew) and the agony at Gethsemane (14,33). Perhaps this makes them to ask for more, the privilege to sit on Jesus' right and left in his glory (10,37). Apart from those associated with James, John's name is mentioned in Mark when he discusses with Jesus regarding the man who exorcises in Jesus' name without authorisation (9,38). As reported in Acts 12,1-2 James was put to death by Herod during his violent attack against the church. John alongside Peter later came to exercise leadership in the primitive church (Acts 3-4; Gal 2,9). Mark 10,39 seems to be implying that John too was martyred.

The participle καταρτίζοντας explains what they are by profession. Zebedee and his sons are all fishermen. They seem to be well to do, as they own a boat (ἐν τῷ πλοίῳ) and the nets (τὰ δίκτυα), and they can afford to employ workers; theirs is a family business. The Zebedee brothers put the nets in order (by cleaning, mending, folding together[66]) for the next fishing expedition[67]. So Jesus sees the Zebedee brothers not while fishing proper but while preparing for fishing.

---

[66] BAGD, 417.

[67] G.R. WYNNE, «Mending their Nets», 282-85. For J. Gnilka the fishing activity of Simon and Andrew takes place during the day whereas that of the Zebedee brothers takes place during the night. The nets are mended during the day and the fishermen go

3.3 *Jesus Calls those whom he Sees*

Without any room for conversation or dialogue Jesus calls James and John whom he sees (καὶ εὐθὺς ἐκάλεσεν αὐτούς). Whereas in the case of Simon and Andrew the adverb εὐθύς qualifies their leaving (ἀφέντες), in the story of the Zebedee brothers it refers to the instantaneous call of Jesus (εὐθὺς ἐκάλεσεν). As soon as Jesus sees them (εἶδεν) he knows that they are the people whom he wants to call and he calls them. The καὶ αὐτοὺς in v. 19 with the epexegetic καί are complements of the verb εἶδεν[68]. The composition of the phrase has already prepared the reader to understand that Jesus «sees» only the sons of Zebedee and calls them (αὐτούς) only. Jesus does not address his call to Zebedee nor to the employees.

The narrative does not present the exact words addressed to them. The concise phrase καὶ εὐθὺς ἐκάλεσεν αὐτούς sums up what transpired. κάλειν is a frequently used verb used 144 times in the NT (Matt 25, Mar 4, Luke 43, John 2, Acts 18, Paul 30, Heb 6, Jas 1; Pet 7, Rev 8). The verb has different meanings such as summoning (Matt 2,7; 20,8), naming (Matt 1,21; Luke 1,13 etc.), inviting (Matt 22,9; Luke 7,39 etc.) and calling to a higher vocation (Matt 4,18; 9,13; Mar 1,20; 2,17; Luke 5,32; Rom 8,30 etc.). Mark, except once (Mark 11,17), uses the verb only in the last sense of a call to discipleship[69]. In the Pauline

---

fishing by night. Cf. J. GNILKA, *Markus I*, 72. It need not be so since the nets they use and the boat they have cannot be compared to that of the modern day. With a small boat and small net at their disposal it must have been normal to do fishing by day as well. For further details on fishing in Palestine cf. W. WUELLNER, *Fishers of Men*, 26-63.

[68] S. LÉGASSE, *Marc*, 118, n. 31.

[69] Apart from καλεῖν, if we take into account other words also used by Mark to refer to Jesus' calling , it is possible to enumerate several people who have been called by Jesus. The references are mainly to the disciples. Thus Jesus called Simon and Andrew (1,17: Δεῦτε ὀπίσω μου); as well as James and John (1,19: ἐκάλεσεν); Jesus also called (προσκαλεῖται) to him those whom he desired and appointed «the Twelve» (δώδεκα). The feeding of the four thousand is preceded by Jesus calling (προσκαλεσάμενος) his disciples to him (8,1). On four occasions the reader is informed that Jesus called his disciples or the Twelve to himself, and then said something to them concerning the demands of discipleship (8,34; 10,42; 12,43: προσκαλεσάμενος; 9,35: ἐφώνησεν). It is reported twice that Jesus called the crowd to himself. At 7,14 Jesus calls (προσκαλεσάμενος) the crowd to him before the parable on defilement; and at 8,34 Jesus calls (προσκαλεσάμενος) the multitude with his disciples and presents the demands on discipleship. Other individuals called by Jesus are Levi (2,14: Ἀκολούθει μοι), and Bartimaeus whom Jesus calls through the agency of others (φωνήσατε). Thus Jesus calls to himself both the disciples (or the Twelve) as individuals and as a

letters too this idea is predominant[70]. Peter in his letters, except for once (1Pet 3,6), uses the verb exclusively in this sense[71].

In the OT narratives the one who calls is God[72] (Exod 3,4; 1Sam 3,4.6.8; Isa 49,1). Even when intermediaries like an angel (Judg 6,12-13) performs this task, the call issues ultimately from God. In the references that we have cited from the Pauline writings as well as from the letters of Peter too, the one who calls is always God. In Mark 1,20 Jesus on his own authority calls and the disciples respond without hesitation or further clarification. In fact only the Gospels (Matt 4,18; Mark 1,20) speak of this authority of Jesus. That, calling people to a different mode of living is part of Jesus' own mission, is substantiated by his claim reported by all the Synoptics, «I came not to call the righteous but sinners» (Matt 9,13; Mark 2,17; Luke 5,32).

Neither the promise of Jesus nor the mission the disciples are to undertake are repeated again in this story of the Zebedee brothers. Since it follows close on the heels of the story of Simon and Andrew, it is implied that even this pair of brothers are called to the same task. Jesus would make them also «become fishers of men».

3.4 The Reaction of those whom Jesus Sees

So compelling is the force of Jesus' seeing and call that James and John do not think twice before responding. Even though the favourite Markan adverb εὐθύς is not used to speak of their decision without delay, it can be presumed that as in the former scene, the Zebedee brothers' response too has been immediate. That such is the case is obvious from the fact that they leave their father in the boat itself (ἐν τῷ πλοίῳ) with hired employees and follow him.

There is however another dimension to their leaving (ἀφέντες). The narrative stresses the fact that the brothers leave their father for good. Mark expressly mentions Zebedee (τὸν πατέρα αὐτῶν Ζεβεδαῖον) who, as noted above, is named normally to distinguish his son James from other persons of the same name in the Gospel, in order to emphasise the radicality of their decision. Besides, they leave the boat and the nets

---

group, the crowd and some individuals who stand out from the wider circle of followers.

[70] Cf. Rom 8,30; 9,12.24; 1Cor 1,9; 7,15.17.18.21; Gal 1,6.15; 5,8.13; Eph 4,1.4; Col 3,15; 1Thess 2,12; 4,7; 2Thess 2,14; 2Tim 1,9; 6,12.

[71] Cf. 1Pet 1,15; 2,9.21; 3,9; 5,10; 2 Pet 1,3.

[72] M. HENGEL, The Charismatic Leader, 17, 73.

which were the tools of their daily occupation as well as the employees (μισθωτῶν) who work with them and commit themselves exclusively to Jesus. While the story of Simon and Andrew emphasises the promptness of their response that of the Zebedee brothers stresses the completeness of their renunciation[73]. So there is a progression in the cost of following. James and John have to leave behind their family ties as well as financial security.

The terse expression ἀπῆλθον ὀπίσω αὐτοῦ refers to the action of following Jesus and forms an inclusion with Δεῦτε ὀπίσω μου (1,17)[74]. As noted above ἀπέρχεσθαι ὀπίσω like ἀκολουθεῖν, is a technical expression for discipleship. The verb occurs some 21 times in the Gospel of Mark. The preposition ἀπό with ἔρχεσθαι, a verb denoting motion, already expresses the idea of separation and moving away. In 1,20 the compound verb ἀπέρχεσθαι occurs with the preposition ὀπίσω, the only such occurrence in the NT, and it has the sense of following someone after having moved away and separated oneself from all that ties him down to the present state. It refers to the disciples' commitment to the person of Jesus and their setting out on a journey that is totally uncertain but has the guarantee of the one who saw them and called them.

3.5 *Summary*

Jesus' seeing is once again the decisive element in the second scene in which Jesus wins another pair of brothers to follow him. Jesus in his perceptive seeing chooses them and invites them for a life of discipleship. The use of the verb κάλειν in the narrative which reflects the idea of God's call, while identifying Jesus' call with God's call, also emphasises that the disciples' response corresponds to that of so many prophets of OT. It also suggests that the call addressed to them is for a mission. The reaction of the Zebedee brothers is one of instantaneous obedience. This whole-hearted response, though painful as it may be, as the cost of following is ever more accentuated, illustrates their faith in Jesus who sees and calls them and their readiness to join themselves to him.

---

[73] A. STOCK, *The Method and Message*, 69.

[74] For this very reason providing the content of the call in the case of the Zebedee brothers is perhaps superfluous. It is to be understood that the content of the call issued in 1,17 is valid for both pairs of brothers.

4. He Saw Levi

Jesus' seeing Levi is quite distinguishable in the whole Gospel. For this is the only story narrated concerning Levi and he never reappears in the Gospel. But his story gains importance because he is portrayed as a representative figure, a sinner and tax collector.

4.1 *Synoptic Comparison*

4.1.1 Mark 2,14 and Matt 9, 9[75]

Matthew does not provide a summary, which functions as an introduction in Mark 2,13, before presenting the story, nor does he refer to Jesus' movement along the sea. A connection with the preceding narrative is established with the usage of an adverb of place: παράγων [...] ἐκεῖθεν. For Matthew (also for Luke) nothing intervenes between the episode of the healing of the paralytic and the call of Matthew. This way he highlights the vocation of Matthew. While following Mark in the construction of the sentence for the most part, Matthew makes a significant change. Whereas in Mark, Jesus sees a tax collector named Levi; in Matthew Jesus sees a man called Matthew[76]. Mark also qualifies Levi by providing the name of his father Alphaeus but Matthew does not follow suit, he just names the person.

4.1.2 Mark 2,14 and Luke 5,27-28

Luke provides a link with the preceding narrative of the healing of the paralytic by the use of the phrase καὶ μετὰ ταῦτα ἐξῆλθεν. But he, like Matthew, does not refer to Jesus' progress along the sea, the gathering of the crowd and Jesus' teaching them which are reported by Mark (2,13). Luke's narrative also lacks the crucial verb for seeing εἶδεν, instead he uses the verb ἐθεάσατο (cf. Luke 5,27; 7,24; 23,55; Acts 1,11; 21,27; 22,9)[77]. Luke agrees with Mark both regarding the name of the person Levi and his profession. He also adds an important

---

[75] The analysis shall be limited to the account of Jesus' seeing the person and calling him since our focus is not on the ensuing narrative of the dinner.

[76] See below for further analysis on the matter.

[77] We have already noted that Lukan vocabulary does not correspond to Markan usage in several instances. Besides Luke does not seem to attach any special meaning to the use of εἶδεν for Jesus.

dimension to Levi's following that is lacking in Mark, that of Levi «leaving everything» and rising and following Jesus.

4.2 Preliminary Observations

Mark presents a third episode patterned on the narrative of Jesus' seeing and winning the first two pairs of disciples. The Gospel of Mark contains in fact many threefold patterns[78]. Markan fondness for three may have had a role to play in presenting the story of Levi. However that would be slight compared to the importance Mark attaches to the following of a representative figure like Levi whom Jesus sees and calls.

Delimitation of the pericope that deals with Jesus' seeing Levi is not clear-cut. Translations and commentaries take either 2,13 and 2,14[79] or

---

[78] Thus, there are: three seed parables (4,3-20: the parable of the sower; 4,26-29: the parable of the growing seed; 4,30-32: the parable of the mustard seed); three popular opinions about John (6,14-14); three popular opinions about Jesus (8,27-28); three predictions of passion (8,31; 9,31; 10,33-34); three failures of the disciples to stay awake in the Garden (14,32-42); three denials of Jesus by Peter (14,66-72). Other patterns of three include: three episodes showing the authority and power of Jesus (1,21-28 [29-34]; 1,40-45; 2,1-12); three positive responses to Jesus' call (1,16-18; 1,19-20; 2,14); three rejection of Jesus (2,1-12; 2,15-28; 3,1-6); three declarations of the full identity of Jesus (1,11; 9,7; 15,39). Scholars have also noted an insertion technique or sandwich technique as it is popularly known (cf. R. EDWARDS, «Markan Sandwiches», 193-216; D. RHOADS – J. DEWEY – D. MICHIE, Mark as Story, 51-52; T. SHEPHERD, «Markan Intercalation», 522-540) that Mark employs to fit other episodes into the middle of a story, thus forming a three-step progression:
i) 5,21-24: healing of Jairus' daughter
    5,25-34: healing of the woman who touched Jesus' garment
    5,35-43: healing of Jairus' daughter
ii) 6,7-13: mission of the Twelve
    6,14-29: beheading of John
    6,30: return of the Twelve
iii) 8,22-26: healing of a blind man at Bethsaida
    8,27-10,45: Jesus' instructions to his followers
    10,46-52: healing of blind Bartimaeus
iv) 11,12-14: cursing of the fig tree
    11,15-19: cleansing of the temple
    11,20-25: lesson from the withered fig tree.
For further details cf. L.T. JOHNSON, The Writings of the New Testament, 162-164.
[79] Novum Testamentum Graece (27th Edition); RSV; W.L. LANE, Mark, 99; E. LOHMEYER, Markus, 54-55; R. PESCH, «Levi-Matthäus», 43-45; V. TAYLOR, St. Mark, 202-203; etc.

the whole of 2,13-17 as a unit[80]. There are also speculations that 2,13-14 and 2,15-17 belong to independent traditions[81] or that Mark took the name from the tradition on the festive meal at Levi's house (2,15-17) and constructed the call of Levi on the lines of 1,16-18[82]. Evidently, within the pericope itself, it is possible to distinguish three scenes:

i) Jesus' departure to the seaside, the gathering of the crowd and Jesus' teaching them (2,13)
   ii) Jesus' seeing Levi and calling him to discipleship (2,14)
iii) Jesus' table fellowship with the toll collectors and sinners, the scribes' questioning such behaviour and Jesus' reply (2,15-17).

All three scenes are distinguished by change of place (2,13: the seaside; 2,14: passing on further [coastal town of Capernaum?]; 2,15-17: Levi's house), time, actors (2,13: Jesus and the crowd; 2,14: Jesus and Levi; 2,15-17: Jesus, his disciples, tax collectors and sinners and the scribes), and action (2,13: teaching; 2,14: seeing Levi and calling him; 2,15-17: eating and discussing).

However, a close look at the pericope shows that 2,13-17 has a thematic and literary unity, placed well within the context of Jesus' public ministry in Galilee. «I came not to call the righteous, but sinners» (v. 17) sums up the theme of the pericope. The particular episode of Jesus' seeing Levi and calling him and his unconditional response is portrayed as a concrete example of the theme. Thus while on the one hand the pericope focuses on Jesus' initiative and mission on the other hand it emphasises discipleship as an unconditional response to the call of Jesus. The other aspect of the theme that is

---

[80] The Greek New Testament (Fourth Revised Edition); Einheitsübersetzung (EHS); La Sacra Bibbia; Syriac Bible (UBC; 1979); C.E.B. CRANFIELD, *St. Mark*, 101; J. ERNST, *Markus*, 93; G.G. GAMBA, «Considerazioni», 212-218; J. GNILKA, *Markus I*, 103; R.A. GUELICH, *Mark* 97; R.H. GUNDRY, *Mark*, 123; B.M.F. VAN IERSEL, *Mark*, 151; etc.

[81] C.E.B. CRANFIELD, *St. Mark*, 101; J. ERNST, *Markus*, 94; J. GNILKA, *Markus I*, 104; V. TAYLOR, *St. Mark*, 201-204; etc.

[82] J.D.G. DUNN, «Mark 2.1-3.6», 398; R. PESCH, «Levi-Matthäus», 43-44. E. Best argues that either Mark has found in the tradition a story of Levi, but using 1,16-20 as model he then composed 2,14 to provide a positive example of the invitation of Jesus as given in 2,17 or that the tradition contained a detailed story of Levi which Mark streamlined into the pattern he had used in 1,16-20. Cf. E. BEST, *Following Jesus*, 176.

treated is Jesus' relationship to tax collectors and sinners demonstrated through his eating with them.

That the pericope is permeated by ideas of discipleship, is also clear from the particular vocabulary relating to it (ἀκολουθεῖν, καλεῖν, μαθηταῖς). There are also several obvious literary connections that hold the pericope *together*. While καὶ ἐξῆλθεν πάλιν παρὰ τὴν θάλασσαν of v. 13a brings Jesus to the sea-shore, the παράγων of 14a pictures Jesus in movement along/from the sea-shore. ἠκολούθησεν αὐτῷ of 14c is in response to the command of Jesus «'Ακολούθει μοι» (v. 14b) The ἠκολούθουν αὐτῷ of v. 15 takes up the ἠκολούθησεν αὐτῷ of v. 14; so is the τελῶναι connected to the τελώνιον of v. 14. The τελῶναι καὶ ἁμαρτωλοί of v. 15 is twice recalled in v. 16 and ἁμαρτωλούς in v. 17 establishes the link between the τελωνῶν καὶ ἁμαρτωλῶν of v. 16.

Our analysis will focus on the incident of Jesus' seeing Levi and calling him to be a disciple. The narrative itself is devoid of any superfluous elements, but it is described with brevity as well as clarity[83]. It is modelled after the accounts in 1,16-20. There are thematic as well as semantic similarities between the two pericope (2,14 and 1,16-20).

4.3 *Circumstances of Jesus' Seeing Levi*

2,13 presents the particulars that preceded Jesus' seeing Levi. There are three constitutive elements that make up the narrative. They are i) Jesus' going out again beside the sea ii) the crowd gathering about him iii) Jesus' teaching them.

i) The phrase in v. 13a καὶ ἐξῆλθεν πάλιν παρὰ τὴν θάλασσαν takes Jesus from the house in which he was since his arrival at Capernaum (2,1) and transports him to the seaside, which provides the spatial background for Jesus as in 1,16-20 to see and select his followers. The adverb πάλιν clearly refers back to the movement of Jesus along the sea of Galilee in 1,16[84].

---

[83] E. Schweizer qualifies the conciseness as follows: «V. 14 erzählt in holzschnitt-artiger Knappheit, alles auf das Wesentliche reduzierend, und ist darin 1,16-20 [...] sehr ähnlich». Cf. E. SCHWEIZER, *Markus*, 30.

[84] The adverb πάλιν here has also the function of marking the beginning of a new narrative. In contrast in 8,13 it has the function of signalling the conclusion of the narrative. πάλιν occurs some 26 times in the Gospel of Mark, of which 13 times it is used of Jesus, referring mainly to his movements.

ii) The reference to the gathering of the crowd takes up the coming together of the crowd on previous occasions (1,32-33.45; 2,2). But here for the first time the gathering takes place on the sea-shore and ever since such meetings takes place by the sea quite frequently (3,7; 4,1; 5,21)[85].

iii) The other information that Jesus taught the crowd that gathered there, in this case without furnishing the content of his teaching, is akin to 1,14-15 where he preaches the Gospel of God[86]. The movement of Jesus and that of the crowd ceases when Jesus begins to teach (1,21.22.38). The reference to Jesus' teaching the crowd has another function in context. The first reference to his preaching is followed by the account of Jesus' seeing the two pairs of brothers and calling them (1,16-20). Here once again the reference to Jesus' teaching is followed by the story of Jesus' seeing Levi and calling him (2,14). Call to discipleship is thus preceded by reference to Jesus' preaching or teaching[87].

4.4 *Jesus' Seeing Levi*

Jesus' seeing Levi transpires with minimal details. The narrative parallels 1,16.18 both verbally and structurally. The evangelist this way indicates that Jesus' seeing Levi has the same features of his seeing of the first four disciples.

4.4.1 Jesus is Still on the Move

In his characteristic way Mark refers to the movement of Jesus before talking of Jesus' seeing the person whom he wants to call. Whereas in v. 13 the three phrases with finite verbs present a simple structure,[88] when narrating the story of Levi, Mark reverts to his style

---

[85] Note also the use of the adverb πάλιν while referring to such gatherings.

[86] It is true that the activity of Jesus in both these instances are described differently. While in 1,14 it is κηρύσσειν, in 2,13 it is διδάσκειν. But in both instances reaching out to people with words of authority and power are involved. It may be noted that in 1,14-15 it is not said who are the recipients of the preaching. 2,13 is clear in this regard. «All the crowd» is explicitly mentioned as those receiving the teaching.

[87] These three elements: the movement of Jesus, the gathering of the crowd and Jesus' teaching them, have been already mentioned separately in 1,14–2,12. But in 2,13 for the first time they are mentioned together.

[88] For further details of the construction of the whole pericope see G.G. GAMBA, «Considerazioni», 202-203.216-218.

of using a participle to prepare for the decisive action of Jesus' seeing, followed by the verb of seeing itself and the object of seeing (cf. 1,16-20). The participle παράγων takes up the παρά of v. 13 and refers to Jesus' passing along the sea[89].

4.4.2 Jesus' Seeing is the most Important Factor

The finite verb εἶδεν expresses Jesus' decisive action of seeing. This fourth occurrence of the verb in the Gospel also carries the same weight of meaning as in the stories of the two pairs of brothers. The importance that the verb obtains can be seen from the verbs used of Jesus in vv. 13-14. The verb εἶδεν assumes central position in the narrative; everything hinges on Jesus' seeing Levi:

He *went out (ἐξῆλθεν)* again beside the sea;
and all the crowd gathered about him,
    and he *taught (ἐδίδασκεν)* them.
        And as he *passed on (παράγων)*,
            he *saw(εἶδεν)*
            Levi the son of Alphaeus sitting at the tax office,
        and he *said (λέγει)* to him,
    «*Follow ('Ακολούθει)* me».
And he rose and followed him.

The seeing of Jesus in this case could have been one of faultfinding given his profession[90]. Instead it is a seeing that does not accuse, nor reprove him for what he does, rather it is a seeing that arouses spontaneous confidence in Levi; it is also a seeing that chooses. Jesus' seeing is so powerful that it has an irresistible effect on Levi.

---

[89] Jesus' coming to the seaside is interpreted by many as Jesus' entrance into the sphere of forces which manifest their hostility to God. E.g., U. MAUSER, *Christ in the Wilderness*, 124-128; W.L. LANE, *Mark*, 100. However it is an exaggeration. Jesus does not go to the seashore in order to confront the evil forces. It is quite usual for Jesus to take a break and go to the sea-shore (3,7; 5,21; 7,31). In many instances it is the locale of Jesus' missionary activity (2,13; 4,1).

[90] See below for explanation. See also G. FISCHER – M. HASITSCHKA, *Auf dein Wort hin*, 101.

4.4.3 Description of Levi

The name Levi has been attested to by all major witnesses[91]. Mark further specifies that he is the son of Alphaeus (Λευὶν τὸν τοῦ Ἀλφαίου). The Western texts in fact read Ἰάκωβον τὸν τοῦ Ἀλφαίου[92]. There is a near unanimity that the reading of the Western witnesses shows the influence of 3,18 where Ἰάκωβον τὸν τοῦ Ἀλφαίου is included among the Twelve[93]. But Mark does not include Levi among the Twelve[94].

Luke also has the story of Jesus' seeing Levi the tax collector and calling him. But he does not say that Levi is the son of Alphaeus (5,27-28). Luke also does not include Levi in the list of the Twelve. Matthew in his parallel account names the person whom Jesus sees at the tax office as Matthew (Matt 9,9) and moreover when giving his name in the list of the Twelve calls him «Matthew the tax collector» (10,3). Mark and Luke also have Matthew in the list of Twelve apostles but do not identify him as the tax collector (3,16f.)[95].

---

[91] Λευίν as in Luke 5,27 is read by $\mathfrak{P}^{88}$, $\aleph^2$, B, C, L, W, f^1, etc. Whereas Λευί is read by $\aleph^*$, A, Δ, 28, etc. However it only accounts for a minor change and it is not considered as something of importance.

[92] Ἰάκωβον is read by D, Θ, f^{13}, 565, it, Diatessaron, Origen, etc.

[93] B.M. METZGER, A Textual Commentary, 66. The witnesses that read Levi are much more reliable compared to the western texts whose evidence is weak. Moreover, the Lukan parallel (5,27) that retains the Markan name «Levi», has no variant reading.

[94] For an alternative attempt to bring Levi into the list of the Twelve see B. LINDARS, «Matthew, Levi, Lebbaeus», 220-222. Lindars points out that some Western texts have the Greek «Lebbaeus» or the Latin «Labbaeus» for «Thaddaeus» in the list of the Twelve in the Gospels of Mark (3,18: D and Itala) and Matthew (10,3: D, the African Old Latin «k», and the Latin version of Origen). Some later Greek authorities, namely the Caesarean and Syrian (Koine) texts, have τὸν του Λεββαῖος ὁ ἐπικληθεὶς Θαδδαῖος, and the Ferrar group reverse the names. The argument is based on the assumption that i) Lebbaeus can be identified with Levi; ii) that the change from Thaddaeus to Labbaeus at Mark 3,16 was first made in Old Latin manuscripts and then in Greek (Ms D is bilingual Greek and Latin) iii) that these manuscripts predate the manuscripts that tried to change «Levi the son of Alphaeus» to «James the son of Alphaeus» at Mark 2,14, since the latter would cancel the necessity of the former.

[95] On the position that the evangelist Matthew has changed Levi to Matthew and designated him as tax collector see D.C. DULING, «Matthew», 618-622; U. LUZ, Matthäus, 42-43; R. PESCH, «Levi-Matthäus», 42-56; A. SAND, Das Gesetz, 196. For a critique of this position see R.H. GUNDRY, Matthew, 166.

As far as the Gospel of Mark is concerned Levi is just Levi and nobody else[96]. He does not belong to the Twelve (3,16-19)[97]. E. Best in great detail has shown the care which Mark has taken in his list of the Twelve. He comes to the conclusion that Mark did not consider «Levi» to have been one of the Twelve[98]. This is a position that seems to be tenable; Jesus sees and calls him in his own right[99]. Mark in his Gospel makes a distinction between the Twelve and the disciples. We shall take it up for some examination later. For the moment it suffices to say that Jesus' seeing and calling Levi is probably understood by Mark as an example of a call to discipleship as distinct from apostleship or Twelveship. From a theological point of view this clarification is important because by Jesus' seeing and calling this representative figure for what he is, Jesus' call to communion is not limited to the Twelve but it is extended to other followers as well.

As is his wont after naming the person Mark hastens to speak of what he is engaged in at the time of Jesus' seeing him. Levi is «sitting at the tax office» (καθήμενον ἐπὶ τὸ τελώνιον). καθήμενον by itself does not indicate his daily occupation, but the fact that he is sitting at τὸ τελώνιον means that he is carrying out some function by sitting there. τελώνιον means revenue or tax office[100]. Levi's tax office is located probably at Capernaum which is the first important place in Herod Antipas' territory that travellers from Herod Philip's territory or Decapolis would pass through, coming round the north end of the

---

[96] Though Levi is not mentioned anywhere else in the NT other than in Mark 2,14 and Luke 5,27.29, his name appears once in the Gospel of Peter. «But I, Simon Peter, and my brother Andrew took our nets and went to the sea. And there was with us Levi, the son of Alphaeus, whom the Lord - (had called away from the custom-house)». *Gos. Pet.* 14,60. Quoted from W. SCHNEEMELCHER, *New Testament Apocrypha I*, 226.

[97] Even this is a much disputed matter. For instance, R.P. Meye thinks that Mark saw the tax collector as one included in the Twelve at the time of their appointment. Cf. R.P. MEYE, *Jesus and the Twelve*, 142.

[98] E. BEST, *Following Jesus*, 176-177.

[99] Two significant differences between the calling of the four (1,16-20) and that of Levi are evident. First, no missionary task («fishers of men») is given to Levi. Second, Levi «arises» whereas the four brothers «leave» everything to follow Jesus. The calling of the four seems to be different. See also R.A. GUELICH, *Mark*, 100; J. KIILUNEN, *Die Vollmacht*, 134; K. STOCK, *Boten*, 199-203.

[100] BAGD, 812.

Lake[101]. Levi as a tax-collector is perhaps not an official, but a private person who has hired a toll where he collects the required tax[102].

In the Judaism of Jesus' days, the tax-collectors were always under suspicion of uncleanness; it was even debated whether or how far a house becomes unclean when tax-collectors and thieves enter it. The publicans and tax-collectors were regarded as thieves or even robbers. Such classification of tax-collectors and tax-farmers with the thieves and robbers was because of their exactions and extortions. They collected more than was appointed them (Luke 3,13), or exacted tolls by deception (Luke 19,8)[103]. Thus Levi by his profession belonged to a class of people that was abhorred by the society.

4.5 Jesus Calls Levi whom he Sees

What Jesus communicates to him is introduced with a historical present καὶ λέγει αὐτῷ . The parallel in 1,17 has instead the aorist εἶπεν. This has led M. Zerwick to caution against an emphatic historical present tense in 2,14[104]. But the force of a historical present can very well be noticed here; the use of which gives a vividness to the narrative and raises interest in what Jesus tells Levi.

The words that Jesus utters are brief and to the point; Jesus does not enter into a discussion with Levi but just says to him, Ἀκολούθει μοι. It is an invitation akin to Δεῦτε ὀπίσω μου of v. 17 and echoes the statement that Simon and Andrew ἠκολούθησαν αὐτῷ (1,18). Ἀκολούθει is a present imperative and has the force of an emphatic

---

[101] C.E.B. CRANFIELD, St. Mark, 103; J. GNILKA, Markus I, 105; W.L. LANE, Mark, 101.

[102] B.M.F. VAN IERSEL, Mark, 151. J.R. Donahue has shown that although Levi belongs to a group commonly known as «tax collectors», the name «toll collectors» may come closer to identifying this group. Cf. J.R. DONAHUE, «Tax Collectors and Sinners», 42.

[103] O. MICHEL, «τελώνης», 101-105. The noun τελώνης occurs 20 times in the NT: Matt 8, Mark 2, Luke 10. Interestingly the term does not appear outside the Synoptic Gospels, more particularly the Johannine tradition has no reference to this category of people. The Gospel of Matthew has traces of a negative estimation of tax collectors and it is all the more curious because Matthew is the only one to be called «tax collector» in the list of the Twelve. The Gospel of Luke while mentioning the fact of their conversion implicitly alludes to how much they require conversion. Cf. O. MICHEL, «τελώνης», 104. Mark has reference to the tax collectors only in the story of Levi and the subsequent meal. Here, the fact that the Scribes take offence at Jesus fellowship with them indicates the prevalent aversion towards them.

[104] M. ZERWICK, Untersuchungen, 65.

summoning. The aorist imperative on the other hand seems to be less emphatic as in 14,13 (ἀκολουθήσετε αὐτῷ) where following somebody other than Jesus is in view[105]. The only other occurrence of the phrase in Mark is when Jesus summons the rich young man to follow him (10,21). But here a long discussion precedes Jesus' invitation unlike in the case of Levi.

4.6 Levi's Unconditional Response

Levi's unconditional response to Jesus' seeing him and calling him, has been paraphrased in the words καὶ ἀναστὰς ἠκολούθησεν αὐτῷ. The aorist participle ἀναστάς is used in the Gospel five times; mainly to refer to Jesus' rising and going to a new location (1,35; 7,24; 10,1; cf. also 16,9 meaning resurrection). The high Priest's standing up also is described by the same participle (14,60). In the story of Levi, his rising up (ἀναστάς) is the prelude to his movement and contrasts with his earlier «sitting down» (καθήμενον). His sitting at the tax office implies that he is firmly entrenched behind his money box, but after the call he stands and moves away from it.

Although the Markan favourite adverb εὐθύς is missing in the narrative, Levi's rising from the seat from which he carried out his daily occupation is thought to be as immediate as the other disciples' response. ἀναστάς would thus explain Levi's unconditional renunciation. The other missing element is a reference to Levi's «leaving» everything. Commentators view Levi's renunciation as greater than that of the four disciples (1,16-20) since on occasion they could return to their fishing. Levi's decision was instead once for all[106]. Hence ἀναστάς corresponds to «leaving their nets» (1,18) and «leaving their father Zebedee» (1,20) and once again highlights Jesus' power to induce the giving up of an occupation[107].

By saying ἠκολούθησεν αὐτῷ the narrative emphasizes the literal carrying out of Jesus' command «ἀκολούθει μοι». It stresses not only Levi's complete obedience but also the power of Jesus' words which elicits such a response. The verb ἠκολούθησεν in the aorist tense equates Levi's following with that of the disciples' (1,18 also 1,20:

---

[105] R.H. GUNDRY, Mark, 123-124; S.E. Porter explains that the present tense does not indicate linear action so much as it «presents» an action more forcefully, more emphatically. Cf. S.E. PORTER, Verbal Aspect, 326, 354-355.

[106] V. TAYLOR, St. Mark, 203.

[107] R.H. GUNDRY, Mark, 124.

ἀπῆλθον) and distinguishes it from that of the many disciples who «followed» Jesus (ἠκολούθουν)[108] in 2,15. Even though Levi belongs to the large circle of disciples which followed Jesus, his following stands out; it is not limited to entering his house [109]; it implies a life long

---

[108] It is much debated if the explanatory phrase ἦσαν γὰρ πολλοὶ καὶ ἠκολούθουν αὐτῷ refers to the disciples of Jesus or to the tax collectors and sinners. That both Matthew and Luke do not have this phrase in their parallel accounts has only added to the confusion. It is evident that the difficulty was noted early enough because some manuscripts like ℵ, L, (Δ), 33 it[b] etc. removed the period after αὐτω and read: ἦσαν γὰρ πολλοί. καὶ ἠκολούθουν αὐτω καὶ οἱ γραμματεῖς τῶν Φαρισαίων; 2,16 καὶ ἰδόντες. B.M. Metzger argues that since in the Gospels the verb ἀκολουθεῖν is used of Jesus' disciples, never of those who were hostile to him, a full stop should follow αὐτω. B.M. METZGER, A Textual Commentary, 67. R.A. Guelich contests this and says that the verb ἀκολουθεῖν occurs elsewhere in the Gospel in a non technical sense (3,7-8; 5,24; 10,32; 11,9; 14,13.54). Cf. R.A. GUELICH, Mark, 98.

Those who take the phrase to refer to the disciples include, C.E.B. CRANFIELD, St. Mark, 104; M. HENGEL, The Charismatic Leader, 81-82, n. 163; B.M.F. VAN IERSEL, Mark, 152-53; K. STOCK, Boten, 202-203, n. 517; V. TAYLOR, St. Mark, 205. The main reasons put forward are: i) the disciples are mentioned in the immediate sentence preceding it ii) it is for the first time that the disciples are mentioned in the Gospel; so a short explanatory phrase is in order iii) that the tax collectors and sinners were many is already said at the beginning of v. 15 iv) the reader has so far met the verb ἀκολουθεῖν only in reference to the attitude and activity of the followers of Jesus (1,18; 2,14), so he can hardly understand it differently in v. 15 v) In 3,13-14 it is said that Jesus «called to him those whom he desired», 2,15 is the only place where Mark refers to a large group of disciples from which he could choose the Twelve. These points seem to be reasonable and convincing.

For those who understand the phrase as referring to the tax collectors and sinners see, R.A. GUELICH, Mark, 98.102; R.H. GUNDRY, Mark, 125; R.P. MEYE, Jesus and the Twelve, 142-145; F. VOUGA, Jésus, 60-66. The reasons for the argument are: i) the verbs of v. 15 ἠκολούθουν along with συνανέκειντο and ἦσαν that refer to the persons who eat at Levi's house are imperfect and parallel. The imperfect indicative points to past time ii) Mark gives no impression of their following Jesus subsequently, nor does he make any later reference to such following iii) since the representative toll collector and sinner Levi has followed Jesus in v. 14, it is only natural that those who are many and follow him in v. 15 are other toll collectors and sinners.

[109] Admittedly, τῇ οἰκίᾳ αὐτοῦ is a bit ambiguous here. The Matthean rendering ἐν τῇ οἰκίᾳ (9,10) does not clarify it either. Only Luke expressly states that it is Levi's house that is in question (Luke 5,29). Most scholars take «his house» in Mark to refer to Levi's house. E.g., C.E.B. CRANFIELD, St. Mark, 102-103; J. DEWEY, Markan Public Debate, 81; R.H. GUNDRY, Mark, 124; B.M.F. VAN IERSEL, Mark, 151-152; W.L. LANE, Mark, 103; D.M. MAY, «Mark 2.15», 147-149; J. PAINTER, «When is a House not Home?», 499-500; V. TAYLOR, St. Mark, 99; etc. But there are some who understand «his house» to mean the house of Jesus. In a very detailed study E.S. Malbon proposes that the house in question belongs to Jesus. Cf.

journey in faith and total surrender to the one who saw him and called him.

But as noted above, Mark does not include Levi among the Twelve. So what does Jesus' seeing and calling him and Levi's unconditional following imply? It is evident that there is a very significant message involved in the following of Levi at this stage of the Gospel. Levi's story has all the elements of the story of the two pair of disciples whom Jesus sees and calls (1,16-20). But there is something more: Levi is not a fisherman, but a tax collector. In calling Levi, the tax collector, Jesus summons a man most despised among the Jews and Levi takes up the invitation to be a follower; to partake of all that such a following would entail. For Jesus, discipleship cuts through all the barriers of conventional religion. He sees someone and knows him to be the one whom he wants to call. It is his seeing, his selective look that is the determining factor. Hence Jesus calls him, regardless of whether he is perceived by others as worthy or not. This way v. 17: «I came not to call the righteous, but sinners» explains Levi's story. Jesus came to call; this basic truth is illustrated through the concrete example of Levi[110]. Luke would have a similar story to narrate in the episode of Jesus' encounter with Zacchaeus (19,1-10) which also concludes with a saying: «for the Son of man came to seek and save the lost» (19,10).

This aspect is highlighted by placing Levi's story in the literary context of 2,1-3,6, a context made up of a series of five controversies (healing of a paralytic, eating with tax collectors and sinners, question about fasting, plucking grain on Sabbath, and healing the man with a

---

E.S. MALBON, «Mark 2.15 in Context», 282-292; see also E. LOHMEYER, *Markus*, 55: «Und es geschieht, daß er beim Mahle liegt in seinem Hause». It is said quite frequently that Jesus enters or stays at a house. In some cases the owner of the house is mentioned (1,29: 5,38; 14,3.14;), but in many cases not (2,1; 3,20; 7,17; 9,28.33; 10,10). However, it is never mentioned in the Gospel that Jesus has a house in Capernaum, nor that he has a house that he can call his own. Jesus is rather portrayed as a wandering preacher. Cf. E. BEST, *Following Jesus*, 175; R.H. GUNDRY, *Mark*, 124; B.M. F.VAN IERSEL, *Mark*, 152. The fact that soon after calling Simon and Andrew, Jesus accepts hospitality at their house (1,29-31) also makes one to think that it was normal for Jesus to accept the hospitality of Levi who would like to honour Jesus whom he decided to follow with a meal.

[110] F.J. MOLONEY, «The Vocation», 507-508; G. SCHMAHL, *Die Zwölf*, 116. Taking the v. 17 as an explanation would negate seeing the pericope as «apothegm» as R. BULTMANN (*Synoptic Tradition*, 61-69) would call it or pronouncement story (a pericope which leads to a final pungent word from Jesus: cf. F.J. MOLONEY, «The Vocation», 506).

withered hand on the Sabbath) where Jesus enters into dispute with his adversaries as he freely infringes their law. The gist of Jesus' claim in all these is that Jesus cannot be contained within the *correct and proper* limits of any conventional religion. Any universal set of values by which men think they can control God and religion is not in harmony with what Jesus stands for. For Jesus what is of utmost importance is the human person. Respect for human person and his dignity must have precedence over other considerations. In the case of the call, there is an added dimension; the important feature is not the identity of the ones being summoned, but the identity of the one who calls[111].

4.7 *Jesus' Seeing Levi Contrasts with the Seeing of the Scribes*

The story of Levi also speaks of the seeing of someone else (2,16). The verb in question is ἰδόντες,[112] the aorist active plural nominative participle of ὁρᾶν. The subjects of the verb are οἱ γραμματεῖς τῶν Φαρισαίων[113]. Here the participle ἰδόντες prepares for the main verb ἔλεγον. The object of seeing is expressed by the explanatory ὅτι that describes Jesus' eating with sinners and tax collectors. ἰδόντες (2,16) stands in direct contrast with εἶδεν (2,14).

The verb εἶδεν (2,14) denotes Jesus' seeing an individual, with a proper name, practising his daily trade, whom he calls to follow him. The Scribes of the Pharisees also see (ἰδόντες), but the focus of the seeing is not on the person of Jesus but on one of his activities. The preceding activities of Jesus in 2,13-14, that of teaching the crowd or calling Levi, are not the object of their seeing. They single out his table fellowship with tax collectors and sinners. They fail to grasp what it means to share bread with the outcasts of the society; their reaction is one of disapproval of the behaviour of Jesus. A look at three narratives

---

[111] F.J. MOLONEY, «The Vocation», 508. All the same, the call of Levi and the admission of the tax collectors and sinners to table fellowship with Jesus (2,15) have to be understood also in the context of the call of Jesus beginning with the clarion call: «repent and believe in the Gospel» (1,14-15). It is plausible that the saying «I came not to call the righteous, but sinners» (2,17) seen in the overall context of the mission of Jesus thus becomes a call to the scribes themselves, provided they consider themselves as «sick» as well as «sinners».

[112] Some Western texts read εἶδαν instead of ἰδόντες.

[113] οἱ γραμματεῖς τῶν Φαρισαίων: this reading which is supported by B is to be preferred, since the tendency of the scribes would have been to insert καί after οἱ γραμματεῖς which is attested by many witnesses like A, Θ, C, *f*¹, *f*¹³, etc. Cf. B.M. METZGER, *A Textual Commentary*, 67.

of seeing with identical structure illustrates the futility of the scribes' seeing.

Mark 2,16	Mark 12,18	Mark 15,19
– καὶ οἱ γραμματεῖς τῶν ει Φαρισαίων ἰδόντες	εἷς τῶν γραμματέων ἰδὼν	Ἰδὼν δὲ ὁ κεντυρίων
– ὅτι ἐσθίει μετὰ τῶν ἁμαρτωλῶν καὶ τελωνῶν	ὅτι καλῶς ἀπεκρίθη αὐτοῖς	ὅτι οὕτως ἐξέπνευσεν
– ἔλεγον	ἐπηρώτησεν αὐτόν	εἶπεν,
– Ὅτι μετὰ τῶν τελωνῶν καὶ ἁμαρτωλῶν ἐσθίει;	Ποία ἐστὶν ἐντολὴ πρώτη πάντων;	Ἀληθῶς οὗτος ὁ ἄνθρωπος υἱὸς θεοῦ ἦν

In the first instance (2,16), what Jesus does raises curiosity; and the resultant reaction is to see what he does. What is perceived by those who see is crucial. The Scribes of the Pharisees see Jesus eating with the sinners and tax collectors which is unthinkable of a teacher and they perceive that it is unbecoming of him; so they protest to the disciples; they lack courage to confront Jesus[114]. The Scribe in the second case (12,28) sees that Jesus answers well. What he perceives is Jesus' ability to handle disputes. But one suspects that even this man like the Sadducees is antagonistic towards Jesus. But the compliment that Jesus renders to him (12,34) makes clear that Jesus detects in him some propensity towards openness. But that does not lead him to faith. The story of the Centurion (15,39) on the other hand is different. His is a journey from seeing to faith; a faith that flows out in proclamation. It is the Centurion who is the model for seeing in the Gospel.

A comparison of Jesus' seeing with that of the Sadducees shows that Jesus' seeing is precise, accurate, personal, elective, and compelling. The Sadducees on the other hand do not see the person, only his eating; their seeing is casual; it remains on the superficial level and even when

---

[114] It appears that they have learned from experience (2,8). They have also witnessed the demonstration of his power over against their criticism. Cf. H.B. SWETE, *Mark*, 42; R.H. GUNDRY, *Mark*, 126.

it is purposive, intended only to dispute with Jesus or his followers[115]. It lacks that initiative or appeal that can motivate people to follow them or to give assent to their teaching.

4.8 *Summary*

Levi's story amply demonstrates that Jesus' seeing is absolutely different from normal human seeing. It is amazing that an apparently disreputable figure like Levi becomes the object of the seeing of Jesus. But the truth of the story is that Jesus' seeing in reality is similar to the «love at first sight». His penetrating eyes see Levi and recognise him as the person whom he wants to call. Jesus also seems to know him as someone who is open and disposed to change. Therefore Jesus calls him, responding to which call implies not merely a change of heart (1,15), but a radical following whose point of reference is Jesus himself ('ακολούθει μοι). Levi cannot resist the seeing of Jesus nor his command to follow. Like in the case of the two pairs of brothers, Levi too responds without hesitation and delay. His decision is final and total. He sets out on a journey of faith with Jesus.

5. **Decisiveness of Jesus' Seeing**

The three narratives that speak of Jesus' recruiting the first of the disciples have the seeing of Jesus as the most important factor. That does not mean that the call was unimportant. But Mark places his focus on Jesus' seeing. The call issues forth from that seeing. The decisiveness of Jesus' seeing can be further brought out by comparing the narrative with the OT parallels, the Johannine account of the call of the disciples and the other call narratives in Mark.

5.1 *Old Testament Patterns*

There are two OT narratives that could be considered as parallel to the story of the disciples which Mark narrates, they are the Elijah-Elisha story (1Kgs 19,19-21) and the story of the choice of David as king over Israel (1Sam 16,1-13).

---

[115] E. BOSETTI, «Un cammino per vedere»,128.

5.1.1 1Kgs 19,19-21

Scholars almost in unison hold that the episodes of Jesus' seeing the two pairs of brothers as well as Levi and calling them are modelled after the Old Testament pattern of Elijah calling Elisha (1Kgs 19,19-21)[116]. They point out as evidence the parallelism that exists between the stories. A. Schulz identifies three stages in the account of the vocation of Elisha that the Markan stories follow:

i) situation data; the movement of Elijah, his seeing Elisha who is going about his daily work

ii) Elijah challenges Elisha to follow him by a symbolic act

iii) Elisha obediently leaves his work, rises up and follows Elijah and ministers to him[117].

A broad parallelism can certainly be established between the narratives of 1,16-20, 2,14 and 1Kgs 19,19-21:

Parallelism	Mark 1,16-18	Mark 1,19-20	Mark 2,14	1Kgs 19,19-21
– a reference to movement	Καὶ παράγων παρὰ τὴν θάλασσαν τῆς Γαλιλαίας	Καὶ προβὰς ὀλίγον	καὶ παράγων	καὶ ἀπῆλθεν ἐκεῖθεν
– a verb of seeing	εἶδεν	εἶδεν	εἶδεν	καὶ εὑρίσκει
– portrayal of persons	Σίμωνα καὶ Ἀνδρέαν τὸν ἀδελφὸν Σίμωνος	Ἰάκωβον τὸν τοῦ Ζεβεδαίου καὶ Ἰωάννην τὸν ἀδελφὸν αὐτοῦ	Λευὶν τὸν τοῦ Ἀλφαίου	τὸν Ελισαε υἱὸν Σαφατ

---

[116] T.L. BRODIE, *The Crucial Bridge*, 91; S. LÉGASSE, *Marc*, 113; M. HENGEL, *The Charismatic Leader*, 16-18; B.M.F. VAN IERSEL, *Mark*, 130; R. PESCH, «Berufung», 9f.; A. SCHULZ, *Nachfolgen*, 100-103; E. SCHWEIZER, *Markus*, 22. Cf. C. COULOT, *Jésus et le Disciple*, 146.150-151, see especially p. 159: «Pour mettre en valeur la figure du maître, le rédacteur fait appel au personnage d'Elie. Il recourt à une typologie afin d'élaborer sa christologie. Cette typologie ne joue pas seulement pour Jésus, le maître, mais encore pour le disciple: il doit imiter Elisée. Il quittera sa famille et ses biens pour se mettre au service de son maître et continuer son oeuvre».

[117] A. SCHULZ, *Nachfolgen*, 100-103.

– description of profession	ἀμφιβάλλοντας ἐν τῇ θαλάσσῃ· ἦσαν γὰρ ἁλιεῖς.	καὶ αὐτοὺς ἐν τῷ πλοίῳ καταρτίζοντας τὰ δίκτυα,	καθήμενον ἐπὶ τὸ τελώνιον,	καὶ αὐτὸς ἠροτρία ἐν βουσίν δώδεκα ζεύγη βοῶν ἐνώπιον αὐτοῦ καὶ αὐτὸς ἐν τοῖς δώδεκα
– call	καὶ εἶπεν αὐτοῖς ὁ Ἰησοῦς, Δεῦτε ὀπίσω μου, καὶ ποιήσω ὑμᾶς γενέσθαι ἁλιεῖς ἀνθρώπων.	καὶ εὐθὺς ἐκάλεσεν αὐτούς.	καὶ λέγει αὐτῷ, Ἀκολούθει μοι.	Καὶ ἐπῆλθεν ἐπ᾽ αὐτὸν καὶ ἐπέρριψε τὴν μηλωτὴν αὐτοῦ ἐπ᾽ αὐτόν
– leaving	καὶ εὐθὺς ἀφέντες τὰ δίκτυα	καὶ ἀφέντες τὸν πατέρα αὐτῶν Ζεβεδαῖον ἐν τῷ πλοίῳ μετὰ τῶν μισθωτῶν	καὶ ἀναστὰς	Καὶ κατέλιπεν Ελισαιε τὰς βόας καὶ κατέδραμεν ὀπίσω Ηλιου καὶ εἶπεν καταφιλήσω τὸν πατέρα μου καὶ ἀκολουθήσω ὀπίσω σου
– following	ἠκολούθησαν αὐτῷ.	ἀπῆλθον ὀπίσω αὐτοῦ.	ἠκολούθησεν αὐτῷ.	Καὶ ἀνέστη καὶ ἐπορεύθη ὀπίσω Ηλιου

A close study of the story of Elisha makes it clear that the Markan stories go beyond the limits of the parallelism[118]. Thus:

i) the story of Elisha is much more detailed than the Markan stories.

ii) the verb of movement used to denote Elijah's movement is less picturesque than that used of Jesus.

iii) From our point of view what is of utmost importance is the verb that expresses Elijah's seeing of Elisha. The narrative has καὶ εὑρίσκει τὸν Ελισαιε υἱὸν Σαφατ.

iv) Elijah performs the symbolic action of casting his mantle upon Elisha; Jesus instead calls the disciples and in the first instance a promise and a mission accompanies the call (1,17: «I will make you become fishers of men»).

v) In the OT the person who calls is ultimately God himself. In the story of Elisha, Elijah just follows the command of God in 19,16: «and Elisha the son of Shaphat of Abelmeholah you shall anoint to be prophet in your place». Jesus' call on the other hand cannot be traced back to any other source; he calls on his own authority.

vi) Elisha's following is not described as immediate; he obtains permission from Elisha to bid farewell to his parents. Besides, he also throws a farewell party for his people. Jesus allows no such delay (cf. Matt 8,21f. // Luke 9,59f.). Immediate and unconditional following of Jesus is the response of the men whom Jesus sees and calls.

vii) It is not at all clear if the reception of a teaching from Elijah formed an essential part of Elisha's following him; and this is clearly of great importance in the case of the disciples of Jesus.

Elijah is reported to have found (εὑρίσκει)[119] Elisha the son of Shaphat. The verb εὑρίσκειν and its derivatives occur in the LXX some 761 times. The third person singular in the present tense occurs only 3 times, all in 1Kings (1Kgs 19,19; 21,36.37). The verb means to find someone as a result of searching for him. Though accidental finding also could be expressed by the same verb it is generally used to refer to finding after seeking. The one who looks for someone does it with the intention of finding him. The fact that Elijah is pictured as carrying out the command of God in 19,16 shows that his passing by the field where Elisha is ploughing is not accidental[120]. Dramatically, Elijah lets eleven

---

[118] E. BEST, *Following Jesus*, 168; M. HENGEL, *Charismatic Leader*, 17; R.P. MEYE, *Jesus and the Twelve*, 95.

[119] On the use of εὑρίσκει in the Gospel of John see below.

[120] The disparity that exists with 1Kgs 19,16 is all too obvious. God's command was «to anoint» Elisha prophet. However, the symbolic act of throwing the mantle

yoke of oxen pass him, and when he finds Elisha casts the mantle on him.

In contrast, Jesus does not find (εὑρίσκει) the disciples whom he calls; he sees (εἶδεν) them. His seeing is presented as a spontaneous reaching out that culminates in a wholehearted following on the part of the disciples. Jesus is not carrying out a preordained command of God; nor are the disciples selected beforehand. It is Jesus' seeing that is crucial and in his seeing Jesus is able to recognise them as the persons whom he wants to call. In short it is a selective seeing which in no way can be compared to Elijah's finding Elisha.

5.1.2 1Sam 16,1-13

A clue to what the seeing of God, and by extension that of Jesus, amounts to is provided by the OT episode surrounding the anointing of David (1Sam 16,1-13). God orders Samuel to go to Bethlehem and anoint one of the sons of Jesse, whom He would indicate, king over Israel. Jesse parades all his sons in review before Samuel, beginning with the first, but each is rejected because he has not been chosen, despite the favourable outward impression he conveys. God explains to Samuel: «for the Lord sees not as man sees; man looks on the outward appearance, but the Lord looks on the heart» (1Sam 16,7: כִּי לֹא אֲשֶׁר יִרְאֶה הָאָדָם כִּי הָאָדָם יִרְאֶה לַעֵינַיִם וַיה וה יִרְאֶה לַלֵּבָב = ὅτι οὐχ ὡς ἐμβλέψεται ἄνθρωπος ὄψεται ὁ θεός ὅτι ἄνθρωπος ὄψεται εἰς πρόσωπον ὁ δὲ θεὸς ὄψεται εἰς καρδίαν).

The narrative contains extensive use of the verb «to see». As seen in the first chapter, God's seeing in OT is commonly expressed by the Hebrew verb רָאָה which the LXX generally translates with the verb ὁρᾶν/ὄψεσθαι/ἰδεῖν. Here two verbs are employed to denote seeing, βλέπειν (ἐμβλέπειν) as well as ὁρᾶν (ὄψεσθαι) both translating the Hebrew verb רָאָה. In fact the key root ראה illustrates superbly the progress of the narration[121]. The imperfect יִרְאֶה occurs three times in v. 7 to express the contrast between God's and man's way of seeing: God is concerned with the heart; he alone is capable of seeing man's innermost being and discerning his purposes (cf. also Jer 17,10; 20,12), whereas man can only «see» the outward side of man, an allusion to

---

does in no way amount to anointing. S.J. DeVries observes that 1Kgs 19,16 is from a different tradition. Cf. S.J. DeVries, *I Kings*, 239.

[121] Only in God's warning to Samuel there is an occurrence of the root נבט, a synonym of ראה with a notion of «showing regard to».

Saul's impressive appearance. People are impressed by what is on the surface; God perceives what the person is really like[122].

From a theological point of view the pericope establishes that David, the youngest son of Jesse would be anointed king over Israel because God has selected him; He has seen David's heart, He knows David through and through, He is not concerned with David's external appearance. It also establishes that kingship depends solely on God's seeing and selection (cf. 2Sam 7,8). The great Samuel is reported to be seeing Eliab the eldest son of Jesse (1Sam 16,6: εἶδεν[123] τὸν Ελιαβ = וַיַּרְא אֶת־אֱלִיאָב); but his seeing is not «divine»; in fact God upbraids him for his «human» conduct. Samuel's seeing is superficial and it cannot be selective.

The episode (1Sam 16,1-13) serves to emphasise that Jesus too «sees not as man sees». His seeing is equal to God's seeing that is not concerned with external stature and attractiveness of a person. Jesus' seeing also contrasts with Samuel's seeing which is human. Unlike Samuel, Jesus does not receive any instruction as regards to the selection of the disciples. He on his own authority sees them and calls them.

5.2 The Johannine Account of the Call of the Disciples: 1,35-51

The Johannine account of the call of the first disciples of Jesus is quite different from the Synoptic account, even though two of the same characters, Peter and Andrew are involved. According to John the call seems to have taken place at Bethany but for the Synoptics it took place on the Sea of Galilee where the first disciples were fishing. John tells that the first disciples were former disciples of John the Baptist. The Synoptics give no information in this regard[124]. The fourth Gospel also

---

[122] M. KESSLER, «Narrative Technique in 1Sm 16,1-13», 549-50; R.H. KLEIN, 1Samuel, 160-161.

[123] The appearance of the same verb εἶδεν here does not mean that it conveys the kind of significance that Mark attributes to Jesus' seeing.

[124] The general attempt at harmonisation is that Jesus first called the disciples as John narrates but that they were subsequently permitted to return to their normal life in Galilee until Jesus came there to call them decisively to full-time discipleship, as the Synoptic Gospels narrate. However, there is no Gospel evidence to support this view. Cf. C.K. BARRETT, St. John, 179; R.E. BROWN, John, 77.

provides no time period in which the disciples come in contact with Jesus[125].

The Johannine account (1,35-51) is permeated by the idea of seeing. All verses except vv. 35, 37, 40, 44 and 49 contain a verb of seeing. In the first scene (1,35-39) all the characters are reported to be seeing: John looks at (ἐμβλέψας) Jesus as he is walking (v. 36), Jesus sees (θεασάμενος) the two disciples following him[126] (v. 38) and invites them to come and see ("Ερχεσθε καὶ ὄψεσθε: v. 39); they accept his invitation; their action literally corresponds to the command of Jesus. They go and see (ἦλθαν οὖν καὶ εἶδαν)[127]. It is evident that the initiative does not rest with Jesus. It is not his seeing that is the determining factor in the disciples' following.

In the second scene (1,40-42) Andrew expresses what his seeing really signifies. He tells his brother Simon Peter:[128] «We have found the Messiah» (Εὑρήκαμεν τὸν Μεσσίαν: v. 41). It was a finding, result of their personal seeking. When Peter is led to Jesus, it is reported that Jesus looks at (ἐμβλέψας)[129] Peter (v. 42). Jesus is not said to be taking the initiative and *seeing* him. All the same it is a look that transcends the superficial; proceeding directly to the heart, penetrating his conscience. As a result Simon receives a new name, Cephas; he is transformed.

The story of Philip (1,43), is akin to the Synoptic account of the call of the disciples. The account is limited to the essentials. John narrates that Jesus found (εὑρίσκει) Philip and invited him to follow him. Jesus seizes the initiative. However, the verb used (εὑρίσκει) is entirely different from what Mark employs (εἶδεν) and the significance he

---

[125] The expression Τῇ ἐπαύριον which occurs in 1,43 seems to be having only a stylistic meaning which occurs also in 1,29 and 1,35 in the first chapter of the Gospel of John. Cf. A. SCHULZ, *Nachfolgen*, 111-112.

[126] In other references in John (1,43; 8,12; 10,4.27; 12,26; 21,19.20.22) ἀκολουθεῖν means to follow as a disciple; but it also has a neutral meaning (e.g., 11,31). Here and in 1,38.40 John is perhaps playing on both meanings. The two disciples' following is the first step to faith and it leads to «staying with» Jesus. Cf. C.K. BARRETT, *St. John*, 180; R. SCHNACKENBURG, *St. John* I, 308.

[127] For the disciples seeing amounts to knowing. They gain insight into who Jesus is and thus grow in faith in the person of Jesus. In John 14,9 Jesus himself would refer to this when he asks Philip, «Have I been with you so long, and yet you do not know me Philip? He who has seen me has seen the Father».

[128] John has a preference for the double name, Simon Peter.

[129] This is the same kind of gaze that John had directed on Jesus (1,36). Jesus fixes his gaze on Peter and looks with penetration and insight. Cf. R.E. BROWN, *John*, 74.

attaches to that verb cannot be ascribed to Jesus' «finding»[130] Philip in John 1,43.

Philip in turn finds (εὑρίσκει) Nathanael[131] (1,45) and describes his encounter with Jesus as finding (εὑρήκαμεν) him. He invites the sceptical Nathanael to come and see ("Ερχου καὶ ἴδε) Jesus of Nazareth (v. 46). Jesus is reported to see (εἶδεν) Nathanael coming to him (v. 47) and tells a wonder-struck Nathanael that he saw (εἶδόν) him when he was under a fig tree (v. 48). Even though Jesus is not the one taking the initiative in this meeting, the verb used of his seeing is the same as that of Mark. However, there is an essential difference. Here Jesus' seeing refers to an activity, Nathanael's coming to him or his being (or sitting) under the fig tree. It is not a selective seeing aimed at the person of Nathanael and it does not have the scope of calling him to discipleship.

So except in the case of Philip (1,43) the initiative rests solely with the disciples; it is not Jesus who goes out in search of them, but the disciples themselves either find him (1,37-39) or are led to him on the basis of blood relationship (1,40-42) or friendship (1,44-51)[132]. In short there is no sense of a call to communion that is implied in the Markan account of the call.

The witnesses who lead other would be disciples to Jesus give a dogmatic description of his person; he is the Lamb of God (1,36), Rabbi (1,38), Messiah (1,41), of whom Moses in the Law and also the Prophets wrote (1,45), Son of God, King of Israel (1,49). The act of seeking as expressed by the verb εὑρίσκειν, involves an assent of faith though preliminary as it may be, that would grow to a complete trust on meeting Jesus. The Markan account gives no room for such a development. Even though the disciples' following is based on their conviction of Jesus as someone different, perhaps a man of God, it is Jesus' seeing and the resultant call that effect such a deep faith that they abandon themselves to him, leave everything and follow him.

---

[130] For R.E. Brown the term εὑρίσκει has no special significance here. He argues that it is used here as well as in 1,41 to introduce a character. Cf. R.E. BROWN, *John*, 82.

[131] Nathanael is known only to John. His name does not appear in any list of the Twelve.

[132] Even in the case of Philip it is said that «Philip was from Bethsaida, the city of Andrew and Peter» (1,44). It refers to Philip's personal acquaintance with the first disciples of Jesus, which may have provided a motive for his decision to follow Jesus. Cf. A. SCHULZ, *Nachfolgen*, 111.

Apart from the above mentioned differences between the Markan (also Synoptic) and the Johannine accounts, it may also further be noted that in the Johannine account of the call of the disciples an important element is missing. Jesus in the Johannine account never invites his disciples to partake of his mission[133]. Mission in the Synoptic accounts is inseparably connected to the call (Mark 1,17; 3,14; Matt 4,18; 10,1; Luke 5,10-11; 9,59-60).

The fourth Gospel alludes to the fact that «Jesus was making and baptising more disciples than John» (John 4,1)[134]. Jesus is presented as practising a baptism independent of John (cf. 3,22) and the disciples of John (3,26) as well as the Pharisees take note of Jesus making more disciples than John: Ἰησοῦς πλείονας μαθητὰς ποιεῖ καὶ βαπτίζει ἢ Ἰωάννης (4,1). Here the comparative πλείονας is the object of both μαθητὰς ποιεῖν as well as βαπτίζειν. So there appears to be a narrow link between making disciples and baptising. Thus John refers to an external sign through which the disciples enter into the community of disciples of Jesus[135]. The Synoptics do not know of any such initiatory rite[136].

5.3 Human Initiative is not the Decisive Factor

The Gospel of Mark contains even other «call narratives» that are conspicuous by the characters' initiative. Four of them could be identified as relevant for examination. They are: i) the Gerasene demoniac (5,18-20) ii) the rich man (10,21-22) iii) blind Bartimaeus (10,51) iv) the young man who fled (14,51-52).

5.3.1 The Gerasene Demoniac (5,18-20)

The Gerasene man who earlier spoke for the demons as they had him in their grip (5,10-12), once liberated of the demons that possessed him

---

[133] A. SCHULZ, Nachfolgen, 114-115.

[134] John 4,2 («although Jesus himself did not baptise, but only his disciples») is widely accepted as a gloss inserted later to avoid the embarrassment at the information that Jesus was baptising.

[135] A. SCHULZ, Nachfolgen, 116. In John 4,1f. the term disciples may perhaps embrace a group larger than the Twelve; however, it is not improbable according to the witness of the Gospel that even these first disciples too may have undergone the rite of baptism.

[136] However, it is not difficult to identify the command of the risen Lord in Matt 28,19: πορευθέντες οὖν μαθητεύσατε [...] βαπτίζοντες αὐτούς, with the actual practice as narrated in John 4,1f.

by the saving power of Jesus, comes up to Jesus with a plea. He begs Jesus' leave to be with him (5,18)[137]. His desire to be with Jesus matches the very purpose for which Jesus chose the Twelve: ἵνα ὦσιν μετ' αὐτοῦ (3,14). This apparently positive development occurs in a scene replete with negative sentiments towards Jesus. The demons are plainly antagonistic to him and attempt to fend him off (5,7.10.12), the demoniac's compatriots are afraid (5,15) and request that Jesus leave their neighbourhood (5,17). In stark contrast the ex-demoniac wants to share Jesus' company.

Jesus does not agree to the ex-demoniac's request. The strong adversative ἀλλά and the historical present λέγει emphasise the authority of the contrary command[138] to go home and report to his family and friends[139] how much the Lord has done for him and how he has had mercy on him (5,19)[140].

Mark does not supply any reasons for Jesus' refusal to let the ex-demoniac be with him. To think that Jesus did not want an ex-demoniac or a born pagan in his company does not make sense. Nor is it plausible to imagine that Jesus wants to leave a witness in the region. That Jesus thinks it premature to start gathering in the Gentiles (cf. 7,27) is also

---

[137] Matthew does not report this fact. He speaks of two demoniacs who meet Jesus. His narrative ends with the request of the people that Jesus should leave their neighbourhood (Matt 8,28-34). Luke follows Mark's story more faithfully and the differences are only slight (8,26-39).

[138] R.H. GUNDRY, Mark, 254.

[139] πρὸς τοὺς σούς is a unique phrase in the NT. Some take it to mean «your family» in the narrow sense, e.g., W. WREDE, The Messianic Secret, 140. Cf. also J. GNILKA, Markus I, 206-207. J. Gnilka understands that the purpose of the commission to announce is to reintegrate the ex-demoniac into his family. But most understand the phrase to mean «a circle wider than the man's family», e.g., J. ERNST, Markus, 157-158; R.A. GUELICH, Mark, 285; R.H. GUNDRY, Mark, 264; J. MARCUS, Mark, 353-354; V. TAYLOR, St. Mark, 284. R. PESCH, Markusevangelium I, 294 calls it the man's own, pagan «Milieu». A broader reading is more likely because i) Jesus' command to the ex-demoniac is to announce what the Lord has done; he in obedience does the proclamation in Decapolis (5,20) ii) the herdsmen flee and tell in the city and in the country what has taken place (5,14); so even this non-evangelistic proclamation has a wider audience.

[140] Scholars note the completeness and permanence of Jesus' action expressed by the perfect tense of πεποίηκεν. Its parallel, the aorist ἠλέησέν can also be considered to be assuming the force of a perfect. The chiasm that puts the personal pronoun at the extremes of   σοι πεποίηκεν καὶ ἠλέησέν σε stresses personal benefit. cf. R.H. GUNDRY, Mark, 264. For Mark's penchant for such duality expressed with the help of καί cf. M. REISER, Syntax, 134-136.

questionable. It is probably best to say that he refuses the ex-demoniac's request because being «with» Jesus belongs as a privilege only to the Twelve. They have been specifically called to «be with him» (3,14). So Jesus' denial simply means that the ex-demoniac is not called[141].

We have noted that it is Jesus who determines whom he would like to be with him;[142] the decisive factor of which is his seeing. It is Jesus alone who takes the initiative. Human aspirations come to naught when the divine will is absent. Not being one of the Twelve is not the main point. Levi for instance (2,14) does not belong to the Twelve, yet Jesus sees and calls him. Vocation springs up from an efficacious, creative act of God; it is basically a gift which calls for a resolute response. The ex-demoniac has not been blessed with it.

Yet he has a role to play. One of the important tasks of the disciples, including that of the Twelve is to «preach» (3,14; cf. also 1,45; 6,12). The ex-demoniac carries it out with great success according to 5,20. But it happens only because it is Jesus who directs him to the task. The initiative must always lie with Jesus. In fact everything in the realm of man's relationship with God has its initiative in God[143]. In the Gospel he is the only person healed by Jesus who also receives from him the mandate to preach. The man becomes thus a messenger of the «good news» of the advent of God's kingdom (1,14-15).

---

[141] R.A. GUELICH, *Mark*, 285-286; R.H. GUNDRY, *Mark*, 264-65. W. Wrede's view that Jesus refuses the ex-demoniac's request out of fear that the man might betray the messianic secret and so sends him to his family where the secret may be guarded does not hold water (Cf. W. WREDE, *Messianic Secret*, 140-141). Firstly, Jesus has explicitly asked the man to tell his people what has happened. Secondly, he has not asked the man to guard a secret. Thirdly, the people in the city and in the country know about it (5,14), so it is no more a secret. G. Theissen appeals to Mark's understanding of «home» as a place of secrecy (7,17.24; 9,28; 10,10). Cf. G. THEISSEN, *The Miracle Stories*, 146-147. But in all these instances pointed out by Theissen except for 10,10 the narrative after giving information about the house explicitly adds a point of privacy; e.g., 7,17: «and left the people»; 7,24: «and would not have anyone know of it»; 9,28: «his disciples asked him privately». So privacy is not implicit in the location itself. Moreover, ἀπάγγειλον means much more than «to give thanks for his cure» as Theissen thinks. So R.A. GUELICH, *Mark*, 286-287.

[142] K. Stock, commenting on Mark 5,18-20 puts it beautifully: «Nicht menschlicher Wunsch entscheidet über dieses Mit-ihm-Sein, sondern allein sein auswählender Wille». Cf. K. STOCK, *Boten*, 18. We might as well add «sondern allein sein auswählender Blick».

[143] F.J. MOLONEY, *Disciples and Prophets*, 135-136.

5.3.2 The Rich Man (10,17-22)

The story of the rich man[144]serves to highlight another dimension to the demands of discipleship, that of renunciation of wealth. But above all it emphasises that discipleship entails a double movement; the divine one consisting of election and call, and the human one which involves wholehearted renunciation and following[145]. A concentric structure could be detected in the story of rich man and Jesus (1,17-22)[146].

    a. a rich man runs up to Jesus with a question (v. 17)
      b. Jesus answers with the requirements of the Law (vv. 18-19)
        c. the man responds citing his observance of the Law (v. 20)
      b'. Jesus answers with his own demands (v. 21)
    a'. the man goes away sorrowful unwilling to follow Jesus (v. 22)

The concluding narrative (10,21-22) has been marked by both similarity and contrast in relation to the narrative on the call of the disciples (1,16-20; 2,14).

By way of similarities between the narratives it can be pointed out that:

i) a verb of seeing precedes Jesus' call:

10,21: ὁ δὲ Ἰησοῦς ἐμβλέψας αὐτῷ ἠγάπησεν αὐτὸν	1,16: Καὶ παράγων [...] εἶδεν Σίμωνα καὶ Ἀνδρέαν
	1,19: Καὶ προβὰς ὀλίγον εἶδεν Ἰάκωβον [...] καὶ Ἰωάννην
	2,14: καὶ παράγων εἶδεν Λευὶν

---

[144] Only in Matthew he is described as a young man (Matt 19,20.22). Luke calls him a «ruler» (Luke 18,18).

[145] The story itself forms part of a wider treatment on riches and its relationship to discipleship (10,17-31). The whole pericope is made up of three conversations: i) the dialogue between Jesus and the rich man (10,17-22) ii) the dialogue between Jesus and his disciples (10,23-27) iii) the dialogue between Jesus and Peter (10,28-31). Two movements of Jesus frame the pericope. In 10,17 Jesus leaves the house (10,10) and resumes the journey; 10,32 again says that they were on the road, going up to Jerusalem. What transpires in 10,17-31 is presented as taking place in the same place and is framed by an inclusion referring to eternal life: ζωὴν αἰώνιον (10,17.30). The story of the rich man is delimited by his arrival and subsequent departure. Our analysis will limit itself to the encounter between the rich man and Jesus and Jesus' call to follow him.

[146] C. COULOT, *Jésus et le Disciple*, 98-99; F. MANNS, *Essais*, 52-53.

ii) the call itself is introduced by the solemn phrase καὶ εἶπεν (10,21; 1,17; 2,14: καὶ λέγει αὐτῷ).

iii) the call in 10,21 is a combination of 1,17 and 2,14: καὶ δεῦρο ἀκολούθει μοι:

10,21: καὶ εἶπεν αὐτῷ,	1,17: καὶ εἶπεν αὐτοῖς ὁ Ἰησοῦς,
Ἕν σε ὑστερεῖ· ὕπαγε, ὅσα ἔχεις	Δεῦτε ὀπίσω μου,
πώλησον καὶ δὸς [τοῖς] πτωχοῖς,	1,19: καὶ εὐθὺς ἐκάλεσεν αὐτούς.
[...] καὶ δεῦρο ἀκολούθει μοι.	2,14: καὶ λέγει αὐτῷ, Ἀκολούθει μοι.

iv) a promise in the future tense accompanies the call:[147]

10,21: καὶ ἕξεις θησαυρὸν	1,17: καὶ ποιήσω ὑμᾶς γενέσθαι
ἐν οὐρανῷ,	ἁλιεῖς ἀνθρώπων.

The contrasts are also equally revealing:

i) In Markan usage the verb of seeing ἐμβλέψας[148] does not assume the characteristics of the verb εἶδεν. There are four occurrence of the verb ἐμβλέπειν in the Gospel of Mark (8,25; 10,21.27; 14,67). In 8,25 ἐνέβλεπεν in the context of the healing of the blind man at Bethsaida means to *have a clear vision of everything*. The ἐμβλέψασα following ἰδοῦσα in 14,67 referring to the maid who spots Peter warming himself is actually redundant[149]. In 10,21 and 27 the participle ἐμβλέψας means to *look at, fix one's gaze upon somebody*. Jesus' seeing here is not elective. In other words Jesus does not «see» the rich man, so he would not become a disciple. The main verb ἠγάπησεν[150] further explains the

---

[147] The promise here breaks the sequence of imperatives ὕπαγε, δός, δεῦρο ἀκολούθει μοι. But it concerns directly with the rich man's question in v. 17: τί ποιήσω ἵνα ζωὴν αἰώνιον κληρονομήσω;. It is noteworthy that the rich man uses the verb in the future tense (κληρονομήσω), Jesus too replies in the same future tense (ἕξεις). The concept of having treasure in heaven is further explained in Jesus' dialogue with Peter in 10,28-31. There it is identified with eternal life (ζωὴν αἰώνιον), the subject matter of the man's query. Thus the two references to ζωὴν αἰώνιον in v. 17 and v. 30 form an inclusion.

[148] Among the Synoptics only Mark mentions Jesus' benevolent and loving seeing of the rich man.

[149] C. COULOT, *Jésus et le Disciple*, 115.

[150] S.T. Lachs says that ἠγάπησεν should be translated as «pitied» following the Aramaic meaning of the root רחם and not according to the Hebrew meaning which would be «loved». Cf. S.T. LACHS, *A Rabbinic Commentary*, 331. While not negating

scope of Jesus' intentive look. It evokes in Jesus sentiments of love for the man; for Jesus understands him. Jesus apparently sees both his inner longing for eternal life as well as the attachment that enslaves and strangles him, thereby blocking his capacity to be open to the surprises and wonders that God can work in him.

ii) a discussion regarding the commandments that precede reduces the immediateness that characterises the disciples' call.

iii) the contrast is most evident in the last verse (10, 22):

10,22: ὁ δὲ στυγνάσας ἐπὶ τῷ λόγῳ ἀπῆλθεν λυπούμενος· ἦν γὰρ ἔχων κτήματα πολλά.

1,18: καὶ εὐθὺς ἀφέντες τὰ δίκτυα ἠκολούθησαν αὐτῷ.
1,20: καὶ ἀφέντες τὸν πατέρα αὐτῶν [...] ἀπῆλθον ὀπίσω αὐτοῦ.
2,14: καὶ ἀναστὰς ἠκολούθησεν αὐτῷ.

Whereas the disciples wholeheartedly respond to Jesus and follow him without delay, the rich man's reaction is just the opposite: ὁ δὲ στυγνάσας ἐπὶ τῷ λόγῳ ἀπῆλθεν λυπούμενος (10, 22). The disciples' immediate reaction is expressed by the participles ἀφέντες (1,18. 20) and ἀναστάς (2,14). The aorist participle στυγνάσας expresses the rich man's outward expression of the inner disposition. It means to *be or become gloomy*[151]. The word of Jesus (λόγος) meets with sadness in him. His inner feeling is indicated by the present participle λυπούμενος. All the three Synoptics mention his sadness (Luke however does not speak of his action of going away). Instead of heeding to Jesus' call to follow him, the rich man goes away from him (ἀπῆλθεν). The reason for such a reaction is made evident: ἦν γὰρ ἔχων κτήματα πολλα (10, 22). His problem is described by the verb ἔχειν (cf. also 10,21: ὅσα ἔχεις πώλησον). The periphrastic construction emphasises the rich man's strong and persistent attachment to his possessions.

---

an element of sympathy for the man in v. 21 the predominant sentiment must be understood as one of love, because Jesus' invitation is not yet given nor has the man declined it, which would perhaps evoke pity. Moreover, the other occurrences of the verb ἀγάπαν (12,30.31.33) in the Gospel always refer to love; love for God and love for man.

[151] BAGD, 771.

The rich man's story is an unsuccessful call narrative[152]. It serves to once again highlight the point that only divine initiative meets with success, however earnest the human striving may be. The story also emphasises a particular aspect of discipleship. Being with Jesus is equally important as fulfilling the commandments of God. A personal belonging to Jesus is implied in the call to follow[153]. The rich man's refusal would amount to a rejection of that intimate relationship which would develop out of his following[154].

Even when Jesus calls someone it is a call to a total following. God wants the person called whole and entire. In view of Jesus' invitation to follow him, and the rich man's incapacity to respond positively, it becomes evident that the man's observance of the commandments (10,20) is empty and devoid of fervour, because love of riches puts a stranglehold on him so that love of God and neighbour «with all heart, with all soul and with all might» is neither possible nor conceivable[155]. «Jesus names no concrete preconditions for discipleship, adds no Eleventh Commandment; rather he only underlines a principle that will remain valid in all life-situations. Renunciation of possessions is not "discipleship in itself" but a means toward realisation»[156].

5.3.3 The Blind Bartimaeus (10,52)

The story of blind Bartimaeus is the last healing miracle in the gospel of Mark. It is also the first and the only miracle Jesus performs in Judah. It is important both in its content, and in the position in which Mark places it in his gospel. It is hardly accidental that the final healing miracle in the gospel involves the giving of sight to a blind man. But it is much more than a miracle of healing. A number of important ideas are fused in this incident and serves as a climax of Jesus' teachings before his triumphal entry into Jerusalem.

---

[152] V. TAYLOR, St. Mark, 430: «This is the only story in the Gospels in which the command of Jesus to follow Him is even tacitly refused. Mark makes no comment on the fact, but merely records what happened».

[153] A. SCHULZ, Nachfolgen, 76-77; E. SCHWEIZER, Markus, 22.

[154] J. DONALDSON, «Called to Follow», 70-71, n. 7: «The young man may not have come seeking discipleship, but Jesus was certainly asking him to accept it. The fishermen (Mk 1:16-20) and Levi (2:14) were not seeking discipleship either, but accepted it».

[155] R. PESCH, Markusevangelium II, 141.

[156] A. STOCK, The Method and Message, 273.

The blind Bartimaeus, on hearing that Jesus was passing by cries out, «Jesus Son of David, have mercy on me» (10,47). The many who accompany Jesus take the cry as a nuisance. So they ask him to keep quiet, but Bartimaeus cries out all the more (10,48) and his insistent plea catches the attention of Jesus who asks them to call him (10,49). Encouraged by the crowd Bartimaeus approaches Jesus (10,50). On Jesus' inquiry Bartimaeus expresses his deep desire to receive sight (10,51). Jesus grants his heart's desire and dismisses him by saying, «Go your way; your faith has made you well» (10,52a). What Bartimaeus had hoped for is being fulfilled in his encounter with Jesus: καὶ εὐθὺς ἀνέβλεψεν (10,52b). But this encounter also gives his existence a new direction as he follows Jesus on the way: καὶ ἠκολούθει αὐτῷ ἐν τῇ ὁδῷ (10,52c) The healing power of Jesus comes to the rescue of the blind man and he is made whole. It also gives him an impetus to follow Jesus.

καὶ ἠκολούθει αὐτῷ ἐν τῇ ὁδῷ contrasts with Jesus' command ὕπαγε. But Bartimaeus is not being disobedient, here ὕπαγε is more of a farewell dismissal, «you may go»[157]. He could not be following Jesus unless he was seeing again. The contrast between: τυφλὸς προσαίτης, ἐκάθητο παρὰ τὴν ὁδόν (v 46) and καὶ εὐθὺς ἀνέβλεψεν καὶ ἠκολούθει αὐτῷ ἐν τῇ ὁδῷ (v 52) points up the miracle. In v 52 ἠκολούθει has the full force of a durative imperfect. Its use draws attention to the significance of the act and connotes an enduring way of life rather than a single journey to Jerusalem (cf. 2,15; 9,38; 15,41)[158].

The phrase ἐν τῇ ὁδῷ occurs in the first verse of this section of the journey to Jerusalem (8,27) as well as here in the last verse (10,52) and thus forms an inclusion. Many interpreters take the occurrence of ὁδός in 8,27 as the first in a series (7 times in the journey section; 16 times in the gospel of Mark) in which this word represents the way of discipleship through following Jesus to the Cross[159]. The overall atmosphere of a journey in this section (8,27–10,52) and the repetition of the phrase ἐν τῇ ὁδῷ make clear that the reference is not merely to Jesus' and his group's movement from one place to the next. So even as he goes to his passion Jesus still finds a disciple in the person of Bartimaeus. The healing from blindness opens for Bartimaeus a new

---

[157] R.G. BRATCHER – E.A. NIDA, *Mark*, 340.
[158] C.D. MARSHALL, *Faith as a Theme*, 142; R. PESCH, *Markusevangelium* II, 174.
[159] E. BEST, *Following Jesus*, 15-18; W.H. KELBER, *The Kingdom*, 69-70.

perspective of life. Even as the healing itself is a testimony of his abiding faith, it articulates itself in his whole-hearted following of Jesus.

Many similarities can be noticed in the narrative of Bartimaeus story and that of Jesus' seeing and calling the four fishermen (1,16-20) and Levi (2,14). A comparison with these pericopes shows that the Bartimaeus story is permeated with elements that characterise discipleship.

– reference to the movement of Jesus:	1,16: Καὶ παράγων παρὰ τὴν θάλασσαν τῆς Γαλιλαίας εἶδεν 1,19: Καὶ προβὰς ὀλίγον εἶδεν 2,14: καὶ παράγων εἶδεν	10,46: Καὶ ἔρχονται εἰς Ἰεριχώ. καὶ ἐκπορευομένου αὐτοῦ ἀπὸ Ἰεριχὼ
– the name of the persons:	1,16: Σίμων καὶ Ἀνδρέας 1,19: Ἰάκωβος καὶ Ἰωάννης 2,14: Λευί	10,46: Βαρτιμαῖος
– the name of the father:	1,19: Ζεβεδαίος	10,46: Τιμαίος
– occupation:	1,16: ἀμφιβάλλοντας	10,46: προσαίτης
– Jesus' calling them:	1,17: Δεῦτε ὀπίσω μου, καὶ ποιήσω ὑμᾶς γενέσθαι ἁλιεῖς ἀνθρώπων. 1,20: καὶ εὐθὺς ἐκάλεσεν αὐτούς 2,14: Ἀκολούθει μοι	10,49: Φωνήσατε αὐτόν
– they leave everything:	1,18: καὶ εὐθὺς ἀφέντες τὰ δίκτυα 1,20: καὶ ἀφέντες τὸν πατέρα αὐτῶν	10,50: ὁ δὲ ἀποβαλὼν τὸ ἱμάτιον αὐτοῦ ἀναπηδήσας ἦλθεν πρὸς τὸν Ἰησοῦν

– they follow Jesus: 1,18: ἠκολούθησαν   10,52: καὶ ἠκολούθει
αὐτῷ   αὐτῷ ἐν τῇ ὁδῷ
1,20: ἀπῆλθον ὀπίσω
αὐτου
2,14: καὶ ἀναστὰς
ἠκολούθησεν αὐτῷ

In fact 1,16-20 and 10,46-52 seem to form an inclusion around the whole activity of Jesus before his arrival in Jerusalem. Jesus begins his activity with the call of the first disciples and ends it with addition of another disciple[160]. There have been many attempts to interpret the Bartimaeus narrative as a call story (even modelled in the form of OT call stories)[161]. But perhaps it is an exaggeration. Conformity to other examples of the genre is far from complete[162]. We might say that Bartimaeus is not called to be an apostle or a «disciple» in the technical sense. Jesus does not see (εἶδεν) him, nor is he called. The «disciples» follow Jesus full time and Jesus really requires it of them (1,17-18.20; 2,14; 10,21). Even Levi (2,14) who is not included in the list of the Twelve, is seen and called very personally. In the case of Bartimaeus Jesus not only does not command Bartimaeus to follow him, he orders him instead to «go» (10,52). So here Mark is not implying that Bartimaeus is becoming an apostle. The point Mark is making is that Bartimaeus, whom Jesus dismisses even as he restores his sight, uses this gift of sight to join the crowd of people accompanying Jesus as he journeys on his way to Jerusalem. Bartimaeus' following falls into a category of a kind of following less than that required of the apostles. However, he is a special disciple though he joins the wider circle of believers.

5.3.4 The Young Man who Fled (14,51-52)

The story of the young man is not a call narrative, but it is still a story of discipleship based on human initiative. At a very critical moment in the life of Jesus when his disciples who wholeheartedly followed Jesus, forsake him and flee (καὶ ἀφέντες αὐτὸν ἔφυφον

---

[160] C.D. MARSHALL, *Faith as a Theme*, 141; J. ROLOFF, *Kerygma*, 126.

[161] P.J. ACHTEMEIER, «And He Followed Him», 133-136; D.A. KOCH, *Die Bedeutung*, 130: he refers to Mark 10,46-52 as a «Nachfolgeerzählung»; M.G. STEINHAUSER, «Bartimaeus Narrative», 583-595.

[162] J.D. KINGSBURY, *The Christology*, 104 ff. n. 159.

πάντες: 14,50), the narrative talks of someone who follows him for a little longer before fleeing naked[163]. He is described as a young man (νεανίσκος) who is reported to be «following along with Jesus», «following close to him»: συνηκολούθει αὐτῷ (14,51). The imperfect -ηκολούθει insists that the young man was not fleeing with the eleven. The prefix συν-, prepares for a contrast with Peter's following from afar (μακρόθεν ἠκολούθησεν) as Jesus is being led away (14,54)[164].

The compound verb συνακολουθεῖν occurs only once more in the Gospel in 5,37, when three disciples follow Jesus into the house where Jairus' daughter is raised from death. Though in 5,37 the verb could mean both a temporal as well as religious following, in 14,51 it implies the religious following of Jesus. But the following here has to be differentiated from the following demanded of the first disciples of Jesus. The narrative does not report that Jesus saw (εἶδεν) him and called him. His following is based entirely on personal initiative. Not that there is any trace of refusal but obviously he does not belong to the close circle of disciples.

5.4 *Summary*

Our investigation has shown that it is Jesus' seeing which is the crucial element in his choice of his disciples. A look at the parallel with

---

[163] The narrative does not provide any information regarding the young man's antecedents. Attempts to establish his identity have been manifold. He has been identified with John Mark who is the author of the Gospel. Cf. e.g., L. JOHNSON, «Who was the Beloved Disciple», 158; S.R. JOHNSON, «Neaniskos in Mark», 126. 134-135; W.L. LANE, *Mark*, 527; and several others with different possible interpretations for the linen and lack of other clothing. For the lack of widespread tradition in the early church that the young man was John Mark cf. J. WEISS, *Das älteste Evangelium*, 405-407. For some he represents a figure of desertion, a typical deserter. Cf. H. FLEDDERMANN, «Naked Young Man», 412-418; F. KERMODE, *The Genesis of Secrecy*, 55-64. R.H. Gundry holds that the young man together with the young man at the tomb represent Jesus in his death, burial and resurrection. Cf. R.H. GUNDRY, *Mark*, 863. A. Vanhoye views in the young man at Gethsemane and in the young man at the tomb a counterpoint to Jesus, both in his arrest and resurrection. Cf. A. VANHOYE, «La fuite», 404. According to M.J. Haren the young man in question is Lazarus whom Jesus raised from the dead. Cf. M.J. HAREN, «The Naked Young Man», 527-531. Most of these are conjectures, the fact is that Mark did not want to name the young man. It would be reasonable to consider the young man as belonging to the wider circle of Jesus' disciples. He must have been dressed up for the night shown by the minimum clothing he had. But he stands out in his perseverance in following Jesus even in the face of obvious danger .

[164] R.H. GUNDRY, *Mark*, 862.

Elijah's call of Elisha (1Kgs 19,19-21) has been instructive in highlighting the importance of that seeing of Jesus (εἶδεν) as opposed to Elijah's finding (εὑρίσκει) of Elisha. John's penchant for εὑρίσκει in his account of the call of the disciples is noteworthy. But the verb communicates the notion of seeking before finding. It does not express the wealth of meaning denoted by εἶδεν used by Mark for Jesus' seeing. The other Markan «call narratives» make clear that discipleship is anchored in Jesus' initiative alone, on his selective seeing. Individual initiative does not obtain success when that element is missing. It is Jesus alone who sees, chooses and calls his disciples.

6. The Significance of Jesus' Seeing and Calling the Disciples

Jesus' seeing of his prospective disciples as we have established is no casual event. An element of selection can certainly be read into that action of Jesus. The subsequent call that he issues to them have a two-fold orientation. Jesus first and foremost asks them to follow him (Δεῦτε ὀπίσω μου [...] ἠκολούθησαν αὐτῷ). They are called to an exclusive engagement with him. The point of reference to the disciples' following is Jesus himself. It is this aspect that comes to the fore in all three instances of Jesus' seeing the disciples (1,16.19; 2,14). Secondly, Jesus promises them that they would be enabled to become partakers of a mission that has the whole humanity as its object. In the following analysis we shall treat these two facets of Jesus' seeing and calling of the disciples.

6.1 Jesus' Seeing Implies an Invitation to Communion

For Jesus, his seeing the heavens torn apart and the Spirit descending upon him was undoubtedly a moment of communion with the Father and the Spirit that confirmed his identity as the Son. The same eyes that witnessed that extraordinary event now see the disciples. In his penetrating and all knowing seeing Jesus selects them, and subsequently issues a call to follow him. This seeing and call have the scope of inviting them firstly and more importantly to enter into communion with Jesus himself. Secondly, it is an invitation to enter into communion with God because entering into communion with Jesus by consequence implies entering into communion with God. Thirdly, it is a call to foster communion among the disciples themselves.

6.1.1 Communion with Jesus

Communion with Jesus would imply for the disciples sharing or exchanging the same thoughts or feelings of Jesus. For the disciples it would mean a life long schooling, a journey both literal and figurative which they need to undertake to grasp both the person of Jesus and· the secret (μυστήριον) of the kingdom of God (4,11). In analysing the disciples' life of communion with Jesus we shall first investigate Jesus' relationship with the disciples whom he sees and calls. Subsequently we shall examine how the Gospel of Mark portrays the disciples in general as entering into communion with Jesus, how they fail and as a result communion is interrupted, and how the communion is restored.

a) *Jesus' Rapport with those whom he Sees and Calls*

The disciples whom Jesus sees and calls except Levi are portrayed as closely associated with him in the Gospel. As individuals and as a group of four or the more restricted group of three, they play prominent roles. The number of times they are named in the Gospel is an indication of their importance (Peter - 25 times [19 times Peter and 7 times Simon]; James - 9 times; John - 10 times and Andrew - 4 times). Other than these four and apart from the list of the Twelve (3,16-19), Judas Iscariot is the only other disciple expressly named in the Gospel (14,10.43), presenting him as the betrayer.

+ Jesus and the Four

Apart from the pericopes which deal with their call (1,16-20) and the listing of the Twelve (3,16-19), on two more occasions the narrative mentions the presence of the four disciples Peter, Andrew, James and John together. In 1,29 Jesus is reported to be entering the house of Simon and Andrew with James and John[165]. The plural (εἰσπορεύονται) in 1,21 already suggests indirectly that the four disciples do accompany Jesus to Capernaum. Now in 1,29 Mark again uses the plural verbs (ἐξελθόντες ἦλθον) to show that they are still present. The explicit reference to them «implies the continued effectiveness of his calling all

---

[165] Both Matthew (8,14-17) and Luke (4,38-41) do not speak of the presence of these four disciples as he entered Peter's house. They use only a singular verb (Matthew: ἐλθών; Luke: ἀναστὰς εἰσῆλθεν) and speak of Jesus alone entering the house of Simon.

four to follow him (1,16-20)»[166]. After witnessing the exorcism which Jesus performs in the synagogue at Capernaum, the Four disciples have the chance to experience Jesus' concern in a gesture demonstrating divine care and attention to human suffering. That the person healed happens to be Peter's mother-in-law underlines his thoughtfulness and regard for the intimacy that characterises family life.

The four disciples are mentioned together once more in 13,3. As Jesus sits on the Mount of Olives, opposite the temple, they come up to Jesus and inquire about the end times (13,3-4)[167]. The placing of Andrew last (as against 1,16-20) has prompted the suggestion that his name has been added to the inner circle of the three[168]. But Andrew may be placed last because of the close association of Peter, James and John in other instances (5,37; 9,2; 14,33)[169]. Besides, the order of names just follows the list in 3,16-19. Precisely because his name appears along with the three, it can not be considered redactional. It has also been suggested that Jesus' addressing the four emphasises the secret nature of the discourse that follows[170]. That it is a private discourse is made clear from the use of the phrase κατ' ἰδίαν, and that seems to be the main point of interest in naming the four disciples. The

---

[166] R.H. GUNDRY, *Mark*, 86. It is also suggested that the reference to James and John was added by Mark to link this passage with 1,16-20. Cf. R.A. GUELICH, *Mark*, 61; J. MARCUS, *Mark*, 198.

[167] In Matthew's account (Matt 24,3-14) the interrogators are the disciples in general, and not the four disciples as in Mark. Their questions concern both the destruction of the temple as well as the sign of Jesus' coming and of the close of the age. Luke also does not mention the four disciples (21,7-19). The question is put without specifying who asks it (ἐπηρώτησαν). The question also concerns immediately to the destruction of the temple. In Mark the question seems to refer exclusively to the destruction of the temple, rather than to the Apocalyptic events as a whole. Ταῦτα points back to the prophecy of the destruction of the temple, and taken by itself ταῦτα πάντα has the same meaning. But in the context of the chapter ταῦτα πάντα appears to point forwards and the common interpretation takes it in this sense. Cf. V. TAYLOR, *St. Mark*, 501-502.

[168] E. LOHMEYER, *Markus*, 267-268.

[169] V. TAYLOR, *St. Mark*, 502. For a treatise on Andrew see, E.V. HARRISON, «Jesus and Andrew», 170-178; see also P.M. PETERSON, *Andrew*.

[170] E. HAENCHEN, *Der Weg Jesu*, 436; G. SCHILLE, *Kollegialmission*, 124; A. STOCK, *The Method and Message*, 325; R. Pesch also holds that they receive the teaching in view of giving an orientation to the Church after the destruction of the temple. Cf. R. PESCH, *Markusevangelium* II, 276: «Die vier erhalten Jesu eschatologische Belehrung, die der Orientierung der Kirche in der Zeit des Evangelisten, nach der Zerstörung der Jerusalemer Tempels dienen soll».

first disciples of Jesus are the privileged recipients of such an important teaching. However, it is evident that the message of the discourse is also meant for all the disciples as 13,37 makes clear: «and what I say to you I say to all: watch».

+ Jesus and the Three

Three of those whom Jesus sees and calls, Peter, James and John form the inner circle of Jesus' disciples[171]. Their relationship with Jesus is entirely different from that of the other disciples. Their names occupy the pride of place in the list of the Twelve (3,16-19)[172]. Peter the first among them receives that name from Jesus at the time of the appointment of the Twelve (3,16). James and John, the Zebedee brothers, also receive a new surname from Jesus; they are designated as Boanerges, i.e., sons of thunder (3,17). These three are the only ones who are said «to be with» Jesus all through his ministry. They are witnesses to events which others have no access to.

The first time the trio is mentioned is at the raising of Jairus' daughter (5,37). There is no reason to think that Mark introduces them into this scene as some speculate[173]. Their presence here should be ascribed to their prominence among the Twelve as well as to the standing they enjoy in the tradition[174]. Jesus by excluding the large crowd (5,37)[175] and the sympathisers at Jairus house (5,40), maintains a near privacy under which he performs the awesome miracle, which

---

[171] V. TAYLOR, St. Mark, 294: «The Three form an inner ring in the apostolic band».

[172] J. Marcus reads an eschatological significance in the portrait of a select group of three within the larger body of Twelve. They stand for the patriarchs within the new Israel (Abraham, Isaac and Jacob + 12). He acknowledges that strictly speaking the Markan inner circle has a 3 + 9 organisation rather than a 3 + 12 one, but he points out that the numbers three and twelve are the prominent ones in the Gospel. Cf. J. MARCUS, Mark, 268.

[173] J. GNILKA, Markus I, 217; R. PESCH, Markusevangelium I, 307; G. SCHMAHL, Zwölf, 129-130.

[174] J. ERNST, Markus, 160; R.A. GUELICH, Mark, 301; R.H GUNDRY, Mark, 282-283.

[175] In Matthew's account (Matt 9,25-26) the crowd and the mockers are put out at the house, just before performing the miracle. However, neither the disciples nor the girl's parents witness the miracle. In Luke (8,49-56) the crowd is not dismissed until they reach Jairus' house. The three disciples as well as the parents of the girl are present to witness the miracle.

some call a «divine epiphany»[176]. They have the privilege to witness such a mighty deed and thereby come to a fuller comprehension of Jesus and his mission.

The next occasion Peter, James and John are singled out from the group of disciples is when Jesus takes them with him (παραλαμβάνει) and leads them up (ἀναφέρει) a high mountain apart by themselves (κατ᾽ ἰδίαν μόνους) for the transfiguration (9,2)[177]. The verb παραλαμβάνειν[178] is used in Mark's Gospel only six times. In four instances Jesus is the subject of the verb (5,40; 9,2; 10,32; 14,33). Once the disciples are said to be taking Jesus with them in the boat (4,36). The other usage of the verb takes the second meaning to refer to the Pharisaic and Jewish observance of the tradition of the elders (7,14). In three of the four instances where Jesus is the subject, the verb refers to Jesus' picking up the trio on special occasions that are characterised by their privacy (5,40; 9,2; 14,33; in 5,40 «those who were with him» should certainly refer to the trio; but in this instance the girl's parents are also taken along with them). The atmosphere of privacy in the case of the transfiguration is highlighted by the phrase κατ᾽ ἰδίαν μόνους[179]. What transpires on the mountain is a spectacular revelation of the glory of Jesus and it is fitting that Jesus should choose his close associates to witness it. The three have a representative role. They represent the disciples not only in their failure to grasp the true identity of Jesus, but more importantly they are also representative witnesses, who have a

---

[176] A. STOCK, *The Method and Message*, 173-174. Cf. J. GNILKA, *Markus* I, 216-217: «göttliche Epifanie».

[177] Both Matthew (17,1) and Luke (28,1) agree with Mark on the presence of the three disciples at the transfiguration.

[178] The verb has two meanings: firstly, it means *to take with or along*, with the accusative of the person; secondly, it can mean, *to take over or receive*. Cf. BAGD, 619.

[179] The presence of only Peter, James and John, and the use of the expression κατ᾽ ἰδίαν μόνους, makes A. Stock to describe it as «an extraordinary threefold evocation of the wilderness isolation». Cf. A. STOCK, *The Method and Message*, 243. R. Pesch draws a parallelism between Jesus' taking Peter, James and John up a high mountain and Moses' going up to the Lord on the mountain along with Aaron, Nadab, and Abihu, and seventy of the elders of Israel (Exod 24,1.9). Cf. R. PESCH, *Markusevangelium* II, 71. But the parallelism is not quite correct. It is not said that Moses takes the others with him, they just go up together; the presence of the seventy elders multiplies the number of those going up; the group sees God on the mountain and eats and drinks (Exod 24,11). In Mark the focus is on Jesus; it is Jesus who takes the trio with him and goes up the mountain; it is he who is transfigured; the trio are just eyewitnesses of his glory.

glimpse of the everlasting glory that is reserved to Jesus after his passion, death and resurrection (8,31). In this way, they appear to be the ones who are privileged to see the kingdom of God coming with power as foretold by Jesus (9,1; cf. also 9,9)[180].

For the last time in the Gospel Jesus takes the trio aside from the group of disciples (14,33), not to witness a moment of glory but in a moment of extreme anguish[181]. It would seem that Jesus turns to this inner circle of his disciples for their companionship[182]. Jesus bids them to watch (14,34) and pray (14,38). Whether they are expected to share, in their measure, in Jesus' messianic suffering is an open question (10,39; 8,34)[183]. However, they fail to do the minimum for Jesus, for as Jesus himself admits, «the spirit indeed is willing, but the flesh is weak» (14,38). The story of Jesus' communion with the three is only contrasted by their failure and ultimately even these three along with the other disciples abandon him and flee (14,52).

---

[180] R.H. GUNDRY, *Mark*, 457; E. NARDONI, «Mark 9:1», 365-384; E.W. STEGEMANN, «Zur Rolle», 372. For a contrary view see, C. BREYTENBACH, *Nachfolge*, 219f.

[181] Matthew too reports Jesus' taking the three aside at the moment of great anguish and sorrow (26,37). Luke refers only to the presence of the disciples on the Mount of Olives. Jesus withdraws from them unaccompanied by anyone and prays (22,39-46).

[182] R.H. GUNDRY, *Mark*, 853-854; B.M.F. VAN IERSEL, *Mark*, 432; V. TAYLOR, *St. Mark*, 552. Cf. J. ERNST, *Markus*, 428: «Die drei Männer, die Jesu Hoheit "geschaut" haben, erleben nun seine Niedrigkeit». Cf. also A. STOCK, *The Method and Message*, 366.

[183] V. TAYLOR, *St. Mark*, 552. E.W. Stegemann, proposes that the Peter, James and John are presented as the inner circle of Jesus' disciples because they are known to the reader of the Gospel not only as those who witnessed the extraordinary miracles he performed, as those who have seen the revelation of Jesus' divinity and glory but also as those who have shared in Jesus' passion and death. The reader knows that they also partook of Jesus' destiny by embracing martyrdom. The advice of Jesus to «watch and pray that you may not enter into temptation» (14,38) perhaps implicitly refers to their martyrdom. Cf. E.W. STEGEMANN, «Zur Rolle», 371-374. The close association of these disciples with Jesus is well noted. The early community also knows of the martyrdom of James (Acts 12,2). Perhaps the reader would also know that Peter and John were also martyred. Apart from this fact the three were considered and respected as prominent among the disciples. Markan account seems to be faithful to the tradition. But it is difficult to establish if an allusion to martyrdom really is implied here.

+ Jesus and the Zebedee Brothers

The Gospel account presents Jesus' special relationship to the Zebedee brothers (1,19-20; 3,17) only as part of the inner circle of three. Apart from those instances already referred to, the two brothers are presented together on one occasion[184]. They come up to Jesus and request privileged seats «on his right and on his left in his glory» (10,35-37). Where Peter seems to have heard only about the approaching passion and death of Jesus (8,32) in foretelling his destiny (8,31), James and John give the impression that they have heard only about what he has said about his resurrection (9,31)[185]. Their reference to his glory appears to stem from their own experience at the Transfiguration (9,2-8) as well as from Jesus' prediction regarding the coming of the Son of man «in the glory of his Father with the holy angels» (8,38). They also seem to have conveniently forgotten what Jesus has instructed them regarding position of honour: «If anyone would be first, he must be last of all and servant of all» (9,35). The Zebedee brothers betray their incomprehension of Jesus and his ministry in spite of their close association with him. But their craving for position is also shared by the other disciples, because the others when they hear the brothers' demand, become indignant or rather jealous of the brothers (10,41). This gives an occasion to Jesus to instruct them on the demands of service and discipleship.

+ Jesus and Peter

Among the disciples Peter is the most towering personality delineated in the Gospel. He is named so frequently either as one of the close associates of Jesus (1,29; 5,37; 9,2; 13,3; 14,33) or as spokesman for the disciples (8,32; 9,5; 10,28; 11,21), or as self-styled faithful follower of Jesus (14,29f.54), or as one who disowns his master (14,66-72)[186]. He is called Simon (1,16.29.30.36) till Jesus changes his name

---

[184] John is mentioned once in the Gospel as speaking up for the disciples when he calls Jesus' attention to the unauthorised exorcist (9,38). But there is no reason to think that John does it because he is more confident that Jesus would listen to him. Mark may want to present an irony here. What the disciples themselves recently fail to accomplish (9,18) an independent exorcist is capable of doing successfully.

[185] B.M.F. VAN IERSEL, Mark, 333.

[186] Since most of the texts that pertain to Peter are either treated already or will be dealt with subsequently, only a limited analysis is envisaged here. For a treatise on the tradition and redaction of the Petrine texts cf. E. BEST, «Peter», 547-558. For other

to Peter at the appointment of the Twelve (3,16). Peter is the first of the four disciples whom Jesus sees and calls. He stands out as the most prominent member of the inner circle of three.

The picture of Peter that emerges from the Gospel is of a down-to-earth person, at times impulsive, but most earnest about following his master. The Gospel presents a story of his discipleship that is coloured with ups and downs, successes and failures. But his is also a story of close relationship with Jesus that matures into a deep communion with him.

+ Jesus and the Twelve

The first four disciples whom Jesus sees and calls, belong to the group of Twelve. Even though it is possible to ascribe a close association of these disciples with Jesus, only as belonging to the group of Twelve or as part of a wider circle of disciples can the story of their discipleship be fully traced.

– The Twelve and the Wider Circle of Disciples

Having seen and called some disciples (1,16-20; 2,14) and after having gathered more followers (2,15) Jesus proceeds to form a band of closely knit followers. They are commonly designated by the term «the Twelve». In 3,13-14 where Jesus appoints the Twelve it is not so evident if he selected them out of a wider group of disciples. However, the indications are that Jesus exercised his will to choose from among those he called. The lack of a definite article with δώδεκα in v. 14 shows that those called are not the Twelve, but Jesus appointed the Twelve from the wider group of followers whom he called[187]. In 4,10 where the Twelve next appears, a large number of followers is with Jesus. Mark presents the Twelve as part of this large group. At the same time Mark also takes pains to distinguish them from this group: in 4,10 they are expressly named as a group standing out from those about Jesus; in 6,7 the Twelve are called out from the disciples who followed

---

studies on Peter see, e.g., R.E. BROWN, *Peter in the New Testament*; O. CULLMANN, *Peter*; P. DSCHULNIGG, *Petrus im Neuen Testament*; R. PESCH, *Simon Petrus*; T.V. SMITH, *Petrine Controversies*; W.S. VORSTER, «Characterisation of Peter», 57-76; T. WIARDA, «Peter as Peter», 19-37.

[187] R.H. GUNDRY, *Mark*, 167; J. MARCUS, *Mark*, 266. Against R.P. MEYE, *Jesus and the Twelve*, 147f. R.P. Meye's position is that the Twelve whom Jesus appoints is the same as those whom he summoned. So there is no selection involved.

him (6,1) and sent out on missionary work; in 9,35 the Twelve are called out again from the group of disciples (9,31) and given a teaching on leadership; in 10,32 the Twelve are distinguished from those following him; in 11,11 the Twelve are the ones who go with Jesus to Bethany as distinct from «those who went before and those who followed» (11,9) and in 14,17 the Twelve alone, not the disciples (14,12) accompany Jesus to the upper room to eat the Passover. In 14,10.20.43 the Twelve are portrayed as a group out of which emerges the betrayer.

Therefore a distinction may be made between the Twelve, and the wider circle of disciples. Scholarly opinion is divided on this distinction[188]. Even though the distinction is not as neat as one would expect as in Luke (that Jesus chose the Twelve from a wider circle of disciples: 6,13), in Mark's Gospel these two groups are not identical[189].

---

[188] It is supported among others by Luke 6,13; J. ERNST, *Markus*, 113; R.A. GUELICH, *Mark*, 157.164-165; R.H. GUNDRY, *Mark*, 167; M. HENGEL, *Charismatic Leader*, 81; E. LOHMEYER, *Markus*, 74-75; J. MARCUS, *Mark*, 266; K.H. RENGSTORF, «μαθητής», 450; K. STOCK, *Boten*, 200; V. TAYLOR, *St. Mark*, 230; etc.

Many others on the other hand hold that the term «disciples» in Mark refers to the Twelve or that both terms are synonymous: Matt 10,1; S. FREYNE, *The Twelve*, 109-114; R.P. MEYE, *Jesus and the Twelve*, 137-172; R. PESCH, *Markusevangelium* I, 204; K.-G. REPLOH, *Lehrer*, 47; etc.

E. Best's position seems to be ambivalent. At some places he holds that the terms «the Twelve» and the «the disciples» are interchangeable. Cf. E. BEST, *Disciples and Discipleship*, 131-161; E. BEST, «The Role», 380: «the Twelve is normally to be understood as signifying the wider group, the "disciples"». But at other places he seems to be supporting a distinction between the Twelve and the disciples. Cf. E. BEST, «Mark's Use of the Twelve», 32. In making such a distinction he shows great interest in separating what is basically traditional (the twelve) and what is basically redactional (the disciples). The pericope that deals with the Twelve, and more specially that deals with the appointment of the Twelve (3,13-19) is considered by many as fruit of editorial work. The extent of Mark's redaction is however, debatable. Some scholars hold that Mark combined two traditions, the one pertaining to the call of the disciples and the other a listing of the Twelve. Cf. e.g., J. GNILKA, *Markus* I, 137; K.-G. REPLOH, *Lehrer*, 46-48. For others Mark took the list of the Twelve and gave it a redactional setting. Cf. R. PESCH, *Markusevangelium* I, 202-203; G. SCHMAHL, *Zwölf*, 46-49; K. STOCK, *Boten*, 50-52; V. TAYLOR, *Mark*, 329.

[189] The Gospel does not contain the names of all the disciples of Jesus belonging to the wider circle of followers, but who do not belong to the Twelve. However, it names a few. Levi is perhaps the most prominent among them. But there are so many minor characters in the Gospel who stand out as examples of true discipleship. The Gerasene demoniac (5,20) is the first missionary preacher in the Gospel. The unauthorised exorcist does seem to be a true follower (9,38-39). The blind Bartimaeus

But having made this distinction one has to hasten to add that the Gospel of Mark does not contain compartmentalised treatment of these two categories of people. All that is pertinent to the disciples apply to the Twelve as well; and all that is required of the disciples is demanded of the Twelve too. What distinguishes them from the disciples is not their relationship to Jesus alone, but as we shall see later their special task in relation to the people. The Twelve are to be seen as the nucleus of the circle of disciples[190].

– The Purpose of Appointing the Twelve: to be with Jesus (3,14)

In 3,14 the purposive ἵνα introduces two subordinate clauses, that explain why Jesus appointed (ἐποίησεν) the Twelve. They are appointed to be with Jesus (ὦσιν μετ' αὐτοῦ) and to be sent out to preach (ἀποστέλλῃ αὐτοὺς κηρύσσειν). Here we shall deal with the first of these intentions. The phrase «being with someone» (εἶναι μετ' αὐτοῦ/ῶν) is also found elsewhere in Mark's Gospel (1,13; 2,19; 3,14; 4,36; 5,18; 14,67). In all these instances the reference is to the presence of Jesus with others (1,13; 2,19) or the presence of others with Jesus (3,14; 4,36; 5,18; 14,67). What is involved is real physical presence of Jesus and experiencing his company[191]. It is precisely this privilege that is denied to the Gerasene demoniac (5,18), and it turns out to be the maid's charge regarding Peter: «You also were with the Nazarene, Jesus» (14,67).

---

certainly qualifies for discipleship (10,51). The passion narrative also speaks of some outstanding disciples. The young man who does not immediately take to flight with the disciples and then flees naked (14,51-52) is one of them. The man from Cyrene who comes from the field and bears Jesus' cross (15,21) is the other. Joseph of Arimathea who asks for Jesus' body after he has been crucified and thus remains faithful to Jesus even beyond his death (15,43-46) is the third person. But the Roman Centurion perhaps is the most conspicuous of all. He facing Jesus as he breathed his last says, «Truly this man was the Son of God» (15,39). All these men together with the women, who followed Jesus and ministered to him (15,40-41; cf. also 16,1) fulfil what Jesus demands in his first passion prediction: to follow him on the way, to risk arrest and danger, to carry the cross, and not to be ashamed of confessing him as the Son of Man.

[190] K. STOCK, *Boten*, 203.

[191] K. STOCK, *Boten*, 17-18. Stock points out that the expression in Mark is used exclusively for being with Jesus. Cf. K. STOCK, *Boten*, 18, n. 22.

Therefore the Twelve are chosen for a special relationship with Jesus[192]. Right through the gospel they are constantly with Jesus in order to know him and to learn from him what is necessary to grasp the mystery that has been given to them and to become instruments in making it known later (1,11.22). In the process their relationship with Jesus grows and matures into full communion with him. However, it is mainly as part of the wider circle of disciples that Mark portrays them as entering into communion with Jesus. So in the following treatment otherwise clearly mentioned the term «disciples» include the Twelve as well.

b) *The Disciples Entering into Communion*
    as Portrayed in the Gospel

The Gospel of Mark contains a detailed itinerary of the disciples' entering into communion of life with Jesus[193]. Since the three instances

---

[192] E. Best rejects the idea of a special relationship between Jesus and the Twelve. Cf. E. BEST, «Mark's Use of the Twelve», 34. His main contention is that when Jesus spells out the role of the Twelve (6,7-13) no reference is made to that relationship. But Best fails to appreciate the fact that preaching is preceded by a preparation which involves sharing of life experience and communion of life. The disciples do receive it from Jesus before they depart on missionary journey. Even the Gerasene demoniac receives the command to preach only when he has experienced the saving work of Jesus.

[193] Three streams of thought could be identified in Mark's portrayal of the disciples (the Twelve included):

i) Mark presents them as positive role models of discipleship past, present and future. It is a view advocated by scholars like, S. Freyne (*The Twelve*), G. Schmahl (*Zwölf*), K. Stock (*Boten*) and several others.

ii) The disciples are presented as a group characterised by their inability or refusal to understand; nevertheless they are entrusted with the teaching and mission of Jesus. The disciples are called upon to a deep commitment of faith in Jesus. Cf. e.g., E. BEST, «The Role», 377-401; C. FOCANT, «L'incompréhension», 161-185; Q. QUESNELL, *The Mind of Mark*, 114-125; H. RÄISÄNEN, *Das Messiasgeheimnis*, 119-141; K.-G. REPLOH, *Lehrer*; R.C. TANNEHIL, «The Disciples in Mark», 386-405.

iii) The disciples in Mark represent a heretical group within the author's community. Faced with a false eschatology that has arisen in the community (a *theios aner* Christology and discipleship) Mark uses the disciples to expose the question or express the false teaching and then puts the correct teaching on the lips of Jesus. The disciples are seen totally in the negative light. Unperceptivness (1,16–8,26), misconception (8,27–14,9) and rejection (14,10–16,8) characterise their story of discipleship. Cf. J.R. DONAHUE, *Are you the Christ?*; W. KELBER, *The Kingdom*; N. PERRIN, «Towards an Interpretation», 1-78; W.R. TELFORD, *The Theology*, 131-137; T.J. WEEDEN, «The Heresy», 145-158; ID., *Mark*. The last position is held

of Jesus' seeing the disciples and calling them onward they are portrayed as constantly being in the company of Jesus. The only exception is when they are on a special mission (6,13-30). On three occasions Jesus withdraws himself from the disciples for short periods. But it is with a purpose. For Jesus these are moments of intimate communion and prayer (1,35; 6,46; 14,32.35.39).

The narrative itself besides the express references to the presence of the disciples, in a very unique way refers to their presence with Jesus through philological means. Mark uses the third person plural of verbs (e.g., ἔρχομαι) without specifying the subject of the verb (1,21.29; 5,1-2.38; 6,32.53; 8,22; etc.). It has the appearance of an impersonal plural but it is not. The subsequent clauses or the context makes it amply clear that Jesus, his disciples and some times even the crowd are involved[194]. Hence the communion of life with Jesus is developed first and foremost by continually being in his presence. The picture that the Gospel paints of the disciples' association and more importantly the fellowship of the Twelve (or those belonging to the Twelve) with Jesus, is private in nature. This is indicated by a whole series of special meetings which are intimate and secluded. The privacy of the meetings is also emphasised in many instances by the adverb κατ᾽ ἰδίαν.

The disciples' being with Jesus and the schooling they receive from him can be divided into three phases, which correspond to the Galilean ministry of Jesus, his journey towards Jerusalem, and the days of his presence in Jerusalem. The first phase is a period of profound interaction in which the disciples gradually become aware of the identity of Jesus. The second phase is dedicated to Jesus' instruction of the disciples on the way to Jerusalem. The last and the final phase is a time of intense communion as Jesus institutes the supreme mode of communion.

---

mainly by American Scholars and is the least tenable. Each view has its own merits. A detailed analysis is beyond the scope of this study. Our basic position is that the Markan presentation takes into account both positive and negative aspects of their story of discipleship. But the story ends on a positive note; the disciples' following takes on a new dimension after the resurrection; the risen Jesus supplies for what is lacking in them; all is forgiven and the story of discipleship continues with new vigour, supported by the ever abiding presence of Jesus.

[194] C.H. TURNER, «Marcan Usage», 225. In the gospel of Mark 15 times the plural of ἔρχεσθαι or one of its compounds is used to denote the coming and going of Jesus and his disciples.

+ The Disciples Recognise the Identity of Jesus

For the disciples being with Jesus signifies a continual schooling[195]. Theirs is an active presence in Jesus' company during his Galilean ministry (1,21–8,30). As eyewitnesses to the miraculous events brought about by Jesus and as attentive hearers of his teaching they are to perceive his identity; they are required to learn about the master; but much more they are to learn from the master.

In the context of the teaching in parables in chapter 4 it is made amply clear that Jesus wishes his disciples[196] to grasp the significance of what he teaches in parables (4,11). They are given the «secret of the kingdom of God». The parables do contain a mystery. They have much to do with the advent of God's rule (1,15). They have been given[197] to the disciples because they are those with him (3,14) who do God's will (3,34-35). The same section on parables presents Jesus once again explaining all the parables in private to his disciples (4,34). Jesus' concern is the Kingdom of God and he makes his disciples sharers of the mystery concerning God's rule. As far as the disciples are concerned it means consistent effort to grasp this mystery; a process that would last till the end of the Gospel and beyond.

The instruction in parables is followed by the event demonstrating Jesus' authority over the wind and sea (4,35-41)[198] that for the first time

---

[195] The term «μαθητής» (Matt 72, Mark 46, Luke 37, John 78, Acts 28) which Mark uses to refer to the disciples in general (it is not so clear sometimes whether a particular occurrence really refers to the Twelve or to the large circle of disciples) literally means *pupil, apprentice*. Cf. BAGD, 485. So the disciple is one who learns. Jesus on the other hand is the teacher (διδάσκαλος).

[196] In 4,10 Mark mentions the Twelve as well as those who were about him, to make it clear that the Twelve are also recipients of the instruction that Jesus gives. «Those were about him» do not refer to Peter, James, and John and possibly Andrew (against R.P. MEYE, *Jesus and the Twelve*, 152-156). Nowhere else Mark does such identification for these four men. «Those who were about him», must be those declared by Jesus to be his new family, those who do God's will (3,31-35). Cf. R.A. GUELICH, *Mark*, 204; R.H. GUNDRY, *Mark*, 196; J. MARCUS, *Mystery*, 81.

[197] A. Stock argues that the secret of the kingdom had been given to the intimate disciples as early as the call to discipleship in 1,16-20. Cf. A. STOCK, *Call to Discipleship*, 120. That would be an exaggeration and an over-interpretation of the verb δέδοται. We have seen that Jesus' call and the disciples' following are neither preceded nor immediately followed by a discussion or instruction. Besides, coming to know the secret of the kingdom entails a life-long process; not given in an instant.

[198] In W. Kelber's view the main point of the story is the failure of the disciples; their fear is the fear of Jesus' rebuke; their question is one of ignorance concerning Jesus' identity. Cf. W. KELBER, *The Kingdom*, 49-50. If the narrative has to be «good

provokes a question in the mind of the disciples concerning the identity of Jesus: «Who then is this, that even wind and sea obey him?» (4,41)[199]. It is an open-ended question that the disciples have to grapple with all through their discipleship, following Jesus. In this incident Jesus for the first time alludes to the need for faith: «Why are you afraid? Have you no faith?»[200]. For the disciples therefore entering into communion with Jesus also signifies entering into a life-long journey of faith in Jesus.

The episode of Jesus' walking on the sea (6,45-52)[201] which forms an inclusion[202] with the other extraordinary event of Jesus' calming the sea (4,35-41) unsettles the disciples so much that Mark explains, «for they did not understand about the loaves, but their hearts were hardened» (6,52). The terrified (ἐταράχθησαν) reaction of the disciples in crying

---

news» it has to do with spelling out who Jesus is, his authority and his impact on the disciples. The disciples' fear is therefore a reverential fear, awe before his power rather than fright at rebuke. Cf. R.H. GUNDRY, *Mark*, 244; V. TAYLOR, *St. Mark*, 277. For a two-fold nuance to the disciples' fear cf. M. MATJAŽ, *Furcht*, 89: «sie ist einerseits Ausdruck ihrer tiefen Erfahrung der Heiligkeit Gottes im Handeln und in der Person Jesu, andererseits aber erweist sie das Herausfordertsein des Menschlichen (vgl. 8,33 τὰ τῶν ἀνθρώπων), was schließlich bedeutet, sich durch das Göttliche prägen zu lassen, d. h. Jesus bedingungslos zu vertrauen und zu gehorchen».

M.A. Tolbert argues that since Jesus has already explained «everything» to the disciples, the present fear of the disciples is ironical. Cf. M.A. TOLBERT, *Sowing the Gospel*, 101,166. Explaining the parables is certainly different from coming to know the identity of Jesus. So the disciples' awe-filled response in the face of such stunning demonstration of Jesus' power is understandable.

[199] J. Ernst would view such a question to be answered later after Easter. Cf. J. ERNST, *Markus*, 151. For J. Gnilka the question is answered by Peter at Caesarea Philippi. Cf. J. GNILKA, *Markus* I, 197. Mark seems to introduce the question early in the Gospel in order to portray the disciples' gradual understanding of the person of Jesus. This is a question which the reader is also called upon to answer.

[200] S. FREYNE, *The Twelve*, 124-125: «God would no longer manifest himself to men in mysterious ways, outside man's ordinary capacity to perceive. He would reveal himself now in and through a human person. Respectful, awesome fear before the power which one could not comprehend was no longer a sufficient human response to such a manifestation. Man must have faith, trust in the power of God, and accept the person he had sent».

[201] For a detailed study of this pericope see J.P. HEIL, *Jesus' Walking on the Sea*, 67-75,118-144; P.J. MADDEN, *Jesus' Walking on the Sea*. For Mark 6,52 see Q. QUESNELL, *The Mind of Mark*.

[202] R.A. Guelich understands that the story was used by the collector of the miracle cycle underlying Mark 4-6 to form an inclusion with the first miracle of the cycle, the stilling of the storm in 4,35-41. Cf. R.A. GUELICH, *Mark*, 347, 353. Cf. also P.J. ACHTEMEIER, «Miracle Catenae», 282-284.

out (ἀνέκραξαν) when they see him walking on the sea and their utter astonishment (ἐξίσταντο) when the wind ceases is attributed to two reasons: firstly, their incomprehension of the multiplication of loaves (6,35-44) and secondly, their hardness of heart (ἦν αὐτῶν ἡ καρδία πεπωρωμένη)[203]. The latter has to do with the rigidity of mind which does not let itself be moulded by the experience with Jesus, which does not adapt itself to the reality of Jesus but maintains fixed ideas and attitudes regarding him. Their astonishment shows that Jesus' walking on the sea does not correspond to the idea which they have formed of him[204]. Mark however, does not say in explicit terms what the disciples should have learned from the miraculous feeding. But it is evident that it has to do with the proper understanding regarding Jesus. What is important is the connection between the two events. Both the multiplication of the loaves as well as the walking on the sea have the common scope of leading the disciples to a proper comprehension of the person of Jesus[205]. The first miracle on the sea was the context of the disciples' question, «who then is this, that even wind and sea obey him?» (4,41). What Jesus says to the terrified disciples answers to a certain extent that question, «It is I» (ἐγώ εἰμι - 6,50). It is a self-identification akin to God's revelation in the OT (Exod 3,14; 34,6)[206].

---

[203] The same verb πωροῦν is used again in 8,17 where Jesus puts this question to the disciples: «Are your hearts hardened?» (πεπωρωμένην ἔχετε τὴν καρδίαν ὑμῶν;). Cf. also John 12,40. S. Freyne suggests that the perfect participle used with an auxiliary verb in both cases has the force of a continuous state. It also alludes to the progressive revelation of Jesus and we would say it alludes to the slow and painful nature of the disciples' comprehension of the person of Jesus. Cf. S. FREYNE, *The Twelve*, 130-131.

[204] K. STOCK, «I discepoli», 22.

[205] K. STOCK, «I discepoli», 22-23. Q. Quesnell holds that the disciples did not comprehend the Eucharistic significance of feedings. Q. QUESNELL, *The Mind of Mark*, 224-229. F.J. Matera suggests that the disciples do not understand that the miracle of the multiplication of the loaves manifests Jesus to be the messianic shepherd after the pattern of Ezek 34,11.23. Cf. F.J. MATERA, «The Incomprehension», 163-171. It would be too much to expect from the disciples to grasp such connection with the Old Testament. The writers of the New Testament or the later readers, reading the OT in the light of the Christ-event may come to such conclusions. But the disciples are called upon to observe the mighty works he performs and perceive who he is. For a criticism of the eschatological interpretation of Jesus' walking on the sea, see E. BEST, *Following Jesus*, 232.

[206] The epiphanic character of this statement has been widely acknowledged. Cf. e.g., J. GNILKA, *Markus*, I, 270; R.A. GUELICH, *Mark*, 351; R.H. GUNDRY, *Mark*,

Nevertheless, right comprehension of what it means eludes the terrified disciples at this stage.

A boat scene is repeated (8,14-21)[207] after the second multiplication of the loaves (8,1-10). No wondrous events take place at this time. But on Jesus making a reference, with a symbolic force, to the «leaven»,[208] the disciples interpret it literally as an allusion to their dearth of physical bread. In response Jesus unleashes several questions to the disciples concerning their lack of understanding and hardness of heart (8,17)[209]. Jesus is concerned that the disciples form a clear and right understanding regarding his identity. That is the only way that they can enter into communion with him. Unlike in 6,52 where the evangelist Mark refers to the connection between the loaves and the proper understanding, here Jesus himself very clearly establishes the link between the two. The multiplication of the loaves should have been a very crucial experience enabling the disciples to comprehend rightly. Jesus insists on the responsibility of the disciples to draw conclusions from their experience.

336; J.P. HEIL, *Jesus' Walking on the Sea*, 69-71; J. MARCUS,   *Mark*, 430-434; R. PESCH, *Markusevangelium* I, 362; V. TAYLOR, *St. Mark*, 330.

[207] For a detailed analysis see N.A. BECK, «Reclaiming a Biblical Text», 49-56; W. COUNTRYMAN, «How Many Baskets Full?», 643-655.

[208] Jesus' reference to the «leaven of the Pharisees and leaven of Herod» (Matt 16,6: «leaven of the Pharisees and Sadducees»; Luke 12,1: «leaven of the Pharisees») has been variously understood. A common view is that it refers to «evil inclinations» (see 1Cor 5,6-8), cf. J. MARCUS, *Mark*, 507, 510-511. For some scholars, Jesus warns the disciples against false messianic hope and narrow nationalism. Cf. J. ERNST, *Markus*, 226; R. PESCH, *Markusevangelium* I, 413. Others take it as referring to the intense hostility toward Jesus from the part of the religious and political leaders, cf. E. HAENCHEN, *Der Weg Jesu*, 288. For some it represents unbelief, the failure to recognise Jesus as the one in whom God is at work, cf. J. GNILKA, *Markus* I, 311; R.A. GUELICH, *Mark*, 423-424; Q. QUESNELL, *Mind*, 254-255; K.-G. REPLOH, *Lehrer*, 83. Considering the context in which Jesus' warning occurs, a context that speaks of the disciples dangerously close to unbelief regarding the identity and mission of Jesus, the leaven most probably refers to unbelief reflected in one's response to Jesus.

[209] As noted above the verb used is the same as in 6,52. These two uses of the verb πωροῦν referring to the hardness of heart of the disciples equates their attitude to that of those who were in the synagogue (Pharisees: 3,6) whose «hardness of heart» (πώρωσις) caused Jesus much grief (3,5). Jesus' questions also imply a certain identification of the disciples with the «outsiders». «Having eyes do you not see, and having ears do you not hear?» (8,18). The outsiders were the ones who «may indeed see but not perceive, and may indeed hear but not understand» (4,12). Now the disciples' behaviour is not much different from theirs.

Every instance of Jesus' questions regarding the disciples' incomprehension up until this point were indeterminate questions, without an object. What the disciples were supposed to comprehend was never clearly specified. Jesus' question to the disciples at Caesarea Philippi (8,27-30), after the healing of the blind man at Bethsaida (8,22-26), in no ambiguous terms clarifies what he implies. Jesus puts a direct question to the disciples: «Who do men say that I am?» (8,27). It is made evident that the identity of Jesus is the object of comprehension.

The incident at Caesarea Philippi has the central position in the Gospel of Mark. This position is not merely spatial in that it is narrated in the eighth chapter of the Gospel which has sixteen chapters, and is found more or less in the middle of the 11229 words that constitute the Greek text of the Gospel. Caesarea Philippi marks the finale of Jesus' Galilean ministry as well as the point of departure for the journey that will take Jesus to Jerusalem for the fulfilment of his mission. It is during the Galilean ministry that Jesus tried to initiate the disciples to proper understanding through instructions and miracles. Now he wants a feedback on what they comprehend regarding his identity[210]. It is not enough that they repeat what others say; they are called upon to give a personal opinion.

Peter as a spokesman for the disciples answers, «You are the Christ» (Σὺ εἶ ὁ Χριστός: 8,29; cf. also 1,1; 9,41; 14,61-62)[211]. Peter's confession is correct as it flows out of his experience and conviction. Peter has experienced Jesus as one who preaches, teaches, heals, exorcises demons and performs other awesome miracles. Peter and other disciples called to be with him, have engaged in the same activities of preaching (3,14; 6,12), teaching (6,30) healing (6,13), and casting out demons (3,15; 6,7.13) as extension of Jesus' own ministry. So Peter can sense God's hand in his works, he can infer from all these

---

[210] The importance of the question is aptly expressed by K. STOCK, «Il discepolo di Gesù», 94: «Riconoscerne l'identità è il primo e più importante compito dei discepoli. Il significato di Gesù, come pure tutto il senso del loro discepolato, dipende dalla sua identità».

[211] Only Mark has the absolute ὁ Χριστός in Peter's reply . Matthew modifies it to include a fuller understanding of Jesus' identity: Σὺ εἶ ὁ Χριστὸς ὁ υἱὸς τοῦ θεοῦ τοῦ ζῶντος (Matt 16,16). Luke too adds τοῦ θεοῦ (Luke 9,20). Mark in keeping with his portrayal of a gradual realisation of the identity of Jesus from the part of various characters in the Gospel, only towards the end of the Gospel presents such a complete understanding. It is the Centurion who really grasps who Jesus is. He proclaims, «'Αληθῶς οὗτος ὁ ἄνθρωπος υἱὸς θεοῦ ἦν» (15,39).

that Jesus is God's anointed one, his «Messiah»[212]. The disciples have grasped well. Though the subsequent narratives show that it is insufficient, there is no more scolding of their lack of understanding. The process of entering into communion with Jesus is on right course. Now a new phase of their formation begins; Jesus will be at pains to make them grasp it.

+ The Instruction on the Way to Jerusalem (8,31–10,52)

Caesarea Philippi marks the beginning of the journey to Jerusalem, but for the disciples it also marks the beginning of a new schooling not only on the identity of Jesus but also on the demands of discipleship. During the journey Jesus gives his whole attention to instruct them. In fact only rarely Jesus does address the crowd (cf. 8,34; 10,1).

Peter's confession of Jesus as the Messiah in Caesarea Philippi is a turning point in the Gospel. While accepting the correctness of the title ascribed to him he has to correct their misconception of his identity. He is no earthly Messiah, triumphant, glorious and kingly, according to the biblical tradition, particularly kept alive by the nationalistic aspirations given the political situation in the country. He shall be a poor, weak, suffering Messiah. Jesus has to drive home this point. Three times in this section Jesus predicts his passion, death and resurrection (8,31; 9,31; 10,33-34). Each time it is met with incredulity and objection from the disciples (8,32; 9,32-34; 10,35-37). In all three instances it provides

---

[212] J.D. KINGSBURY, *Christology*, 92-93. Χριστός as an appellative means the Anointed One, the Messiah, the Christ. For more literature on Χριστός, see BAGD, 886-887; W. GRUNDMANN, «The Christ-Statements», 527-580. According to R. Pesch, Peter's confession does not allude to the Jewish ideas of a political Messiah, but rather implies the prophetic tradition of the Anointed One of God. Cf. R. PESCH, *Markusevangelium* II, 33: «Mit dem vernünftigerweise nur als reflektierte, sich von den Volksmeinungen absetzende Stellungnahme auslegbaren Messiabekenntnis kann Petrus als Sprecher der Jünger nicht auf jüdische nationalpolitischen Messianismus festgelegt werden. Vielmehr dürfte seine Messiasprädikation Jesu eher an prophetische Traditionen vom Gesalbten Gottes anknüpfen, mit dem Jesus als vollmächtiger, mit dem Geist Gottes gesalbter Lehrer, Prophet, Offenbarer gewürdigt werden kann. Im Unterschied zu den Volksmeinungen bekennt sich Petrus zur definitiven eschatalogischen Autorität Jesu als des Gesandten Gottes».

But Peter's confession has to be considered first and foremost as grounded on his personal experience with Jesus, his person, his mission and his teaching. It would not be wrong to suppose that for Peter, Jesus also represents the fulfilment of Israel's hopes and expectations.

Jesus an occasion for a discourse concerning the demands of following him (8,33-9,1; 9,35-50; 10,38-45).

The first passion prediction is met with strong objection from Peter. Jesus in no uncertain terms points out that he is on the side of man, his is human thinking, not in conformity with divine will (8,33)[213]. It prevents him from entering into communion with Jesus. So he indicates to Peter what he should do; he should «get behind» him (8,33). That is the place of the disciple, behind the master, to follow the way he indicates (cf. 1,17; 2,14)[214]. Jesus' instruction following the first passion prediction emphasises the inevitability of suffering in discipleship. Denying oneself and accepting the cross are the essential conditions Jesus puts for the disciple willing to follow him (8,34).

No one lays the cross on the disciple. Just like his following, taking up his cross is completely a voluntary act. «To take the cross is to take an active step in the direction of suffering and endurance»[215]. It is in the light of the cross that the nature of discipleship becomes evident[216].

Denying oneself means more than denying things to oneself. It calls for a denial of what one takes oneself to be at the deepest level. «For whoever would save his life will lose it; and whoever loses his life for my sake and the gospel's will save it» (8,35). If the disciple is to deny or lose himself, he can only achieve this through dedication to Jesus and the gospel. It is Jesus who calls and facilitates the disciples'

---

[213] On the opposition to God's ways that places Peter on the same level with the demons and Jesus' adversaries see K. STOCK, «La conoscenza dei demoni», 101-104.

[214] E. BOSETTI, «Un cammino per vedere», n. 25; J. ERNST, *Markus*, 238-239; B.M.F. VAN IERSEL, *Mark*, 285-286. Cf. K STOCK, «I discepoli», 25: «Sin dalla chiamata: "Su, dietro di me!" (1,17) e immutabilmente il posto giusto del discepolo è dietro al maestro; Pietro invece si è messo davanti a Gesù per manifestargli la sua opposizione al cammino scelto. Ma proprio la scelta del cammino spetta al maestro ed è compito del discepolo seguirlo. Pietro cerca di cambiare queste competenze e Gesù lo rimanda al posto che gli spetta in quanto discepolo».

[215] E. BEST, *The Gospel as Story*, 86. Luke adds a particular detail to the phrase when Jesus demands of the disciple to «take up his cross *daily*» and follow (Luke 9,23). Apart from the idea of martyrdom, the phrase implies a self-giving that is less visible, but not less challenging, that of daily life. One's adhesion to the way of the cross passes through every minute and every hour of the day; lived out in complete fidelity to the will of God.

[216] A. Stock adds that Mark's holding back the teaching on discipleship till after Jesus predicts his passion and resurrection is done on purpose. The disciples could not understand Jesus prior to his cross and resurrection; therefore it is fitting to present Jesus both as teaching the disciples the way of the cross and literally showing the way as he is walking towards the cross. A. STOCK, *Call to Discipleship*, 141.

following; and he is the means through whom the disciple realises his self-giving. The disciples' life is to be a life of communion with Jesus[217]. This way of life has to determine every choice which the disciple makes. Aligning his thoughts to Jesus' thoughts and yielding his will to Jesus' will is a pre-requisite to such a way of life. Hence, a perfect communion with Jesus in the glory of the Father (8,38) is the scope of his discipleship.

The second prediction does not meet with an open opposition from the disciples. The Evangelist comments: «but they did not understand the saying, and they were afraid to ask him» (9,32). Besides the fear, a kind of disinterestedness characterises their behaviour. The subsequent narrative shows that they are not concerned with the fate of Jesus but their own affairs: «who is the greatest» among them (9,34). This gives an occasion for Jesus to instruct them regarding their relationship with each other. The secret of maintaining communion among themselves is to be seen in the spirit of service (9,35). Jesus also makes evident that communion with him is formed through service to fellowmen: «Whoever receives one such child in my name receives me; and whoever receives me receives not me but him who sent me» (9,37)[218]. Communion with men is essential for communion with God.

The theme of service is taken up again in the instruction following the third prediction. Twice Jesus reiterates its importance: «Whoever would be great among you must be your servant, and whoever would be first among you must be slave of all» (10,43-44). The disciple is required to be a servant and slave. The chiasm of (a) μέγας (b) γενέσθαι (c) ἐν ὑμῖν (c') ἐν ὑμῖν (b') εἶναι(a') πρῶτος dramatises the demand made on the disciples[219]. Jesus himself provides the model for the disciples. «For the Son of man also came not to be served but to serve, and to give his life as a ransom for many» (10,45). In this definition of his mission Jesus not only changes the sense of the title

---

[217] K. STOCK, «I discepoli», 25: «La vera vita consiste proprio nella permanente comunione di vita con Gesù. Chi mantiene la comunione con Gesù rinnegando se stesso e portando la sua croce, sopportando il rifiuto dei contemporanei (8,38), sarà riconosciuto da Gesù quando verrà nella gloria del Padre suo (8,38) e parteciperà alla vita gloriosa di Gesù. La meta del cammino di Gesù è la gloria del Padre, è la partecipazione perfetta alla vita di Dio».

[218] E. BEST, *The Gospel as a Story*, 88: «True greatness consists in receiving the unimportant such as the child in antiquity». For the low status of the children in society see J. JEREMIAS, *New Testament Theology*, 227.

[219] R.H. GUNDRY, *Mark*, 581.

Messiah (8,29) but corrects the disciples' false expectations. The disciple is invited to imitate the master as regards service[220]. The disciple does not have to give his life as a ransom for many. But he is required to follow the master in his mission of service. By giving his life as a ransom for many Jesus liberates humanity enslaved to sin and death and restores it to full communion with God. Jesus' mission of service is necessary to bring about this liberation and reconciliation with God and men. In imitation of the master the disciples too in their mission of service have to strive to bring about communion with God and with one another[221].

+ Institution of the Supreme Mode of Communion

In sharp contrast to Jesus' absorption with the instruction of the disciples on the way to Jerusalem, his entry into Jerusalem is marked by scant attention given to them. The disciples are always present with Jesus following him (11,12.15.19. 20.27 etc.), but they are mentioned only rarely in chapters 11-13 (11,1.14; 12,43)[222]. Jesus still instructs them separately (11,20-25; 12,43-44; 13,3-37: the eschatological discourse is reserved to Peter, James, John, and Andrew). But the last supper (14,12-32) is a very intimate moment which Jesus spends exclusively with the disciples and more accurately with Twelve. Everything that Jesus utters on this occasion is solely devoted to his relationship with them. Though the theme of betrayal at first dominates the conversation at the meal (14,17-21), soon the atmosphere changes and what follows is centred on the bond of communion between Jesus and the disciples.

During the meal Jesus institutes a new and perpetual mode of communion with the disciples (14,22-24). In the form of bread and wine he offers his own body and blood, to be eaten and drank, as sign of his permanent communion with men, which will reach its fullness in the kingdom of God (14,25). Jesus' presence in the bread and wine will be a new mode of his being with the disciples. With the words

---

[220] Cf. 1Pet 2,21-24 where Peter recommends «following in his footsteps». For when Christ departed he left behind an example for them to follow (cf. also John 13,14-15: foot washing). However, the concept of imitation is not so strong in Mark's idea of discipleship. He proposes some thing more profound, which the disciple in communion with Jesus would do.

[221] K. STOCK, «I discepoli», 28.

[222] S. Freyne notes that their being «with him» is now more to witness his fate than to receive any positive instruction. Cf. S. FREYNE, The Twelve, 133.

«Take, this is my body» (14,22), and «This is the blood of the covenant, which is poured out for many» (14,24), Jesus binds the same disciples into a covenant with himself, by calling them to share in the saving benefits of his sacrificial death[223].

The account of the last supper points back to the miracles of feeding (Mark 6,35-44; 8,1-9). Those incidents were for the disciples opportunities to comprehend Jesus' true identity in order to develop a relationship of communion with him. Now in the last supper Jesus gives his body and blood as spiritual nourishment that would preserve and enhance that communion of life with him[224].

c) *The Disciples' Incomprehension and Interruption of Communion*

The disciples' itinerary of faith and communion with Jesus is also littered with stories of their failure. A shadow is already cast at the outset as Mark names those appointed to be with Jesus (3,14-19). Judas Iscariot is already presented as one «who betrayed him» (3,19). For the first time Jesus refers to their incomprehension when he expresses an exclamation of surprise: «Do you not understand this parable? How then will you understand all the parables?» (4,13). A note of impatience can be detected in Jesus' tone as he confronts a terror stricken lot of disciples with the question, «Why are you afraid? Have you no faith?» (4,40). The disciples' reaction of fear in the next boat scene draws a comment from the Evangelist: «for they did not understand about the loaves, but their hearts were hardened» (6,52). In the final boat scene Jesus' criticism of their lack of understanding grows louder, he repeatedly asks, «Do you not yet perceive or understand?» (8,17.21).

The strategy Jesus has been employing thus far was of teaching in parables and speaking through actions. The disciples do not yet seem to rise to Jesus' expectations. However, after Peter's confession at Caeserea Philip Jesus no more criticises their lack of understanding, but resorts to direct teaching on discipleship. All three predictions of passion, death and resurrection are followed by such teachings because the disciples do not comprehend the sense of the predictions. They choose the easy way out (8,32), or they do not just understand (9,32) or their concern is about their own position (10,35-45).

---

[223] F.J. MOLONEY, *Disciples and Prophets*, 148.

[224] We shall deal with the idea of communion in the miraculous feeding in some detail in the next chapter.

After Jesus' entry into Jerusalem, the disciples almost fade into the background till the last supper. The atmosphere over the supper is one of tension as Jesus reveals that one from the intimate group of Twelve would betray him (14,18). It points to the total rupture of communion which Jesus painstakingly built with the disciples. Jesus' saying that the betrayer is, «one who is dipping bread into the dish with me» (14,20), heightens the sense of break-down of relationship. Jesus predicts that even the rest of the eleven would desert him: «You will all fall away; for it is written, "I will strike the shepherd, and the sheep will be scattered"» (14,27),[225] and that Peter would deny him three times (14,30). The disciples fail to watch and pray even «one hour» with Jesus (14,37-38; 40. 41). The disciples' failure reaches its climax when Judas does betray him (14,45) and they all forsake him and flee (14,50). Even Peter who dares to follow Jesus at a distance, right into the courtyard of the high priest (14,54) breaks down when challenged by a maid. He has no qualms to deny Jesus when faced with peril (14,66-72). The break down of communion is total. What has been foretold come to pass. Not one disciple perseveres in following Jesus. Except for the women followers (cf. 15,40-41.47) not one follows him to Golgotha. Jesus has to walk the way of the cross all alone.

---

[225] The quotation would imply that both the dispersion of the disciples and the death of Jesus are in fulfilment of the scriptures. Cf. S. FREYNE, The Twelve, 136; F.J. MOLONEY, Disciples and Prophets, 148. For E. Best in this adapted quotation from Zacharia 13,7, the one who strikes the shepherd is God; the shepherd is Jesus; the sheep are the disciples. Judgement ought to fall on the sheep who have sinned, but it falls instead upon the shepherd. On the cross Jesus cries «My God, my God, why hast thou forsaken me» (15,34). Jesus stands outside the mercy of God because he bears the judgement of God. E. BEST, The Gospel as a Story, 69-70. It has been suggested that the disciples' «falling away» (σκανδαλισθήσεσθε) would refer to their reaction at the onset of eschatological tribulation. See, e.g., J. JEREMIAS, The Central Message, 49-50. But Jesus is clearly referring to his death. The quotation is used to support Jesus' statement that they will all fall away; the scattering of the sheep is caused by what happens to the shepherd. L. Schenke opines that «scattered» here means «shepherdless» rather than the disciples' going in different directions. Cf. L. SCHENKE, Studien, 387-388. But it is hard to imagine that the disciples would separate themselves together from Jesus as a group. Scattering would certainly imply a dispersal in different directions. But it is possible that they regroup themselves after the initial shock.

d) *Communion Restored*

The flight of the disciples and the death of Jesus on the cross is not the end of the story of discipleship. Even while announcing the extreme failure of the disciples Jesus still holds out a glimmer of hope: «after I am raised up, I will go before you to Galilee» (14,28). The purpose of this «going before» (προάξω) is not specified. The women who come to the tomb with the intention to «anoint» the mortal remains of Jesus (16,1) are told by the young man[226] at the empty tomb to do something different. The young man at the empty tomb recalls the same promise of Jesus when he commands the women: «But go, tell his disciples and Peter that he is going before [προάγει] you to Galilee; there you will see him, as he told you» (16,7). The two imperatives ὑπάγετε εἴπατε that follow the adversative ἀλλά, express the commission to search out the «scattered» disciples and remind them of the promise Jesus made to them while he was still alive[227].

+ The Meaning of προάγειν in 14,28 and 16,7

The young man announces that the fulfilment of Jesus' prediction (14,28) is in course: «he is going before you to Galilee» (16,7). Προάγειν which is in the future tense in 14,28 (προάξω) takes the present tense (προάγει) in the address of the young man (16,7) thereby noting the actual stage of its fulfilment. There are only 5 occurrences of

---

[226] The young man is identified as an angel (cf. Tob 5,3-7; 12,15; 2 Macc 3,26.33; Luke 24,4; *Gos. Pet.* 13,55). White robe is traditional for angels (Acts 1,10; Rev 6,11; 7, 9). His sitting on the right side indicates his authority. For the right side is the side of favour. Cf. W. GRUNDMANN, «δεξιός», 37-40. On the idea that the young man is invested with omniscience and power see R. VIGNOLO, «Cercare Gesù», 96: «Quale figura celeste è dotata di onniscienza e potere: riconosce lo stato d'animo delle donne, interpreta le loro intenzioni, affida loro un messaggio, [...] conosce il destino di Gesù e la sua promessa ai discepoli, dispone e prevede il loro ricongiungimento con il maestro».

[227] Peter is expressly mentioned. Peter seems to have separated himself from the rest by his three-fold denial of Jesus (14,66-72). So he requires an open reinstatement. Cf. E. SCHWEIZER, *Markus*, 206: «Mit der besonderen Nennung des Petrus wird wahrscheinlich auf seine Verleugnung zurückgewiesen». Both Luke 24,34 and 1Cor 15,5 actually speak of a separate appearance to Peter. But above all the mention of his name by the young man implies that Peter would equally qualify for what Jesus offers to his disciples in Galilee.

the verb προάγειν[228] in Mark's Gospel. In the first instance (6,45) it is used in the temporal sense to speak of Jesus making the disciples to go before him to Bethsaida. In 10,32 the sense is spatial as the verb expresses Jesus' walking ahead of those who accompany him. In 11,9 the verb is used to distinguish «those who went before» from «those who followed» Jesus. The other two occurrences are used in the promise of Jesus (14,27) and the young man's reference to it (16,7).

It has been suggested that the verb προάγειν in 14,28 and 16,7 means «to lead the way». The risen Christ would then be understood as leading the disciples from Jerusalem to Galilee[229]. But the Markan usage of the verb does not suggest such a meaning[230]. Nor is it tenable to read the shepherding imagery into it[231]. For Mark προάγειν is not a «technical term» for the shepherd's work. He does not attach such meaning in the other occurrences of the verb. Apart from 14,28 and 16,7 the only other use of the verb referring to Jesus is in 10,32. There Jesus' προάγειν stands in close relation to the ἀκολουθεῖν of those following him. It is the same sense that is denoted in these instances too. The risen Jesus' προάγειν entails as well as makes possible the disciples' ἀκολουθεῖν[232]. The master goes before, he precedes the

---

[228] Προάγειν in the transitive sense means to *lead forward, lead or bring out* someone etc. Intransitively it means to *go before, lead the way, precede*. Cf. BAGD, 702.

[229] See for e.g., E. BEST, *The Gospel as a Story*, 74; C.F. EVANS, «"I will Go before You"», 3-18; R. PESCH, *Markusevangelium* II, 381; R.H. SMITH, *Easter Gospels*, 38; J. WEISS, *Earliest Christianity*, 18. The promise is that the disciples will see him only in Galilee. If Jesus were to lead them to Galilee they will see him already from the place of departure.

[230] Many scholars hold that the verb here means to precede, e.g., C.E.B. CRANFIELD, *St. Mark*, 429; J. ERNST, *Markus*, 424; R.H. FULLER, *Resurrection Narratives*, 61; E. HAENCHEN, *Der Weg Jesu*, 488; W. MARXSEN, *Mark*, 86; L. SCHENKE, *Studien*, 375; E. SCHWEIZER, *Markus*, 168; R.H. STEIN, «A Short Note», 450; K. STOCK, *Boten*, 165.171-173; V. TAYLOR, *St. Mark*, 549.

[231] J. JEREMIAS, *The Parables of Jesus*, 121, n. 26; also «ποιμήν», 492-493. John 10,4 can not be used to defend this view because the verb used there is different (πορεύομαι).

[232] L. SCHENKE, *Studien*, 375-76: «Offenbar ist προάγειν in 14,28 wie in 16,7 in zeitlichem Sinn zu verstehen (vgl. 6,45); daß Jesus die Jünger erst sammeln und dann "an ihrer Spitz" nach Galiläa ziehen will, ist als Meinung des Evangelisten kaum anzunehmen». Neither would it be correct to conclude that Jesus' going ahead of the disciples presupposes their not being scattered. Cf. M. WILCOX, «The Denial-Sequence», 428. It is hard to think that Jesus' prediction to that effect, based on the scriptures would not take place (14,27).

disciples. The disciples are to follow him. The call to follow when Jesus first saw the disciples (1,16-20; 2,14) is still valid. In spite of the incomprehension and repeated failure of the disciples the risen Christ renews in effect that invitation to follow him. As for the disciples a new manner of following Jesus is being inaugurated here.

+ «There you will see him» (16,7)

The young man also clarifies what the purpose of Jesus' preceding to Galilee would be: «there you will see him» (ἐκεῖ αὐτὸν ὄψεσθε). In 14,28 this fact is not explicitly mentioned[233]. But 16,7 with the phrase καθὼς εἶπεν ὑμῖν also makes clear that it was implicitly intended. The actual meaning of 16,7 together with 14,28 has been the subject of long debate. One suggestion is that it is an invitation to Gentile mission. The reference to Galilee is understood as short hand for «Galilee of the Gentiles» (Isa 8,23 LXX; Matt 4,15)[234]. Yet unlike Matthew, Mark nowhere speaks of Galilee of the Gentiles. Neither does Mark portray Jesus' ministry in Galilee as a Gentile ministry. In Mark's Gospel the term Galilee does not seem to have any theological import[235]. Since

---

[233] It has led some scholars to speculate that Mark has fabricated 14,28 out of 16,7 and there added «as he told you». Scholars in general hold that these two verses are Markan redactions. E.g., R. BULTMANN, *Synoptic Tradition*, 285; M. DIBELIUS, *From Tradition to Gospel*, 190; W. MARXSEN, *Mark*, 75-81; V. TAYLOR, *St. Mark*, 549; T.J. WEEDEN, *Mark*, 46. Matthew also establishes this connection between Jesus' prediction (26,32) and the angel's message (28,7). It is absent in Luke. Luke does not have any Easter message which the women should communicate (24,6-7). All the same the women returning from the tomb narrate what happened at the tomb to the eleven and to all the rest (24,8- 9).

[234] G.H. BOOBYER, «Galilee», 334-348; J.-M. VAN CANGH, «La Galilée», 67-75; C.F. EVANS, «I Will Go before You», 3-18; M. KARNETSKI, «Die Galiläische Redaktion», 252-257; R.H. LIGHTFOOT, *Locality*, 55-65; J. Schreiber holds that Galilee in Mark includes Tyre, Sidon, etc. to emphasise its Gentile character. Cf. J. SCHREIBER, *Theologie des Vertrauens*, 172-184. But see E.S. MALBON, «Galilee and Jerusalem», 251f. for the distinction between Jewish Galilee and the foreign lands surrounding it.

[235] It is true that Jesus inaugurates his ministry in Galilee, but his mission is largely among his own people. Even when Mark alludes to Jesus' Gentile mission, it is rendered through Jesus' travels to foreign lands surrounding Galilee, not his Galilean ministry as such. For a detailed analysis see, R.H. GUNDRY, *Mark*, 849. G.D. Kilpatrick argues that Mark is remarkably reserved with regard to the Gentile mission. Cf. G.D. KILPATRICK, «The Gentile Mission», 145-158; C.D. MARSHALL, *Faith as a Theme*, 40-42.

Lohmeyer first interpreted it as referring to the parousia,[236] several other scholars have come to similar conclusions[237]. But this position does not appear to be defensible[238].

Several factors favour considering these references as promising a resurrection appearance in Galilee:[239]

---

[236] E. LOHMEYER, *Markus*, 356; ID., *Galiläa und Jerusalem*, 10-14.

[237] C.F. EVANS, «I will Go before you», 3-18; R.H. LIGHTFOOT, *Locality and Doctrine*, 55-65; W. MARXSEN, *Mark*, 75-95.111-116; N. PERRIN, «Towards and Interpretation», 37-45; M.A. TOLBERT, *Sowing the Gospel*, 248, n. 54; T.J. WEEDEN, *Mark*, 111-117.

[238] It is not within the scope of this work to enter into a very detailed study of this position. However, the main arguments to support this view may be summed up as follows: i) ὤφθη is a *terminus technicus* for seeing the risen Christ (cf. 13,26; 14,62). The future tense ὄψεσθε in 16,7 shows that Mark is referring to the parousia. ii) Since there is no resurrection accounts in Galilee, the verses 14,28 and 16,7 should be referring to an imminent event for the church to which Mark is writing and that would be parousia. iii) A climatic event after resurrection that is so predicted should be the parousia and not a resurrection appearance iv) 14,28 should be understood as interpreting 14,27. The gathering of the «elect» (13,26-27), the «scattered sheep» (14,27) would take place at the parousia. v) Mark ends the Gospel at 16,8 without an account of a resurrection appearance, but only with a promise of seeing which is yet to take place at the time of writing the Gospel.

For a critique of this position see T.A. BURKILL, *Mysterious Revelation*, 252-257. It may be pointed out that i) ὄψομαι is not a terminus technicus in Mark or in the NT. Just from two references (Mark 13,26 and 14,62) such conclusions should not be drawn. Neither did chapter 13 locate the second coming of Jesus in Galilee. Cf. R.H. GUNDRY, *Mark*, 1008; R.H. STEIN, «A Short Note», 446-447 ii) The resurrection accounts in Matthew and John could not be considered as fabricated under the influence of Mark 14,28 and 16,7 (against W. MARXSEN, *Mark*, 82). iii) In each of the predictions regarding Jesus' fate (8,31; 9,31; 10,33-34), passion and resurrection are very closely associated and no mention is made at all about the parousia. The three predictions, instead would lead us to expect 14,28 and 16,7 to refer to a resurrection appearance. Consequently it is hard to think that parousia is the climatic event in the Gospel. Cf. E. BEST, *The Gospel as a Story*, 76-77; R.H. STEIN, «A Short Note», 447-448 iv) The Gospels as well as the NT bear witness to the fact that the gathering of the scattered disciples does indeed take place after the resurrection. It does not have to wait for the parousia. The accounts of the resurrection appearances to the disciples testify to that (Matt 28,16f. Luke 24,13f. 36f.; John 20,19- 21,23; 1Cor 15,5f. v) the abrupt ending at 16,8 does not invalidate taking 14,28 and 16,7 as reference to resurrection appearance. Moreover by the time the Gospel was written the disciples have left to different directions for preaching; Peter probably has died in Rome. 16,7 includes him among those who have to go to Galilee. Cf. R.H. GUNDRY, *Mark*, 1008.

[239] Many scholars support this view. Cf. for instance, E. BEST, *The Gospel as a Story*, 72-78; R. BULTMANN, *Synoptic Tradition*, 285; T.A. BURKILL, *Mysterious Revelation*, 255 f.; C.E.B. CRANFIELD, *St. Mark*, 469; J. ERNST, *Markus*, 488;

i) The theme of the fulfilment of the prediction is a strong argument to support this view. 16,7 has the verb προάγειν in the present tense (προάγει) whereas 14,28 has it in the future (προάξω). So what is predicted is already taking place. A reference to parousia would still require the verb in the future tense.

ii) It has also been noted that Mark's use of μετά with the infinite in the Gospel (1,14) and for that matter the NT usage of the same construction[240] always imply an event coming shortly after the event just mentioned. 14,28 the only other occurrence of the expression in Mark should also be understood as referring to an imminent event[241].

iii) The three predictions of Jesus' destiny (8,31; 9,31; 10,33-34) clearly refer to the promise of resurrection. It is logical to expect a resurrection appearance.

iv) The community, which had stories of the appearances of the risen saviour, could understand Mark's narrative only as referring to resurrection appearance. The antiquity of 1Cor 15,5 and its possible Semitic origin add weight to the argument[242].

v) The command that the women receive expressly mentions Peter (16,7) who should be told along with the disciples to go to Galilee where they will see Jesus. If Mark were written after A. D. 65 as generally believed, Peter is already dead in Rome. It is not probable that a dead Peter would be told to proceed to Galilee to experience the future parousia[243].

vi) From our point of view Mark's use of the verbs for «seeing» would provide one of the strongest clues for taking the prediction of Jesus (14,28) and the command of the young man (16,7) literally:

J. GNILKA, Markus II, 343; E. HAENCHEN, Der Weg Jesu, 545-546; B.M.F. VAN IERSEL, Mark, 430.497-500.505-506; L. SCHENKE, Studien, 372.454-456; E. SCHWEIZER, Markus, 203.206; R.H. STEIN, «A Short Note», 449-452; A. STOCK, Call to Discipleship, 60f.; ID., The Method and Message, 426-430; K. STOCK, «I discepoli», 30-31; ID., Boten, 171-173; H.B. SWETE, Mark, 339; R.E. TANNEHILL, «The Disciples in Mark»,403-404; V. TAYLOR, Mark, 549.607-609.

[240] It is found 13 times in the NT: Matt 26,32; Mark 1,14; 14,28; Luke 12,5; 22,20; Acts 1,3; 7,4; 10,41; 15,13; 19,21; 20,1; 1Cor 11,25; Heb 10,15.26 (perhaps an exception).

[241] R.H. STEIN, «A Short Note», 449-450.

[242] E. SCHWEIZER, Markus, 212; R.H. STEIN, «A Short Note», 50. Cf. also E.L. BODE, The First Easter Morning, 90-104. Bode (p.103) puts the date of the formulation of the tradition by the end of the thirties.

[243] R.H. GUNDRY, Mark, 1008; R.H. STEIN, «A Short Note», 50-51.

«there you will see him» (ἐκεῖ αὐτὸν ὄψεσθε). It is to verify it that we shall now turn.

+ The Disciples shall indeed See the Risen Jesus as Sign of Restoration of Communion

We shall develop the argument that Mark's reference to seeing itself shall give a clue for taking the reference in 16,7 to the disciples' actual seeing of the risen Jesus, firstly by examining the use of the verb ὁρᾶν for the disciples' seeing, and secondly by establishing that the major sections of the Gospel of Mark conclude by a reference to seeing.

– The verb ὁρᾶν referring to the disciples connect seeing with understanding

The future form ὄψεσθε (16,7) is the last occurrence of the verb ὁρᾶν in Mark's Gospel. In our analysis of the verb it has been noted that the verb in its various forms has been used primarily to refer to Jesus' seeing. But among the other characters who are said to be seeing, the disciples are prominent among them. Four times the verb refers to their seeing (6,49.50; 9,8.9).

The first two instances occur in the context of Jesus' walking on the water where the disciples see him (6,49: ἰδόντες; εἶδον 6,50:) but fail to see well, in other words they could not conceive that it was Jesus. So they are utterly terrified. That reaction, as we have already seen, invites the comment of the Evangelist: «for they did not understand [συνῆκαν] about the loaves, but their hearts were hardened» (6,52)[244]. Thus the narrative when speaking of the seeing of the disciples, connects it also with right understanding or rather, lack of it.

In the next two instances where the disciples' seeing is referred to (9,8.9), Peter, James and John are the protagonists. They see the transfigured Jesus (9,2), his glistening garments (9,3) as well as Moses and Elijah who appeared (ὤφθη) to them and talking to Jesus (9,4). It is

---

[244] The narrative here draws up a link between the disciples' seeing, their reaction and the reason for such reaction i.e. lack of understanding:

Action	Reaction
ἰδόντες	ἀνέκραξαν
εἶδον	ἐταράχθησαν

Reason
οὐ γὰρ συνῆκαν

the sum total of this experience on the mountain that is referred to by Jesus when he enjoins them not to tell anyone what they had seen (ἃ εἶδον) until after the resurrection (9,9). But as all good things, this experience too is short-lived. Looking around they see (εἶδον) only Jesus (9,8). Their not seeing anyone else points up the fact that it is Jesus alone who merits their attention, something which the voice from heaven had expressly asked the disciples, «This is my beloved Son; listen to him» (9,7)[245]. The disciples are to combine their seeing with listening, which means they should strive to gain right understanding. Once again the narrative makes an express link between the disciples' seeing and understanding. From that moment onwards Jesus commits himself to instructing the disciples regarding the implications of following him. In the process the disciples are also given a better understanding of the identity and mission of the master himself[246].

16,7 also, which is the last reference to the disciples' seeing, needs to be read in the light of such linkage between the disciples' seeing and their acquiring proper understanding. The young man at the tomb promises the disciples that they will indeed see the risen Jesus. The narrative however, makes no explicit linkage with understanding. But it can be presumed that the disciples will finally begin to see and gain right understanding.

Notwithstanding their failure, and their abandonment of Jesus, the prospect of meeting the risen Jesus, of seeing him in person and finally arriving at a mature understanding of Jesus' identity and their own discipleship is held out for the disciples. But above all there is the sure hope of re-establishing the interrupted communion with Jesus. Whenever Jesus is the object of disciples' seeing, their reaction is one of fear, terror (6,49.50), awe (9,6) etc. Though such reactions by themselves may be considered normal, the expectation is that finally at this meeting anything negative in such reactions would be overcome

---

[245] According to M.A. Tolbert the fulfilment of 9,1 is found in 9,7. Thus the kingdom of God comes in power, not through the wonderful visual experience of transfiguration but through listening to the word of Jesus. Cf. M.A. TOLBERT, *Sowing the Gospel*, 206-207. But 9,1 really contains a promise of seeing and it is precisely the fulfilment of that promise that is narrated subsequently (9,2.4.8.9).

[246] J. Schmidt argues that the promise of seeing is in fact an invitation to recall to mind an instance of *seeing* that took place in Galilee at the transfiguration, which the disciples were charged not to tell anyone, until the Son of man should have risen from the dead (9,9). So 16,7 has to be understood as referring back to what they had seen on the high mountain. Cf. J. SCHMIDT, *Das Gewand der Engel*, 41-43 . But a promise has to do with something that will take place in the future!

and a positive rapport of communion would be established. Hence it is going to be a meeting which guarantees forgiveness, encouragement, consolation, and strength that would enable them to bear witness to Jesus[247]. Moreover a new manner of Jesus' presence to his disciples and consequently a new way of entering into communion with the risen Lord also begins here.

- The major sections of Mark's Gospel conclude
  with a reference to seeing

An argument based on the whole structure of the Gospel of Mark also supports taking the promise of the young man at the tomb literally. Mark ends each of the three great sections of his Gospel with the a significant reference to seeing. The public ministry of Jesus in Galilee (1,14–8,26) closes with the story of the blind man at Bethsaida who sees (8,22-26). The man gains his sight by a two-stage healing, which is interpreted as symbolic of the disciples' gradual recognition of Jesus' identity[248]. Mark seems to be indirectly using the first stage of healing to distinguish the disciples' limited sight from the blindness of the «outsiders» (4,11), including his own hometown and family (6,1-6) as well as «Pharisees and Herod» (8,14). The primary focus of the story however, is on the man's total healing. The disciples too show themselves to be in need of the second touch from the Great Physician, Jesus. Mark's Gospel does not narrate their receiving it, but the promise is held out at the end of the Gospel (16,7)[249].

The story of Bartimaeus (10,46-52) that concludes the journey section (8,27–10,52) is also a miracle of healing from blindness. The blind beggar by his sheer perseverance and open expression of faith in «Jesus, Son of David» (10,47.48) invites the attention of Jesus, who in turn, moved by his «blind faith» gives sight to him. In his profession of faith he was already able to see into the mystery of Jesus' identity; now he sees him with his own eyes. Bartimaeus uses his newly gained gift of sight to follow Jesus on the road to Jerusalem (10,52). The once

---

[247] J. ERNST, Markus, 488: «Das Zeugnis der Jünger ist in den persönlichen Begegnungen mit dem Auferstandenen, im "Sehen" des Auferstandenen begründet, das Hören vom leeren Grab hat stützende und sichernde Bedeutung für Glaubensschwache».

[248] For various interpretations of the two-stage healing and the symbolism involved see E.S. JOHNSON, «Mark VIII. 22-26», 379-83; F.J. MATERA, «The Incomprehension», 167-171.

[249] R.A. GUELICH, Mark, 434-436.

blind man becomes a disciple capable of «seeing» (ἀνέβλεψεν). His «seeing» thus anticipates what Peter and the other disciples can obtain only after the resurrection when they return to Galilee (ὄψεσθε: 16,7). All the others go up to Jerusalem without knowing Jesus sufficiently, they accompany him only later to abandon him (14,50.66-72). Only this once blind beggar along with the women of 15,40-41 go up to Jerusalem in a positive way. He represents all the believers who, reinforced by the light of Easter, can begin in Galilee the journey that will lead to the kingdom[250].

The third major section of the Gospel (11,1–16,8)[251] also closes with an important reference to seeing (16,7)[252]. The unseeing and non-

---

[250] X. PIKAZA, *Marco*, 285-286.

[251] The ending of Mark's Gospel has been the subject of extensive research. For a clear and concise presentation of the textual criticism see, B.M. METZGER, *A Textual Commentary*, 102-106. Without entering into the details it suffices to affirm with Metzger that, «on the basis of good external evidence and strong internal considerations it appears that the earliest ascertainable form of the Gospel of Mark ended with 16.8». But that has serious consequences for our interpretation of the disciples' seeing the risen Jesus in Galilee. For 16,8 states that the women «went out and fled from the tomb; for trembling and astonishment had come upon them; and they said nothing to anyone, for they were afraid». So Mark does not speak of the women transmitting the message to the disciples and Peter. As a result it could mean that communion is not re-established, the disciples do not see, the story of discipleship ends on a negative note. A good number of scholars subscribe to this view. The alternative possibility is to consider the reaction of the women as temporary, short-lived, and a typical response to an act of divine power. The women subsequently do communicate the message of reconciliation to the disciples and Peter, the disciples do indeed see, consequently communion is re-established, the story of discipleship continues on a positive note, they embrace the way of Jesus, (cf. R. PESCH, *Markusevangelium* I, 60: «Der Auferstandene sammelt seine Gemeinde in Galiläa, sein Weg mündet in ihren Weg, bzw. ihr Weg wird zum Weg der Nachfolge») they go forth to take up their ministry. R. Vignolo sums up what the abrupt end of the Gospel means for the reader. Cf. R. VIGNOLO, «Cercare Gesù», 99: «Questo finale originario di Marco - enigmatico per molti aspetti - impegna la mente del lettore, lasciando a lui l'impegno di colmare il vuoto narrativo del testo. Un finale sorprendente, reticente, ironico, costruito su di un duplice scarto: uno *kerygmatico* (con cui Marco esalta la maggior grandezza della risurrezione del crocifisso, mistero irriducibile a una sorte di lieto fine); e l'altro *narrativo*: rinunciando a narrare le apparizioni del Risorto, e limitandosi a predirle, il narratore marciano costringe il lettore a ripensare l'intera storia di Gesù e lo obbliga a farne lui stesso una parafrasi integrativa, guadagnandone una più profonda intelligenza. Il testo del racconto finisce, ma in realtà la storia di Gesù continua: in una nuova relazione a Dio, nella vita dei discepoli, nel *kerygma*, nella mente e nell'esistenza dello stesso lettore!».

perceiving disciples are promised that they will see the risen Jesus in Galilee. A word of movement, as a verb of preparation always preceded Jesus' seeing the disciples (1,16; 2,14: παράγων; 1,19: προβάς). Even in 16,7 a verb of movement (προάγει) indicates the preparation of the decisive event of seeing. Jesus in a definitive way (shown by the indicative mood of προάγει) does the preparation himself, and traces out the way. But there is a difference, it is no more Jesus who sees; that role passes on to the disciples. Jesus' mission is complete. He is no more said to be seeing. Now the disciples have the capacity to see. The expectation is that the disciples would at long last really see and that communion with Jesus would be re-established.

6.1.2 Communion with God

The analysis above has established the «Jesus-centredness» of communion that the disciples enter into. Nevertheless, Jesus' seeing the disciples has also to be conceived in the light of his seeing the heavens being torn apart and the Spirit descending upon him like a dove (1,9). That was for Jesus a great moment of intense communion with God. Jesus' seeing the disciples and calling them is an invitation to a communion of life and fellowship with him and through him to enter into a communion of life with God the Father and the Spirit. Hence the disciples' being with him, and fellowship with him is not only Christo-centric but also Theo-centric. God enters into the world of the disciples in Jesus and through him the disciples gain access to the divine. Jesus is the pivot of God reaching out to man and man reaching out to God.

Making known God and his kingdom determines Jesus' own ministry (1,14-15). Even before the people acknowledge the authority of Jesus in his «new teaching» (1,27), and recognise the hand of God at work in the powerful works of Jesus (2,12), the disciples do respond to Jesus' call and thereby recognise his authority. Jesus subsequently reveals that discipleship itself is grounded on one's willingness to do the will of God (3,35). God calls man to a new allegiance that may even lead to

---

Cf. also T.K. HECKEL, *Viergestaltigen Evangelium*, 32-62; M. MATJAŽ, *Furcht*, 292-312, especially 308-312; R. VIGNOLO, «Una finale reticente», 129-189.

[252] This reference itself is preceded by the account of the remarkable seeing of the Roman Centurion. Thus even the third section itself can be said to be coming to a close with the seeing of a stranger. He sees Jesus breathing his last by letting out an extraordinarily loud cry and declares his profession of faith in Jesus, «Truly this man was the Son of God» (15,39). This outsider is the first man who is given the grace to «see» rightly, comprehend fully and confess freely Jesus' divine sonship.

the disavowal of demands of one's natural family which fails to take into account «the will of God». Jesus' instructions to the disciples are geared to teach them to be «on the side of God» and not of men (8,33). By way of example he presents the obligation to embrace his own fate as fulfilment of divine imperative (8,31; 9,31; 10,32-34), and while undergoing the extreme agony he seeks not what he wills, but the will of the Father (14,36). The disciples are also encouraged to trust actively in God (11,22), for an unconditional faith combined with the willingness to forgive wrongs (11,25) evokes a ready hearing from the Father. Thus the schooling which the disciples receive from Jesus is always oriented towards God. Ultimately it is God who is the point of reference to their discipleship. God himself explicitly directs the disciples to listen to Jesus (9,7). Communion with God is established by listening to Jesus, by a life of faith in him, and by a wholehearted following of his footsteps.

The disciples are enabled to gain access not only to God the Father but also to the Holy Spirit. In our interpretation we have seen that the Spirit manifests itself pre-eminently in the ministry of Jesus. The disciples' response to Jesus' call can already be thought of as having been caused by the movement of the Spirit in them. In so far as the disciples are to continue the ministry of Jesus, the self-same active presence of the Spirit would characterise and determine their involvement in the world. It would be the Spirit speaking through them (13,11) and acting through them. Hence the aspect of communion between Jesus and those whom he sees and calls do embrace a Theocentric dimension. Jesus becomes the mediator of communion between God and the disciples.

6.1.3 Communion among Themselves

The narrative emphasises another aspect of Jesus' seeing the first disciples. Except in the case of Levi, Jesus is said to be seeing always a pair of brothers; Simon and his brother Andrew (1,16) as well as James and his brother John (1,19). In so doing, the blood relationship could not be the main point that is stressed. For the Markan narrative, it is not probable that Jesus' elective seeing would be governed by any considerations like kinship, acquaintance, or familiarity. The concept of communion could again explain the reason for seeing and calling in twos. The call narrative already at the outset seems to be highlighting the communitarian aspect of discipleship.

The group is not formed by a random coming together of men because they share a common interest; it is the coming together of those whom Jesus sees and calls and appoints (3,14). Divine initiative stands behind their fellowship. Those who respond to the call do it because they believe in his word as God's word and follow him because they see it as carrying out God's will. Belonging to the group requires leaving everything (1,18.20; 2,14), renouncing the natural family (3,32-35), and detachment from wealth (10,21). The Gospel makes it abundantly clear that they come together precisely for the sake of Jesus and the Gospel (10,29) and that reward would not be wanting for those who do it (10,30)[253]. The graphic description of those whom Jesus calls as following and moving with him always as a group illustrates the distinctiveness of the group and the personal relationship that should exist between them. Nourished by faith in Jesus and supported by love, the group grows into a closely-knit community which has communion with him at the very core of their common life. Communion with Jesus by consequence implies communion among themselves.

The Gospel in a subtle way emphasises the corporate aspect of their communion in that it seldom brings to the fore any individual disciples except Peter. Jesus deals with them as a group (also of fours and threes) and he insists on the need to learn to live in community: «If anyone would be first, he must be last of all and servant of all» (9,35). The chiastic positions of ἔσχατος and διάκονος strengthen the contrast between firstness and lastness. Here the question is one of rank not merely in relation to Jesus but also in relation to one another[254]. The same theme is taken up once again when Jesus exhorts them not to aspire for position of authority: «but whoever would be great among you must be your servant, and whoever would be first among you must be slave of all» (10,43-44). Jesus does not necessarily imply that any disciple should exercise authority. Whoever wishes to do it should be a

---

[253] E. Best argues that there is no direct connection between the rich man's story (10,17-22) and Jesus' promise of reward for those who renounce it (10,28-31). E. BEST, *Following Jesus*, 110-111. Jesus invitation to the rich man to sell his possessions, to give it to the poor and then to follow him (10,21) presupposes a group, a community to which he can subsequently belong. It is to this group that Jesus makes the promise of a hundredfold reward. There is a direct line stretching from the story of the rich man to the teaching on wealth, to Peter's remark, to the promise of reward. See also D.O. VIA, *The Ethics*, 142-143.

[254] R.H. GUNDRY, *Mark*, 509.

servant and a slave, and a person in that position is not expected to exercise authority.

As preaching the advent of God's kingdom determined Jesus' mission, the disciples too as a community and as individuals, are called to preach the coming of God's kingdom in Jesus. The communitarian aspect characterises not only their being together, but also their ministry. Jesus sends them out in pairs on their missionary journey. Neither Matthew (10,5) nor Luke (9,2) mention this aspect. The significance of sending them in pairs may be that it conforms to the law of two or three witnesses (Deut 19,15; 17,6; 2Cor 13,1; 1Tim 5,19; etc.)[255]. The good news has to be preached on the authority of two witnesses; the presence of two preachers motivates the hearers to be convinced of the truth of the message[256]. At the same time, they are also able to provide each other both personal and moral support[257].

6.1.4 Summary

Jesus' seeing the disciples and issuing the call to follow him have the purpose of offering the disciples the possibility to enter into a relationship of communion with him. Jesus wishes to share with them and extend to them his experience of communion with God. Communion with Jesus is established by «being with him», listening to his teaching, witnessing his mighty works, having a glimpse of his glory and forming a right understanding regarding his true identity. The story of the disciples' being with him is also marked by doubt, incomprehension, failure and flight. But the story does not end on a negative note but on the positive promise of seeing the risen Jesus in Galilee. The disciples are finally enabled to see; the risen Lord would

---

[255] J. JEREMIAS, «Paarweise Sendung», 133-35. In fact, the early Christian mission practice does seem to correspond to this manner (e.g., Acts 13,1-3). It would not be wrong to think that the church may have gained this lesson from Jesus.

[256] K. STOCK, Boten, 87.

[257] Neither Mark nor the other Evangelists present explicitly the concept of fellowship and communion as lived out by the disciples. Only after the resurrection they are faced with the problems surrounding it. The Acts of the Apostles bear witness to the common life of the inceptive church which to this day stands as a model of basic Christian communities (Acts 2,42.44f.; 4,32f.). Paul on the other hand has a developed theology of communion and fellowship perhaps most lucidly expressed by the verb κοινωνία (1Cor 10,16; 2Cor 13,14). Paul's concept of communion involves vertically communion with God through Jesus and horizontally communion with one another. The first letter of John also develops the theme of the two-pronged communion to some extent (1 John 1,3).

make up for what is wanting in them; discipleship can continue with renewed vigour.

Communion with Jesus also enables the disciples to enter into communion with God. Through Jesus the disciples gain access to God's own life of communion. But that opens up a new dimension to their being together as a group. The disciples enter into a life of communion with each other. Life of communion henceforth reflects their following and belonging to Jesus.

6.2 Jesus' Seeing Implies an Invitation to Share in the Mission

It is significant that Jesus' seeing the disciples and calling them is the next thing he does on coming to Galilee preaching the gospel of God (1,14-15). It is to be inferred that a close link does really exist between Jesus' preaching and the calling of the disciples. Even while stressing that their following is exclusively directed towards him (1,17: Δεῦτε ὀπίσω μου), Jesus already indicates that it has a specific scope directed precisely towards men (1,17: ποιήσω ὑμᾶς γενέσθαι ἁλιεῖς ἀνθρώπων). This very fact is reiterated at the appointment of the Twelve (3,13-19). Apart from the primary purpose of «being with him», the Twelve are also appointed «to be sent out to preach and have authority to cast out demons» (3,14-15: ἵνα ἀποστέλλῃ αὐτοὺς κηρύσσειν καὶ ἔχειν ἐξουσίαν ἐκβάλλειν τὰ δαιμόνια).

6.2.1 The Sending of the Disciples (3,14-15)

The second subordinate clause introduced by the purposive ἵνα in 3,14 indicates that the Twelve are to be sent out: ἀποστέλλῃ[258]. Of the 13 uses of the verb in 5 instances the disciples are the object of the

---

[258] Several scholars have pointed out the tension that exists between the two purpose clauses. The Twelve are appointed both «to be with» Jesus as well as «to be sent out». J. Marcus notes that the tension can be resolved by interpreting 3,14 and 3,15 sequentially: now the disciples are with Jesus, but later he will send them out to preach and exorcise (cf. 6,7.12-13) . Cf. J. MARCUS, Mark, 267. Some resolve the tension by assigning the clauses to different periods in the life of the Twelve, before and after the resurrection. Prior to the resurrection they are in the company of Jesus; after the resurrection they become his missionaries. Cf. C.E.B. CRANFIELD, St. Mark, 128; J. ERNST, Markus, 113; K.-G. REPLOH, Lehrer, 45-46; E. SCHWEIZER, Markus, 40.67. Nevertheless many have rightly viewed these two clauses as complementary. Their being in the company of Jesus provides them with the basis for their mission, to proclaim Jesus and what he stands for. The Twelve's ministry is thus an extension of Jesus own ministry. Cf. R.A. GUELICH, Mark, 159; R.H. GUNDRY, Mark, 168.

verb, the verbal form is present active and the one who sends them is Jesus (3,14; 6,7; 11,1.3; 14,13). But only in two cases their sending implies an assignment directed at others implicitly: 3,14; 6,7. The use of the present subjunctive in 3,14, the absolute use of the infinitive κηρύσσειν and the fact that the recipients of the disciples' activity are indefinite, all suggest that here ἀποστέλλειν should not mean just a single act of commissioning. It should rather signify a real designation that has lasting effect[259]. Thus the phrase οὓς καὶ ἀποστόλους ὠνόμασεν[260] denotes the status of the disciples based on their designation (cf. also 6,30).

6.2.2 Mandate to Preach

The disciples are sent out with the specific purpose of preaching (κηρύσσειν)[261]. The verb κηρύσσειν occurs 12 times in the Gospel of Mark (Matt 9; Luke 9; John 0; Acts 8). It is used to refer to the preaching of John the Baptist (1,4.7); of Jesus (1,14.38.39); of the disciples (3,14; 6,12); and of those who experience healing from Jesus (1,45; 5,20; 7,36). Twice it is used in the passive form without specifying who will be the subject of preaching (13,10; 14,9).

John the Baptist preaches «a baptism of repentance for the forgiveness of sins» (1,4) and the coming of the mighty one (1,7). Jesus preaches the Gospel of God (1,14). Those healed preach the fact of their healing (1,45; 5,20; 7,36). The Gospel is the subject matter of preaching in 13,10 and 14,9. But the verb also occurs without object. The content of Jesus' preaching in 1,38.39 is not indicated nor is it pointed out in the case of the disciples in 3,14; 6,12[262]. As for Jesus' preaching in 1,38.39 it is quite obvious that what he preaches is the same as in 1,14. It is to be inferred that the same holds true for the disciples. Following their master, they preach what he preaches. Being with Jesus, they learn from him and about him. So the message they

---

[259] K. STOCK, *Boten*, 19; K.-G. REPLOH, *Lehrer*, 54; G. SCHMAHL, *Zwölf*, 74-75.

[260] It is considered an interpolation from Luke 6,13. However, it is supported by ℵ, B, (C*), Θ, *f*[13], etc. Metzger notes that «the external evidence is too strong in their favour to warrant their ejection from the text». Cf. B.M. METZGER, *A Textual Commentary*, 69.

[261] B. Friedrich says that «to preach» is a poor translation of the verb κηρύσσειν. Its true sense is «to proclaim». B. FRIEDRICH, «κῆρυξ», 703.

[262] In 3,14 some manuscripts like D, W, (lat), bo^pt, try to make up for the lack of object by adding κηρύσσειν τὸ εὐαγγέλιον καὶ ἔδωκεν αὐτοῖς. Cf. NESTLE-ALAND, *Novum Testamentum Graece*, 96.

carry to others naturally has as its content the message of Jesus[263]. However, it is to suspected that they would add some thing regarding the bringer of that message as well. On the other hand it is possible that the non-specification of the content of their preaching is done on purpose. What is emphasised is their preaching; the content of their preaching is left open for the reason that it is different before and after the resurrection of Jesus[264]. The Gospel itself gives evidence to it. While 1,1 refers to the post-resurrectional preaching, 1,14-15 is to be considered the pre-resurrectional preaching.

6.2.3 Authority over the Unclean Spirits

The Twelve are sent out with the additional purpose of having authority to cast out demons (3,15: καὶ ἔχειν ἐξουσίαν ἐκβάλλειν τὰ δαιμόνια)[265]. 6,7 establishes that Jesus does give the Twelve such authority, a fact confirmed by the other Synoptics as well (Matt 10,1; Luke 9,1)[266]. The authority is expressed by the word ἐξουσία. The word occurs 10 times in Mark (Matt 10; Luke 16; John 6). Except once (13,34: used of the servants in a parable) it always refers to Jesus (1,22.27; 2,10; 11,28[2].29.33) or the Twelve (3,15; 6,7). While Jesus' authority is manifested in his teaching (1,22.27), in forgiving sins (2,10) and in a general way in his deeds (11,28f.), the Twelve have the authority specifically to cast out demons (3,15) and over the unclean

---

[263] S. FREYNE, The Twelve, 143; R.A. GUELICH, Mark, 159; C.D. MARSHALL, Faith as a Theme, 40; K. STOCK, Boten, 25-26.

[264] K. STOCK, «Theologie», 132.

[265] This second infinitive clause has the function of explaining the nature of the mission of the Twelve. But as it stands in the sentence it is quite clumsy in style and content. Its awkwardness has been noted by many scholars, e.g., E. LOHMEYER, Markus, 74, K.-G. REPLOH, Lehrer, 45-46. Someone is sent to perform an action not to have an ability. Cf. R.A. GUELICH, Mark, 159; K. STOCK, Boten, 23. Mark's editorial hand is to be suspected in the construction of this sentence. Cf. R.A. GUELICH, Mark, 159-160; R PESCH, Markusevangelium I, 203; K.-G. REPLOH, Lehrer, 46; G. SCHMAHL, Zwölf, 58-59.

[266] According to Matthew the Twelve receive from Jesus authority both over unclean spirits as well as to heal every disease and every infirmity (10,1). Luke mentions about such authority not at the constitution of the Twelve, where it is only said that Jesus named them apostles (6,13), but before commissioning them on missionary journey. Luke also confirms that they receive authority over all demons and to cure diseases (9,1). Mark does not speak about the authority to cure diseases at their appointment, but later reports that along with casting out demons they anointed with oil many that were sick and healed them (6,13).

spirits (6,7). What is characteristic of Mark is the emphasis on the authority of the Twelve over the demons. Only Mark among Synoptics insists that casting out demons forms an essential part of their ministry during their missionary journey (6,13).

The phrase ἐκβάλλειν τὰ δαιμόνια appears almost like a fixed expression referring to Jesus (1,34.39; 3,22) and the Twelve (3,15; 6,13). ἐκβάλλειν (occurring 11 times) is never used with «unclean spirits» (πνεῦμα ἀκαθάρτον: the expression occurs 11 times), but in most cases the verb is employed in the phrase or in the context of casting out demons (δαιμόνιον: the word occurs 10 times)[267]. The phrase has another peculiarity. It occurs three times in conjunction with preaching (1,39: referring to Jesus; 3,15 and 6,13 referring to the Twelve). 1,39 and 6,13 are summary statements regarding the ministry of Jesus and the Twelve respectively. The ministry of the Twelve is thus portrayed as an extension of the ministry of Jesus. When speaking of authority it may be specified that, it is an authority over unclean spirits (1,27) and it is Jesus who gives (ἐδίδου) the authority to the Twelve at their commissioning (6,7). Jesus is not a mere possessor of such authority, but he is capable of transmitting it to the subordinates. At 3,15, «to have authority» (ἔχειν ἐξουσιαν) presupposes possession of authority given only at 6,7. So it is probable that the actual commissioning of the Twelve at 6,7 may have influenced the formulation of 3,14-15[268].

However, the point of emphasis here is that at the appointment of the Twelve their ministry is already envisaged as participating in the ministry of Jesus. The content of their preaching is the same as that of Jesus; moreover they also share in the accompanying activity that characterises Jesus' mission, that of casting out demons. In fact after calling the four men to become «fishers of men» (1,17), Jesus opens his

---

[267] The close connection between ἐκβάλλειν and δαιμόνια alone explains why 3,15 has, «and have authority to cast out demons» whereas at their commissioning Jesus gives «them authority over the unclean spirits» (6,7). The change from «demons» to «unclean spirits» seems to be the result of linguistic habit. Cf. R.A. GUELICH, *Mark*, 66; R.H. GUNDRY, *Mark*, 91.

[268] K. STOCK, *Boten*, 23-24: «Die Absicht, einerseits in Abhängigkeit von "aussenden" das Wirken der 12 mit der Formel für das Wirken Jesu (1,39) zu beschreiben und andererseits die Autorisierung für die Dämonenaustreibung herauszustellen, dürfte zu der nicht ganz befriedigenden Formulierung von 3,15 geführt haben». R.A. GUELICH, *Mark*, 160: Mark «combined a formulaic expression ("to cast out demons") with the idea of authorisation ("to have authority") to round out the summary of the Twelve's mission ("to preach" and "to cast out demons")».

public ministry with them in Capernaum, exactly with an astounding, authoritative teaching (1,21-22.27) which expresses itself in exorcising an unclean spirit (1,23-26). The summary statement in 1,39 which concludes the ministry of Jesus from 1,21 onward and refers back to his preaching in 1,14-15 highlights the essential elements of Jesus' mission and establishes a close link between preaching and casting out demons[269]. At 3,14-15 the purpose of the appointment of the Twelve are presented as involving the same essential elements, reiterated later in the statement that sums up the ministry of the Twelve (6,12-13). The Twelve are thus portrayed as both participating in and continuing the mission of Jesus.

6.2.4 Seeing, Communion and Mission

By inaugurating Jesus' ministry with the seeing and call of the four men (1,16-20), and by presenting it in its two-fold essential elements of preaching and casting out demons Mark sets the tone for Jesus' relationship with the Twelve. It is basically that relationship which provides the foundation of all that the Twelve would be capable of doing. Actually the principal purpose of Jesus' calling them as defined by 3,14 is «to be with him». The secondary motive of calling them which is the continuation of Jesus' mission is envisioned as flowing from the first. We have defined «to be with him» as entering into communion with Jesus. So it may be said that the mission of the Twelve emanates from communion with him. It is by being with Jesus that they learn about him, it is their continued presence with him that enables them to comprehend who he is and what he stands for.

We have seen that ever since Jesus called the four men to follow him, he has been instructing them both by words and deeds on his proper identity. Entering into communion with Jesus has been inextricably bound up with the acknowledgement of the identity of Jesus and accepting the way of the cross, death and resurrection. This alone would make them fitting heralds who could proclaim the εὐαγγέλιον which after the resurrection involves announcing the advent of God's kingdom, in the person of Ἰησοῦ Χριστοῦ υἱοῦ Θεοῦ (1,1). Communion with Jesus, an abiding relationship with him, nurtured and sustained by the ability «to see» which the disciples acquire from the risen Lord, coupled with deep faith and commitment in him would

---

[269] K. STOCK, *Boten*, 24-25.

enable the disciples to become effective missionaries, efficient «fishers of men»[270]. This fact highlights not only the importance of the preparation of missionaries but also the obligation of maintaining a lifelong relationship with Jesus.

6.2.5 The Mission of the Twelve

After the appointment of the Twelve, their sending itself is not verified up until 6,7 where the second scope of the calling of the Twelve seems to be realised. This is the only instance during the lifetime of Jesus, when the Twelve carry out what is inherent in their calling. Jesus calls them (προσκαλεῖται, same verb as in 3,14) and begins to send them out (καὶ ἤρξατο αὐτοὺς ἀποστέλλειν δύο δύο). ἤρξατο + ἀποστέλλειν in the present tense here has an iterative sense[271]. What is implied is not a repetition of the mission of the Twelve,[272] but it is iterative with respect to Jesus' sending one pair after another. This communitarian aspect of their being sent is the new element added to the narrative on commissioning the Twelve. In pairs of two they are sent out (ἀποστέλλειν δύο δύο)[273]. However, one must hasten to add that the missionary mandate of the Twelve does not exhaust itself with this one episode. They are not appointed (3,14) and commissioned (6,7) just for this isolated mission. But they have a lasting role to play as apostles of Jesus (6,30). That could account for the omission of a missionary mandate at the end of the Gospel[274]. The promise of «seeing» in Galilee while reinstating them as disciples following the master also confirms them in their ministry which forms part and parcel of their status. There is no need of a second appointment or commissioning. Jesus' authority and power is most visible in making

---

[270] K. STOCK, «Theologie», 144: «Die Missionare sollen ganz von der Person Jesu geprägt sein und sich an ihm orientieren. So sind sie vorbereitet, die Frohe Botschaft zu verkünden, wie die Königsherrschaft Gottes sich in Jesus, dem Christus, dem Sohn Gottes gezeigt hat».

[271] For a detailed analysis see K. STOCK, Boten, 85-86.

[272] The Gospel does not speak of any other instance of their missionary activity. It is also improbable that 6,7-13 is the summary of repeated missionary forays by the Twelve. It narrates an episode in the life of Jesus and of the Twelve. The narrative on the return of the Twelve and the feed back they give to Jesus (6,30) suggests that it indeed was a single episode.

[273] For a consideration on the distributive δύο δύο as Semitism see E.C. MALONEY, Semitic Interference, 152-154.

[274] K. STOCK, Boten, 86.

effective missionaries of those men prone to failure and incomprehension, but sincere in their unconditional following.

The Twelve are sent out equipped with authority over unclean spirits (καὶ ἐδίδου αὐτοῖς ἐξουσίαν τῶν πνευμάτων τῶν ἀκαθάρτων). The imperfect ἐδίδου (as opposed to aorist ἔδωκεν of Matt 10,1 and Luke 9,1) may indicate that Jesus repeats the action of giving authority to each pair separately[275]. By giving «authority over the unclean spirits» another of the objectives of their being sent out is fulfilled. At this point no reference to the fulfilment of the primary objective, that of preaching is made. The focus is on the participation in the authority of Jesus. Just as Jesus' authority is manifested in his power over the demons, the Twelve would be capable of announcing the good news accompanied by a demonstration of the same authority over the demons. They are given the authority by Jesus, they are only messengers and executives of the one who commissions them.

Jesus recommends the Twelve to take the minimum of travel provisions (6,8-9)[276]. They are permitted to take one staff, wear sandals and put on one tunic. The demands seem to be less rigorous than in Matthew (or rather Q; Matt 10,10; cf. also Luke 9,3)[277]. What is evident is that they should be completely free for their mission. Renunciation which has characterised their following Jesus (1,18.20; 10,28) should govern their missionary involvement. The messengers should be completely dependent on providence and the generosity of the beneficiaries of their ministry for their maintenance.

The Twelve are to behave with humility, seeking neither their convenience nor comfort (6,10). If any place refuses to receive them it would be dangerous for its inhabitants. Welcoming the messengers and accepting their message is seen as decisive for their salvation (6,11; cf. Matt 10,15 and Luke 10,12 for more explicit saying). Any refusal of the messengers would tantamount to rejecting the one who sent them. This

---

[275] R.A. GUELICH, *Mark*, 321; K. STOCK, *Boten*, 88; V. TAYLOR, *St. Mark*, 303. Cf. also R.H. GUNDRY, *Mark*, 301. R.H. Gundry speculates also that giving may be considered as taking an oral form. This could explain the imperfect form of the verb as verbs of speaking often take the imperfect form (cf. ἔλεγεν in 6,10).

[276] Matthew (10,5-15) and to a lesser extent Luke (9,3-6) have more detailed instructions for the Twelve, including the note of eschatological urgency. For comparisons of the parallels see F. HAHN, *Mission*, 42-46; H.K. NIELSEN, *Heilung*, 82-85. See J. MARCUS, *Mark*, 389, for possible parallels with Exodus tradition.

[277] For an explanation on the provisions see V. FUSCO, «Missione universale», 113-119; for the historical reasons suggested for the prohibitions see R.H. GUNDRY, *Mark*, 308-309.

way the message is identified with the messengers and the messengers are identified with the one who sent them, Jesus[278].

The summary report of the activity of the Twelve (6,12-13) stresses the faithful carrying out of what they are sent for and brings out the parallelism between the activity of Jesus and that of the Twelve. The Twelve preach just as Jesus preaches (1,14-15.38-39.45). The content of the preaching as has been noted corresponds to Jesus' preaching (1,14-15). Their preaching also involves a call to conversion. However, announcing the message precedes such a call[279]. Their call to conversion places them in line with the Baptist's (1,4) and Jesus' (1,15) call to repentance and makes them the mediators of new relationship with God.

The Twelve also cast out (6,13) demons just like Jesus (1,25-26.34.39). The authority with which Jesus invested them has been effective. The imperfect ἐξέβαλλον suggests the repeated success of exercising their authority over the demons. The new element added is that the Twelve also heal many sick (the verb ἐθεράπευον is again in the imperfect). The parallelism with Jesus' ministry is complete (1,34). The chiasm that places the objects at the extremes makes them to stand out as recipients of the power of Jesus mediated through the Twelve:[280]

δαιμόνια πολλὰ   ἐξέβαλλον,
                  ἤλειφον ἐλαίῳ   πολλοὺς ἀρρώστους
                  ἐθεράπευον (6,13).

The mention of the word ἄρρωστοι while establishing a connection with Jesus' own healing of the sick people (6,5), highlights also the contrast between the resounding success of the Twelve and a less than successful ministry of Jesus in his home town[281]. Oil is known to have a therapeutic quality (cf. Isa 1,6) but anointing with oil for healing is not known elsewhere in the Gospels. It may bear the influence of early Christian practice of anointing the sick with oil (cf. Jas 5,14-15)[282].

In the mission of the disciples, Jesus' ability to predict and the fulfilment of that prediction stands out conspicuously. When Jesus sees

---

[278] K. STOCK, *Boten*, 92-93.

[279] K. STOCK, *Boten*, 94: «Die Umkehr steht nicht für sich allein, sie ist Antwort auf die Botschaft wie in Mk 1,15».

[280] R.H. GUNDRY, *Mark*, 303.

[281] Z. KATO, *Die Völkermission*, 66f.

[282] J. GNILKA, *Markus* I, 240; R.A. GUELICH, *Mark*, 323.

the first of his disciples, he makes a promise which would become reality only in the future: «I will make you become fishers of men» (1,17). At the appointment of the Twelve the objectives of doing it are spelt out: «to be with him, and to be sent out to preach and to have authority to cast out demons» (3,14-15). Being with him, communion with him is the pre-requisite for the secondary purpose of being sent out. The commissioning of the Twelve presupposes Jesus' conviction of their sufficient preparation. With the dispatch of the pairs Jesus gives them authority over the unclean spirits (6,7). The first thing the Twelve do on going out is to preach (6,12). Preaching precedes demonstration of authority over demons (6,13). The success of the Twelve in preaching, casting out demons and healing the sick point to Jesus' own success in making them «fishers of men» (1,17).

6.2.6 Universal Mission

The content of the preaching of the Twelve is the Gospel. Mark emphasises it in no uncertain terms at the start of the narrative (1,1). Here Jesus is the content of the Gospel; his life, ministry, suffering, death, and resurrection form the good news. At 1,14-15 Mark presents Jesus preaching the Gospel of the fulfilment of time and the advent of the kingdom of God. In so far as Jesus is the bringer of the good news and represents the fulfilment of time and the advent of the kingdom of God the content of the Gospel points to Jesus as well. Therefore the primary task of the Twelve is to proclaim Jesus.

However, nowhere in Mark's Gospel is it specified who should be the beneficiaries of the preaching and ministry of the Twelve. Both at their appointment (3,14-15) as well as at their commissioning (6,7f.) the beneficiaries are indeterminate[283]. When Jesus sees and calls the first disciples, his promise speaks of making them «become fishers of men» in generic terms (1,17). However, 13,10 stipulates that «the Gospel must first be preached to all nations»[284]. Even though 13,10

---

[283] In Matt 10,5f. it is explicitly prohibited to go to the Gentiles and the Samaritans, they should rather go to the lost sheep of the house of Israel (cf. Matt 15,24). Luke 9,6 without being specific speaks of their going through the villages, preaching the Gospel and healing everywhere.

[284] There is near unanimity among scholars that the command refers to universal mission. Cf. e.g., F. HAHN, *Mission*, 116-19; D. SENIOR, «The Struggle to be Universal», 63-81; D. SENIOR – C. STUHLMUELLER, *Biblical Foundations*, 217-225; K. STOCK, «Theologie», 131-132.139-140; J.F. WILLIAMS, «Mission in Mark», 142-151. But isolated contrary views are not lacking. See for instance, T.J. WEEDEN, «The

together with 9,9 and 14,9 may reflect the post-Easter preaching of the community, two points may be read into that injunction. Firstly, it can be assumed that the Twelve have a particular responsibility to carry out that task. Since the Twelve have already an experience in doing it (6,7-13.30) it can be considered as an invitation to resume it with added zeal. The promise of seeing the resurrected Jesus in Galilee (16,7), confirms that the Gospel does not end on a negative note, but on the positive experience of renewal of communion and a commitment to follow the way Jesus has traced out for them. Taking up this challenge necessarily involves proclaiming Jesus. Secondly, the newness of the command is that the sphere of their preaching and missionary activity is now spelt out to include «all nations». The Twelve are to be fishers of men in all nations.

The ministry of Jesus itself provides the basis for the disciples opening to the Gentiles. Although the Galilean ministry of Jesus is primarily directed towards the people of Israel (7,27), he does travel outside Galilee and go into Gentile territory and reach out to those who seek his help (5,1-20; 7,24–8,9.22-26). The rejection of Jesus by his own household at Nazareth (6,1-6), and the controversy over purity (7,1-23) leads to mission activity beyond Israel's borders. The response of faith and sincere action on the part of the Gentiles persuade Jesus to rethink the «Israel first» strategy[285].

With Jesus' entry into Jerusalem, the temple-theme comes to the fore. The cleansing of the temple and Jesus' subsequent prophetic opening of the temple «for all the nations» (11,17)[286] leads to further rejection by the Jewish leaders (11,18.28). Ironically the opening to the Gentiles is ever more closely tied to the rejection of Jesus by Israel. The parable of the vineyard (12,1-9) once again highlights Jesus' mission, his rejection and opening to the Gentiles. The imperative on universal mission (13,10) is presented as connected to the fate of the temple (13,2). The subsequent narrative of Jesus' passion and death culminates with report of the tearing of the temple-veil (15,38) and the

---

Heresy», 145-158; ID., *Mark*, 167-168. Cf. also G.D. KILPATRICK, «Gentile Mission», 145-158. According to Kilpatrick 13,10 refers to a mission among Diaspora Jews.

[285] For detailed analysis see W. KELBER, *The Kingdom in Mark*, 45-65; D. SENIOR – C. STUHLMUELLER, *The Biblical Foundations*, 218-20; K. STOCK, «Theologie», 141; J.F. WILLIAMS, «Mission in Mark», 144.

[286] Both in Matthew (21,13) and in Luke (19,46) this phrase «for all the nations» is absent.

positive presentation of a Gentile Centurion who «sees» and confesses his faith in Jesus (15,39).

As witnesses to Jesus' ministry, his disputes with the Jewish leaders, his rejection, his gradual opening to the Gentiles and finally his death, the Twelve could already discern that their preaching and ministry could not limit itself to the «Israel first» strategy. In their modus operandi, «The *heilsgeschichtlich* πρῶτον of Mark 7,27a is [to be] replaced by the eschatological πρῶτον of 13,10»[287]. The Twelve are to assume the bounden responsibility to preach the good news that is Jesus Christ with no regard for any sort of boundaries that separate peoples. The thrust of their activity is to proclaim the nearness of God in Jesus, to invite everyone, irrespective of race, colour, social status, to enter into relationship with God, to enter into communion with him.

6.2.7 Summary

The disciples' experience of communion with Jesus is not meant to be zealously guarded and enjoyed all for themselves. It is meant to be shared with others; to be proclaimed. So they have a mission, a mission oriented towards men (1,17); just as Jesus proclaimed the inbreak of the kingdom of God, they are to proclaim by word and deed the nearness of God to humanity, his entering into human realm in the person of Jesus Christ the Son of God (1,1). They are to hold out to all who repent and believe (1,15) the possibility of entering into communion with God.

7. Conclusion

Our attempt has been to establish that Jesus' seeing, expressed by the verb εἶδεν in Mark's gospel, is the most crucial element in the choice and call of the disciples. It is that seeing alone which would explain the immediateness of the call as well as the immediateness of the response. The discipleship of Simon, Andrew, James and John who form part of the group of Twelve, and that of the representative figure Levi, has its origin and foundation in the person of Jesus and in his seeing.

Jesus' seeing the heavens being torn apart and the Spirit descending upon him is a moment of intense communion with God, and the Spirit. The same event also established his links with humanity and his role as the Son. The eyes which see that extraordinary event at Jordan now see

---

[287] F. HAHN, *Mission in the New Testament*, 119.

the five men while they are engaged in their daily work. That is a special seeing which provides Jesus the insight that they are the persons whom he wants to call. Hence he calls them. Jesus wishes to extend to them that experience of communion with God and the Spirit which he himself experienced. In doing so he invites them first and foremost to belong to him, to form a community with him, to enter into communion with him, and through him to experience communion with God.

Jesus accepts that his disciples, who leave everything and follow him, need time to experience and to form the right understanding of himself, his identity, his mission. Jesus also expressly instructs them on the «way» that they need to tread if they are to follow him. The disciples prove to be frail human beings whose adventure with Jesus is replete with awe-inspiring experiences, successes, as well as misunderstandings, failure and desertion. But the story of their discipleship after resurrection continues on a more positive note, with deeper understanding and renewed vigour.

But the disciples have another role to play. After entering into communion with Jesus, God, and one another, they are required to be instruments reaching out to the people proclaiming the advent of the kingdom in Jesus, they are to preach Jesus Christ. They have to invite men to enter into communion with God. They have to win men for God, they have to be fishers of men, they have to bring mankind near to God and God near to them.

CHAPTER IV

He Saw a Great Crowd (Mark 6,34)

The fifth and the final occurrence of the verb εἶδεν in the Gospel of Mark is used to refer to Jesus' seeing of the crowd. On coming ashore in an attempt to find rest for himself and for the weary disciples, they are met by a great throng. The narrative quite characteristically speaks of Jesus «seeing» them. There is no trace of agitation on his part at not being able to get away from the public. Instead his seeing is replete with positive disposition towards the crowd. In treating this important event in the life of Jesus we shall first deal with the context of 6,34 which speaks of Jesus' seeing the crowd. Subsequently we shall analyse the verse proper, examining the object of the verb of seeing, εἶδεν, the effect of that seeing and the consequent activities of teaching and feeding which Jesus engages in, moved by that seeing.

1. Placement of Mark 6,34

Mark 6,34 which speaks of Jesus' seeing the crowd is closely bound together to the preceding (6,30-33) as well as to the subsequent narrative (6,35-44). The former supplies information regarding the return of the disciples (6,30), Jesus' invitation to rest for a while (6,31), their tentative attempt to go to a lonely place (6,32), and the coming together of the crowd (6,33). The latter flows naturally from 6,34 and speaks of Jesus miraculously feeding the crowd (6,35-44). Because of the logical progression of thought several scholars take the whole complex stretching from 6,30-44 as one single pericope[1]. All the same

---

[1] E.g., R.M. FOWLER, *Loaves and Fishes*, 68f.; J. GNILKA, *Markus* I, 254f.; R.A. GUELICH, *Mark*, 336f.; R.H. GUNDRY, *Mark*, 321f.327; E. HAENCHEN, *Der Weg*

many scholars have divided this material into two parts, consisting of a summary report and a miracle story. The pericope does begin by providing a summary of what transpires on the disciples' return to Jesus[2]. But there is no unanimity on where the summarising ends and where the story proper begins[3]. A clear-cut division between the summary report and the story of the feeding is not as explicit as some scholars understand[4].

Precisely because of the close and logical progression from one verse to the other beginning from 6,30, drawing the line between the summary and the miracle story proper can become forced and arbitrary. What can be said with confidence is that 6,30 is necessary to introduce Jesus and the Twelve into the scene. Their attempt to go to a «lonely place» is what brings also the crowd into that part of the world (6,31-33). Jesus' seeing them is directly connected to their unexpected presence there (6,34). It also occasions Jesus' teaching (6,34) and subsequent feeding (6,35-44). Thus it may be better to view the whole pericope 6,30-44 as holding together as a unity. There is a very good blending of material here that the story progresses very logically

---

Jesu, 243f.; P. LAMARCHE, Marc, 169f.; E. LOHMEYER, Markus, 122f. (30-32.33-34.35-44).

[2] Markan style of providing the so-called summary reports at various points in the Gospel has been widely detected by scholars. We may refer only to the major works on this; for example, C.H. DODD, «The Framework», 1-11; W. EGGER, Frohbotschaft; N. PERRIN, The New Testament; K.L. SCHMIDT, Der Rahmen. The list of K.L. Schmidt who perhaps for the first time identified them has been accepted by N. Perrin too: 1,14-15.21-22.39; 2,13; 3,7-12; 5,21; 6,6b.12-13.30-33.53-56; 10,1. W. Egger's list: 1,14-15.21-22.32-34.39.45; 2,1-2.13; 3,7-12; 4,1-2; 6,6b.30-34.53-56; 10,1. W. Egger omits 5,21 and 6,12-13 from K.L. Schmidt's list and adds four more: 1,32-34.45; 2,1-2; 4,1-2. Interestingly except 10,1 all summaries are found in the first six chapters of the Gospel.

[3] Some draw the division between 6,31 and 6,32; e.g., P.J. ACHTEMEIER, «Miracle Catenae», 280; J. ERNST, Markus, 188f.; R. PESCH, Markusevangelium I, 345f.; E. SCHWEIZER, Markus, 71f.; others put the division between 6,33 and 6,34; e.g., C.E.B. CRANFIELD, St. Mark, 213f. L. SCHENKE, Wundererzählungen, 217-222; K.L. SCHMIDT, Der Rahmen, 190f., and yet others place the division between 6,34 and 6,35; e.g., W. EGGER, Frohbotschaft, 121-131; B.M.F. VAN IERSEL, Mark, 224f.; V. TAYLOR, St. Mark, 318f.; W. TOOLEY, «The Shepherd», 16.

[4] J. DELORME, «Mc 6,30-34», 44-58; W. EGGER, Frohbotschaft, 121f. W. Egger's scholarly work recognises the transitional character of the summary report. But W. Egger rounds off the pericope at 6,34 as it refers back to the teaching theme of 6,30. But we would like to stress that the verse is equally forward looking since an important theme is developed there.

coming to a conclusion by noting the spectacular success of Jesus' activity[5].

Within this literary unit verse 34 has a pivotal role[6]. Without reference to Jesus' seeing the crowd the story would have come to an end, or it would have taken another turn, narrating perhaps the retreat Jesus and his weary disciples enjoyed. Every thing that Jesus does subsequently in this pericope therefore hinges on this important verse.

2. Situation

The situation that is described in the pericope includes the return of the disciples (6,30), Jesus extending to them an invitation to rest (6,31), the movement of Jesus and the disciples in order to realise it (6,32) and the movement of the crowd who note the tentative attempt of Jesus and his disciples (6,33).

2.1 *Return of the Apostles*

6,30 returns to the narrative of 6,7-13, on the mission of the Twelve that has been interrupted by the interlude of 6,14-29 which recounts the opinions regarding Jesus (6,14-16) and the death of John the Baptist (6,17-29). Mark in 6,30 gives a concluding report on the missionary activity of the Twelve. By the use of the noun οἱ ἀπόστολοι a direct link is established with Jesus' action of sending (ἀποστέλλειν) the Twelve in groups of two (6,7)[7]. When the Twelve are again with Jesus

---

[5] Closely connected to the placement of 6,34 is the question of tradition and redaction. The difference in opinion on where exactly the summary ends and where the traditional story begins is due to the differing positions on the tradition and redaction of the pericope. We would not want to enter into the intricacies of the debate. R.M. Fowler for instance, after examining 6,30-34 on the basis of vocabulary, style and themes and comparing it with 8,1-10 concludes: «The story is Markan from beginning to end». Cf. R.M. FOWLER, *Loaves and Fishes*, 68. Some scholars support his position. But then there are several others who take 8,1-10 to be later, not earlier than 6,30-44. For a treatise on the tradition and redaction of both stories see S. MASUDA, «The Good News» 191-219.

[6] E. Lohmeyer qualifies the verse with the comment: «Der Satz ist von einzigartigem Gewicht». Cf. E. LOHMEYER, *Markus*, 124.

[7] This is the only instance apart from the variant reading of 3,14 in which the designation οἱ ἀπόστολοι is used of the Twelve. Scholars argue that the term here refers to their role as «those sent». It does not indicate their status as «the Apostles» (so J. DUPONT, «Le nom d'apôtres», 991-992; K.-G. REPLOH, *Lehrer*, 55; G. SCHMAHL, *Zwölf*, 79; E. SCHWEIZER, *Markus*, 71; V. TAYLOR, *St. Mark*, 319). But it can be presumed that by Mark's day the term had indeed become a technical term

(συνάγονται)[8] who sent them out on the mission and gave them authorisation, they report (ἀπήγγειλαν) back to him all they had done and taught (πάντα ὅσα ἐποίησαν καὶ ὅσα ἐδίδαξαν).

«All that they had done and taught» sums up the whole of their missionary activity. Their activity has a twofold character of word and deed (cf. also 3,14 and 6,12-13). But there is no mention of the content of their activity or teaching. All the same, according to 6,13 their deeds consist of casting out demons and healing. 6,12 speaks of their preaching (κηρύσσειν) and the content of the preaching is that men should repent (cf. also 3,14). But 6,30 instead speaks of their «teaching». This is the only instance which speaks of the teaching of the Twelve. In fact Mark uses the verb διδάσκειν exclusively for Jesus and the Twelve[9]. The use of the verb διδάσκειν for the Twelve here, besides implying a making known of facts, also emphasises their role of giving instructions to their hearers[10]. It also stresses the fact that what they teach has the sanction and authority of Jesus. As we have already established the Twelve's activities stand in parallel to Jesus' own activity and they are an extension of Jesus' own mission.

6,30 summarises the conversation between the Twelve and Jesus on their return from the missionary journey. But the verse has certainly a transitional character. It reintroduces the actors, Jesus and the Twelve into the narrative after the digression of 6,14-29. The ensuing narrative is built on 6,30.

---

for the Apostles. So the readers of Mark may understand the term in that light. However, it has to be emphasised that in 6,30 the word is set in the context of mission. It does not refer to any official status. Their function justifies the title. Cf. E. BEST, *Following Jesus*, 193; C.E.B. CRANFIELD, *St. Mark*, 214-215; R.A. GUELICH, *Mark*, 338; R.H. GUNDRY, *Mark*, 327; W.L. LANE, *Mark*, 224; J. ROLOFF, *Apostolat*, 142-143. For the significance of the term ἀπόστολος, see K.H. RENGSTORF, «ἀπόστολος», 414-445; K. STOCK, *Boten*, 98-99.

[8] K. STOCK, *Boten*, 99: «Es [das Wort] drückt weniger die Idee der Rückkehr aus als die Idee der (erneuten) Sammlung um Jesus».

[9] The only exception is of 7,7 which is a citation from Isa 29,13 LXX.

[10] R.P. MEYE, *Jesus and the Twelve*, 56: «Although the disciples are sent out to preach the gospel (6:12), preaching ultimately necessitates teaching; and therefore in Mark's second account of their activity, he notes their *teaching*». While speaking of his ministry Paul too makes the distinction between preaching (1Cor 1,17) and teaching (1Cor 4,17).

2.2 Invitation to Find Rest

A direct address of Jesus to the apostles[11] is introduced by the verb λέγει in the historical present tense. The address begins with Δεῦτε, an imperative in hortatory sense (come!, come away!, come on!)[12], reminiscent of the first call addressed to Simon and Andrew (1,17; cf. also 12,7; 10,21). Here it is an invitation addressed to all the apostles as is made clear by the emphatic ὑμεῖς αὐτοί, meaning «by yourself»[13]. κατ' ἰδίαν[14] (cf. 4,34; 6,32; 9,2.28; 13,3) further stresses the private nature of their retreat. The place they are heading for is described twice in 6,31 and 6,32 as εἰς ἔρημον τόπον thereby underlining the atmosphere of silence and solitude[15]. Jesus' own custom of withdrawing to ἔρημον τόπον seems to have influenced the choice of the place (1,35).

The purpose of going to the lonely place is spelt out by the aorist imperative ἀναπαύσασθε[16]. They are called upon to «rest a while»

---

[11] Both Matthew and Luke do not report any conversation between Jesus and the disciples here. Both record only the fact of Jesus' departure. Luke adds that Jesus took the disciples also along with him (9,10b).

[12] M. ZERWICK, A Grammatical Analysis, 123.

[13] M. Zerwick opines that the αὐτοί added to ὑμεῖς is perhaps to be neglected as in the Latin versions. Cf. M. ZERWICK, Biblical Greek, §198. But the emphasis on the pronoun is quite in order. It brings into focus the disciples who really are the ones in need of rest. According to M. Zerwick there could also be an implication that the apostles need to withdraw to a lonely place just as Jesus did (1,35). So ὑμεῖς αὐτοί could mean: «Now you (sc. in your turn do as I did and)». Cf. M. ZERWICK, A Grammatical Analysis, 123.

[14] For the significance of κατ' ἰδίαν see U. MAUSER, Christ in the wilderness, 119-124. According to him κατ' ἰδίαν in Mark is always connected with a passage indicating either a retreat or a special revelation and in some instances the two elements are joined together. 6,31 displays a combination of these two elements. Jesus invites the disciples to withdraw from the multitude to be all by themselves. The event of the multiplication of the loaves that follows also has a revelatory significance for Mark. But the disciples seem to be lacking the capacity to understand the significance of the feeding miracles (6,52; 8,17f.).

[15] The phrase ἔρημος τόπος occurs 5 times in Mark (1,35.45; 6,31.32.35). It is generally translated as a «lonely place». Three times it occurs in the pericope 6,30-44 alone. Both Matthew and Luke also situate the feeding story in the ἔρημον τόπον. (Matt 14,15; Luke 9,12). Mark however makes a distinction between ἔρημος τόπος (lonely place; deserted place) and ἡ ἔρημος which is desert (cf. 1,3.4.12.13).

[16] The use of the verb ἀναπαύεσθαι is considered to be alluding to the noun ἀναπαύσεως of Ps 22,2 (LXX) and thus hinting at the «Good Shepherd» motif of the OT.

(ὀλίγον)[17]. In an explanatory sentence Mark clarifies why they need rest: «For many were coming and going, and they had no leisure even to eat»[18]. The disciples are really in need of some time to recuperate after their mission; but the coming and going of the crowd[19] does not permit it. This invitation to rest stands out in Mark's Gospel. It reflects Jesus' concern for his disciples akin to Jesus compassionate response to the «sheep without a shepherd» (6,34)[20].

In the previous chapter we have seen that one of the main purposes of appointing the Twelve was «to be with» Jesus (3,16), to enter into communion with himself. Moments of solitude and silence would provide them a chance to enjoy the intimacy and company of Jesus; to

---

[17] W. Egger (*Frohbotschaft*, 126-127) and E. Wendling (*Entstehung*, 64) argue that the command Δεῦτε and the motif of rest are evidences to suggest that the v. 31 is an isolated piece of tradition preserved in domenical saying of Matt 11,28. But scholars agree that Matt 11,28 does seem like a Matthean composition which develops a Mosaic/exodus typology (Exod 33,14). Cf. W.D. DAVIES – D.C. ALLISON, *Matthew* II, 287.296-297; R.H. GUNDRY, *Matthew*, 218-219. If so, Matthew certainly post-dates Mark. Those who do not accept any connection with Matt 11,28 include, S. LÉGASSE, *Marc*, 392; J. GNILKA, *Markus* I, 122; etc.

[18] Mark 3,20 also speaks of the coming together of the crowd and the motif of the inability to eat. R.M. Fowler takes the indefinite «they» here to refer to the crowd (ὄχλος). Accordingly, because of the coming together of the crowd, the crowd could not even eat. In the same way R.M. Fowler understands that even in 6,31 it is the crowd which had no opportunity to eat. The narrator purposely divulges to the reader the insight into the needs of the crowd and prepares him for the ensuing story of feeding. Cf. R.M. FOWLER, *Loaves and Fishes*, 77-78. But the «they» in 3,20 has to refer to Jesus and the Twelve (though not mentioned explicitly, the presence of the Twelve with Jesus is implied from the preceding pericope of their appointment). αὐτούς, a masculine plural accusative can not refer to ὄχλος which is singular. The crowd's inability to eat is not the reason for Jesus' family's attempt to seize him. Similarly, the inability of those who were coming and going to eat is not the reason for Jesus' and his disciples' departure for rest.

[19] H. Montefiore argues that the crowd who were coming and going were engaged in preparations for a Messianic uprising. Jesus escaped with his disciples from the scene of this activity. He made for the desert by the side of the lake. The crowd «from all the towns» reached the destination ahead of Jesus and the disciples. On seeing them Jesus had compassion on them «because they were like sheep without a shepherd» (6,34); meaning «an army without a general», «a nation without a national leader». Under the pressure of the actual situation Jesus knew that he could not be a military leader, so «he began to teach them many things» (6,34b). Jesus had to explain to them why he could not accede to their wish. So the crowd had gone to the desert to initiate a revolt. Jesus thwarted their attempt at a Messianic uprising. Cf. H. MONTEFIORE, «Revolt», 135-141.

[20] R.A. GUELICH, *Mark*, 339.

get to know him better in an atmosphere of dialogue and peace. The rest envisaged here therefore is not empty, but dense and brimming with revelation.

There is another nuance to the retreat to the lonely place. Jesus seems to be stressing the need to complement action with contemplation. Contact with the crowd need to be alternated with contact with Jesus. That alone would guarantee the success of the ministry of the disciples[21].

2.3 *Movement of Jesus and the Disciples*

The first step towards the realisation of their plan is taken when Mark reports that «they went away in the boat to a lonely place by themselves» (6,32)[22]. Mark utilises a chiastic structure to refer to the destination as well as to stress the private nature of their withdrawal[23].

6,31: κατ᾽ ἰδίαν   εἰς ἔρημον τόπον
6,32: εἰς ἔρημον τόπον   κατ᾽ ἰδίαν

The departure by boat recalls the other boat journeys of Jesus (4,35-41; 5,1-2.18.21) and prepares for the contrastive movement of the people on foot (6,33). The verse has also a very clear parallel in 1,35.

1, 35: καὶ ἀπῆλθεν   εἰς ἔρημον τόπον
6,32: καὶ ἀπῆλθον ἐν τῷ πλοίῳ εἰς ἔρημον τόπον

---

[21] Ora et labora, the golden rule of monasticism and for that matter true Christian living, may find its origin in these lines of the scripture!

[22] Matthew speaks of Jesus withdrawing (ἀνεχώρησεν) from there in a boat to a lonely place apart (14,13). There is no mention of the Twelve going with him. But they reappear in the following story of the feeding of the five thousand (14,15). Luke on the other hand reports that Jesus took the disciples and withdrew (ὑπεχώρησεν) apart to a city called Bethsaida. So their destination is not a lonely place but a city and there is no mention of a journey by boat.

[23] F. Neirynck considers the phrase εἰς ἔρημον τόπον κατ᾽ ἰδίαν as an example of Markan duality. Cf. F. NEIRYNCK, *Duality in Mark*, 95, 115, 119. For R.M. Fowler the repetition of it in v. 32 marks the end of the first Markan insertion in 6,30f. Cf. R.M. FOWLER, *Loaves and Fishes*, 78. U. Mauser finds in the phrase ἔρημον τόπον a typology of God's people gathered in the wilderness as in olden times. Cf. U. MAUSER, *Christ in the Wilderness*, 104-105. But it has to be noted that the reference here is to ἔρημος τόπος, a lonely place, a deserted place surrounded by «farms and villages» (6,36) as distinct from the ἐρημία, which is wilderness. So the typology is faulty.

The parallelism is evident not only in the vocabulary but also in the circumstances surrounding both episodes. Jesus' retreat to a lonely place takes place after a busy day of great works (1,21-34); the Twelve are also invited to rest after their exacting ministry. Just as Simon and those who are with him pursue Jesus (1,36), so also the crowd follow Jesus and the Twelve. It is expressly stated in 1,35 that Jesus went out to a lonely place, «and there he prayed». In 6,31 the purpose of going to a lonely place is to «rest a while». It can only be guessed from the parallelism that it would have been quite possible that they would spend some time in prayer. The parallelism between 1,35 and 6,31 serves to view the beginning of the ministry of Jesus and that of Twelve as linked together in close relationship[24].

The mention of the destination in 6,32 also looks forward to the following story as it already situates what is going to happen in the ἔρημος τόπος (6,35). This way, along with what transpires in 6,33-34, Mark effects a smooth transition from the return of the Twelve to the episode of the feeding of the five thousand.

2.4 *Movement of the Crowd*

Many people see Jesus and the apostles going and they run there on foot ahead of them (6,33)[25]. Their running on foot contrasts with Jesus' and the apostles' travelling by boat. It is possible to imagine that more people join the group while they are running as explained by Mark: they come «from all the towns»[26]. προῆλθον completes the setting by

---

[24] Cf. K. STOCK, *Boten*, 104.

[25] The phrases καὶ εἶδον αὐτοὺς ὑπάγοντας καὶ ἐπέγνωσαν πολλοί have created some difficulty. The difficulty concerns mainly in understanding the meaning of the phrase καὶ ἐπέγνωσαν πολλοί and its relationship to what precedes it. Some variant readings have the verb ἐγνώσαν (B*, D, *f*¹). It is perhaps best to take the verb ἐπέγνωσαν here to mean in the sense of «to take note of, to notice» (cf. Mark 2,8; 5,30). This way the verb will have a redundant effect with εἶδον. So the phrase would read, «Many saw them going, and took note of it». Cf. S. LÉGASSE, *Marc*, 393, n.15. Such a reading would mean that the seeing of the many (crowd) expressed by the verb εἶδον remains on a level that differs greatly from Jesus' own seeing. Matthew's account speaks of the crowds hearing about (ἀκούσαντες) Jesus' withdrawing to a lonely place apart (Matt 14,13b). He also speaks of the crowds following (ἠκολούθησαν) him «on foot from the towns». Luke on the other hand speaks of the crowds learning (γνόντες) about Jesus' and the apostles' withdrawing to the city of Bethsaida, and they follow (ἠκολούθησαν) him (9, 11).

[26] W. Egger speculates that in the narrative of 6,31-33 two groups of people are involved. The first group gathers around Jesus already at 6,31b. They see both Jesus

having the crowd on hand when Jesus disembarks[27]. The four verbs (εἶδον, ἐπέγνωσαν, συνέδραμον, προῆλθον) crowded together in v. 33 highlight on the one hand the striving of the crowd to flock to Jesus and on the other their great need which only Jesus can discern and satisfy.

3. Jesus' Seeing the Crowd

In Mark's presentation of 6,32 expectation was already raised by giving information on Jesus' and the apostles' going away (ἀπῆλθον) in the boat. The ἐξελθών[28] of 6,34 responds to that expectation and refers to Jesus' coming out of the boat on to the shore. From the plural of ἀπῆλθον the focus narrows down to the singular of ἐξελθών bringing Jesus to the centre of the narrative. The aorist participle at the same time prepares for the all important verb εἶδεν. In keeping with his style Mark pictures Jesus on the move and the movement can be understood

---

and the Twelve going away in a boat (καὶ εἶδον αὐτοὺς ὑπάγοντας). Two more phrases from 6,33 are also ascribed to them: καὶ πεζῇ - προῆλθον αὐτούς. The rest of the verse καὶ ἐπέγνωσαν πολλοί - ἀπὸ πασῶν τῶν πόλεων συνέδραμον ἐκεῖ refers to the second group. W. Egger also cites 6,54f. (ἐπιγνόντες αὐτὸν περιέδραμον ὅλην τὴν χώραν ἐκείνην) as a parallel to prove the existence of the second group. However, it is clear that breaking down each verse and ascribing it to different traditions (so also E. LOHMEYER, *Markus*, 124) does injustice to the author and his intention of writing the narrative. It is quite logical to think that the πολλοί of 6,33 does refer to the πολλοί of 6,32 (those who were coming and going and those who saw them going and knew them are the same).

[27] R.A. GUELICH, *Mark*, 340. How the crowd could overtake Jesus and the Twelve who travelled by boat has puzzled many. Even the textual variants show their uneasiness at this and try to resolve it; D and it, for instance have: ἐκεῖ καὶ συνῆλθον αὐτοῦ; L has: ἐκεῖ καὶ προσῆλθον αὐτούς (Δ Θ αὐτοῖς) etc. Matthew follows the Markan account (14,13a). Luke situates the destination at Bethsaida (9,10). The common opinion is that the destination was not on the east coast of the sea but along the west coast. So the journey by boat must have been between the coves along the western shores of the sea between Tiberias and Bethsaida. In that case it is possible to think of an enthusiastic crowd managing to reach the destination before the boat. Cf. B. BAGATTI, «Dove avvenne», 293-298; J. GNILKA, *Markus* I, 259; R.A. GUELICH, *Mark*, 340; S. LÉGASSE, *Marc*, 393; R. PESCH, *Markusevangelium* I, 349.

[28] P.J. Achtemeier is of the opinion that ἐξελθών here is directly connected to 5,43 and means his coming out of the house of Jairus. This way Jesus emerges from the house, sees the crowd milling about and feeds them, as he had commanded the little girl to be fed (5,43). Cf. P.J. ACHTEMEIER, «Miracle Catenae», 281; Cf. also R. PESCH, *Markusevangelium* I, 346-347. But Mark uses the verb even before in 5,1-2. He also employs it in 6,54. So it may have more to do with his style than being a hint that he returns to the source that continues the narrative from 5,43.

to come to a halt when he next speaks of Jesus' decisive seeing in the aorist indicative (εἶδεν).

3.1 The Crowd as Object of Jesus' Seeing

So far in the pericope Mark has employed the generic term πολλοί to refer to those who were «coming and going» (6,31) and those who saw Jesus and the apostles going away in the boat and ran there on foot (6,32). Now for the first time in the present pericope Mark refers to these people as the crowd (ὄχλον) and qualifies it as a «great crowd» (πολὺν ὄχλον).

3.1.1 Reference to the Crowd in the Gospel

Right from Jesus' ministry in the synagogue at Capernaum (1,21f.) Mark implies the presence of many people wherever Jesus goes (1,22.27.32.34; 2,2.3 etc.). Reference to them is made in a variety of ways:

i) Mark has often recourse to the third plural verbs (1,22.27.32.45; also 6,54.55) to imply their presence.

ii) Different forms of the adjective πολύς indicate the innumerable number of people who gather about Jesus (1,34; 2,2; 3,10; 6,2.31.33; also 9,26; 10,31.48; 11,8; 12,25; 13,6; 15,41). Another adjective that is used to refer to the people in general terms is πᾶς (πάντες: 1,37; also 6,42; 7,14; πάντων: 2,12; πάντας: 1,32; 2,12; 5,40; also 6,39).

iii) The people are also referred to by the noun πλῆθος (3,7.8). It seems to be a synonym of the ὄχλος in 3,9.

iv) λαός which is a Lukan favourite is employed by Mark twice: in 7,6 which is a citation from Isa 29,13 (LXX) in the sense of the «people of Israel»; in 14,2 the chief priests and scribes refer to the people as λαός, and probably it connotes the people of God as in LXX[29].

v) The crowd is referred to by the noun ὄχλος 38 times in the Gospel of Mark (Matt 50, Luke 40, John 20, Acts 22, Rev 3, rest of NT 0). The word is used in the Gospel to denote a crowd of people[30]. However, ὄχλος is not used to identify any particular group of people. It is also

---

[29] V. KÜSTER, Jesus und das Volk, 51, 56.

[30] But in 14,43 ὄχλος does not mean the usual sense of the word but rather refers to a detachment of the temple guard (cf. 14,47: «τὸν δοῦλον τοῦ ἀρχιερέως»). Cf. B. CITRON, «The Multitude», 413; V. KÜSTER, Jesus und das Volk, 50.

not clear if it refers always to the same people[31]. The Gospel itself hints that tax collectors and sinners (τελῶναι καὶ ἁμαρτωλοί: 2,15) belong to the group. Women (γυναῖκες: 15, 40f.) and children (παῖδες: 9,36f.) also formed part of the group[32].

So the noun ὄχλος which by far is the most prominent name for the crowd, dwarfs all other nouns and references used to speak of the throng of people. The term «denotes for the most part the anonymous background to Jesus' ministry»[33].

3.1.2 Characterisation of the Crowd

As noted above, though the Evangelist in various ways notes the presence of a throng of people wherever Jesus goes, a mention of the crowd by the term ὄχλος is done for the first time in the Gospel at 2,4. Ever since they are mentioned several times till 6,34. The characterisation of the crowd up until this point in the Gospel (6,34) is illuminating.

i) The crowd gather about Jesus. What is said mainly about them is that they flock to him. They gather about Jesus by the sea side (2,13; 4,1), they come together at his home (3,20.32), they congregate round Jesus on crossing the sea by boat (5,21, cf. also for further gatherings 8,1; 9,14.15.17.25; 10,1).

ii) At times their crowding together is suffocating. In order to get to Jesus those who are carrying the paralytic have to remove the roof above him (2,4). Jesus himself takes precautions not to be crushed by the thronging of the crowd (3,9). The disciples once call Jesus' attention to the crowd pressing around him (5,31).

---

[31] During Jesus' trial and passion the ὄχλος appear three times (15,8.11.15). The attitude of the ὄχλος in these instances is diametrically opposed to what is presented in the course of the Gospel. The chief priests and the scribes and the elders (11,27) who were afraid of the people (11,32; 12,12) seem to have won them over. Now they are able to stir them up (ἀνέσεισαν: 15,11; cf. also Luke 23,5). Such a change of attitude from the part of the crowd makes one inclined to question if not in these instances the reference is to another group of people hostile to Jesus. However commentators in general believe that it is the same group of people. For the contrary view see P.S. MINEAR, «Audience Criticism», 87.

[32] V. KÜSTER, *Jesus und das Volk*, 63. It is not very evident whether in 12,41 the rich people also belong to ὄχλος. The rich (πλούσιοι) are here clearly contrasted with the poor widow (12,42f.). All the same it seems that ὄχλος is used here to refer to both the rich and the poor alike (Against V. Küster. Cf. V. KÜSTER, *Jesus und das Volk*, 63-64).

[33] R. MEYER, «ὄχλος», 586.

iii) The crowd transmit to Jesus the message of the arrival of his family (3,32).

iv) Mark also refers to the crowd following Jesus (5,24; also 10,46).

v) Individual supplicants are said to emerge from the crowd (5,27.30; also 9,17).

The picture that is delineated of the crowd is of a huge number of people milling about Jesus wherever he goes. It is a disorderly and distraught group that attracts the attention and care of Jesus. Unlike the scribes and the religious leaders, they are a people of faith and of unadulterated enthusiasm, ready to be instructed, willing to follow Jesus who has not only words of wisdom, but has the power to liberate them from their infirmities. It is this kind of crowd that Jesus sees as he lands with his disciples on the sea-shore in pursuit of some rest.

3.1.3 Jesus' Interactions with the Crowd Prior to his Seeing them

The first time the ὄχλος is referred to by name is in the context of a notable healing performed by Jesus (2,4). The large crowd are described as blocking access to Jesus, so much so that the four men who carry the paralytic have to let him in through an opening on the roof (2,4). Their extraordinary initiative is described as faith (2,5). However, the scribes grab the attention of Jesus with their hostile and critical attitude. With them comes controversy and polemic. But Jesus uses the occasion to demonstrate his authority and power. The amazing feat performed by Jesus produces in the crowd great awe and they glorify God (2,12). «The pericope ends, then, with a recognition of his power as God-given»[34]. The lack of faith of the scribes is only matched by the abundant faith of the suppliants and the crowd[35].

The crowd are reported to be coming together several times and the most common response of Jesus to their coming together is to teach them (2,13; 4,1; cf. also 6,34; 10,1). His presence draws the crowd to him, and Jesus discerns their primary need and teaches them. They present themselves as fertile soil ready to be instructed. Responding to that need, as we shall see, is the basic priority of Jesus' ministry. They hear from Jesus words that they long to hear; they view him as someone who would not betray their trust like their religious leaders;

---

[34] R.H. GUNDRY, *Mark*,115.

[35] It is difficult to imagine that the πάντας in 2,12 includes the scribes too as Gundry thinks. Cf. R.H. GUNDRY, *Mark*,115. It is very unlikely that they would be converted by the time Jesus performs the miracle!

they see him so like themselves, yet so different in his relationship to God. It may be noted that in these instances the Evangelist usually refers merely to the fact of Jesus teaching them without providing the content of the teaching of Jesus.

The presence of a large crowd is again described in 3,9. Here, Jesus' great works of healing (3,10) has attracted many people. The crowd suspect in Jesus' works God's hand at work. They in their turn want to be healed of their infirmities. So they press upon him to touch him (3,10).

In 3,20 information is given regarding the gathering of the crowd. The narrative without specifying what transpires there reports that as a result they (Jesus and the disciples)[36] could not even eat. The implication is that both Jesus and the newly formed community of disciples were busy tending to the needs of the crowd. It must have included both healing and exorcism (3,22) as well as teaching as the ensuing «sandwiched story»[37] tells (3,22-30). However, their sitting about him proves again a hindrance for the family of Jesus to approach him. But the crowd act as the intermediaries that pass the message to Jesus that his family is asking for him outside (3,32). Jesus on hearing that looks around (περιβλεψάμενος) on those who sat about him and pronounces one of the most thought-provoking comments uttered by him, «Whoever does the will of God is my brother, and sister, and mother» (3,35). «The clear implication is that this crowd is made up of such obedient doers and that they belong to Jesus' family»[38]. In other words what constitutes this ὄχλος is obedience to God's will. Interestingly neither Jesus' physical family members nor his disciples earn such words of appreciation from Jesus[39].

A large crowd flock to Jesus on his return from Decapolis (5,21). Without reporting what takes place there, the narrative then talks of the visit of Jairus, the president of a synagogue (5,22). While Jesus makes the journey to Jairus' house in response to his request to restore his daughter, the crowd follow him, throng about him, and press around

---

[36] The «they» (αὐτούς) is odd there, because the disciples play no further role in the story. Besides it conflicts with «he went into a house». J. Marcus opines that Mark included the disciples in order to tie this story with the previous one by sustaining the image of the Twelve as a group chosen «in order that they might be with him». Cf. J. MARCUS, *Mark*, 278-279.

[37] J. MARCUS, *Mark*, 278.

[38] J. MARCUS, *Mark*, 286.

[39] P.S. MINEAR, «Audience Criticism», 82.

him (5,24.31). But that journey occasions the performance of another miracle. A supplicant emerges from the crowd (5,27) and with her sheer faith in Jesus obtains healing from her bleeding.

Thus the picture of Jesus' interaction with the crowd before his decisive seeing at 6,34 is very positive[40]. The crowd in reality provide the background to Jesus' ministry. On Jesus' part they pose no nuisance, his approach to them is characterised by warmth and understanding. There is a progression in Jesus' attitude towards them. At first they are mere recipients of his ministry, but their enthusiastic response and obedience to God's will induces him to count them worthy of being called his family.

It is possible to note also a progression in the crowd's attitude towards Jesus. They at first witness the mighty works performed by Jesus with authority; faith is born in the crowd; they recognise that God's hand is at work in him and in response they glorify God (2,12). The crowd also gather around him gladly, to listen to his teaching (2,13; 3,20.22; 4,1) and to obtain healing (3,9). They thus earn high esteem from Jesus as meriting to be called his true family (3,35). Individual supplicants begin to emerge from the crowd, and obtain their heart's desire with faith in Jesus. Thus «they constituted no heterogeneous mass of bystanders or drifters but a continuing audience of committed believers»[41]. But 6,34 contains another dimension to the status of the crowd. Jesus in his seeing is able to detect it and respond accordingly. We shall develop this in the course of our analysis of Jesus' seeing.

3.2 Characteristics of Jesus' Seeing

As Jesus comes ashore he sees (εἶδεν) a great crowd. None of Jesus' previous interaction with the crowd begins with his seeing. At 3,34 it is said that Jesus looking around those who sat about him uttered a word of appreciation. The verb used is the participle περιβλεψάμενος. Though it is used exclusively for Jesus in the Gospel,[42] the verb does not carry the meaning of an aorist finite εἶδεν. 6,34 is the first and the only time

---

[40] Apart from the above references there is one instance where mention is made regarding Jesus taking leave of the crowd (4,36; cf. also 6,45). But it provides only the information that Jesus concluded the day's activity of teaching in the evening, left the crowd and went over to the other side of the sea.

[41] P.S. MINEAR, «Audience Criticism», 87.

[42] See above p. 29.34-35.

that the crowd become the object of Jesus' seeing expressed by the verb εἶδεν. For that reason there is something unique to his seeing here.

The presence of the crowd in this «lonely place» is wholly unexpected for Jesus and his weary disciples. The great crowd which besiege the place they land, in reality act as an obstacle to be overcome in order to realise what they had set out to do (6,32). The expected reaction would be one that is aimed at getting rid of the nuisance posed. Instead no such attempt is made; the Evangelist reports that Jesus sees them. As in the case of the seeing of Jesus' first disciples, his seeing is not casual[43]. It is a seeing that is able to look beyond one's own interests and discern the needs of the others. In other words his seeing is other-centred.

According to the Jewish Philosopher Martin Buber, the most decisive step in the life of Moses was the going out to his people and *seeing* them (Exod 2,11)[44]. Moses' seeing results in a first hand knowledge of the condition of his people which impels him to act in defence of his people. Jesus' seeing the crowd too is active and quite decisive in that their thronging to him even in the unexpected place gives him an insight into their condition.

In so far as the crowd outmanoeuvre Jesus and the disciples the initiative rests with them. But once on the shore Jesus seizes the initiative which begins with his seeing. For the rest of the narrative the crowd are only the passive recipients of the activity of Jesus.

One of the most important features of Jesus' seeing the crowd is that it forms a sequence with the seeing of Andrew, Peter, James, John and Levi. The importance of such a linkage is too strong to be neglected[45]. It is our position that there exists a connection, denoted by the verb

---

[43] We have noted earlier that when referring to a casual seeing of Jesus, or seeing that is a preparation for the main action the evangelist usually uses the aorist participle ἰδών but never the aorist indicative.

[44] M. BUBER, *Moses*, 52: «Die Erzählung davon, wie Mose zu seinen Brüdern ausging (Exodus 2,11-15), der Anfang der eigentlichen Lebensgeschichte, ist in echt biblischer Komposition auf einem dreimal wiederkehrenden "er sah" und auf einem zweimal, reimhaft wiederkehrenden "seine Brüder" aufgebaut [...]». TM uses the verb ראה to express Moses' seeing (מֹשֶׁה וַיֵּצֵא אֶל־אֶחָיו וַיַּרְא בְּסִבְלֹתָם). וַיַּרְא ב means «and he saw into» and indicates Moses' firsthand exposure to the oppression. Cf. J.I. DURHAM, *Exodus*, 19. LXX which usually translates וַיַּרְא with εἶδεν, uses here a verb (κατανοήσας) which means more to observe carefully, consider, contemplate etc.

[45] B. CITRON, «The Multitude», 415: «The "seeing of the multitude" forms the sequence to the "seeing" of Peter and Andrew, James and John at the Lake of Galilee [...]».

εἶδεν, not only with Jesus' seeing of the disciples but also with his seeing of the heavens torn apart.

4. Effect of Jesus' Seeing: Compassion

Jesus' seeing the crowd at that unexpected place leaves profound effects on him. Mark has a neat phrase, ἐσπλαγχνίσθη ἐπ' αὐτούς which describes the crowd as the object of Jesus' strong emotion denoted by the verb σπλαγχνίζεσθαι.

4.1 The Meaning of the Verb σπλαγχνίζεσθαι

In Greek usage the verb derives its meaning from the noun σπλάγχνα which means the «inner parts» of a sacrificial victim. The reference is to the noble parts, i.e., the heart, liver, lungs, and kidneys which are separated in the sacrifice and consumed by the participants at the beginning of the sacrificial meal. So the verb σπλαγχνίζεσθαι means «to eat the inner parts» at the sacrificial meal. In the Bible, the inner parts or «the entrails» stand for whatever is deepest and most intimate (Prov 26,22). The emotions are considered to be located in the entrails since they are most intimate and hidden. There are also hints in Biblical usage which suggest that σπλάγχνα might be regarded as the seat of the positive stirring of pity (Prov 12,10; Wis 10,5). The verb therefore means to be moved with pity, to have compassion. This becomes the predominant meaning in the NT[46].

The Latin *misericordia* perhaps expresses accurately the meaning of the verb σπλαγχνίζεσθαι. *Misericordia* is composed of two roots: *misereor* and *cor*. It is a sentiment of pity and compassion born in the heart of someone from the consideration of the miserable human condition. *Misericordia* is always aimed at the other. It is not only a human sentiment, but also represents God's behaviour towards human beings. For «the Lord is merciful and gracious, slow to anger and abounding in steadfast love» (Ps 103,8).

The verb σπλαγχνίζεσθαι occurs 4 times in Mark (Matt 5, Luke 3, rest of NT 0). In three instances Jesus is the subject of the verb (1,41;

---

[46] Cf. H. KÖSTER, «σπλαγχνίζομαι», 548-551; LSJ, 1628; C. SPICQ, «σπλαγχνίζο-μαι», 273-275. It is good to note that the neither the verb nor the noun are all too common in the LXX. The verb occurs only twice (Prov 17,5 and 2Macc 6,8). In neither case is there a Hebrew original. In the 15 occurrences of the noun, Prov 12,10 has רַחֲמִים, Prov 26,22 has בֶּטֶן and in other cases there is either the Hebrew equivalent missing or the Greek is the original.

6,34; 8,2). The other occurrence is a prayer, an imperative addressed to Jesus by the father of the boy with the unclean spirit (9,22). Where the crowd are the object of the verb (6,34; 8,2) the ensuing stories deal with the multiplication of bread. In the other two instances the verb (1,41; 9,22) occurs in healings. The verb thus denotes Jesus' inner feeling of pity for the condition of the recipients of his ministry, making him to want to help them.

Even in the other Synoptic Gospels except for the three uses in the parables (Matt 18,27; Luke 10,33; 15,20) the verb is always attributed to Jesus. It expresses Jesus' feeling for the crowd (Matt 9,36; 14,14; 15,32) the blind men (Matt 2,34), and the widow who lost her son (Luke 7,13).

4.2 Meaning of the Verb σπλαγχνίζεσθαι in the Parables

Jesus prefers to express himself by similes and parables. His emotions, feelings and dispositions come across in a powerful way through this established language of symbols. Three Synoptic parables in an impressive manner illustrate the sentiment of compassion. In the parables the verb σπλαγχνίζεσθαι denotes a specific attitude on the part of men. But in two of the parables this human attitude is ultimately to be understood as representing divine disposition.

4.2.1 The Parable of the Unforgiving Servant

In answer to the prayer of the wicked servant the Lord of that servant is moved with compassion (σπλαγχνισθείς), releases him (ἀπέλυσεν) and forgives him (ἀφῆκεν) the debt (Matt 18,27)[47]. The aspect of forgiveness is brought to the fore since the parable, as presented by Matthew, is told in answer to Peter's question, «Lord, how often shall my brother sin against me, and I forgive him? As many as seven times?» (18,21). However on analysing the motif for the forgiveness of the debt of the servant, it becomes clear that it is intrinsically connected to the Lord's feeling of compassion. The feeling of compassion – sorrow at the condition of the servant – translates itself into forgiveness. So the parable suggests that compassion involves forgiveness. But forgiveness is also brought about by mercy as is made evident by the Lord in the parable when he upbraids the servant for not

---

[47] According to BDF § 176,1 the verb «probably only appears to take the gen. of the person pitied [...] since ὁ κύριος τοῦ δούλου ἐκείνου [...] is to be taken together».

showing mercy (οὐκ ἔδει καὶ σὲ ἐλεῆσαι) just as he received mercy (ὡς κἀγὼ σὲ ἠλέησα:18,33)[48]. The Lord's sentiment of compassion involves also showing mercy, kindness and restraint to the servant whom the Lord has had the right to punish.

The parable exhibits Matthew's desire to make the king represent Jesus as Lord. The man who is king is designated as ὁ κύριος. This appellation echoes the designation of Jesus as Lord in the narrative leading up to the parable (18,21) and, indeed throughout the Gospel[49]. Besides, the verb προσεκύνει which expresses the action of falling on the knees and imploring (18,26) in the case of the first servant contrasts with the verb παρεκάλει (18,29) referring to the fellow servant doing the same action. προσκύνειν means more *to (fall down and) worship*[50] than to implore. Elsewhere in the Gospel of Matthew this verb is used only in reference to Jesus. It describes various characters like, the Magi (2,11), a leper (8,2), the ruler (9,18), the Canaanite woman (15,28), and the disciples (14,33; 28,9.17) worshipping Jesus. The Lord's feeling is to be understood as manifesting Jesus' own disposition. 18,35 indicates that Matthew also has in mind the heavenly Father: «So also my heavenly Father will do to every one of you, if you do not forgive your brother from your heart».

4.2.2 The Parable of the Lost Son

The strongest expression of the human emotion of compassion is described by Luke in the parable of the lost son. In fact, it is the father, and not the returning son, who is the central figure in the parable. The focus is on his compassion and love. It is for that reason that J. Jeremias would like to call the parable as the «parable of the Father's love»[51].

The verb ἐσπλαγχνίσθη gives insight into the character of the father. It reflects the compassionate heart, a compassion which precedes the son's confession[52]. The subsequent behaviour of the father expresses in vivid detail how the father's compassion is translated into action,

---

[48] Matthew makes it abundantly clear elsewhere in the Gospel too that only the merciful shall receive mercy (5,7). Plea for mercy is a constant refrain on the lips of those who approach Jesus for favour. Cf. Matt 9,27: two blind men; 15,22: The Canaanite woman; 17,15: a man; 20,30.31: two blind men of Jericho.

[49] R.H. GUNDRY, *Matthew*, 373.

[50] BAGD, 716.

[51] J. JEREMIAS, *The Parables*, 128.

[52] W. FORBES, *The God of Old*, 138

thereby revealing the nature of his compassion. The father runs, something unusual and undignified for an aged oriental,[53] embraces the son, kisses him, instructs to dress him up well and orders a grand feast. The father's heart goes out to the son, he forgives him, suffocates him with love, takes concrete steps to remedy the son's situation, and rejoices.

The expressions used like ἐνώπιόν σου, ἐσπλαγχνίσθη, ἐντολή are meant to reveal that in his love and compassion the father is an image of God[54]. In the atypical actions of the father, we encounter the extraordinary nature of God's pardoning love and acceptance[55]. Jesus mirrors the character and actions of God. So we would expect that the images used of God would therefore be applicable to Jesus himself. The father's compassion could be understood as reflecting Jesus' own compassion for the crowd.

A comparison between Luke 15,20, which narrates the father's character and feeling and Mark 6,34 which expresses Jesus' sentiment for the crowd, would establish that both narratives have very important parallels:

i) The perspective in the parable shifts from that of the son to that of the father: the going (πορεύσομαι) of v. 18 in the soliloquy of the son becomes a coming (ἦλθεν) in v. 20. The same change of perspective is evident in the Markan narrative. The focus changes from the actions of the crowd (εἶδον, ἐπέγνωσαν, συνέδραμον, προῆλθον) to the action of Jesus (ἐξελθών).

ii) Both narratives refer to some kind of movement, expressed by a participle, in preparation for the main action: in the parable it is the movement of the son that is highlighted (ἀπέχοντος); in the Markan narrative the focus is on Jesus' movement (ἐξελθών).

iii) Both narratives emphasise the point that the initiative is seized by the father and Jesus.

iv) The main action in both narratives is one of seeing and the verb that expresses it is the aorist εἶδεν.

v) The sentiment that is aroused by the seeing in both cases is described by the verb ἐσπλαγχνίσθη.

vi) The feeling of compassion moves both the father and Jesus to act promptly and decisively in favour of the objects of compassion.

---

[53] J. JEREMIAS, *The Parables*, 130; E. SCHWEIZER, *Lukas*, 164.

[54] J. JEREMIAS, *The Parables*, 128.

[55] W. FORBES, *The God of Old*, 254.

vii) The son in the parable and the crowd in the Markan narrative have no right to the compassion of the father or that of Jesus. They, as passive recipients, receive it as a gracious gift.

The parallelism reveals that Jesus' compassion for the crowd can be compared to the father's compassion for the son. It reflects Jesus' goodness, his grace, his boundless mercy (underlined by his clarion call to conversion: 1,15), his promptness and his abiding love.

4.2.3 The Parable of the Good Samaritan

In the illustrative parable of the good Samaritan, σπλαγχνίζεσθαι is shown to be the basic and decisive attitude in human and hence in Christian acts[56]. The sight of the stricken man makes feelings of compassion to well up in the foreign Samaritan (10,33). The verb σπλαγχνίζεσθαι, is «the fulcrum upon which the story turns»[57]. Compassion moves the Samaritan to identify with him, and act for his benefit. The term σπλαγχνίζεσθαι signifies exactly the same as the «love» described in 10,27: 'Αγαπήσεις κύριον τὸν θεόν σου [...] καὶ τὸν πλησίον σου ὡς σεαυτόν. But it is more. The lawyer, in answering Jesus' question on who proves to be the real neighbour, admits that it is the Samaritan and points to his action as showing mercy (10,37). Therefore the Samaritan's compassion also implies mercy.

4.3 *Markan Portrayal of Jesus' Compassion*

The parables help to determine the nature of the sentiment of compasssion. Matthew makes clear that compassion involves forgiveness, showing mercy, kindness and restraint. Luke has a better knack for detailing actions that express positive emotions. He illustrates that compassion implies goodness, grace, boundless mercy, promptitude and whole-hearted and unconditional love. Markan portrayal of Jesus' compassion for the crowd can be understood as taking on these same features. It describes and characterises the divine nature of Jesus' acts.

We may emphasise above all that it is Jesus' seeing that evokes compassion for the crowd. In analysing the first instance of Jesus'

---

[56] H. KÖSTER, «σπλαγχνίζομαι», 553-554. In fact, Luke 10,33 is the only instance where the verb is clearly used of men.

[57] J. NOLLAND, *Luke 9: 21-18: 34*, 594. Basing on word count as well as use of verbs, M.J.J. Menken establishes that σπλαγχνίζεσθαι is the central word in the narrative. Cf. M.J.J. MENKEN, «The Position», 111.

seeing expressed by the verb εἶδεν we have noted that at his seeing the heavens being torn apart and the Spirit descending upon him, Jesus is fully conscious of his relationship to God as well as to humanity. It is that consciousness of his relationship to humanity that is at the back of his compassion for the crowd when he sees them, when he sees their precarious condition. The same eyes that saw the events at baptism see the crowd and the result is that Jesus is filled with compassion.

It is noteworthy that in 6 of the 12 occurrences of the verb σπλαγχνίζεσθαι in the Synoptics what produces compassion in the persons is their seeing (Matt 9,36; 14,14; Mark 6,34; Luke 7,13; 10,33; 15,20). In three instances the participle ἰδών is used to refer to that seeing (Matt 9,36; Luke 7,13; 10,33). The aorist εἶδεν is used by Mark 6,34, the Matthean parallel (14,14), and Luke 15,20.

Jesus' seeing the crowd is what produces compassion in him (6,34). Among the five occurrences of the verb εἶδεν in Mark's Gospel, this is the only instance where the evangelist speaks of the inner feelings of Jesus caused by his decisive seeing[58]. Mark has one more instance where he expressly refers to the emotions of Jesus resulting from his interaction with someone (10,21).

10,21: ὁ δὲ Ἰησοῦς ἐμβλέψας αὐτῷ ἠγάπησεν αὐτόν
6,34: καὶ ἐξελθὼν εἶδεν πολὺν ὄχλον καὶ ἐσπλαγχνίσθη ἐπ' αὐτούς

The parallelism here is obvious. Jesus is the subject in both cases and a verb of seeing in each instance is followed by a verb that reveals the inner feelings of Jesus for the persons whom he sees. The difference is that in the first case it is merely a looking (ἐμβλέψας) expressed by a participle which is only a preparation for his loving him. In the latter case however, the aorist indicative εἶδεν expresses Jesus' decisive action of seeing. The focus here is mainly on his seeing. The feelings of compassion that his seeing evokes in him is pictured as more intense

---

[58] It is pointless to ask how did the Evangelist or the disciples know the feelings of Jesus. It may be that Jesus gave vent to his feeling of compassion in direct speech as in 8,2 «I have compassion on the crowd, because they have been with me now three days, and have nothing to eat [...]». In that case the statement in 6,34 may be an indirect exclamation of the feelings of Jesus. The direct speech may sound, «I have compassion on the crowd, because they are like sheep without a shepherd».

since it points to an enduring concern for the crowd on account of their present situation[59].

5. The Reason for Jesus' Compassion

The Gospels are consistent in providing in each instance the reason for Jesus' feeling of compassion. In Matthew's Gospel once Jesus' pity is evoked by the condition of the two blind men (20,34). Jesus' feeling for them moves him to come to their aid. As a result they receive their sight. Three times the crowd (ὄχλος) becomes the object of Jesus' compassion: 9,36; 14,14//Mark 6,34; 15,32//Mark 8,2. The reason for being moved with compassion in the first instance (9,36) is the plight of the crowd, «because they were harassed and helpless, like sheep without a shepherd». In the second instance (14,14) which parallels Mark 6,34 the reason as can be inferred from Jesus' subsequent activity of healing is that there were many in the crowd that needed healing. The third instance (15,32) too parallels Mark 8,2. Here the compassion of Jesus is aroused from the need he identifies in the crowd, they are hungry.

In the Markan account Jesus' compassion is said to be growing out of his concern for the crowd as «sheep without a shepherd» (ὅτι ἦσαν ὡς πρόβατα μὴ ἔχοντα ποιμένα). As noted above Matthew too uses this image to explain the reason for Jesus' compassion for the crowd. The plight of the crowd deeply moves Jesus. They are compared to a sheep and they do not have a shepherd, a true leader. The image of «sheep without a shepherd» is familiar in the Bible. In the following investigation we shall look at the OT understanding of the metaphor and examine its Synoptic usage.

5.1 *The OT Background to the Metaphor of the Sheep without a Shepherd*

Throughout the biblical period tending flocks was one of the main occupations of the people[60]. The herding of the sheep was considered a

---

[59] Another possible example is Mark 7,34. In the story of the healing of the deaf and dumb man Mark says that looking up (ἀναβλέψας) to heaven, Jesus sighed (ἐστέναξεν). Here the reference is to looking as distinct from seeing. Jesus' sighing does not seem to be a means of exorcism. It is an expression of emotion, just as in 8,12. We have no clear clues to Jesus' emotions there. In 8,12 one may suspect hints of frustration.

responsible job. The picturesque image of the shepherd leading a flock of sheep provided the inspiration to apply the «shepherd-sheep» image to both those who had leadership roles in the community and the community of Israel itself. This same imagery also provides the basis for the negative metaphor of «the sheep without a shepherd».

5.1.1 Occurrences of the Metaphor

There are four occurrences of the metaphor in the OT that correspond to the Markan rendering: Num 27,17; 1Kgs 22,17; 2Chr 18,16; Zech 10,2 (for the same idea cf. also, Isa 13,14; Ezek 34,5.6.8)[61]. Only in Num 27,17 the metaphor is employed in a positive way, i.e., steps are taken to avoid the situation of the sheep having no shepherd. The story of the king of Israel and the prophecy of Micaiah (1Kgs 22,17 // 2Chr 18,16) only serves to emphasise that without the leader the people will be scattered. Zech 10,2 reflects the actual situation of the people of Israel as sheep without a shepherd.

In Num 27,17 Moses prays God that someone replace him as leader of the community: «Let the Lord, the God of the spirits of all flesh, appoint a man over the congregation, who shall go out before them and come in before them, who shall lead them out and bring them in; that the congregation of the Lord may not be like sheep without a shepherd» (οὐκ ἔσται ἡ συναγωγὴ κυρίου ὡσεὶ πρόβατα οἷς οὐκ ἔστιν ποιμήν)[62]. The prayer outlines the role of the shepherd but at the same time gives insight into the role Moses himself played in Israel.

«Who shall go out before them and come in before them» (וַאֲשֶׁר יוֹצִיאֵם וַאֲשֶׁר יְבִיאֵם) is probably technical terminology from the military sphere (cf. Josh 14,11; 1Sam 18,13-16; 2Sam 5,2; 1Kgs 3,7

---

[60] In fact the people of Israel are depicted as being of shepherd origins. The Patriarchs themselves are said to have been shepherds (Abraham - Gen 13,2; Isaac - Gen 26,14; Jacob - Gen 30,29-30; 31,38-40; Rachel - 29,9: רֹעָה; Joseph - Gen 37,2). Moses was said to be keeping the flock of his father-in-law, Jethro (Exod 3,1). David was also keeping the sheep before he was anointed king (1Sam 16,11; 17,34).

[61] Strictly speaking there is one more instance of the image, employed in the book of Judith (11,19). Here the Babylonian Holofernes whom Judith tricks is compared in a flattering way to a would be leader of sheep that have no shepherd. Even this example helps to understand that the metaphor was quite widely used.

[62] Scholars generally ascribe this part of the narrative to the P authorial-editorial school. It is also argued that the death of Moses was originally recorded in Num 27,12-23. But its postponement was dictated by the need to include the Deuteronomic law and complete some unfinished business in the final chapters of Numbers. Cf. J. BLENKINSOPP, *The Pentateuch*, 167, 229-232.

etc.). The hiphil of the verb יצא in conjunction with the hiphil of בוא are frequently used with military overtones[63]. However the same expression «go out and come in» is also used (mostly with priests as the subjects) in the sense of «perform cultic acts» (Exod 28,35; 33,37; 34,34; Lev 9,23). In addition, it is not uncommon to use the expression as an inclusive pair of antonyms to indicate totality: «be able to do something/everything,» or simply «do something» (Deut 28,6.19; 31,2; 2Kgs 11,8; Ps 121,8; Isa 37,28; Jer 37,4)[64]. This last idea perhaps best explains the role of Moses as shepherd. The Pentateuch indeed portrays Moses as a true leader who directs and governs the people in every sphere of their life. Moses therefore takes care to appoint a successor (Joshua) knowing well that without a successor who shares «some of his authority» (Num 27,20) and charism in order to shepherd the people of Israel, they, like sheep without a shepherd, would go astray.

The fact that without that leadership Israel is prone to being scattered, is reiterated in the prophecy of Micaiah to king Ahab: «I saw all Israel scattered upon the mountains, as sheep that have no shepherd» (1Kgs 22,17). The parallel version in 2Chr 18,16 also presents the same imagery. Even though it is an unfavourable prophecy, contradicting what the four hundred prophets told the king of Israel and Jehoshaphat king of Judah, Micaiah feels compelled to relate to them what Yahweh truly intends. Micaiah's vision of Israel as a scattered sheep, and the sheep returning home without their masters signify the death of the masters[65]. Zech 10,2 takes up that theme and refers to «the people [who] wander like sheep; they are afflicted for want of a shepherd». The situation that is presented is one of a leaderless, shepherdless flock. This scenario induces us to examine the portrayal of Israel as sheep and to pose a question, who are the shepherds of Israel and what are their roles?

5.1.2 The Portrayal of Israel as Sheep

Numerous are the references in the OT which present the people of Israel as sheep. In the early references «Israel» and «sheep» stand in parallelism: 2 Sam 7,8; 1Chr 17,7; 1Kgs 22,17; 2Chr 18,16. In a number of passages Israel is compared to sheep (Num 27,17; 1Kgs 22,17; 2Chr 18,16; Ps 44,11.22; 77,20; 78,52; 80,1; Isa 53,6; Mic 2,12;

---

[63] P.J. BUDD, *Numbers*, 306; H.D. PREUSS, «יצא», 229, 236.

[64] H.D. PREUSS, «יצא», 229.

[65] S.J. DEVRIES, *1Kings*, 268.

5,8; Zech 10,2). Explicit references to Israel as sheep gives insight into the intimate relationship that exists between Yahweh and the people (Ps 74,1; 79,13; 100,3: «sheep of thy pasture» ; 95,7: «sheep of his hand»; Mic 7,14: «flock of thy inheritance»; Zech 9,16: «flock of his people»; cf. also Zech 11,4.7.17; 13,7). As sheep Israel belongs to God. God himself says in Ezek 34,31: «you are my sheep, the sheep of my pasture, and I am your God».

But the sheep are entrusted to the care of the shepherds. However, especially after the division of the kingdom, the shepherds of Israel have neglected the sheep. Hence God complains in Jer 50,6: «My people have been lost sheep; Jer 50,17 laments: «Israel is a hunted sheep driven away by lions» (cf. also Jer 13,20; 23,1.2; 27,6). In Ezek 34,2f. the shepherds of Israel are condemned for not feeding the sheep. They did not care for the sheep nor did they attend to them (Jer 23,2; Zech 11,16), they have taught them to swear by Baal (Jer 12, 16; cf. Ezek 22,26), they have scattered them (Jer 23,1; Ezek 34,5.6.8); the sheep have become a prey, food for all the wild beasts, since there was no shepherd (Ezek 34,8). So God intends to rescue the sheep from their mouths (Ezek 34,10) becoming himself the shepherd of his sheep (Ezek 34,11-16)[66].

So the picture that emerges of the sheep is one of being God's own inheritance, liberated, protected and sustained by God himself. But they have also their own shepherds, who after the glorious era of the leading shepherds of Israel, in reality do not prove themselves to be true leaders because they neglect their sheep. Self interest takes precedence over the common good of the community. As a result, the sheep go astray, go after other gods, do not follow God's ways for want of direction.

5.1.3 The Shepherds of Israel

We shall briefly determine the prominent shepherd figures of OT. In doing so we shall also look into their role as shepherds.

a) *God as the Principal Shepherd*

The OT projects God as the principal shepherd of Israel. The image of the shepherd describes eminently the behaviour of God, his interest in the affairs of his folk Israel, and his taking care of them. However, the title «shepherd» is attributed to God only in 4 instances: Gen 48,15;

---

[66] Cf. also N. CACHIA, *Good Shepherd*, 52.

49,24; Ps 23,1; 80,1. Though few, these examples bring out an important truth, that God behaves with his people as a good shepherd does with his flock. Along with the title shepherd there are also a number of verbs that are attributed to God expressing his activity of shepherding his flock. We would like to single out the following activities of God as shepherd:[67]

i) Israel's liberation from Egypt is perhaps the most important activity of God as shepherd. OT contains manifold references to God's marvellous deed of bringing out Israel from slavery. A variety of verbs like עלה (Exod 3,17; Lev 11,45 etc.), יצה (Deut 8,14), בוא (Judg 2,1), הלך (Ps 105,43) in hifil express this saving deed.

ii) Connected to God's action of liberating is the concept of Yahweh leading and guiding Israel. נחה (Gen 24,27; Exod 13,17. 21 etc.), נהג (Ps 78,52; 80,1), נהל (Exod 15,13; Isa 40,11) are the main verbs that express Yahweh's loving and gentle act of leading them.

iii) Another important role ascribed to Yahweh is that of feeding his people. The miraculous feeding in the desert has been a constant theme of remembrance (אכל- hifil: Exod 16,32; Deut 8,3.16 etc.). This is an activity which is also expressed by the verb רעה the root for the noun רעה, shepherd (Isa 40,11)[68].

iv) Gathering of the scattered sheep is also a very significant idea celebrated in the OT (שוב - Deut 30,3; קבץ - Isa 56,8; Ezek 11,17; 28,25; 29,13; 37,21, etc.).

b) *Moses as Shepherd of Israel*

The OT contains other positive as well as negatives pictures of the shepherds who are the leaders of Israel. Moses is the foremost of the shepherds of Israel. His ministry as seen above has been all embracing, covering all aspects of the people's life, military, cultic, legislative, as well as day to day governance[69]. Two roles of Moses could be highlighted, his role as teacher and as the one who feeds the people

---

[67] E. Bosetti emphasises four key activities of God as shepherd: leading, providence, liberation, covenant. Cf. E. BOSETTI, *Il Pastore*, 235-236. N. Cachia's list of the fundamental roles of God as shepherd is as follows: leading, feeding, guarding-presence, gathering-searching-delivering-judging, tenderness-healing, knowing-alliance. Cf. N. CACHIA, *Good Shepherd*, 45-63.

[68] The theme of Psalm 23 is predominantly God's tending his flock, which includes feeding and giving rest.

[69] M. SAMUEL, *The Lord is my Shepherd*, 137-139.

with manna. We shall develop these two roles in the course of our analysis[70].

c) *David the Shepherd-King*

David is also described as the shepherd of Israel: «He chose David his servant, [...] to be the shepherd of Jacob his people, of Israel his inheritance» (Ps 78,70-72). Military and royal overtones to the «pastoral» terms used by the tribes of Israel in designating David as their new king are all too evident: «it was you that led out [ἐξάγων/ יצא-hifil] and brought in [εἰσάγων / בוא-hifil] Israel; and the Lord said to you, "You shall be shepherd [ποιμανεῖς / תִּרְעֶה] of my people Israel, and you shall be prince [ἡγούμενον/ נגיד] over Israel"» (2Sam 5,2)[71]. Political and military leadership comes to the fore in the portrayal of David as shepherd. But the one who appoints David as shepherd is God himself who is the real shepherd of Israel. David carried out his job most faithfully, caring for the flock entrusted to his care. He was seized of a great sense of responsibility for his people so much so that he argues with God to spare his people from the punishment resulting from his own sin of taking a census of Israel (1Chr 21,17; cf. 2Sam 24,17).

d) *Unfaithful Shepherds*

In the book of Jeremiah the term «shepherd» is used for political, and military leaders (Jer 2,8; 3,15; 10,21; 25,34). It is clear that by the

---

[70] Apart from the term shepherd, there are a number of verbs used in the OT which are «pastoral», in the sense that they portray the shepherding carried out by the people concerned. Thus God sent Moses to Pharaoh to bring forth Israel (Exod 3,10.11.12: ἐξαγεῖν/ יצא- hifil). It is further said that he led Israel (Exod 15,22: ἐξαιρεῖν / נסע; Acts 7,10: ἐξήγαγεν); he brought them forth (Exod 14,11; 32,7; 33,1; Num 21,5; Deut 9,12). E. Bosetti holds that Moses' rod (Exod 4,2; 7,20; 9,23; 10,13 etc.) itself is a token of his authority. Cf. E. BOSETTI, *La tenda*, 15-18, 48-49.

[71] J. Jeremias notes that no ruling king in Israel is ever referred to in the OT as «shepherd». Cf. J. JEREMIAS, «ποιμήν», 488. When the term is used in reference to the king it is always before he assumes office (e.g. 2Sam 5,2; 1Chr 11,2: verb תִּרְעֶה - ποιμανεῖς). The reason could be that the Israelite idea of theocracy evidently avoided every title which would seem to lessen the supremacy of God. Cf. G.J. BOTTERWECK, «Hirte und Herde», 344. The king as shepherd installed by the deity with cultic functions and with the responsibility of protecting his people is frequently attested in the ancient Near East since the most ancient period. In Israel too such notions were prevalent. But his functions were not comparable to that of his Mesopotamian counterpart. Cf. J.A. SOGGIN, «רעה», 1248.

prophet's time it was a well-established and regular portrait of the ruling class[72]. It is also probable that the reference applies to the religious leaders as well[73]. Jeremiah and other prophets like Ezekiel and Zechariah (cf. 10,42 for the metaphor) lament that the shepherds have been selfish and neglected their flock. Their failure embraces every sphere, political, social, moral and religious. Ezekiel in particular uses the evil shepherd theme extensively to illustrate irresponsible leadership and how God intends to remedy the situation (Ezek 34)[74].

e) *The Promised Shepherd*

There is a dramatic development in the prophecy of Ezek 34,23-24: «And I will set up over them one shepherd, my servant David, and he shall feed them; he shall feed them and be their shepherd. And I the Lord, will be their God, and my servant David shall be prince among them; I, the Lord, have spoken» (Cf. also Ezek 37,24f.; Mic 5,2-4). God intends to execute his plan through a Davidic shepherd[75]. Jeremiah too predicts God's future plan: «And I will give you shepherds after my own heart, who will feed you with knowledge and understanding» (Jer 3,15). The reference however, is to shepherds in the plural. What is striking is the reference to that with which the shepherds will be feeding: knowledge and understanding. In Zechariah the promise of the future shepherd (Messiah) undergoes a final development. In 13,7 he summons the sword: «Awake, O sword, against my shepherd [...] smite the shepherd, that the sheep may be scattered». Originally the shepherd whom the sword smites was the worthless shepherd of 11,15; in the present context he can only be the one «whom they have pierced» (Zech 12,10) and whose death ushered in the time of salvation (Zech 13,1-6). Thus OT prophecy closes with an intimation of the shepherd who suffers death according to God's will[76].

---

[72] W.L. HOLLADAY, *Jeremiah* I, 89; P. DE ROBERT, *Le Berger d'Israël*, 72; J.W. VANCIL, «Sheep, Shepherd», 1189.

[73] R. RUMAINEK, *Dio pastore*, 10.

[74] All the same, the scattering of Israel is also the result of their own actions. When Israel does not follow God's ways and sin against him, God himself scatters them (Lev 26,33; Deut 4,27; 28,64; 1Kgs 14,15; Neh 1,8; Isa 24,1; Jer 9,16; 13,24; Ezek 12,15; 20,23; 22,15; Bar 2,29).

[75] J. Jeremias says that, «with the title "shepherd" Ez. seeks to guard against a one-sidely political understanding of the figure of the future ruler, and also to leave the manner of the fulfilment of the promise to God». Cf. J. JEREMIAS, «ποιμήν», 488.

[76] J. JEREMIAS, «ποιμήν», 488.

5.1.4 Summary

The sentiment of compassion that is produced in Jesus on seeing the crowd is caused by Jesus' insight into the condition of the crowd as «sheep without a shepherd». An examination of the OT use of the imagery clarifies that the OT places great expectations on the shepherds, the leaders of Israel. They are to shepherd their flock without fail. God's own role as Chief shepherd in liberating, leading, guiding, feeding, and gathering the people, provided the role-model for the other shepherds of Israel to emulate. Moses was the absolute epitome of a true shepherd, who zealously carried out all that God commanded him, teaching, directing and governing the people and providing for them in time of need. As shepherd-king David too carried out his duties in a commendable fashion. But by the time of the prophets the shepherds, both political and religious, had failed miserably, leaving the people like sheep without a shepherd. However, the prophets held out the hope of God raising a shepherd after his own heart, who will take care of his sheep.

5.2 *The Synoptic Use of the Metaphor*

In the NT only Mark and Matthew (9,36) employ this imagery of the «sheep without a shepherd». However, the Matthean rendering is more expressive in that it also gives clues to the actual situation of the crowd.

5.2.1 The Metaphor in Matthew's Gospel

In 9,36 Matthew specifies that on seeing the crowd Jesus is moved with compassion «because they were harassed and helpless, like sheep without a shepherd»[77]. The idea that comes across is that their leaders both political and religious do not take care of them, instead they exploit them. They are victims, as harassed and cast down (ἦσαν ἐσκυλμένοι καὶ ἐρριμμένοι)[78]. The crowd cannot turn to them to be instructed regarding the ways of God. Matthew seems to be deliberately alluding to the OT picture of God's people not having a shepherd[79].

---

[77] Matthew imports the imagery from Mark 6,34 expands it and links it up with the imperative in 10,6: «Go rather to the lost sheep of the house of Israel».

[78] σκύλλειν (ἐσκυλμένοι: perfect passive participle) means to *weary, harass*. Cf. BAGD, 758. ῥίπτειν (ἐρριμμένοι: also perfect passive participle) means literally «lying on the ground». Cf. BAGD, 736. But here it must mean helpless and cast down. Cf. also W.D. DAVIES – D.C. ALLISON, *Matthew* II, 147.

[79] R.H. GUNDRY, *Use of the OT*, 32-33. ID., *Matthew*, 181.

Jesus wants to remedy the situation, he wants to take care of the crowd. He tells his disciples, «the harvest is plentiful, but the labourers are few; pray therefore the Lord of the harvest to send out labourers into his harvest». Probably Matthew is presenting the notion that Israel is waiting for her true shepherd, Messiah and he has finally arrived in the person of Jesus[80]. He will take care of them; teach (9,35), heal (Matt 14,14) and feed them (Matt 15,32). He will also enlist the collaboration of others to minister to them (10,5-15)[81].

5.2.2 Mark's Use of the Metaphor

Mark's use of the metaphor first and foremost characterises the crowd as sheep without a shepherd. But it also indirectly attributes the title shepherd to Jesus.

a) *Characterisation of the Crowd as Sheep without a Shepherd*

What Matthew has explicitly stated is implicit in the Markan rendering regarding the predicament of the crowd (6,34). But elsewhere in the Gospel Mark too presents the state of abandonment of the crowd. He alludes to the egoistic behaviour of the Scribes for instance when Jesus criticises them and denounces their hypocrisy and deception (12,38-40; cf. Ezek 34,2-8)[82]. The leaders teach «as doctrines the precepts of men» (7,7); they pay scant regard for the «commandment of God, and hold fast the tradition of men» (7,8)[83]. They are one of the major causes of the people's downfall. Consequently the people are harassed, burdened, exploited and left to themselves with no one to

---

[80] W.D. DAVIES – D.C. ALLISON, *Matthew* II, 148.

[81] D.A. HAGNER, *Matthew*, 261: «The real need of these troubled and bewildered people, who have no master to lead them out of their plight, is met by the fundamental reality Jesus has come to bring. But a universal need of this kind, a harvest this great, requires workers to extend the proclamation of the good news».

[82] Widows were usual victims of extortion. H. Fleddermann associates the long prayers with the temple cult and holds that the scribes use the cult as a pretext for robbing the widows of their financial resources. Cf. H. FLEDDERMANN, «Warning», 61-66.

[83] R. Pesch placing this reading in the broader context of Jesus' ministry, reads «the commandment of God» to mean the great commandment of Deut 6,4-5 to love the Lord God with all one's heart, soul, and might. Cf. R. PESCH, *Markusevangelium* I, 373. But in the context of 7,9-13 it would rather point to God's law as written law in contrast to tradition. But the point in either case is that God's love is being neglected. Cf. R.A. GUELICH, *Mark*, 306.

guide them[84]. However, Matthew's elaboration and precision (9,36) of the Markan text helps to get a better understanding of the plight of the people as narrated by 6,34. Upon Jesus' seeing the crowd what causes Jesus' compassion is not «the abundance of sickness he has seen but rather the great spiritual need of the people, whose lives have no centre, whose existence seems aimless, whose experience is one of futility»[85].

b) *Jesus as Shepherd in Mark 6,34* [86]

Jesus' seeing the condition of the people moves him to act in their favour. Mark pictures Jesus as immensely interested in their affairs, so that finally they have someone to guide them and to take care of them. The implication is that Jesus is the authentic shepherd for the shepherdless flock. It is true that Mark does not actually compare Jesus to a shepherd whereas the crowd are compared to sheep without a shepherd. But in the light of the life, ministry and death of Jesus, such a role can, without hesitation, be ascribed to Jesus[87]. Jesus is the Davidic

---

[84] W. HENDRIKSEN, *Mark*, 250: «No animal is as dependent as is a sheep. Without someone to guide it, it wanders, is lost, becomes food for wolves, etc. Without someone to graze it, it starves. Jesus knows that the people are like that: their leaders fail to give them reliable guidance. They do not supply their souls with nourishing food. The minds of the would-be guides are too occupied with legalistic niceties about Sabbath restrictions, fast, phylacteries, tassels, etc., to be concerned about souls». Cf. also J. ERNST, *Markus*, 191: «Das Mitleid Jesu ist nicht in einer konkreten Notlage (vgl. 1,41; 8,2; 9,22), sondern in dem geistig-religiösen Zustand eines Volkes, das ohne Führung ist, begründet».

[85] D.A. HAGNER, *Matthew* I, 260.

[86] The image of the shepherd occurs only twice in Mark: 6,34 and 14,27. It is also not quite frequently used for Jesus in the NT. There are just 15 instances of the term employed, six of which are in John's Gospel which by far has a very developed theology of the good shepherd (John 10,2.11[2].12.14.16). Luke does not apply the image of the shepherd to Jesus. In Matthew's Gospel the term occurs three times, two of which are Markan parallels (Matt 9,36 // Mark 6,34; Matt 26,31 // Mark 14,27). The other instance refers to the role of the Son of Man at the last judgement where his task of separating is akin to the shepherd's separating the sheep from the goats (Matt 25, 32). The letter to the Hebrews calls Jesus «the great shepherd of the sheep» (13,20). Peter goes further and uses the designation «chief shepherd» for Jesus (1Pet 5,4; cf. also 2,25). The book of Revelation calls the Lamb in the midst of the throne as shepherd (7,17).

[87] On the text of Mark 6,34 L. Legrand has the following to say: «The reference to the "shepherd" is not just an *obiter dictum*. It constitutes a caption that makes of the entire section that will follow a veiled description of the Messiah as one whose role will be to gather, lead and feed the "crowds" and turn them into a messianic people, healed, appeased sated and united». Cf. L. LEGRAND, «The Good Shepherd», 237.

Messiah, the promised shepherd of God (cf. Ezek 34,23-24; 37,24f. Mic 5,2-4 etc.)[88]. But what underlies 6,34 is more the Mosaic aspect of the shepherd image. In Num 27,17 it is the departure of Moses which occasions the concern as well as remedial steps so that Israel «may not be like sheep without a shepherd». Here the reader is called upon to view Jesus as taking up the Mosaic office of shepherding the flock. This idea gains strength when considering that some Jews without doubt expected the last redeemer, Messiah to be like the first redeemer Moses[89].

The main roles of God as shepherd in the OT that we have highlighted are liberating, leading/guiding, feeding, and gathering[90]. It can be assumed that such roles are fused in the public ministry of Jesus which reflects an actualisation of the selfsame saving activity. However, in his presentation of the activity of Jesus as shepherd, Mark highlights just two of these roles. Following Jesus' seeing which caused sentiments of compassion in Jesus, he begins to teach them many things. Answering the spiritual need of the people is the priority. Subsequently he feeds them. We shall elaborate these roles later. Mark seems to be implying that the messianic times foretold by the prophets find their fulfilment in the ministry and person of Jesus (Isa 35, 5-6; Ezek 34,11-16).

c) *Jesus as Shepherd in Mark 14,27*

The second and the last instance of the shepherd imagery in the Gospel of Mark gives insight into how Jesus takes on that role in relation to his disciples. Jesus says to them in 14,27: «You will all fall away; for it is written, "I will strike the shepherd, and the sheep will be scattered"». Jesus is using a quotation from Zech 13,7[91]. In the OT the

---

[88] J. MARCUS, *Mark*, 406

[89] W.D. DAVIES – D.C. ALLISON, *Matthew* II, 148; J. MARCUS, *Mark*, 406, 417.

[90] God is never called shepherd in the NT. Jeremias holds that the paucity of such references is due to the great prominence given to the Christological application of the shepherd figure. Cf. J. JEREMIAS, «ποιμήν», 491. However, comparison of God with a shepherd is made in the parables. In the parable of the lost sheep (Luke 15,3-7 // Matt 18,12-14) God is pictured as full of joy at the conversion of a sinner. Peter instructs the fellow-elders to «tend the flock of God» (1Pet 5,2). This expression seems to be attributing to God the idea of shepherd in an indirect way. The flock ultimately belongs to God. Even the chief shepherd, Jesus Christ is accountable to God (1Pet 5, 4). Cf. E. BOSETTI, *Il Pastore*, 206.

[91] For textual comparisons see R.H. GUNDRY, *Use of the OT*, 25-28.

quotation is in the form of a command: «smite the shepherd, that the sheep may be scattered» (LXX: πατάξατε τοὺς ποιμένας καὶ ἐκσπάσατε τὰ πρόβατα, TM: הַךְ אֶת־הָרֹעֶה וּתְפוּצֶיןָ הַצֹּאן). But in Jesus' use of the quotation the emphasis falls on the prediction, «I will strike», and on the agreement between Jesus' imminent fate and the text from Zechariah[92]. As seen above originally the shepherd who is smitten is the worthless shepherd of Zech 11,15. But Jesus adapts it to apply to himself projecting himself as the one «whom they have pierced» (Zech 12,10) and whose death ushers in the time of salvation (Zech 13,1-6). The striking of the shepherd refers to Jesus' passion. The sheep being scattered points to the disciples' fleeing (14,50).

Important parallels underlie the narratives of 6,34 and 14,27:

i) Both narratives emphasise the shepherd motif. In 6,34 Jesus does not present himself explicitly as the shepherd, but his subsequent activities motivated by his compassion on seeing the condition of the crowd, explain that he takes upon himself that role for the shepherdless crowd. But in 14,27 applying the OT quotation to himself, Jesus in no uncertain terms presents himself as shepherd of his disciples.

ii) The narratives present instruction and dialogue as the basis of interaction between both Jesus and the crowd as well as Jesus and the disciples. In 6,34 explicit reference is made to Jesus' activity of teaching the crowd. Jesus' use of the quotation in 14,27 is in the context of the supreme instance of communion and dialogue before his passion (14,17-31).

iii) In both instances the feeding motif comes to the fore. Jesus' teaching activity in 6,34 is followed by his activity of feeding the crowd (6,35-44). Jesus presents himself as shepherd in 14,27 after having fed his disciples with his own body and his own blood (14,22-25).

iv) Both narratives shed light on another important activity of Jesus as shepherd, that of gathering the scattered. The notion of gathering the

---

[92] Cf. H. ANDERSON, «The Use of OT», 292; R.H. GUNDRY, Mark, 845. Gundry also points out that the shift from the command to the future, «I will strike», keeps the quotation from implying that Jesus' enemies will obediently and therefore blamelessly carry out the command of God. The fact that the striker is not identified also keeps God from blame. See also R.T. FRANCE, Jesus and the OT, 107-108, who argues that the change from imperative to the indicative is a necessary grammatical adaptation to the NT context. According to E. BEST, Gospel as a Story, 69, the shift from «you» to «I» means that God will strike the shepherd with judgement which would otherwise fall on the sheep. But the «I» is not here identified as Yahweh!

scattered is quite evident in 6,34 and in the subsequent narrative (6,39-40). Jesus, by his appeal and charisma, has caused the crowds to gather around him (πολὺς ὄχλος)[93]. Jesus' application of the OT quotation to himself in 14,27 is followed by a promise, «But after I am raised up, I will go before you to Galilee» (14,28)[94]. The cross and death are the inevitable consequence of Jesus' assuming the role of the shepherd. But death would not be the end of the story. An apparent defeat and failure would be transformed into victory at the resurrection. The resurrected Lord will gather his flock and guide them with his abiding presence (cf. 16,7).

Thus Jesus presents himself as shepherd of the crowd who were like sheep without a shepherd. Jesus perceives well their need and responds to it. In the case of the crowd that perception arises from his seeing them. The disciples include those whom he saw and called. He, as their true shepherd knows them well, that without his active assistance they tend to be scattered. His promise (14,28; 16,7) is a pledge of his lasting care and continued guidance of his flock.

5.2.3 Summary

Jesus' seeing the crowd, and his compassion which it arouses in him due to their plight expressed through the imagery of «sheep without a shepherd», provides the basis for Mark's portrayal of Jesus as the true shepherd who takes care of his sheep. Mark's view of the OT promises of a Messianic shepherd fulfilled in the person of Jesus is in keeping with the general NT understanding to that effect. Mark's Gospel being the earliest has perhaps given the lead in seeing in the person of Jesus the authentic shepherd. But Jesus is more than a Mosaic-Davidic shepherd. He came «to give his life as a ransom for many» (10,45). His role reflects God' own role of shepherding his flock.

6. Result of Jesus' Compassion: Teaching

Jesus' compassion for the crowd resulting from his seeing them moves him to identify the crowd's need. It is because they lack shepherds who would feed them with the word of life and satisfy their

---

[93] See above p. 209-212.

[94] On the promise and its realisation see above p. 174f. Cf. L. LEGRAND, «The Good Shepherd», 253: «As a suffering shepherd, he [Jesus] will himself bear the brunt of the distress of the scattered flock. But, as the Risen Lord, he will again lead them into the unity and security of the fold».

inner hunger that they find themselves in the condition of being scattered, exploited and prone to be swayed away by false teachings. So Jesus as true shepherd begins to teach them (καὶ ἤρξατο διδάσκειν αὐτοὺς πολλά)[95]. Jesus takes on the role of the shepherd for the shepherdless crowd and carries out that role first and foremost by teaching them. He discerns that quenching their spiritual thirst is their most important need and it is for that they flock to him[96].

In our analysis of the OT background to th imagery, «sheep without a shepherd», we have noted that in Num 27,17 Moses prays God for a successor, lest Israel be like sheep without a shepherd. The verse, while noting the importance of a successor to his office, also gives a glimpse into the role Moses himself played in Israel. Moses during the wilderness period was the ultimate authority, as revealer, communicator and interpreter of God's will. He not only mediated the Law but also interpreted, taught and administered it. Though a comprehensive judicial system was put in place following advice from Jethro (Exod 18,13-27), Moses was to represent the people before God, continue his teaching function, and deal with cases without precedent in law (cf. Deut 1,5; 4,1; 5,1 etc.)[97]. Moses' role in short was one of shepherding Israel and teaching was basic to carrying out that role. As long as Moses was there the congregation of the Lord was like sheep which have a shepherd.

We have also noted above that Moses typology explains well Mark's portrayal of Jesus assuming the role of shepherd for the shepherdless flock, the crowd. Shepherding the flock implies revealing, interpreting and above all teaching God's will. That is why when Jesus takes on that role, the first thing he does is to begin to teach them. Jesus wants to reveal God's will to them[98]. It would be later testified that what Jesus

---

[95] In the Matthean parallel there is no reference to teaching, instead Matthew reports that Jesus healed the sick (14,14). Luke has «and he welcomed them [the crowd] and spoke to them of the kingdom of God, and cured those who had need of healing».

[96] W. EGGER, *Frohbotschaft*, 130: «die wahre Not des Volkes besteht darin, daß sie keinen Lehrer haben – diese geistige Not ist bedrückender als die leibliche Not». R. PESCH, *Markusevangelium* I, 350: «Daß Jesus das Volk lehrt, deutet e contrario an, daß die Lehrer Israels versagt haben, daß der Hirte als Lehrer gekommen ist [...]».

[97] J. BLENKINSOPP, *The Pentateuch*, 172-173.

[98] E. LOHMEYER, *Markus*, 124: «Jene Führerlosigkeit des Volkes ist in der Art dieser Menschen, die Hilfe durch "Lehre" in der Art des Meisters gegründet; anders gesprochen, dieses Lehren ist ein göttliches Offenbaren, dieser Lehrer ein Meister, der

teaches has the divine sanction. For the heavenly voice expressly commands to listen to him (cf. 9,9: ἀκούετε αὐτοῦ).

6.1 Reference to Jesus' Teaching

The fact of Jesus' teaching is referred to by the verb διδάσκειν which occurs 17 times in Mark (Matt 14; Luke 16; John 9). The verb in the infinitive form occurs four times (4,1; 6,2; 6,34; 8,31) and following Mark's style all of them are used with ἤρξατο[99]. Of all these occurrences of the verb διδάσκειν 15 times it is used of Jesus (the exceptions are 6,30: disciples; and 7,7: Pharisees and Scribes). In responding to the need of the crowd in 6,34, Mark presents Jesus as teaching them «many things» (πολλά). It is Mark's style to use the adverbial accusative πολλά[100] with words of speaking (cf. 1,45; 3,12; 4,2; 5,10.23.38.43; 6,20.34; 8,31; 9,12.26; 15,3). But it fails to provide information as to what exactly Jesus teaches. The content of the teaching remains unspecified.

The most conspicuous activity of Jesus in the Gospel of Mark is his teaching. Apart from the verb διδάσκειν to refer to his activity of teaching, the noun διδάσκαλος is a constant designation for Jesus. The term occurs 12 times in the Gospel (Matt 12; Luke 17; John 8), ten of which are in the vocative case διδάσκαλε (Matt 6; Luke 12; John 3). Jesus is addressed as διδάσκαλε by his disciples (4,38; 9,38; 10,35; 13,1), by one of the crowd (9,17); and by Jewish scholars (10,17.20; 12,14.19.32). διδάσκαλον occurs once on the lips of the servants of Jairus referring to Jesus (5,35). Once the same Jesus refers to himself as διδάσκαλος (14,14).

Such frequency of the verb διδάσκειν together with the noun διδάσκαλος as well as the noun διδαχή referring exclusively to the

---

mit der Weisheit und dem Erbarmen Gottes selber spricht - und vor solcher Höhe sind Hörer immer wie Schafe ohne Hirten».

[99] ἤρξατο plus infinitive is generally considered Armaism. Mark likes to use it quite frequently. Cf. M. ZERWICK, *A Grammatical Analysis*, 104. In 6,34 its usage is considered pleonastic, deliberately employed for effect. Cf. E.J. PRYKE, *Redactional Style*, 80-81. R. Pesch sees it as sign of Mark's editorial hand. Cf. R. PESCH, *Markusevangelium* I, 106.

[100] There is a general agreement that πολλά is adverbial; so it would rather mean «at length». W. EGGER, *Frohbotshaft*, 130, n. 50; R.A. GUELICH, *Mark*, 335; V. TAYLOR, *St. Mark*, 320. R.H. Gundry translates it as «much». For him such usage stresses Jesus' didactic authority by indicating that he holds the crowd under his sway till late in the day. Cf. R.H. GUNDRY, *Mark*, 323.

teaching of Jesus (occurring 5 times: 22.27; 4,2; 11,18; 12,38), amply demonstrate that Mark places great emphasis on Jesus' teaching activity. But Jesus' role as teacher is also brought out by several references to Jesus' disciples as μαθηταί (Mark: 46, Matt: 72, Luke: 37, John: 78), which among other things imply a learner to teacher relationship. Jesus has disciples because he is a teacher. Moreover Mark also employs related didactic terms[101] and expressions[102] for a skilful portrayal of Jesus as teacher.

6.2 Reference to Jesus' Teaching the crowd in the Gospel

Mark's Gospel contains a number of references in which Jesus is said to have taught the crowd[103] without any reference to what Jesus really taught. These references mainly occur in what many scholars have identified as «summary reports» (Sammelberichte)[104]. The summary reports are narrative units in which Mark summarises Jesus' ministry, at the same time emphasising as well as generalising certain aspects of his ministry. Authors have different views on the function of the summaries[105]. It may be said that on the whole they stand alone,

---

[101] Mark employs the Semitic word 'Ραββί three times (Matt 4; Luke 0; John 8). The occurrences in Mark are 9,5; 11,21 (in both cases Peter so addresses Jesus); and 14,45 (here Judas addresses Jesus so). The term essentially carries the same meaning as διδάσκαλος and designates Jesus as teacher. Cf. R.P. MEYE, Jesus and the Twelve, 36-37.

[102] Mark also uses other verbs like λέγειν (usually with αὐτοῖς e.g. 3,23; 4,2.13.21; 7,14, etc.), λάλειν, (ἐλάλει αὐτοῖς τὸν λόγον is a typically Markan expression cf. 2,2; 4,33; 8,32), ἀκούειν, (Mark uses the verb in two ways: firstly, people are said to be hearing about the activity of Jesus; e.g. 2,1; 3,8.21; 5,27; etc. secondly, Jesus directs the attention of the crowd with the verb; e.g. 4,3.9.23; 7,14 etc.) with relatively more frequency than Matthew or Luke. These terms also describe Jesus' didactic activity. Cf. R.T. FRANCE, «Teaching of Jesus», 105-106; R.P. MEYE, Jesus and the Twelve, 48-51; E.S. MALBON, «Markan Characters», 113-117.

[103] The didactic terminology referred to above would perhaps give the impression that Jesus' teaching is primarily for the disciples. But it is good to note that as a rule Mark uses διδάσκειν for the public teaching of Jesus and only on two occasions it is also used for the private instruction given to the μαθηταί (8,31; 9,31). So it is implicit that the crowd too are almost constant recipients of Jesus' ministry of teaching.

[104] See n. 2 above for the various scholars' list of summary reports.

[105] Authors in general consider these to be editorial compositions. Cf. P.J. ACHTEMEIER, «He Taught Them», 474. N. Perrin sees them as transitional structural devices that hold together the Gospel. Cf. N. PERRIN, The New Testament, 147; See also W. EGGER, Frohbotschaft, 164-165. For K.L. Schmidt they are literary devices that tie together individual pericopes rather than providing the basic literary

independent of the pericopes that surround them. However, they introduce new information into the narrative in a general and non-specific way[106]. One of the important features of these summary reports is the reference to the teaching as the primary activity of Jesus. There is also the absolute use of the verb διδάσκειν where the verb is used without either direct object or a ὅτι - clause to specify the content[107]. Besides, they imply that the crowd are the immediate recipients of the teaching[108]. The following pericopes have elements of summarising with special reference to teaching (through didactic terminology) with little clue as to the content of the teaching itself: 1,21-22.39; 2,1-2.13; 4,1-2; 6,6b.30-34; 10,1[109].

Apart from the above mentioned references to Jesus' teaching the crowd, Mark also presents Jesus as teaching in the temple. Reference is made twice to his activity of teaching there: 11,17; 12,35 and once the διδαχῇ of Jesus is referred to (12,38). The audience in the temple is presumably made up of all, Jesus' disciples (11,11.12.15 etc.), the traffickers (11,17), the chief priests, the scribes (11,18a), and definitely the crowd, for Mark very characteristically refers to their amazement and gladness at Jesus' teaching (11,18b; 12,37). That, teaching constituted an important aspect of Jesus' activity in Jerusalem, is brought out by Jesus himself when he reminds his captors, «day after day I was with you in the temple teaching, and you did not seize me» (14,49).

A look at those references where the message of Jesus' teaching the crowd is presented can help us to determine the general thrust of his teaching. But before we establish what exactly Jesus taught we shall point out the essential features of Jesus' teaching in general.

---

structure of the document. Cf. K.L. SCHMIDT, *Der Rahmen*, 13. They could also be thought of as literary conclusions to the preceding as well as literary introductions to the following pericopes. W. Egger for instance holds that 6,30-34 is an introduction to the ensuing story of the multiplication of loaves. Cf. W. EGGER, *Frohbotschaft*, 122.

[106] C.W. HEDRICK, «Summary Statements», 294.

[107] R.T. FRANCE, «Teaching of Jesus», 111; K.H. RENGSTORF, «διδάσκω», 138f.

[108] E.S. Malbon says that it is when speaking of the teaching of the crowd that Mark refers to the teaching of Jesus without giving the content. Cf. E.S. MALBON, «Markan Characters», 113.

[109] Strictly speaking we have to qualify the view that the summaries do not have the content of the teaching of Jesus because 4,1f. do present in parables the content of what Jesus teaches. But it is only an exception.

6.3 *Characteristics of Jesus' Teaching*

The teaching of Jesus as delineated by Mark has very important, salient features. We shall note the most predominant of them.

i) The source of Jesus' teaching is unique. It is indicated in the Gospel by a positive as well as a negative statement by way of contrast: «for he taught them as one that had authority, and not as the scribes» (1,22)[110]. This comment of Mark is the key to gaining an insight into Jesus' teaching as well as understanding his entire presentation of Jesus' conflict with the authorities[111]. The negatively worded portrayal of Jesus' teaching would mean that Jesus' authority was not derived or borrowed. Unlike the Scribes who depended on the Torah and tradition of the elders for its validity and binding power Jesus did not appeal to them[112]. The point that Mark stresses is that their teaching is completely opposed to that of Jesus and so are devoid of authority. Jesus' teaching on the other hand is invested with authority (ἐξουσία). It is the authority of Jesus itself which is the cause of opposition[113]. Jesus' possession of it is intrinsically bound up with his identity as the Son of God (cf. 1,1.11; 9,7). God himself is the source of his knowledge and power and hence of his ἐξουσία.

ii) It is a new teaching. Those who heard Jesus in the synagogue at Capernaum and witnessed the mighty work he performed question among themselves in amazement, «What is this? A new teaching! With authority he commands even the unclean spirits, and they obey him» (1,27). Mark here takes up the motif of διδαχή and ἐξουσία from v. 21, incorporates the mighty work of exorcism he performs into his teaching thus forming a single unity, bases it on Jesus' ἐξουσία and qualifies it as

---

[110] The repeated use of the term διδαχῆ in Mark 1,21-28 is most striking. This pericope sets the tone for the rest of Jesus' public ministry. Cf. J.C. IWE, *Jesus in the Synagogue*. Even here the content of Jesus' teaching is not described, but it underscores what is special to Jesus' teaching.

[111] On religious authorities see M. COOK, *Mark's Treatment*. The author's main concern however is historical. Cf. also D. LÜHRMANN, «Die Pharisäer», 169-185. For Lührmann the Markan confrontations Jesus and his disciples have with Pharisees and scribes reflect the controversy that took place in the Evangelist's own day between his community and contemporary Jewish groups. For a literary - critical study of the Markan story of conflict see J.D. KINGSBURY, «The Religious Authorities», 42-65.

[112] R.A. GUELICH, *Mark*, 56; J. JEREMIAS, «γραμματεύς», 741-742; V. TAYLOR, *St.Mark*, 173.

[113] P. GUILLEMETTE, «Un enseignement», 239-240.

new[114]. The newness of Jesus' teaching consists in his being the Son of God and the authoritative manner in which he gives it[115]. It is new because it is aimed at freeing men from their old ways, from demons, from sins and from their bondage (7,1-16)[116]. «Since his teaching and his miracles unfold under his keynote proclamation of the imminent reign of God (Mark 1: 14-15), every word and action partakes of the announcement that God is, right now, inaugurating the ultimate restoration of all creation to divine rule. This eschatological happening is what the *new* in «a new teaching» refers to (cf. 2: 18-22!)»[117].

iii) Miracles form an essential part of the teaching. «Mark graphically depicts the power of the word of Jesus in his powerful deed»[118]. The mighty works of Jesus appear as the result, the illustration of the depth of effectiveness, and indication of the dimension of Jesus' teaching ministry. In other words they are the proof of the power of Jesus' teaching[119]. Just as Jesus' teaching enables the disciples and the crowd to be «on the side of God», and not of men

---

[114] K. SCHOLTISSEK, *Vollmacht*, 123; K. STOCK, «Machttaten», 200: «Lehre und Handeln Jesus werden in einem unlösbaren Zusammenhang gesehen. Beide werden als Äußerungen seiner Vollmacht erfahren».

[115] The popular acclamation of a «new teaching with authority» is also inseparably connected to the demon's recognition of Jesus status, «I know who you are, the Holy One of God» (1,24). So the first newness is the person of Jesus. Cf. also R.J. DILLON, «Authority», 98; J.C. IWE, *Jesus in the Synagogue*, 104.

[116] R. PESCH, «Eine neue Lehre», 275.

[117] R.J. DILLON, «Authority», 98.

[118] R.P. MEYE, *Jesus and the Twelve*, 47. Though both the teaching as well as the mighty works that Jesus performs are rooted in the ἐξουσία of Jesus, Mark also makes a clear distinction between teaching and doing (cf. 1,21-22 and 1,27; 6,20; 6,30). Both are not identical, neither is doing subordinated to teaching. Some scholars tend to think to the contrary; e.g., E. SCHWEIZER, *Markus*, 24: «Markus benutzt also eine Wundergeschichte (vgl. zu 4,35-41), um die "Dimension" des Lehrens Jesu aufzuzeigen». R. PESCH, «Ein Tag», 127: «In Jesu vollmächtigem Lehren zeigt sich die Nähe der Gottesherrschaft an; eben deshalb ist das Lehren das bleibende Charakteristikum der Wirksamkeit Jesu bei Markus».

[119] A.M. AMBROZIC, «New Teaching», 142; R.P. MEYE, *Jesus and the Twelve*, 46. It may also be noted that the Markan narrative itself creates a link between the title teacher and Jesus' activity as one who performs mighty deeds. See for instance 4,38 where the storm-stricken disciples wake up Jesus by calling him διδάσκαλε. In the midst of the double miracle in 5,21-43 Jesus is again addressed as διδάσκαλος (5,35). Cf. also E.K. BROADHEAD, *Naming Jesus*, 83-85. Broadhead establishes a further narrative link between the debate and controversy which surrounds Jesus and his designation as the Teacher.

(8,33), his mighty works liberate them from domination by Satan and demons and usher in the reign of God[120].

iv) A very important feature of the teaching of Jesus is that it teaches the way of the cross. In the journey section of the Gospel (8,27-10,52) where Jesus devotes himself to instructing his disciples this point is brought out with particular emphasis in the passion predictions (8,31; 9,31; 10,32-34). Mark in fact characterises the passion predictions as teaching (8,31: καὶ ἤρξατο διδάσκειν; 9,31: ἐδίδασκεν; 10,32: καὶ ἤρξατο λέγειν). In his teaching Jesus indicates that the way of the Messiah (8,29) is the way of the cross. Jesus does not limit himself to teaching the way of the cross but he himself treads it willingly, knowing fully well that the inevitable death is not the last word but only a stepping stone to victory and communion with God. For anyone who wishes to be «on the side of God» (8,33), to be thinking the things of God, and willing to follow him, Jesus holds out the same way of the cross (8,34)[121].

6.4 *The Content of Jesus' Teaching*

Though Mark furnishes very little of the content of Jesus' teaching while referring to the fact that he taught the crowd, he does present elsewhere in the Gospel the message Jesus wanted to communicate. We shall briefly deal with the central message of his teaching as can be gathered from elsewhere in the Gospel where the crowd also seem to be recipients of his teaching.

6.4.1 The Good News of the Kingdom of God

Mark opens the narrative on Jesus' ministry referring to his preaching[122] and qualifying it as «good news» (εὐαγγέλιον: 1,14). In

---

[120] The fact that mighty works manifest the kingdom of God is made clear in the instruction Jesus gives to the Seventy-two in Luke's Gospel. Luke 10,9: «Whenever you enter a town [...] heal the sick in it and say to them, "The kingdom of God has come near to you"». Healing is effectively a sign of the presence of the kingdom.

[121] Jesus addresses this teaching both to the disciples as well as to the multitude. So not only the disciples, but anyone who wishes to follow him has to go the way of the cross that he has traced out for them.

[122] This brings us to the classic distinction in Mark between preaching or proclaiming (κηρύσσειν) and teaching (διδάσκειν). For a detailed study see R.P. MEYE, *Jesus and the Twelve*, 52-60. He comes to the conclusion that in spite of hints that both are identical, teaching is attributed to Jesus almost exclusively, while proclaiming is done mostly by others. Besides, Mark never refers to private

addition he reports that what Jesus preaches is the Gospel of God (1,14). So God himself guarantees the content of his preaching. In the subsequent verse (1,15) he gives the definite content of that preaching. In doing so Mark defines the central message of Jesus' preaching addressed to everyone who comes into contact with him.

a) *The Arrival of the Kingdom*

The core of the message as delineated by Mark is present in two declarative and two imperative statements in which he condenses the preaching of Jesus: «The time is fulfilled, and the kingdom of God is at hand; repent, and believe in the gospel» (1,15)[123].

The first declarative statement speaks of the fulfilment of time; Jesus announces the coming to pass of a decisive moment in time. The perfect tense of πεπλήρωται indicates that the event has come to pass with lasting significance; and the passive voice indicates that God is at work in bringing it about[124]. This fact is confirmed by the next

---

proclamation, unlike private teaching. We have already noted that 6,30 is the only instance where the disciples are said to have taught. Otherwise teaching is an activity exclusively done by Jesus. Jesus proclaims the good news of the arrival of the Kingdom (1,15). Subsequently Jesus explains his proclamation. He does so in private to the disciples. Occasionally the crowds are also recipients of such explanation. This explanation and application of the message of his proclamation to life is teaching. Cf. also A.M. AMBROZIC, «New Teaching», 143-149; K. STOCK, *Boten*, 20-21.

[123] Scholars take this as the first summary statement of the gospel, providing the substance of Jesus' message. Cf. W. EGGER, *Frohbotschaft*, 39f.; C.W. HEDRICK, «Summary Statements», 294-295; K.L. SCHMIDT, *Der Rahmen*, 32-35; V. TAYLOR, *St. Mark*, 165. For the programmatic and paradigmatic significance as well as the introductory and paranetic function of 1,14-15 see C.D. MARSHALL, *Faith as a Theme*, 36-43. C.W. Hedrick has the following to say about Mark 1,14-15: «Mark 1: 14-15 is a concise *summary* of the content of the preaching of Jesus, the only one in the Gospel. Its position at the beginning of Jesus' ministry affects the reader's view of the entire narrative. It invites the reader to supply the "general content" of Mark 1:14-15 as the substance of Jesus' message, wherever Jesus is described as preaching or teaching [...] This technique relieves the author of the necessity of repeating the "message" each time Jesus is described as addressing audiences. Unless otherwise informed, the reader would assume (or Mark appears to *intend* that he assume) on the basis of the summary at 1,14-15, that Jesus is preaching and teaching about the Kingdom of God». Cf. C.W. HEDRICK, «Summary Statements», 294-295.

[124] A.M. AMBROZIC, *The Hidden Kingdom*, 21f.; W. EGGER, *Frohbotschaft*, 56; R.A. GUELICH, *Mark*, 43; C.D. MARSHALL, *Faith as a Theme*, 35.

statement: the Kingdom of God has arrived[125]. The presence of the Kingdom is the basic message of Jesus. In the light of that presence urgent action is required as the following imperatives show. Jesus calls to «repent», to make a radical change from one's wayward ways and to turn to God's ways. Jesus further summons to «believe» the Gospel, which is the good news from God[126]. God's intervention in human history thus calls for human commitment.

b) *The Kingdom of God as Motif of the Parables*

We have already observed that the verb διδάσκειν is usually used in the absolute sense, giving no content of the teaching subsequently. In the few cases where the content is given a verbal form of λέγειν is normally added (4,2; 9,31; 11,17; 12,35.38). One such instance is 4,2f. where the crowd are explicitly named as recipients of his teaching (cf. 4,1). The only hitch is that the message of his teaching is expressed in parables[127] («he taught them many things in parables» [128]) which need

---

[125] On the debate as to the exact meaning of the ἤγγικεν, whether it denotes «arrival» or «nearness», see the vast references to the scholars who hold either position in R.A. GUELICH, *Mark*; 43-44. R.A. Guelich's position which he sums up in the following words seems to be tenable. Cf. R.A. GUELICH, *Mark*, 44: «Rather than referring exclusively to the present aspect of the Kingdom [...] or the future [...] the ἤγγικεν of 1: 15 maintains both the present but "hidden" fulfilment of the Kingdom in Jesus' ministry (cf. the "good news" of 1:1 and 1:14) and the future consummation of the Kingdom in power (cf. parables in Mark 4 and 13). Thus the Kingdom of God has "come into history," the appointed time "has been fulfilled," even though the full appearance is yet to come».

[126] For a treatise on the different dimensions of faith called for see, C.D. MARSHALL, *Faith as a Theme*, 49-56.

[127] The parable as a way of teaching reaches back to a flexible, many-faceted form of OT wisdom speech known as מָשָׁל often translated in the LXX as παραβολή. An OT מָשָׁל could be anything from a one-line proverb or aphorism, or a riddle, or oracle, up to a lengthy historical recital, or a short story containing a complicated allegory. The word παραβολή in the Synoptic Gospels likewise carries a wide range of meanings, corresponding fully to its use in the OT and Rabbinic literature, though scholars tend to restrict the English word «parable» to Jesus' narrative parables. Cf. F. HAUCK, «παραβολή», 744 - 761.

[128] The phrase is akin to what we have in 6,34 except for the reference to the parables: καὶ ἐδίδασκεν αὐτοὺς ἐν παραβολαῖς πολλά. πολλά here certainly refers to Jesus' preaching and teaching regarding the kingdom, the theme of the parables. By extension it can be supposed that the πολλά of 6,34 too have their basis in Jesus' teaching of the kingdom. C.E.B. CRANFIELD, *St. Mark*, 217: «the meaning [of πολλά] is not that Jesus taught them a great number of different things, but that he taught the one message of the kingdom of God persistently».

to be deciphered in order to grasp its meaning. Mark records a number of parables narrated by Jesus (2,17-22; 3,23-27; 4,2-9.21-25.26-29.30-32; 7,14-23.27; 9,50; 10,25; 12,1-10; 13,28.34-37). The parables in Mark take up the theme already set out in 1,15; they stimulate thought, provoke reflection and call for decision as well as action in the light of the advent of the kingdom[129].

The parabolic teaching in chapter four concludes by saying that, «with many such parables he spoke the word to them, as they were able to hear it; he did not speak to them without a parable, but privately to his own disciples he explained everything» (4,33-34). It can be presumed that Jesus spoke more parables than Mark records. At the same time, those that are recorded are only a sample of what Jesus spoke to the crowd. Three parables that he records use the seed image to communicate the message of Jesus, they are: the parable of the sower (3-9), the parable of the growing seed (26-29), the parable of the mustard seed (30-32)[130]. The basic thrust of all three seed-parables is the kingdom of God and its character. We shall make a brief analysis of these parables.

+ The Parable of the Sower (4,3-9)

A simple, basic structure[131] of the parable could be drawn around the phrases καὶ καρπὸν οὐκ ἔδωκεν and καὶ ἐδίδου καρπὸν, highlighting

---

[129] V. TAYLOR, St. Mark, 250.

[130] The parables in 4,21-25: the parable of a light under a bushel (4,21-23), and the parable of measure (4,24-25), are different in style and imagery from the rest of the set of parables in chapter four. Scholars argue that the audience of these two parables are also different. Most scholars hold that the disciples are the recipients of this parabolic teaching. Cf. A.M. AMBROZIC, The Hidden Kingdom, 103-104; R.A. GUELICH, Mark 228; K. STOCK, Boten, 79-80. Others hold that Jesus is speaking to the crowds, cf. R.H. GUNDRY, Mark, 211. It is more likely that Jesus is speaking to the disciples here. The change in style is visible; these two parables are not narrated as a story, but one uses the technique of question and answer (21-23) and the other is presented as an exhortation (24-25). They too have link with 4,11 which speaks of the disciples as the recipients of the «secret of the kingdom» (μυστήριον δέδοται τῆς βασιλείας τοῦ θεοῦ). In vv. 21-23 reference is made to what is «hidden» (κρύπτον/ ἀπόκρυφον) establishing a link with μυστήριον and vv. 24-25 speaks of what is given (δοθήσεται) taking up the idea of δέδοται.

[131] For the binary structure of the parable see J. MARCUS, The Mystery, 21-22, and for the triadic pattern see R.A. GUELICH, Mark, 190, 194-195.

thus the theme of failure and success. Though the parable[132] dwells more on the aspect of failure, the threefold failure of the unproductive seeds is finally matched by the spectacular threefold success of the productive seeds[133]. As the definition of the purpose of the parables (4,10-12) as well as the interpretation of the parable (4,13-20) show, Mark uses the parable to explain the rejection of Jesus and his message of the breaking-in of the kingdom of God by some people and the acceptance by others[134]. Despite the failures and obstacles that Jesus' message meets with, the final outcome is going to be positive. So the parable challenges the hearers to reflect on the kind of response that is required in order to bring forth fruit. The parable has shown that there are different responses, different ways of hearing the word spoken by Jesus; the emphasis however, is on the response that is most productive and the hearers are encouraged to take note of it and to act accordingly in view of the advent of God's reign.

+ The Parable of the Growing Seed (4,26-29)

The opening reference to the ἡ βασιλεία τοῦ θεοῦ makes this parable an explicit kingdom parable. Jesus in his parabolic teaching compares the kingdom of God to the seed which a man scatters on the ground[135]. As a kingdom parable, it illustrates the presence and growth of the

---

[132] The title perhaps does not reflect the main focus of the parable. It has been noted that the sower only sets the parable in motion and so he is not the focal point of the parable. Cf. R.A. GUELICH, Mark, 192; J. MARCUS, The Mystery, 20-21; R. PESCH, Markusevangelium I, 231. The contrary view, that the sower plays the main role is also held by many scholars. Cf. C.H. DODD, The Parables, 135-137; J. GNILKA, Markus I, 155; J. JEREMIAS, The Parables, 150-151. Some have identified the sower in the parable as Jesus himself. Cf. J. MARCUS, The Mystery, 37-39.

[133] More dramatically, in the case of the productive seeds, the fact of giving fruit is mentioned even before the coming up of the seed. Besides, in speaking of that success, the verbs employed are imperfect (ἐδίδου, ἔφερεν), not aorist (κατέφαγεν, ἐξηράνθη, ἔδωκεν). Present participles accompany those imperfect verbs giving thus the sense of ongoing productivity and abundance. Cf. also R.H. GUNDRY, Mark, 192.

[134] C.H. DODD, The Parables, 136; R.H. GUNDRY, Mark, 191; J. JEREMIAS, The Parables, 150. Jeremias stresses that the breaking-in of the kingdom of God is compared so often to the harvest.

[135] It is evident that the seed provides the basis of comparison. It is because of that this parable is included in chapter 4 along with other seed parables. The silent but consistent sprouting, growing, and maturing of the seed is the focus of the parable. Some scholars have stressed the role of the man who scatters the seed, thereby making him the point of comparison. Cf. J.D. CROSSAN, «The Seed Parables», 251-253; J. JEREMIAS, The Parables, 151.

kingdom. Just like the seed, the kingdom grows on its own apart from any visible, external causes or forces. No extraordinary ushering in, and enhancement of the kingdom is to be expected; it grows silently on its own despite the disciples' lack of understanding. It is not difficult to detect the hand of God at work in this stage of growth[136]. However, the parable stresses more pointedly the aspect of fruition and harvest. The seed has to produce a harvest. At the opportune time God will harvest the ripe fruit. The word of God that Jesus sows is also intended to produce fruit worthy of harvest[137].

+ The Parable of the Mustard Seed (4,30-32)

The parable opens with a double question seeking a comparison for the kingdom of God (4,30). The answer is given in the form of an antithetical parallelism; highlighting the contrast between the comparatively small size of the mustard-seed (4,31) and the comparatively large size of the grown-up plant (4,32)[138]. This third seed parable explicitly identifies the kingdom of God as the point of comparison. The comparison itself is brought out by accentuating the contrast that exists between the mustard seed which stands for smallness[139] and the full-grown plant which stands for greatness. In Jesus' teaching the parable exposes two basic truths about the kingdom. First, by the image of the seed it describes the almost infinitesimal presence of God's rule as opposed to the popular expectation of the times. This presence of the kingdom was displayed in the life and

---

[136] Several scholars see in the phrase αὐτομάτη ἡ γῆ καρποφορεῖ God's miraculous activity at the time of germination in contrast to human activity. Cf. J. ERNST, Markus, 142; J. JEREMIAS, The Parables, 151-152; R. PESCH, Markusevangelium I, 256. It would follow then, that the parable highlights God's role in bringing about his kingdom, irrespective of any human efforts. Cf. J. ERNST, Markus, 142; J. MARCUS, The Mystery, 172-173; R. PESCH, Markusevangelium I, 256. It may be true that there is little biblical evidence for taking αὐτομάτη to be synonymous with «by God» (Cf. R.A. GUELICH, Mark, 241-242). The parable also values human effort, in spite of emphasising the independence of the seed's growth from the farmer. All the same, God's role is the decisive factor that explains the growth of the seed.

[137] R.A. GUELICH, Mark, 245-246; R.H. GUNDRY, Mark, 221-222.

[138] R.A. GUELICH, Mark, 248.

[139] The smallness of the mustard seed (κόκκῳ σινάπεως) was proverbial in Palestine (cf. Matt 17,20; Luke 17,6). Cf. H. HUNZINGER, «σίναπι», 289. But this claim is highly disputable. But botanical precision is not the point of the parable.

ministry of Jesus. Second, it pointed to the coming of God's kingdom in its greatness in the future[140].

All these three seed parables reflect Jesus' own ministry of sowing the seed/word of the kingdom which, though insignificant it may seem, calls for enthusiastic response. The full flowering of the kingdom, guaranteed by God himself, will embrace amazing dimensions, and that is reason enough to place one's faith in Jesus and in God's rule which is both a present as well as a future reality[141].

6.4.2 The Message of Jesus' Teaching in the Temple

In the narrative of Jesus' activity in Jerusalem (chapters 11-12), on two occasions Mark presents Jesus' activity explicitly as teaching (11,17; 12,35) and once he refers to the διδαχῇ of Jesus (12,38). In these instances the audience is not exactly specified. But from the context (cf. 11,18b; 12,37 b) it can be ascertained that the crowd are the main and immediate recipients of the teaching. We shall examine briefly these references to establish the principal themes of Jesus' teaching of the crowd in the temple.

a) *Teaching of Jesus at his Driving away the Dealers from the Temple (11,17)*

On his second day in Jerusalem (11,12-19),[142] Jesus enters the temple, drives out the traffickers, and does not permit anyone to carry vessels through the temple (11,15-16). To this activity with authority is joined the activity of teaching (11,17)[143]. The verb employed here is once again διδάσκειν along with λέγειν; both occurring together is

---

[140] R.A. GUELICH, *Mark*, 251-253; H.K. MCARTHUR, «The Mustard Seed», 209-210.

[141] C.H. DODD, *The Parables*, 138: «the coming of the Kingdom of God is in the teaching of Jesus not a momentary event, but a complex of interrelated events including His own ministry, His death, and what follows, all conceived as forming a unity».

[142] On the three day structure of the three-fold grouping of texts in chapters 11-12, and on the thematic links between them see, K. STOCK, «Gliederung», 481-515.

[143] An obvious parallelism can be drawn between the episode at the synagogue at Capernaum (1,21f.) and what takes place in the temple in Jerusalem (11,15f.). They include, coming into the city, entry into the synagogue or temple, teaching activity to which interestingly expelling the demon or the traffickers is joined (a demon like opposition of the chief priests and scribes [11,18a] also is a case in point), and the amazement of the crowd at Jesus' teaching.

normally a sign that the content of the teaching follows (cf. 4,2; 9,31;
11,17; 12,35.38)[144]. It is quite logical to think of the αὐτοῖς (11,17) as
referring to those dealers mentioned in 11,15[145]. But the crowd is
present there as shown by 11,18b, and they seem to be the main
audience. It is not certain if the chief priests and the scribes are present
(11,18a); what is said of them is that they «heard» what Jesus taught. It
is also possible that they heard it from someone else.

What Jesus teaches is marked by an antithetical parallelism:[146] «"My
house shall be called a house of prayer for all the nations", but you
(ὑμεῖς δέ) have made it a den of robbers» (11,17). The parallelism is
formed with two texts from the OT, the first clause taken from Isa 56,7
and the second using Jer 7,11. It is evident that in Jesus' teaching the
focus is on the second, which describes what has become of the temple:
a den of robbers. The statement in Jeremiah forms part of his temple
proclamation in which he denounces the behaviour of the people (7,3-
12)[147]. The essence of the proclamation is, «amend your ways and your
doings» (7,3). Making the house of God a «den of robbers» is a
reflection of the present state and behaviour of the people, they behave
like robbers in their whole dealings and conduct. So the prophet calls
upon the people to convert themselves and to change their ways.

Jesus in his teaching takes up the saying about the den of robbers
from Jeremiah and seemingly applies it to justify his action of expelling
the traffickers from the temple[148]. But seen in the overall context of Jer
7,3-12 it is more than that. Jesus, by indicating the condition of the
temple, is evidently referring to the condition of the people. Whereas
Jeremiah begins with the immoral conduct of the people to arrive at the

---

[144] According to V. Taylor, καὶ ἐδίδασκεν καὶ ἔλεγεν may indicate continuous
teaching, in which more was said than is recorded. Cf. V. TAYLOR, *St. Mark*, 463. Cf.
also K. STOCK, «Gliederung», 490-491. See E. SCHWEIZER, *Markus*, 128: «Mit dem
Bericht vom "Lehren" Jesu (vgl. zu 1,21-28) unterstreicht Markus die Bedeutung des
Gesagten; die Griechische Zeitform drückt nämlich ein wiederholtes Tun aus».

[145] Both Matthew (21,13) and Luke (19,46) show that Jesus is addressing exactly
the traffickers in the temple.

[146] However, the teaching here is given in the form of a question and not a
statement as in Matt 21,13 and Luke 19,46. The οὐ plus the indicative mood of
γέγραπται in the question implies that it is written. Cf. R.H. GUNDRY, *Mark*, 640.

[147] For the parallelism between Jeremiah's temple proclamation and Jesus'
teaching in the temple see, K. STOCK, «Gliederung», 503, n. 42.

[148] Matt 21,12 and Luke 19,45 view it that way. Many scholars also hold the same
view, cf. R.H. GUNDRY, *Mark*, 640; R. PESCH, *Markusevangelium*, 198;
E. SCHWEIZER, *Markus*, 128; etc.

condition of the temple, Jesus in reverse order presents the condition of the temple to highlight the wrong behaviour of the people as regards to their relationship with God and with one another. Given such state of affairs Jesus forcefully calls for urgent conversion[149]. Jesus' demand for conversion takes up the theme of his preaching as he entered public ministry (1,15). In the light of the advent of the kingdom of God, and in order to be open to God's reign, one has to change his ways and doings, embracing conversion in every sphere of his life[150].

b) *Teaching of Jesus on Son of David (12,35)*

On the third day of his activity in the temple Jesus seizes the initiative, which rested with his interlocutors since he left the temple on the second day (11,21. 28; 12,14.18.28),[151] and teaches something very important. The audience as noted by v. 37b are the crowd[152]. The question, «how can the scribes say that the Christ is the son of David?», presupposes not only a general scribal agreement on this designation of the expected Christ, but perhaps also the lack of this designation in the OT. But Jesus' exegesis of the psalm is different. From Ps 110,1 he deduces that someone whom David calls «Lord» cannot be «Son of

---

[149] K. STOCK, «Gliederung», 504: «Jesus ist nicht primär am Tempel interessiert, aber in der Art des Jeremias erlaubt ihm der Tempel, das Verhältnis der Israeliten zueinander und ihr Verhältnis zu Gott zur Sprache zu bringen und ganz eindringlich zur Umkehr aufzufordern». The possibility for conversion is always left open. The perfect tense of the verb πεποιήκατε has the scope of indicating that the effect of their past action lasts still, but it does not deny the prospect of a change of heart.

[150] Seen this way Jesus' activity in the temple is much more than what is traditionally spoken of as temple-cleansing, nor is it a disruption (cf. M. BORG, *Conflict*, 171.345, n. 42) since no stopping of sacrificial worship involved. Scholars however note the that incident in the temple was a messianic action. Cf. C.E.B. CRANFIELD, *St. Mark*, 359; J. ERNST, *Markus*, 329; E. LOHMEYER, *Markus*, 237; V. TAYLOR, *St. Mark*, 464; etc. But C.A. Evans argues that there is no convincing evidence to suggest that there were expectations that the Messiah would destroy the temple. The hypothesis that Jesus foreshadowed the temple's destruction through symbolic action, even as a necessary prelude to restoration is at best tenuous. Cf. C.A. EVANS, «Jesus' Action», 237-270.

[151] K. STOCK, «Gliederung», 485.500.501.

[152] In Matthew's account Jesus puts the problem to a particular group, the Pharisees (Matt 22,41). Luke has some of the scribes (20,39) and probably the Sadducees too (20,27) as audience (20,41).

David» as the scribes assume. In his teaching here Jesus is implicitly alluding to his status[153].

c) *Teaching of Jesus on Right Conduct (12,38)*

Just before concluding his teaching activity in the temple, Jesus once again cautions the crowd on the right behaviour that is required in view of the advent of the kingdom[154]. That the audience here is the πολὺς ὄχλος of 12,37 is clear because Mark presents the ensuing warning as διδαχῇ αὐτοῦ (12,38) which is a continuation of the teaching that began in 12,35 (ἔλεγεν διδάσκων)[155]. Whereas in the previous pericope (12,35-37) Jesus teaches the crowd by calling into question what the scribes say, here he teaches them by calling into question what they do (12,38-40)[156].

The teaching itself consists of two parts: the first which begins with the imperative Βλέπετε ἀπό warns the crowd against different aspects of the wrong behaviour of the scribes; while the second, with the future indicative λήμψονται predicts a judgement on them. Jesus thus teaches

---

[153] Jesus' clarification follows Bartimaeus' invoking him by the name, «Son of David» (10,47.48) and more recently the crowd's connecting his coming to the coming of the kingdom of David (11,1-10). Mark does want the reader to infer that the counterpart to «Son of David» in 12,35-37 is «Son of God». This is clear due to three reasons: a) Mark directly associates the title «Son of God» with the title «Messiah» (14,61; 15,39). b) «Son of God» is the title Mark himself employs in his prologue, in order to explain to the reader who Jesus the Messiah is. c) Son of God is also the title by which God knows Jesus the Messiah (1,11). Cf. C. BURGER, *Jesus als Davidssohn*, 64-70; J.D. KINGSBURY, *The Christology*, 112. However, the title Son of David is not rejected. Christ's Davidic sonship does not cease, once David's son he always remains his son (this view is further supported by Rom 1,3-4, where Jesus as son of David κατὰ σάρκα is contrasted to Jesus as son of God). Jesus is more than Son of David. But he does not make a clear statement about it either. Cf. P.J. ACHTEMEIER, «And He Followed Him», 128; J. GNILKA, *Markus*, 171; R.H. GUNDRY, *Mark* 717-719; J.D. KINGSBURY, *The Christology*, 106-114.

[154] For the double themes of the identity of Jesus and the right human conduct, in relationship to God and to one another that permeates the narrative of Jesus' three day-Jerusalem activity in chapters 11-12, see K. STOCK, «Gliederung», 500-509.

[155] In the Matthean account Jesus addresses both the crowds and his disciples (Matt 23,1f.). But later directly addressing the scribes and the Pharisees, he denounces their behaviour in seven «woes» (23,13-36; cf. Luke 11,37-52). Luke presents Jesus as addressing his disciples in the hearing of all the people (20,45).

[156] R.H. GUNDRY, *Mark*, 719; V. TAYLOR, *St. Mark*, 495.

the crowd by analysing and denouncing the wrong behaviour of the scribes, and holding it up as something not to be emulated[157].

6.4.3 The Good News of Jesus Christ

The advent of the kingdom of God is verified essentially in the life and ministry of Jesus Christ. It is his coming that has heralded the reign of God. He is the newness, he is the explicit sign that the time is fulfilled, he is the reason for conversion and faith (1,15). It is true that in his teaching he does not define himself, nor proclaim himself explicitly, but it is up to his audience to hear his message and see in the light of his great deeds, what he stands for and gain an understanding of who he is. Seen in this light Jesus himself is the content of his teaching. That is why Mark can at the outset boldly ascribe the word εὐαγγέλιον to the account of the life and ministry of Jesus Christ, the Son of God (1,1).

6.4.4 Summary

Jesus' seeing which touches off the reaction of compassion for the crowd moves him to explain the message of his coming. In doing so he announces the advent of the kingdom of God and the consequent human response that is required[158]. Jesus reveals and communicates the will of God for the people. In his teaching he takes on the role of the true shepherd who feeds them with the word of life, and satisfies their inner hunger, and fills them with hope. Now we shall turn to Jesus' satisfying the bodily hunger of the crowd.

7. Subsequent Feeding of the Crowd

Jesus' seeing the crowd which caused the sentiments of compassion to well up in him moved him to discern as well as to respond to their basic spiritual need. But Jesus is equally concerned about their bodily need; rather he provides them with a meal as sign of fellowship and communion. In doing so he proves himself to be the true shepherd who

---

[157] K. STOCK, «Gliederung», 509: «Über den Hinweis auf das verkehrte Verhalten der Schriftgelehrten, denen die Verurteilung droht, zeigt Jesus noch einmal, indirekt, was das geforderte richtige Verhalten gegenüber Gott und den Menschen ist».

[158] Luke 9,11 which parallels Mark 6,34 clearly states that Jesus «welcomed them [the crowd] and spoke to them of the kingdom of God». So it is proof enough that the kingdom of God was the theme of Jesus' teaching.

feeds his flock both figuratively and literally. In our analysis of the pericope we do not intend to do a detailed exegesis of the pericope but only to highlight the salient aspects of the miracle.

7.1 *The Account of the Miracle*

The feeding of the five thousand is the only miracle narrated by all four Evangelists (Matt 14,13-21; Mark 6,30-44; Luke 9,10-17; John 6,1-14)[159]. That is indicative of the significance of the event. The role the disciples play in the miracle, Jesus' authority and power displayed in performing such a feat, the reference to this event made by Jesus subsequently (6,52; 8,17-21), and Mark's recording of a sequel to this event, all point out that the Evangelist regarded this event as crucial in the life of Jesus.

7.1.1 The Dialogue between Jesus and the Disciples

The story of the feeding begins with a dialogue between Jesus and the disciples initiated by the disciples. This is the only instance where Mark records a rather long dialogue between Jesus and the disciples. The other instances are mostly one line statements or requests from the part of the disciples (1,37; 4,10; 7,17 etc.)[160]. The disciples take the

---

[159] In Mark and Matthew there is also a separate account of the feeding of the four thousand (Mark 8,1-10 // Matt 15,32-39). Opinion is divided on the historicity of the two accounts. There are those who hold that the two accounts are records of two different events; e.g., C.E.B. CRANFIELD, *St. Mark*, 205; R.H. GUNDRY, *Mark*, 398-401; J. KNACKSTEDT, «Brot-vermehrungen» 313-320. Another theory is that they are two traditions of the same miracle; Those who hold it include, P.J. ACHTEMEIER, «Miracle Catenae», 290-301; J.-M. VAN CANGH, *La multiplication*, 125-128; J. ERNST, *Markus*, 189; R.M. FOWLER, «The Feeding», 101-104; G. FRIEDRICH, «Die beiden Erzählungen», 10; J. GNILKA, *Markus*, 255; R.A. GUELICH, *Mark*, 401-403; B.M.F. VAN IERSEL, «Die wunderbare Speisung», 179; K. KERTELGE, *Die Wunder*, 139-141; E. LOHMEYER, *Markus*, 153; C.G. MONTEFIORE, «Revolt», 140; R. PESCH, *Das Markusevangelium* I, 401-402; L. SCHENKE, *Die Wundererzählungen*, 226; E. SCHWEIZER, *Markus*, 72; V. TAYLOR, *St. Mark*, 630. After a very careful study of the two accounts of the miracle from the viewpoint of vocabulary, style, theme, form and tradition-history, S. Masuda convincingly concludes that «the two accounts are not derived from variants, but from one tradition, the second account being closer to the original form of the tradition than the first». Cf. S. MASUDA, «The Miracle of the bread», 214.

[160] Cf. K. STOCK, *Boten*, 107. The words exchanged between Jesus and the disciples have a tone of sharpness. First, the conversation is characterised by imperative mood (ἀπόλυσον, εἶπεν αὐτοῖς, Δότε, ὑπάγετε ἴδετε). Second, Mark's

initiative with respect to asking that Jesus dismiss the crowd since it is «a lonely place and the hour is now late» (6,35)[161], so that the crowd could «go into the country and villages round about and buy themselves something to eat» (6,36). Unlike in the case of the feeding of the four thousand (8,1-2) where Jesus takes the initiative and calls the disciples, here the disciples identify the problem, they come to Jesus on behalf of the people and suggest a solution[162]. In contrast to the feeding in 8,1f. there is also little hint of urgency here. The people could find provisions for themselves in the surrounding villages and towns.

Jesus' reaction to their suggestion is baffling. Jesus acknowledges that there is a problem to be solved but he does not accept the solution proposed by them. Instead he commands them, «you give them something to eat» (6,37a). The disciples, totally unprepared for that kind of an order, react with astonishment and make another reasonable suggestion of buying two hundred denarii worth of bread to feed the crowd (6,37b)[163]. The disciples who initially sought the dismissal of the crowd in order that they might go and buy bread (ἀπελθόντες ἀγοράσωσιν), now volunteer to buy bread for them (ἀπελθόντες ἀγοράσωμεν δώσομεν). Neither is this suggestion met with Jesus'

---

unusual use of the adversative δέ twice in the pericope is conspicuous, adding an emphasis to the tension in a subtle way. Cf. R.M. FOWLER, *Loaves and Fishes*, 81-82.

[161] It is commonly held that ἤδη ὥρας πολλῆς γενομένης refers to late afternoon near sunset. It means that it was already time for the Jews' main meal. S. Masuda notes the occurrences of ὥρα in Mark's Gospel (12 times) and sees a particular significance in the fact that except for the two instances in the present pericope all other 10 occurrences are in the narrative of Jesus' last week in Jerusalem, referring to the passion and the parousia of the Son of Man. So he infers that the ὥρα in 6,35 alludes to the eucharist and the passion. Cf. S. MASUDA, «The Miracle of the Bread», 192-193. It is not a convincing argument. Not all occurrences refer to Jesus' passion (11,11; 13,11.32). The Passover meal takes place in the evening (ὀψίας γενομένης: 14,17) and not «when it grew late» (ἤδη ὥρας πολλῆς γενομένης: 6,35).

[162] But whether they are moved entirely by altruistic considerations in wanting to dismiss the crowd is open to question. It is not improbable that they are thinking of finally realising what they were originally set out to do (6,31). Cf. R.H. GUNDRY, *Mark*, 324; K. STOCK, *Boten*, 107-108.

[163] According to Matt 20,2f. the denarius was a day's wage for a labourer. Cf. also BAGD, 179. John 6,7 which also refers to the sum of two hundred denarii indicates that it is not sufficient to buy enough bread for everyone in the crowd to get a little (John 6,7). In R.M. Fowler's view the disciples' possession of 200 denarii and five loaves and two fish violates Jesus' command in 6,8-9. Cf. R.M. FOWLER, *Loaves and Fishes*, 114-119. The instruction was given for the missionary journey. Taking along provisions was quite normal as shown by Mark 8,14. John 13,29 testifies also that Jesus and the disciples had a common money box administered by Judas Iscariot.

approval. At his bidding the disciples discover five bread and two fish at their disposal (6,38). With this the dialogue comes to an end. Jesus now takes centre stage. The disciples' service is again called for only in seating the crowd, distributing the food and in collecting what is left over.

7.1.2 Jesus Multiplies Bread and Fish

Jesus takes the initiative to feed the crowd on the spot. He orders the crowds to be seated (ἀνακλῖναι) in companies (συμπόσια συμπόσια)[164] on the green grass (χλωρῷ χόρτῳ)[165]. Then, like the father of a Jewish household Jesus takes (λαβών) the five loaves and two fish, looks up to heaven (ἀναβλέψας εἰς τὸν οὐρανόν), blesses (εὐλόγησεν),[166] and breaks

---

[164] Authors point out the possible reference here to Exod 18,25 where Moses arranged the Israelites into groups of thousands, hundreds, fifties and of tens under the respective leaders. In the Qumran documents these subdivisions are used as eschatological model for their sectarian life (1QS 2,21-22; CD 13,1; 1QM 4,1-5; IQSa 2,11-22). The arrangement points back to the wilderness experience and hints at the eschatological moment of the gathering of Israel. Mark 6,40 speaks of hundreds and fifties, when multiplied together they come to five thousand. Cf. J. ERNST, Markus, 192; J. GNILKA, Markus I, 260-261; R.A. GUELICH, Mark, 341; P. LAMARCHE, Marc, 174; W.L. LANE, Mark, 229; etc.

[165] The mention of the green grass (ἐπὶ τῷ χλωρῷ χόρτῳ) seems to want to evoke the activity of the shepherd: Ps 23,2: «he makes me lie down in green pastures» (εἰς τόπον χλόης). The presence of that theme is all the more probable due to two more allusions of the psalm in the Markan account: just like the shepherd who leads his sheep by restful waters (Ps 23,2: ὕδατος ἀναπαύσεως), Jesus invites his apostles to repose (6,31: ἀναπαύσασθε); just as the psalmist is led by God to a table for a feast (Ps 23,5: ἡτοίμασας ἐνώπιόν μου τράπεζαν), the crowd are invited to recline (6,39: ἀνακλῖναι) for the meal (cf. Ezek 34,26f.). Cf. also R.A. GUELICH, Mark, 341; W.L. LANE, Mark, 229; R. PESCH, Markus-evangelium I, 350; I. DE LA POTTERIE, «La Multiplication des Pains», 315-316; J. ROLOFF, Das Kerygma, 243, n. 144; etc.

[166] Scholars point out that this is the only deviation from the normal practice at a Jewish meal. While praying Jesus looks toward heaven rather than downward as prescribed. Cf. Str-B II, 246. However, Jesus repeats this action before healing the deaf and deaf man (7,34; cf. also John 11,41). It is assumed that a nuance of drawing on the extraordinary power necessary to perform the miracle in both instances is intended. Cf. W.L. LANE, Mark, 230; R. PESCH, Markusevangelium I, 352-353. In the former instance this gesture is accompanied by a prayer which is lacking in the latter. εὐλόγησεν of 6,41 is substituted by εὐχαριστήσας at 8,6. The parallel between εὐχαριστήσας (8,6; 14,23) and εὐλόγησας (8,7; 14,22) favour that εὐλόγησεν at 6,41 means praising God for the bread and fish and not calling down God's power on the bread and fish. So God is the object of blessing. Cf. R.A. GUELICH, Mark, 342; R.H. GUNDRY, Mark, 325-326.

(κατέκλασεν) the loaves and hands (ἐδίδου) them to the disciples to be distributed to the crowd. The verb ἐδίδου is an imperfect of duration and perhaps repetition[167]. The implication would be that Jesus handed repeatedly new bread to the disciples which they passed on to the crowd. The same happened also with the fish. The food increased miraculously till all had their fill.

7.1.3 The Left Over Food Collected

The story of the miraculous feeding concludes with a demonstration of the fact that five thousand men ate to their fill and still had twelve baskets of food left over. Mark is talking only of men whereas Matthew specifies that «those who ate were about five thousand men, besides women and children» (Matt 14,21). So an immense gathering was miraculously fed. The fragments gathered amounted to twelve baskets full[168]. However, there is no note of bewilderment and acclamation of the crowd that accompany most of the miracles that Jesus performs. The crowd seem to be oblivious of the extraordinary feat accomplished by Jesus. The fact that Jesus appeals to the disciples' memory in referring to this event later, is proof that it had not taken place by chance; it was intended to be revelatory (Mark 6,52; 8,19).

7.2 *The Significance of the Miraculous Feeding*

This is a story that is replete with meaning. Its significance has been variously interpreted. We shall here occupy ourselves with examining just two prominent aspects of the miracle: its eucharistic significance and its Christological interpretation.

7.2.1 Eucharistic Significance

The view that Mark understood the miraculous feedings (6,30-44; 8,1-9) as eucharistic meals, or as prefigurements of the eucharist has been quite widely held[169]. The main reason put forward is that there are

---

[167] Cf. M. ZERWICK, *A Grammatical Analysis*, 124.

[168] Numbers abound in this story. Whether twelve baskets correspond to the twelve apostles (or to the twelve tribes of Israel) cannot be proved.

[169] J.-M. VAN CANGH, *La multiplication*, 76-88.100-104; J. ERNST, *Markus*, 192; B.M.F. VAN IERSEL, «Die wunderbare Speisung», 167-194; K. KERTELGE, *Die Wunder*, 136-137; E. LOHMEYER, *Markus*, 127, n. 5; S. MASUDA, «The Miracle of the Bread», 201-203; F.J. MOLONEY, *A Body Broken*, 40; R. PESCH, *Markusevangelium* I, 348; Q. QUESNELL, *The Mind of Mark*; L. SCHENKE, *Wundererzählungen*, 146.227;

close similarities between the feeding narratives and the Markan narrative of the last supper in vocabulary and style[170]. A close look at the narratives indeed shows that the vocabulary is quite similar:

Mark 6,41	Mark 8,6-7	Mark 14,22-23	1Cor 11,23-24
Καὶ λαβὼν τοὺς πέντε ἄρτους καὶ τοὺς δύο ἰχθύας	καὶ λαβὼν τοὺς ἑπτὰ ἄρτους	λαβὼν ἄρτον	ἔλαβεν ἄρτον
εὐλόγησεν	εὐχαριστήσας	εὐλογήσας	εὐχαριστήσας
κατέκλασεν τοὺς ἄρτους καὶ	ἔκλασεν καὶ	ἔκλασεν καὶ	ἔκλασεν καὶ

V. TAYLOR, *St. Mark*, 324. Cf. also J.M. BASSLER, «Loaves», 168-169: he talks of a eucharistic interpretation that will be recognised by the «implied reader».

However, quite a number of scholars argue against the eucharistic interpretation of the feeding narratives. They include: E. BEST, *Gospel as a story*, 63; G.H. BOOBYER, «The Eucharistic Interpretation», 161-171; R.M. FOWLER, *Loaves and Fishes*, 134-147; J. GNILKA, *Markus* I, 261; R.A. GUELICH, *Mark*, 342-343; R.H. GUNDRY, *Markus*, 328-333; F. NEUGEBAUER, «Die wunderbare Speisung», 269; R. PESCH, *Markusevangelium* I, 352; J. ROLOFF, *Kerygma*, 241-246; A. SEETHALER, «Die Brotvermehrung», 108-112.

[170] G.H. Boobyer investigates two more arguments proposed to support the eucharistic interpretation of the miracle of feeding. They are: i) In the Gospel of John the story of the feeding of the five thousand is followed by a discourse on Jesus the bread of life in which Jesus explicitly speaks of eating the flesh and drinking the blood of the Son of man. So the Evangelist views the feeding of the five thousand in some sense as a eucharistic act. ii) In 1Cor 10,1f. Paul associates the manna given to Israel in the wilderness with the Christian eucharist. It is possible that Mark may have understood the miraculous feeding as the Christian equivalent of manna in the desert and following Paul's lead connects the miraculous feedings with the eucharist. Boobyer in responding to the first argument maintains that the main interest in the Johannine discourse is Christological and only once the Evangelist establishes the Christological doctrine does he speak of eating the flesh of the Son of man and drinking his blood. Besides, the Johannine account clearly shows that true eucharist was celebrated in bread and wine (John 6,51-58). Moreover the audience in John's Gospel is the hostile murmuring Jews; so it is unlikely that even something even prefiguring eucharist was celebrated with them. Mark's dependence on Paul is also highly open to question given the divergent version of the last supper in Mark. Neither are there indications to suggest that Mark accepts Paul's exegesis of the manna in 1Cor 10,1-4. Cf. G.H. BOOBYER, «The Eucharistic Interpretation», 161-168.

ἐδίδου τοῖς μαθηταῖς [αὐτοῦ] [...]	ἐδίδου τοῖς μαθηταῖς αὐτοῦ [...]	ἔδωκεν αὐτοῖς καὶ εἶπεν, Λάβετε, τοῦτό ἐστιν τὸ σῶμά μου.	εἶπεν, Τοῦτό μού ἐστιν τὸ σῶμα τὸ ὑπὲρ ὑμῶν· τοῦτο ποιεῖτε εἰς τὴν ἐμὴν ἀνάμνησιν.
καὶ τοὺς δύο ἰχθύας ἐμέρισεν πᾶσιν.	καὶ εἶχον ἰχθύδια ὀλίγα· καὶ εὐλογήσας αὐτα	καὶ λαβὼν ποτήριον εὐχαριστήσας ἔδωκεν αὐτοῖς, καὶ ἔπιον ἐξ αὐτοῦ πάντες. καὶ εἶπεν αὐτοῖς, Τοῦτό ἐστιν τὸ αἷμά μου τῆς διαθήκης τὸ ἐκχυννόμενον ὑπὲρ πολλῶν.	ὡσαύτως καὶ τὸ ποτήριον μετὰ τὸ δειπνῆσαι λέγων, Τοῦτο τὸ ποτήριον ἡ καινὴ διαθήκη ἐστὶν ἐν τῷ ἐμῷ αἵματι· τοῦτο ποιεῖτε, ὁσάκις ἐὰν πίνητε, εἰς τὴν ἐμὴν ἀνάμνησιν.

However, Boobyer has convincingly pointed out that the vocabulary (λαμβάνειν, εὐλογεῖν, εὐχαριστεῖν, κλᾶν ἄρτον, κατακλᾶν ἄρτον) is not necessarily a technical term for eucharist (cf. Acts 27,35)[171]. There are also essential differences between the feeding narratives and the narrative of the last supper: i) In contrast to the feeding narratives, in the narrative of the last supper, number pays no role; no number of bread or participants is furnished. ii) For the feeding narratives fish is an essential item of the meal, at the last supper fish is absent; the last supper is celebrated with bread and wine. iii) The words that Jesus pronounces over the bread and wine at the Lord's supper which lay the foundation for the eucharistic celebration are lacking at the feeding narratives, thus depriving the feedings of their basic sacramental nature. iv) At the feedings the disciples have a role of service whereas at the

---

[171] G.H. BOOBYER, «The Eucharistic Interpretation», 162. Cf. also R.M. FOWLER, *Loaves and Fishes*, 134.139-140. The similarity in language to the beginning of the last supper may very well be due to the use of the language and custom of the Jewish meal in both instances.

last supper they are active table companions of Jesus. v) The gathering of the left over food is reported in the miracle stories, but it has no place in the Lord's supper.

Given such divergences between the two accounts, one should be slow to interpret the feeding miracles as eucharistic[172]. But the miracle itself points to something more than a Jewish meal which Jesus shared with the crowd in exceptional circumstances. It is to determine that we shall now turn.

7.2.2 The Miracle Portrays Jesus as the Good Shepherd

In explaining what takes place at the feeding, reference is often made to the feeding accounts of the OT (Exod 16; 2Kgs 4,42-44). However, there is no basis to suggest that the Markan feeding is a repetition of the feeding with manna and quail in the desert (cf. John 6,30f.)[173]. Jesus' miraculous feeding of the crowd also far exceeds that of Elisha who fed one hundred men with twenty loaves (2Kgs 4,42-44)[174]. This is not to suggest that Jesus' feeding should not be read in the light of the exodus

---

[172] This is not to deny that the Feeding stories have had no bearing on the early Christian eucharist. Bread and fish are represented in the mosaic of Tabgha, near Capernaum, they also appear frequently in early Christian frescos in the catacombs as symbols of the eucharist. The risen Lord is also presented as associated with the symbolism of fish in Luke 24,42f. and John 21,1-14. Cf. I. DE LA POTTERIE, *La Multiplication*, 328; A. RICHARDSON, «The Feeding», 147-148. It is also probable that the Lord's supper liturgy has had influence on the wording of 6,41 as well as in giving prominence to bread throughout the narrative. It may also explain why the fish are relegated a lesser role in 8,1-10 and in the parallel accounts of Matthew and Luke. Cf. R.A. GUELICH, *Mark*, 343; H. PATSCH, «Abendmahlsterminologie», 227-228.

[173] Against A. HEISING, *Die Botschaft*, 39f.; ID., «Das Kerygma», 52-57; S. MASUDA, «The Miracle of the Bread», 207-209. Such a view also tries to harmonise the mention of the two fish equalling them to the quail (Num 11,31; Wis 19,11-12; in antiquity fish and birds were conceived to be having their origin in water). The manna typology also would take the 5 loaves to refer to the 5 books of Moses, 2 fish to refer to the law and the prophets and 12 baskets to refer to the 12 tribes of Israel or the 12 apostles. See also J. GNILKA, *Markus* I, 263; S. MASUDA, «The Miracle of the Bread», 203-06.

[174] For a detailed analysis of the Elisha story and its parallelism to the Markan narrative see A. HEISING, *Die Botschaft*, 18-19; J. MARCUS, *Mark*, 415-416; S. MASUDA, «The Miracle of the Bread», 208-209. The ratio between the bread and the number of people fed vary considerably: Elisha story, 1:5; Jesus' feeding, 1:1000. S. MASUDA, «The Miracle of the Bread», 208: «In the contrast between Elisha and Jesus, Mark is pointing to the far surpassing greatness of Jesus, filled with the Spirit of God».

tradition or the Elisha tradition. But the implication is that both these traditions are surpassed in the person of Jesus.

In fact we explained Jesus' teaching activity resulting from his seeing the crowd on the lines of Moses who, as the pre-eminent shepherd of Israel, reveals, interprets and teaches God's will. Moses' role as shepherd also involved providing for the people. It is to Moses that the people turned when they had no bread (Exod 16), no meat or fish (Num 11,4-34), nor water (Num 20,2f.; 21,5-18). Moses, took upon himself the obligation to present their problem before God and through God's intervention, he was able to satisfy the people. Thus for Moses carrying out his office also meant looking after the physical well-being of the people. It is interesting to note that Jesus too, on assuming the role of shepherd for the shepherdless flock, is equally concerned about their physical well-being. He provides for them after the model of Moses. Jesus thus proves himself a true shepherd of the people. But Jesus is more. He is the new Moses (Deut 18,15),[175] he is the fulfilment of God's promise of a new and faithful shepherd (Ezek 34). Seen this way, it is easy to understand why Jesus did not accept the suggestions put forward by the disciples (6,35-37) but took the initiative to feed the crowd on the spot. By providing food for «the sheep without a shepherd» Jesus shows himself to be God's promised servant David who «shall feed them and be their shepherd» (Ezek 34,23)[176]. The shepherd motif in the feeding story becomes much more explicit considering the possible allusion also to Psalm 23 where God is celebrated as the Shepherd of his people. In Jesus' action what the Psalmist awaits from God himself finds its fulfilment[177].

---

[175] R. PESCH, *Markusevangelium*, 354; A. SEETHALER, «Die Brotvermehrung», 109. Commentators are in general agreement in seeing God's promise of raising up an eschatological prophet fulfilled in Jesus (Deut 18,15.18).

[176] G. ZIENER, «Die Brotwunder», 284: «[Der Speisungsbericht] zeichnet Jesus als den guten Hirten, der das neue Gottesvolk mit seinem Wort und mit (Lebens) Brot nährt. Als neuer Moses gliedert er das Volk in Einzelgemeinden, in seinem Auftrag teilen ihnen die Jünger das Lebensbrot».

[177] See n. 173 above. W.L. LANE, *Mark*, 232-33: «The meal was eschatological to the degree that the people experienced rest in the wilderness and were nurtured by the faithful Shepherd of Israel, but it pointed beyond itself to an uninterrupted fellowship in the Kingdom of God. In the centre of the event stands Jesus, who creates the situation and arranges everything that pertains to the meal. He orders the camp in their groups, takes and breaks the bread and divides the fish, and through his hands the miracle unfolds for those who have eyes to see. If the crowd has been described as

In portraying Jesus as the shepherd of the people Mark is giving the miracle a true explicit Christological interpretation. In other words the episode reveals who Jesus is. As we have noted several times the identity of Jesus is the main concern of the Gospel of Mark (1,1). What is confirmed by the heavenly voice (1,11; 9,7), feared by the demonic world (1,24; 3,11; 5,7), confessed partially by Peter (8,29), suggested by Bartimaeus (10,47.48), implied by Jesus himself (1,1-11; 12,35, 14,61-62) and proclaimed with certainty by the Centurion (15,39) is reiterated through an extraordinary event; here the miracle speaks for itself, it proclaims Jesus' identity as the Messianic Shepherd[178]. For the Evangelist Mark the activity of feeding along with teaching (6,34) thus represent Jesus' mission of being Shepherd to the people. In his teaching Jesus' endeavour has been to talk about the kingdom of God and to reveal himself as the one who would bring it about. The miraculous feeding too proclaims Jesus as the promised, messianic Shepherd. This theme of the Shepherd with the OT prophecy in the background also implies that Jesus is someone equal to God. Hence the whole pericope (6,30-44) has a revelatory character.

The story has at the same time another theme, that of the incomprehension of the disciples. Before this revelation of the mystery of Jesus' identity the disciples remain blind. Mark says, «for they did not understand about the loaves, but their hearts were hardened» (6,52)[179]. By his characteristic γάρ clause Mark here links the amazing story of Jesus' walking on the sea with the equally miraculous feat of

---

sheep without a shepherd, Jesus is presented as the Shepherd who provides for all of their needs so that they lack nothing».

[178] It is true that Mark presents the miracle as taking place as though it were nothing extraordinary. For the crowd do not seem to recognise it as a miracle. So they could not be expected to comprehend the identity of Jesus revealed by the event. But the Evangelist has certainly the reader in mind. It is up to the reader to evaluate the miracle and identify the message it communicates. At the same time the narrative reflects the experience of the early Christian community. Cf. L. SCHENKE, *Die Wundererzählungen*, 230: «In der Erzählung kommt die Glaubenserfahrung zur Sprache, die die urchristliche Gemeinde mit Jesus gemacht hat: unter seine Hirtensorge weiß sie sich gestellt, aus seiner Hand empfängt sie ihr Leben. Sie bekennt ihn als ihren gottunmittelbaren Mittler und Messias, der in Fürsorge über seine Anhänger wacht. So erfährt sie ihn stets aufs neue in ihrem Alltag, in ihren Gottesdiensten und in ihrer Missionstätigkeit».

[179] The same theme is taken up in 8,14-21 where reference is again made to the feedings and interestingly connection is again made between the loaves and the failure to understand. See Chapter 3.

feeding the crowd. The evangelist explains their sheer astonishment at what happens on the sea by pointing to their lack of understanding of the loaves. Such a reaction from the part of the disciples following closely on the heels of Jesus' self-revelation (6,50: ἐγώ εἰμι) indicates that their failure there pertains to their lack of understanding of who Jesus is. By establishing a connection with the loaves at this stage of the narrative Mark tells the reader that the disciples had missed something even in the previous feeding miracle. It is that failure to understand the significance of the miracle that caused the great astonishment at Jesus' actions on the sea. They should have realised that both Jesus' teaching and the subsequent feeding pointed to his identity. They should have seen in his actions that he was taking on himself the role of the promised shepherd for the crowd described as «sheep without a shepherd» (6,34). They should have by now gained an answer to their basic question, «who then is this, that even wind and sea obey him?» (4,41).

8. Jesus' Seeing Ushers in Communion

A train of thought that we have developed through our analysis of the previous occurrences of the verb εἶδεν is that in each instance it was Jesus' seeing that acted as a catalyst in ushering in communion; in the first event communion with God (1,10), and in the subsequent instances (1,16.19; 2,14) communion with the disciples whom Jesus saw and called. The same is applicable even in the instance of Jesus' seeing the crowd (6,34).

Jesus' seeing gave him an idea of the condition of the shepherdless crowd; his heart went out to them, he was moved with compassion. That sentiment of compassion was translated into active action of teaching, in an effective discernment of the real need. In teaching the crowd Jesus was sharing with them what he experienced at the first instance of his seeing (1,10), that of the advent of the reign of God in his own person with its present and future dimensions. Such sharing had the scope of initiating a new relationship between God and the people enabling them to embrace God's ways and to be «on the side of God» (8,33).

The feeding that followed could be seen in the context of sharing and communion. It was for all practical purposes a fellowship meal, a meal shared with the crowd, recipients of Jesus' words of teaching[180]. It was a celebration of togetherness and communion[181]. The crowd may have been oblivious of the significance of the event, but that does not empty it of its meaning. By their intermediary role the disciples too share in this fellowship. In this episode the picture of a community born out of communion and fellowship is complete: God in Jesus reaches out and interacts with the people through the medium of the disciples (cf. Acts 2,42). Thus the whole pericope has not only Christological significance, but also ecclesiological and, as far as the disciples are concerned, even missiological importance.

9. Conclusion

Our investigation into the significance of the use of the verb εἶδεν for Jesus' seeing of the crowd has revealed that the verb expresses a decisive seeing that is rich in meaning. That seeing produced sentiments of compassion to well up in Jesus and gave him an idea of the condition of the crowd as a shepherdless flock. His seeing was a preparation for transforming his tender feeling of compassion into helpful action. By his perceptive seeing, Jesus realised the need to assume the role of the shepherd for them.

In taking up that role of the shepherd to the shepherdless crowd Jesus first and foremost thought of quenching their innermost thirst for the word, which was their primary need. In satisfying that need, Jesus

---

[180] J. GNILKA, *Markus*, 261: «Man wird die Speisung im Kontext der Tischgemeinschaft sehen müssen, die der irdische Jesus Menschen gewährte». J. ROLOFF, *Das Kerygma*, 243: «Das Thema von Mk. 6,34-44 [ist] *die von Jesu gewährte Tischgemeinschaft*».

[181] R.M. Fowler makes a comparison of Jesus' feeding the crowd with Herod's banquet (6,14-29) which immediately precedes it. Cf. R.M. FOWLER, *Loaves and Fishes*, 85-86. He draws a parallel between the three classes of Herod's guests: his courtiers, officers and leading men of Galilee (6,21) and the three groups of people at Jesus' meal: company by company, group by group, one hundred by fifty (6,39-40). Certainly the parallelism does not hold. At Herod's banquet they are three classes of people, but at Jesus' meal the people referred to are the same, the different synonymous used describe the same class of people arranged differently. However, the other contrast R.M. Fowler points out is valid. Herod's banquet concludes with the grisly spectacle of the head of John the Baptist on the platter, while Jesus' meal concludes innocently with the gathering of the leftover food in baskets. We may add that at Herod's banquet there is rupture of human relationships, because blood is spilt, whereas at Jesus' meal there is communion and fellowship stressed by the mention of the satisfaction of those who ate (6,42).

revealed God's will manifested in the fact of the arrival of his kingdom. He taught them the ways of God. The content of Jesus' teaching the crowd also pointed out the kind of response that was required of them, the right conduct that was a prerequisite in order to inherit the kingdom.

The subsequent miraculous feeding too is best explained in the light of Jesus' assumption of the role of shepherd. Jesus fed the crowd not only with the word but also with material food as a sign of communion and fellowship (this episode must have had a great influence on the actual Christian liturgical celebration of the Eucharist, both in its structure and in its sequence, i.e., the liturgy of the Word followed by the liturgy of the Eucharist). However, the miraculous nature of the episode suggests that it was more than a fraternal meal; it was revelatory in character. It once again pointed to the true identity of Jesus. In short it was an episode with Christological implications.

GENERAL CONCLUSION

During the course of the study we have been able to look into the rich concentration of meaning attached to Jesus' seeing expressed by the aorist εἶδεν. The five instances of its occurrence are decisive since these are occasions of great importance. Now we shall sum up our analysis by noting the important aspects of Jesus' seeing.

1. Revelatory Aspect of Jesus' Seeing

From what we have elaborated above, it is evident that Jesus' seeing has extraordinary revelatory traits. Seeing in the five cases we have analysed results in revelation.

1.1 *Seeing as a Moment of Revelation of the Identity of Jesus*

Jesus' seeing is always a moment of revelation to him. Jesus' experience of seeing the heavens being torn apart and the Spirit descending upon him as well as hearing the heavenly voice, confirms his awareness of his relationship to God and the Spirit. It is a moment of revelation. It proclaims the identity of Jesus; it points out his status as beloved Son of the Father (1,11). At the same time it also alludes to his role. It reinforces his insight into his relationship to humanity and the work of salvation he has to undertake on their behalf.

Jesus' seeing his prospective disciples also occasions the revelation of his identity and role. In his seeing these lowly men, Jesus is fully conscious of his role as Master and teacher. Basically it is that consciousness which impels him to call them, to offer them the possibility of being his disciples, to belong to him. As a good master, Jesus promises to form them and to enable them to partake of his own mission.

Jesus' seeing the crowd not only gives him a deep understanding into the desperate situation of the crowd, but also reveals to him his own role that he should assume for their benefit. Hence Jesus takes on the role of the Shepherd for the shepherdless crowd. The subsequent activities he engages in are an eloquent translation of that role into concrete action, of being the promised, messianic Shepherd.

1.2 *Jesus' Seeing Invests the Objects of His Seeing with Identity*

But as far as the disciples are concerned Jesus' seeing occasions the revelation of their own true identity, rather invests them with identity. A casual seeing would prompt someone to brand them as fishermen or tax collector in the case of Levi; people who do not count in the society or rather despised and kept at a distance on account of the trade they practise. But Jesus' seeing is different. In his seeing he is able to have a glimpse into the depth of their inner being and recognise that they are the ones he wants to call. It is like the «love at first sight». Jesus sees not as man sees; man looks on the outward appearance but Jesus sees the heart (1Sam 16,7). Prompted by his seeing he calls them.

Jesus' seeing the crowd reveals to him their predicament. At the same time it also gives him insight into their earnestness, their unbridled enthusiasm in flocking to him as well as their readiness to be instructed, formed, and restored. Jesus wants to invest them with self-confidence and identity of their own. Helped by his seeing Jesus identifies their real need. That motivates him to act in their favour.

1.3 *Jesus' Seeing Occasions a Revelation which Embraces a Double Movement*

Revelation consists of a double movement. It begins with a man-ward movement that has its initiative in God, revealing in the case of seeing, the true identity of the characters involved. Consequently revelation calls for a God-ward movement from the part of man. For Jesus his seeing of the extra-terrestrial reality at his baptism, and the resultant divine communication called for an assent to the God-willed role for him, a commitment in carrying out his part in the work of salvation. Jesus' life and ministry in the rest of the Gospel narrates how Jesus responds to the revelation of his links with God, the Spirit as well as with humanity. Jesus' seeing of the disciples reveals to him that they are the persons whom he really wants to call in order to make them his collaborators. The response to that revelation is manifested in the call he addresses to them. The instance of seeing the crowd reveals to Jesus their plight as well as their openness to receive his words. In response to that revelation Jesus assumes the role of shepherd to them.

The double faceted nature of revelation occasioned by Jesus' seeing is also applicable to Jesus' audience. The revelation of Jesus' identity, his Sonship and his role in the work of salvation is God's way of reaching out to humanity. The consequence of this revelation is an obligation to listen to him (9,7) which means in essence to welcome Jesus, to believe in him, to adhere to him with faith, and to put into practice what he teaches. God comes to man with revelation; man should move towards him with faith. In Jesus' seeing the disciples and calling them, once again an articulation of the selfsame man-ward movement is apparent. Jesus touches the depth of their being with his seeing, reveals to them a glimpse of his power and appeal, makes them realise that it is a seeing filled with authority, fills them with hope, and offers them a proposal to be his followers as well as to share in his ministry towards humanity. His invitation calls for a response that is unconditional and whole-hearted. The disciples rise to the occasion with their «yes» and follow him. The event of Jesus' seeing the crowd and his subsequent activities reveal Jesus' compassionate way of reaching out to them. Their reaching out to Jesus is evident in their enthusiasm to listen to his teaching and in their obedience to him.

2. Jesus' Seeing as Prelude to Communion

Jesus' seeing gains importance when the aspect of communion implied in that seeing is considered. Jesus' experience of communion through seeing is followed by the sharing of that communion with those whom Jesus sees. Sharing of communion is basically a saving act.

2.1 Jesus' Experience of Communion

We hold that the verb εἶδεν which denotes Jesus' seeing the heavens being torn apart and the Spirit descending upon him expresses the way in which Jesus enters into interaction and communion with God and the Spirit. The verb indicates how Jesus has had access to the divine realm when the heavens were torn open. He literally sees the Spirit and hears the Father's voice. Here is God speaking to his Son; the Son experiencing the love of God in the Spirit; the Spirit by His powerful presence moving Jesus to undertake his ministry given by God. Jesus is involved in a state of sharing or exchanging the same thoughts or feelings, and aligning his will to the will of God.

2.2 *Jesus Calls the Disciples to Enter into Communion*

The same eyes that witnessed that extraordinary event at his baptism now see his prospective disciples (1,16.19; 2,14). In his penetrating and omniscient seeing Jesus selects them, and subsequently issues a call to follow him. This seeing and call have the scope of inviting them firstly and more importantly to enter into communion with Jesus himself. Secondly, it is an invitation to enter into communion with God because entering into communion with Jesus by consequence implies entering into communion with God. Thirdly, it is a call to foster communion among the disciples themselves[1]. Communion with Jesus would imply for the disciples sharing or exchanging the same thoughts or feelings of Jesus. For the disciples it means a life long schooling, a journey both literal and figurative which they need to undertake to grasp both the person of Jesus and the message of his proclamation.

2.3 *The Crowd Gain Access to Communion with God*

Jesus' seeing the crowd gives him an idea of the condition of the shepherdless crowd; his heart goes out to them, he is moved with compassion. That sentiment of compassion is translated into active action of teaching, in an effective discernment of the real need. In teaching the crowd Jesus is sharing with them what he experienced at the first instance of his seeing (1,10), that of the advent of the reign of God in his own person with its present and future dimensions. Jesus extends to the crowd his own communion with God and the Spirit. Such sharing has the scope of initiating a new relationship between God and the people enabling them to embrace God's ways and to be «on the side of God» (8,33). The feeding that follows can be viewed from the perspective of sharing and communion. It is a celebration of togetherness and communion. By their intermediary role the disciples too share in this fellowship. In this episode the picture of a community born out of communion and fellowship is complete: God in Jesus reaches out and interacts with the people through the medium of the disciples (cf. Acts 2,42).

2.4 *A Three-fold Structure of Communion*

The dynamics of communion preceded by Jesus' seeing embraces a three pronged dimension. The same concept also gives coherence to our

---

[1] See below for further development of the concept.

investigation into the significance of Jesus' seeing denoted by the aorist εἶδεν. Firstly, Jesus experiences communion with the Father: «as the Father has loved me» (John 15,9a). Secondly, Jesus shares communion with the disciples: «so have I loved you» (John 15,9b). Thirdly, this communion is to be shared and maintained with one another: «love one another as I have loved you» (John 15,12).

Jesus is the pivot on which access to God is established. Both the disciples and the crowd are enabled to enter into communion with God by means of the mediator Jesus. Vertically God reaches out to man through Jesus, man reaches out to God also through Jesus. Jesus envisages a special role for the disciples, that of animating the crowd and making possible communion with God. So horizontally it also implies communion not only among the disciples themselves but also with the crowd, the people of God.

But the one who guarantees communion is the Holy Spirit. The Spirit whom Jesus sees descending upon him is the Spirit of the Father and of the Son, Jesus. The scripture itself refers to him as Spirit of the Father (Matt 10,20; John 15,26), or Spirit of God (Matt 3,16; 12,28; Rom 8,9.14 etc.) as well as Spirit of his Son Jesus Christ (Gal 4,6; Phil 1,19). The Spirit is the bond of communion between the Father and the Son. He is also the fountainhead of every communion, the facilitator and guarantor of both the disciples' and the crowd's communion with the Son Jesus and with God the Father. «So by what is common to them both the Father and the Son wished us to have communion both with them and among ourselves; by this gift which they both possess as one they wished to gather us together and make us one, that is to say, by the Holy Spirit who is God and the gift of God»[2].

3. Vocation is Grounded on Jesus' Seeing

Jesus' seeing is unique. Jesus sees so many people as he moves along the region of Galilee. But when he sees Simon, Andrew, the Zebedee brothers James and John, and Levi, he fixes his eyes on them and calls them. There is undoubtedly something special about Jesus' seeing. The disciples are overwhelmed, compelled within their inner being to leave in haste their profession and family, to respond to the invitation of Jesus. Luke wants his readers to understand that it is the miraculous catch of fish that induced the first four disciples to abandon everything

---

[2] St. Augustine, *Sermones,* 71,18.

and follow him (5,1-11). For Mark the real miracle that takes place is within the disciples, which is caused by the seeing of Jesus, they were seized by the tender but irresistible power of Jesus' seeing (cf. Jer 20,7 [NRSV]: «O LORD, you have enticed me, and I was enticed; you have overpowered me, and you have prevailed»).

Here one of the basic truths that characterises vocation to discipleship is brought out very powerfully: it rests solely on divine initiative. Jesus himself would emphasise this point in the Gospel of John, «You did not choose me, but I chose you» (15,16). In a way, vocation begins with God's seeing the person concerned. God sees the heart of man (1Sam 16,7), discerns its thoughts and intentions (Heb 4,12), and detects the willingness or the lack of it to any offer that he would make. So the vocation of the five prospective disciples is based on Jesus' seeing them. They are called not because they are wise and powerful (1Cor 1,26f.) but because Jesus wants to call them; he wants to form them, enable them to undertake what he has in store for them.

Jesus' seeing them is followed by his call to follow him (1,17: Δεῦτε ὀπίσω μου). The call that is issued by necessity has to meet with a response. Man can refuse or accept the call that is addressed to him. God respects the freedom of man. Those whom Jesus sees and calls respond whole-heartedly, they follow him immediately without hesitation (ἠκολούθησαν αὐτῷ).

The two-fold objectives of the call is defined by Jesus himself when he issues the call: «Follow me and I will make you become fishers of men» (1,17). Jesus calls his disciples to a life of «being with him» as well as to a life of engagement. The time tested principle of *ora et labora* (contemplation and action) is the articulation of the same objectives.

3.1 *Vocation to be with Jesus*

God, who sees and calls a person to follow him, wants that he share a life of intimate union with Him. For the first disciples of Jesus, entering into communion with Jesus was the first step towards entering into union with God. It implied for them a life-long journey of schooling and formation in which they came to gain the right understanding of the identity and mission of Jesus. They learned to align their will to the will of God manifested in Jesus, they learned to be «on the side of God» (8,33). The ultimate goal of a life of discipleship therefore is a progressive growth into the life of Jesus Christ and a genuine imitation of that life through a faithful participation in it. This is brought about by an active pursuit of a life of contemplation and prayer.

Union with God and knowledge of God's ways effected by such a life completely transforms the disciple. St. John of the Cross explains this phenomenon of union:

> The intellect of this soul is God's intellect; its will is God's will; its memory is the eternal memory of God; and its delight is God's delight; and although the substance of this soul is not the Substance of God, since it cannot undergo a substantial conversion into him, it has become God through participation in God, being united to and absorbed in him, as it is in this state. Such a union is wrought in this perfect state of spiritual life, yet not as perfectly as in the next life. Consequently the soul is dead to all it was in itself, which was death to it, and alive to what God is in himself. Speaking to itself, the soul declares in this verse: "In killing you changed death to life." The soul can well repeat the words of St. Paul: *I live, now not I, but Christ lives in me* [Gal.2: 20][3].

The disciple becomes assimilated into the life and love of Jesus Christ, so much so that «he is a new creation; the old has passed away, behold, the new has come» (2Cor 5,17)[4]. Consequently the disciple is also enabled to be a sacrament of Christ in the world, an ambassador and an agent of the ministry of reconciliation (2Cor 5,18-20). This is the way Jesus' promise, «I *will make you become* fishers of men» (1,17), becomes verified in the life of the disciples.

3.2 *Vocation to Active Involvement*

The disciple's transformation into another Christ makes him reach out to the world in like manner. Communion with God is not to be zealously guarded for oneself. It is to motivate the disciple to look at the world through the eyes of Jesus Christ and look with compassion on the world (6,34). The disciple is called upon to proclaim the advent of God's kingdom of mercy and love in the person of Jesus, he is to bring

---

[3] ST. JOHN OF THE CROSS, *The Living Flame of Love*, 2,34.

[4] Masters of spirituality would call the disciple's relationship with God at its deepest and most intimate level as mystical union. Great mystics of Christian Spirituality like John of the Cross, Theresa of Avila, Ignatius of Loyola, Meister Eckhart, and even Vincent Pallotti (founder of Pallottines!), have traced the process of the soul's entering into mystical union with God. The ultimate quest of the soul is to attain the vision of God («beatific vision»). Interestingly vocation which begins with God's seeing the disciple, has its ultimate scope in enabling the disciple to «see» God.

God near to the people and win people for God; he is to become a fisher of man.

That Jesus' disciples whom he saw and called succeeded in becoming «fishers of men» is confirmed by the NT. Rom 10,18 for instance says, «Their voice has gone out to all the earth, and their words to the ends of the world». «And more than ever believers were added to the Lord, multitudes both of men and women» (Acts 5,14). The imagery of being fished out of the sea, was also not absent in the consciousness of the first Christians. They had the sensation of being delivered from a deep sea of darkness, as it were, when they were converted to Christianity and perhaps for this reason they used to refer to themselves as *pisciculi*, little fish caught in the sea. The disciples, by their preaching and by their ministry of reconciliation (2Cor 5,18f.), won them for Christ.

3.3 *Vocation to Common Life*

Jesus' proclamation of the arrival of the kingdom of God (1,14-15) is immediately followed by the formation of a community (1,17.19). Community is born when people with faith, respond to Jesus' call and set out to follow him. The two-fold scope of following Jesus, that of being and doing (1,17; 3,14), also unites the disciples among themselves. They discover the bond of communion that exists between them which in turn enables them to enter into communion with one another. The life of communion to which the disciple is called is lived out in fellowship with others. In the final analysis, every community is the result of the initiative of God.

4. **Ecclesiological Dimension to Jesus' Seeing**

We have emphasised above the vocational aspect of Jesus' seeing and the individual dimension of the disciple's response to the call to communion. However, it is never to be forgotten that the individual is called always as part of a larger faith-community. It is the larger group, the wider circle, the crowd who are the primary objects and recipients of Jesus' ministry. They are the direct recipients of God's involvement in the world. Even the disciple's ministry is oriented towards them (1,17). So in the fifth and the final instance of Jesus' seeing expressed by the verb εἶδεν, Jesus' seeing is described as rightly directed at the crowd. His seeing them, the resulting compassion for them, and the subsequent activities he carries out for them, reflect, his assuming the role of shepherd for them. Jesus translates into concrete action God's own feeling for the crowd. He extends to them God's own love and concern and above all shares with them communion with God.

Thus the crowd are called to experience communion with Jesus, with God, and with the Spirit. But there is always a horizontal dimension to the call to communion; they are to emulate that communion in their own life and existence. Seen this way the church too is a communion, it is catholic not in the sense of being in the whole world but in its striving to be in solidarity with every one. Communion with God presupposes communion with all, even with sinners (Mark 2,17).

The recent Apostolic Letter, *Novo Millennio Ineunte*, in defining what is communion emphasises the corporate aspect of communion. «Communion is the fruit and demonstration of that love which springs from the heart of the Eternal Father and is poured out upon us through the Spirit which Jesus gives us (cf. *Rom* 5:5), to make us all "one heart and one soul" (*Acts* 4:32)»[5]. The Apostolic Letter further adds that «it is in building this communion of love that the Church appears as "sacrament", as the "sign and instrument of intimate union with God and of the unity of the human race"»[6].

So not only the disciples but everyone who belongs to Jesus is also called upon to enter into communion with him, with God and with one another. In order to achieve it the Holy Father's exhortation invites every believer to cultivate and develop a spirituality of communion.

A spirituality of communion indicates above all the heart's contemplation of the mystery of the Trinity dwelling in us, and whose light we must also be able to see shining on the face of the brothers and sisters around us. A spirituality of communion also means an ability to think of our brothers and sisters in faith within the profound unity of the Mystical body, and therefore as "those who are part of me". This makes us able to share their joys and sufferings, to sense their desires and attend to their needs, to offer them deep and genuine friendship. A spirituality of communion implies also the ability to see what is positive in others, to welcome it and prize it as a gift from God: not only as a gift for the brother or sister who has received it directly, but also as a "gift for me". A spirituality of communion means, finally, to know to "make room" for our brothers and sisters, bearing "each other's burdens" (*Gal* 6:2) and resisting the selfish

---

[5] JOHN PAUL II, Apostolic Letter *Novo Millennio Ineunte*, 42.
[6] JOHN PAUL II, Apostolic Letter *Novo Millennio Ineunte*, 42.

temptations which constantly beset us and provoke competition, careerism, distrust and jealousy[7].

The people of God have to discover and live out such a spirituality if the Church is to maintain its relevance in the world. That is accomplished through earnest striving and persevering prayer, «Master, let me receive my sight» (10,51).

---

[7] JOHN PAUL II, Apostolic Letter *Novo Millennio Ineunte*, 43.

ABBREVIATIONS

AASFDHL	Annales Academiae Scientiarum Fennicae Dissertationes Humanarum Litterarum
AB	Anchor Bible
ABD	D.N. FREEDMAN, ed., *The Anchor Bible Dictionary*
al.	alii (and other authors)
AnBib	Analecta Biblica
ATD	Acta Theologica Danica
ATANT	Abhandlungen zur Theologie des Alten und Neuen Testaments
BAGD	W. BAUER – W.F. ARNDT – F.W. GINGRICH – F. DANKER, *A Greek English Lexicon of the New Testament & Other Early Christian Literature*
BDF	F. BLASS – A. DEBRUNNER – R.W. FUNK, *A Greek Grammar of the New Testament and Other Early Christian Literature*
BETL	Bibliotheca ephemeridum theologicarum Lovaniensium
Bib	*Biblica*
BiLe	*Bibel und Leben*
BJRL	*Bulletin of the John Rylands University Library of Manchester*
BS	*Bibliotheca Sacra*
BTB	*Biblical Theology Bulletin*
BTS	Biblisch-Theologische Studien
BU	Biblische Untersuchungen
BZ	*Biblische Zeitschrift*
BZNW	Beihefte zur Zeitschrift für die neutestamentliche Wissenschaft
CBQ	*Catholic Biblical Quarterly*
cf.	confer (see)
ch.	chapter

e.g.	exempli gratia (for example)
DivThom	*Divus Thomas*
EB	*Études bibliques*
ed.	editor/editors
EDNT	H. BALZ – G. SCHNEIDER, ed., *Exegetical Dictionary of the New Testament*
EHST	Europäische Hochschulschriften: Reihe 23, Theologie
EKKNT	Evangelisch-Katholischer Kommentar zum Neuen Testament
etc.	etcetera
ETL	*Ephemerides theologicae Lovanienses*
ExpTim	*Expository Times*
f.	and the following
FB	Forschung zur Bibel
FRLANT	Forschungen zur Religion und Literatur des Alten und Neuen Testaments
Fs.	Festschrift (commemorative volume)
FThSt	Frankfurter Theologische Studien
GTJ	*Grace Theological Journal*
Gos	Gospel
HTKNT	Herders theologischer Kommentar zum Neuen Testament
HTR	*Harvard Theological Review*
Ibid.	ibidem
i.e.	id est (that is)
ICC	International Critical Commentary
ID.	Idem (the same author)
Int.	*Interpretation*
ITS	*Indian Theological Studies*
JBL	*Journal of Biblical Literature*
JR	*Journal of Religion*
JSNT	*Journal for the Study of the New Testament*
JSNTSS	Journal for the Study of the New Testament Supplement Series
JTS	*Journal of Theological Studies*
KD	*Kerygma und Dogma*
LD	Lectio divina
LSJ	H.G. LIDDELL – R. SCOTT – H.S. JONES, *A Greek-English Lexicon*
LXX	Septuagint
MSSNTS	Monograph series. Society for New Testament Studies

MT	Masoretic Text
n.	footnote number
Neot	*Neotestamentica*
NICNT	New International Commentary on the New Testament
NT	New Testament
NT	*Novum Testamentum*
NTAbh	Neutestamentliche Abhandlungen
NTD	Das Neue Testament Deutsch
NTS	Novum Testamentum, Supplements
NTS	*New Testament Studies*
OT	Old Testament
p.	page/pages
par.	parallel/parallels
PSV	*Parola spirito e vita*
RB	*Revue biblique*
RBI	*Rivista Biblica Italiana*
RNT	Regensburger Neues Testament
RSB	Ricerche storico bibliche
RSR	*Recherches de science religieuse*
RSV	Revised Standard Version
SANT	Studien zum Alten und Neuen Testament
SBB	Stuttgarter biblische Beiträge
SBFA	Studium Biblicum Francescanum Analecta
SBLASP	Society of Biblical Literature Abstracts and Seminar Papers
SBLDS	Society of Biblical Literature, Dissertation Series
SBM	Stuttgarter biblische Monographien
SBS	Stuttgarter Bibelstudien
SBT	Studies in Biblical Theology
SJT	*Scottish Journal of Theology*
SNTSMS	Society for New Testament Studies Monograph Series
Str-B	H. STRACK – P. BILLERBECK, *Kommentar zum Neuen Testament aus Talmud und Midrasch*
TDNT	G. KITTEL – G. FRIEDRICH, ed., *Theological Dictionary of the New Testament*
TDOT	G.J. BOTTERWECK – H. RINGGREN, ed., *Theological Dictionary of the Old Testament*
TG.S	Tesi Gregoriana, Serie Spiritualità
TG.T	Tesi Gregoriana, Serie Teologia
TLNT	C. SPICQ, *Theological Lexicon of the New Testament*

TLOT	E. JENNI – C. WESTERMANN, ed., *Theological Lexicon of the Old Testament*
tr.	translator
trans.	translation
TS	*Theological Studies*
TTS	Trier Theologische Studien
TZ	*Theologische Zeitschrift*
v./vv.	verse/verses
WBC	Word Biblical Commentary
WUNT	Wissenschaftliche Untersuchungen zum Neuen Testament
ZKT	*Zeitschrift für katholische Theologie*
ZNW	*Zeitschrift für die neutestamentliche Wissenschaft*
ZTK	*Zeitschrift für Theologie und Kirche*

BIBLIOGRAPHY

1. Commentaries

BARRETT, C.K., *The Gospel According to St. John*, London 1978[2].

BROWN, R.E., *The Gospel according to John (i-xii)*, AB 29, New York 1966.

BUDD, P.J., *Numbers*, WBC 5, Waco 1984.

CRAIGIE, P.C., *Psalms 1–50*, WBC 19, Waco 1983.

CRANFIELD, C.E.B., *The Gospel According to Saint Mark*, Cambridge 1963.

DAVIES, W.D. – ALLISON, D.C., *A Critical and Exegetical Commentary on The Gospel According to Saint Matthew* I-III, Edinburgh 1988-1997.

DEVRIES, S.J., *I Kings*, WBC 12, Waco 1985.

DURHAM, J.I., *Exodus*, WBC 3, Waco 1987.

ERNST, J., *Das Evangelium nach Markus*, RNT, Regensburg 1981.

GNILKA, J., *Das Evangelium nach Markus I*, EKKNT II, Neukirchen – Vluyn 1978.

GRUNDMANN, W., *Das Evangelium nach Markus*, THNT 2, Berlin 1977.

GUELICH, R.A., *Mark 1–8: 26*, WBC 34A, Dallas 1989.

GUNDRY, R.H., *Mark: A Commentary on His Apology for the Cross*, Grand Rapids 1993

GUNDRY, R.H., *Matthew. A Commentary on His Handbook for a Mixed Church under Persecution*, Gran Rapids 1994[2].

HABEL, N. C., *The Book of Job*, London 1985.

HAENCHEN, E., *Der Weg Jesu. Eine Erklärung des Markus-Evangeliums und der kanonischen Parallelen*, Berlin 1968[2].

HAGNER, D.A., *Matthew 1–13*, WBC 33A, Dallas 1993.

HENDRIKSEN, W., *The Gospel of Mark*, Edinburgh 1975.

HOLLADAY, W.L., *Jeremiah* I, Philadelphia 1986.

IERSEL, B.M.F.VAN., *Mark*, Sheffield 1998.

JUEL, D.H, *Mark*, Augsburg Commentary on the New Testament, Minneapolis 1990.

KLEIN, R.H., *1Samuel*, WBC 10, Waco 1983.

LACHS, S.T., *A Rabbinic Commentary on the New Testament. The Gospels of Matthew, Mark, and Luke*, New York 1987.

LAMARCHE, P., *Evangile de Marc*, EB 33, Paris 1996.

LANE, W.L., *The Gospel according to Mark*, NICNT 2, Grand Rapids 1974.

LÉGASSE, S., *L'évangile de Marc*, I-II, LD Commentaires 5, Paris 1997.

LOHMEYER, E., *Das Evangelium des Markus*, Göttingen 1963.

LUZ, U., *Das Evangelium nach Matthäus. 2. Teilband. Mt 8–17*, EKKNT I/2, Zürich 1990.

MANN, C.S., *Mark, A New Translation with Introduction and Commentary*, AB 27, Garden City NY 1986.

MARCUS, J., *Mark 1–8*, AB 27, New York 2000.

MATEOS, J. – CAMACHO, F., *El Evangelio de Marcos. Análisis lingüístico y comentario exegético* I, Cordoba 1993; Italian trans., *Il Vangelo di Marco. Analisi linguistica e commento esegetico* I, tr. B. Pistocchi, Assisi 1997.

METZGER, B.M., *A Textual Commentary on the Greek New Testament*, Stuttgart 1994[2].

NOLLAND, J., *Luke 1–9: 20*, WBC 35A, Dallas 1989.

————, *Luke 9: 21–18: 34*, WBC 35B, Dallas 1993.

PESCH, R., *Das Markusevanglium*, HTKNT II/1-2, Freiburg 1976-1977.

PIKAZA, P., *Para vivir el evangelio. Lectura de Marcos*, Estella 1995; Italian trans., *Il Vangelo di Marco*, tr. M. Zapella, Roma 1996.

PLUMMER, A., *A Critical and Exegetical Commentary on the Gospel According to S. Luke*, ICC, Edinburgh 1901[4].

SCHNACKENBURG, R., *Das Evangelium nach Johannes* I, Freiburg 1965; English trans., *The Gospel According to St John* I, tr. K. Smyth; Wellwood 1968.

SCHWEIZER, E., *Das Evangelium nach Markus* I, Göttingen 1983[6].

STOCK, A., *The Method and Message of Mark*, Wilmington 1989.

SWETE, H.B., *The Gospel According to St. Mark*, London 1908.

TAYLOR, V., *The Gospel According to St. Mark*, London 1966[2].

WATTS, J.D., *Isaiah 34–66*, WBC 25, Waco 1987.

WEISS, B., *Das Matthäus-Evangelium*, Göttingen 1898.

WEISS, J., *Das älteste Evangelium*, Göttingen 1903.

WENHAM, G.J., *Genesis 1–15*, WBC 1, Waco 1987.

WESTERMANN, C., *Isaiah 40–66*, tr. D.M.G. Stalker, London 1969.

YOUNG, E.J., *The Book Of Isaiah* III, Grand Rapids 1972.

2. Books and Articles

ABBOTT, E.A., *From Letter to Spirit*, London 1903.

ABRAHAMS, I., *Studies in Pharisaism and the Gospels*, New York 1967.

ACHTEMEIER, P.J., «"And He Followed Him": Miracles and Discipleship in Mark 10: 46-52», *Semeia* 11 (1978) 115-145.

———, «"He Taught Them Many Things": Reflections on Marcan Christology», *CBQ* 42 (1980) 465-481.

———, «Toward the Isolation of Pre-Markan Miracle Catenae», *JBL* 89 (1970) 265-291.

ADINOLFI, M., *L'apostolato dei Dodici nella vita di Gesù*, Milano 1985.

AMBROZIC, A.M., «New Teaching with Power», in J. PLEVNIK, ed., *Word and Spirit*, Fs. D.M. Stanley, Willowdale 1975, 113-149.

———, *The Hidden Kingdom. A Redaction-Critical Study of the References to the Kingdom of God in Mark's Gospel*, Washington 1972.

ANDERSON, H., «The Old Testament in Mark's Gospel», in J.M EFIRD, ed., *The Use of the Old Testament in the New and Other Essays*, Fs. W.F. Stinespring, Durham 1972, 280-306.

BACON, B.W., «The Prologue of Mark: A Study of Sources and Structure», *JBL* 26 (1907) 84-106.

BAGATTI, B., «Dove avvenne la moltiplicazione dei pani?», *Salmanticensis* 28 (1981) 293-298.

BALZ, H., «συνίημι», *EDNT* III, 307-308.

BARRETT, C.K., *The Holy Spirit and the Gospel Tradition*, London 1947.

BASSLER, J.M., «The Parable of the Loaves», *JR* 66 (1986) 157-172.

BAUER, W., *Griechisch-Deutsches Wörterbuch zu den Schriften des Neuen Testaments und der übrigen urchristlichen Literatur*, Berlin 1958[5]; English trans., *A Greek English Lexicon of the New Testament and Other Early Christian Literature*, tr. W.F. Arndt – F.W. Gingrich – F.W. Danker, Chicago – London 1979[2].

BEASLEY-MURRAY, G.R., *Baptism in the New Testament*, London 1962.

BECK, N.A., «Reclaiming a Biblical Text: The Mark 8: 14-21 Discussion about Bread in the Boat», *CBQ* 43 (1981) 49-56.

BERNHARDT, K. -H., «בְּרָא, Theological Usage», *TDOT* II, 246-248.

BEST, E., *Disciples and Discipleship*, Edinburgh 1986.

————, *Following Jesus*, JSNTSS 4, Sheffield 1981.

————, «Mark's Use of the Twelve», *ZNW* 69 (1978) 11-35.

————, *Mark. The Gospel as a Story*, Edinburgh 1983.

————, «Peter in the Gospel According to Mark», *CBQ* 40 (1978) 547-558.

————, «The Role of the Disciples in Mark», *NTS* 23 (1976-77) 377-401.

BETZ, O., «φωνή», *TDNT* IX, 278-309.

BLASS, F. – DEBRUNNER, A., *Grammatik des neutestamentlichen Griechisch*, Göttingen 1954⁹; English trans., *A Greek Grammar of the New Testament and other Early Christian Literature*, tr. R.W. Funk, Chicago – London 1961.

BLENKINSOPP, J., *The Pentateuch, An Introduction to the First Five Books of the Bible*, New York 1992.

BODE, E.L., *The First Easter Morning. The Gospel Accounts of the Women's Visit to the Tomb of Jesus*, AnBib 45, Rome 1970.

BOOBYER, G.H., «Galilee and the Galileans in St. Mark's Gospel», *BJRL* 35 (1953) 334-348.

————, «The Eucharistic Interpretation of the Miracles of the loaves in St. Mark's Gospel», *JTS* 3 (1952) 161-171.

BORG, M.J., *Conflict, Holiness and Politics in the Teachings of Jesus*, New York 1984.

BOSETTI, E., *Il Pastore. Cristo e la chiesa nella prima lettera di Pietro*, Bologna 1990.

————, *La tenda e il bastone. Figure e simboli della pastorale biblica*, Milano 1992.

————, *Marco. Il rischio di credere*, EDB, Bologna 2000.

————, «Un cammino per vedere. Mc 1,9-10 sullo sfondo dell'intero vangelo», in M. ADINOLFI – P. KASWALDER, ed., *Entrarono a Cafarnao, Lettura interdisciplinaria di Mc I*, Fs. V. Ravanelli, Jerusalem 1997, 123-145.

BOTTERWECK, G.J., «Hirte und Herde im Alten Testament und im Alten Orient», in W. CORSTEN – A. FROTZ – P. LINDEN, ed., *Die Kirche und ihre Ämter und Stände*, Fs. J. Frings, Köln 1960, 339-352.

BOUSSET, W., *Kyrios Christos: Geschichte des Christusglaubens von den Anfängen des Christentums bis Irenaeus*, Göttingen 1921².

BRATCHER, R.G. – NIDA, E.A., *A Translator's Handbook on the Gospel of Mark*, Leiden 1961.

BRETSCHER, P.G., «Exodus 4,22-23 and the Voice from Heaven», *JBL* 87 (1968) 301-311.

BREYTENBACH, C., *Nachfolge und Zukunftserwartung nach Markus. Eine methodenkritische Studie*, ATANT 71, Zürich 1984.

BROADHEAD, E.K., *Naming Jesus. Titular Christology in the Gospel of Mark*, JSNT 175, Sheffield 1999.

BRODIE, T.L., *The Crucial Bridge. The Elijah-Elisha Narrative as an Interpretative Synthesis of Genesis-Kings and a Literary Model for the Gospels*, Collegeville 2000.

BROWN, R.E. al., *Peter in the New Testament*, Minneapolis 1973.

BROWN, R.E., *The Community of the Beloved Disciple*, New York 1979.

BRUGMANN, K., *Griechische Grammatik*, Munich 1913[4].

BUBER, M., *Moses*, Zürich 1948.

BULTMANN, R., *Die Geschichte der synoptischen Tradition*, Göttingen 1964[6]; English trans., *The History of the Synoptic Tradition*, tr. J. Marsh, Oxford 1963.

BURGER, C., *Jesus als Davidssohn*, FRLANT 98, Göttingen 1970.

BURKILL, T.A., *Mysterious Revelation. An Examination of the Philosophy of St. Mark's Gospel*, New York 1963.

BUSE, I., «The Markan Account of the Baptism of Jesus and Isaiah LXIII», *JTS* 7 (1956) 74-75.

BYRNE, B., *Sons of God – Seed of Abraham*, Rome 1979.

CACHIA, N., *«I am the good shepherd. The good shepherd lays down his life for the sheep» (John 10,11). The Image of the Good Shepherd as a Source for the Spirituality of the Ministerial Priesthood*, TG.S 4, Roma 1997.

CALVIN, J., *A Harmony of the Gospels, Matthew, Mark and Luke* I, tr. A.W. Morrison, Grand Rapids 1972.

CANGH, J.-M.VAN., «La Galilée dans l'évangile de Marc: un lieu théologique?» *RB* 79 (1972) 59-76.

————, *La multiplication des pains et l'eucharistie*, LD 86, Paris 1975, 76-88, 100-104.

CERFAUX, L., «La mission de Galilée dans la tradition synoptique», in *Recueil Lucien Cerfaux* I, Gembloux 1954, 425-469.

CHARLES, R.H., ed., *The Apocrypha and Pseudepigrapha of the Old Testament in English* II, Oxford 1969[5].

CHARLES, R.H., ed., *The Testaments of the Twelve Patriarchs*, London 1908.

CITRON, B., «The Multitude in the Synoptic Gospels», *SJT* 7 (1954) 408-418.

CONYBEARE, F.C., «New Testament Notes. (1) The Holy Spirit as a Dove», *ExpTim* (4th Ser.) ix (1894), 451-458.

COOK, M., *Mark's Treatment of the Jewish Leaders*, NTS 51, Leiden 1978.

COULOT, C., *Jésus et le Disciple. Etude sur l'autorité messianique de Jésus*, EB 8, Paris 1987.

COUNTRYMAN, W., «How Many Baskets Full? Mark 8: 14-21 and the Value of Miracles in Mark», *CBQ* 47 (1985) 643-655.

CRANFIELD, C.E.B., «The Baptism of Our Lord – A Study of St. Mark 1.9-11», *SJT* 8 (1955) 53-63.

CROSSAN, J.D., «The Seed Parables of Jesus», *JBL* 92 (1973) 244-266.

CULLMANN, O., *Die Tauflehre des Neuen Testaments. Erwachsenen – und Kindertaufe*, Zürich 1948; English trans., *Baptism in the New Testament*, tr. J.K.S. Reid, London 1950.

————, *Peter: Disciple, Apostle, Martyr*, Philadelphia 1962.

DAUBE, D., *The New Testament and Rabbinic Judaism*, Salem 1984.

DAVIES, P.R. – CHILTON, B.D., «The Aqedah: A Revised Tradition History», *CBQ* 40 (1978) 514-546.

DELORME, J., «Jésus, les apôtres et la foule. Mc 6, 30-34», *AS* 47 (1974) 44-58.

DERRETT, J.D.M., «ἦσαν γὰρ ἁλιεῖς (Mk 1,16). Jesus' Fishermen and the Parable of the Net», *NT* 22/2 (1980) 108-137.

DEWEY, J., *Markan Public Debate. Literary Technique, Concentric Structure, and Theology in Mark 2, 1–3,6*, SBLDS 48, Chico 1980.

DIBELIUS, M., *Die Formgeschichte des Evangeliums*, Tübingen 1971[6].

DIETRICH, W., *Das Petrusbild der lukanischen Schriften*, Stuttgart 1972.

DILLON, R.J., «"As One Having Authority"(Mark 1: 22): The Controversial Distinction of Jesus' Teaching», *CBQ* 57 (1995) 92-113.

DODD, C.H., «The Framework of the Gospel Narrative», in ID., *New Testament Studies*, Manchester 1953, 1-11.

————, *The Parables of the Kingdom*, Glasgow 1961.

DONAHUE, J.R., «Tax Collectors and Sinners. An Attempt at Identification» *CBQ* 33 (1971) 39-61.

————, *Are you the Christ? The Trial Narrative in the Gospel of Mark*, SBLDS 10, Missoula 1973.

DONALDSON, J., «"Called to Follow" A Twofold Experience of Discipleship in Mark», *BTB* 5 (1975) 67-77.

DSCHULNIGG, P., *Petrus im Neuen Testament*, Stuttgart 1996.

———, *Sprache, Redaktion und Intention des Markus-Evangeliums*, SBB 11, Stuttgart 1984.

DUNN, J.D.G., «Mark 2.1–3.6: A Bridge between Jesus and Paul on the Question of the Law», *NTS* 30 (1984) 395-415.

DUPONT, J., «Le nom d'apôtres a-t-il été donné aux Douze par Jésus?», in F. NEIRYNCK, ed., *Etudes sur les évangiles synoptiques* II, Louvain 1985, 976-1018.

EDERSHEIM, A., *The Life and Time of Jesus the Messiah* I, London 1883.

EDWARDS, R., «Markan Sandwiches, the Significance of Interpolations in Markan Narratives», *NT* 31 (1989) 193-216.

EGGER, W., *Frohbotschaft und Lehre. Die Sammelberichte des Wirkens Jesu im Markusevangelien*, FTS 19, Frankfurt 1976.

———, *Methodenlehre zum Neuen Testament*, Freiburg 1987.

ENSLIN, M.S., «John and Jesus», *ZNW* 66 (1975) 1-18.

ERNST, J., *Johannes der Täufer. Interpretation – Geschichte – Wirkungsgeschichte*, BZNW 53, Berlin 1989.

EVANS, C.A., «Jesus' Action in the Temple: Cleansing or Potent Destruction?», *CBQ* 51(1989) 237-270.

EVANS, C.F., «"I will Go Before you into Galilee "», *JTS* 5 (1954) 3-18.

FABRIS, R., *Gesù di Nazareth. Storia e interpretazione*, Assisi 1983[2].

FEUILLET, A., «Le Baptême de Jésus d'après l'évangile selon saint Marc (1,9-11)», *CBQ* 21 (1959) 468-490.

———, «Le symbolisme de la colombe dans les récits évangéliques du baptême», *RSR* 46 (1958) 524-544.

FISCHER, G. – HASITSCHKA, M., *Auf dein Wort hin. Berufung und Nachfolge in der Bibel*, Innsbruck – Wien 1995.

FLEDDERMANN, H., «A Warning about the Scribes (Mark 12: 37b-40)», *CBQ* 44 (1982) 52-67.

———, «The Flight of a Naked Young Man (Mark 14: 51-52)», *CBQ* 41 (1979) 412-418.

FOCANT, C., «L'incompréhension des disciples dans le deuxième évangile», *RB* 82 (1975) 161-185.

FOERSTER, W., «'Iησοῦς», *TDNT* III, 284-293.

FORBES, G.W., *The God of Old. The Role of the Lukan Parables in the Purpose of Luke's Gospel*, JSNTSS 198, Sheffield 2000.

FOWLER, R.M., *Loaves and Fishes. The Function of the Feeding Stories in the Gospel of Mark*, SBLDS 54, Chico 1981.

————, «The Feeding of the Five Thousand: A Markan Composition», SBLASP I, 101-104.

FRANCE, R.T., *Jesus and the Old Testament*, London 1971.

————, «Mark and the Teaching of Jesus», in R.T. FRANCE –D. WENHAM, ed., *Gospel Perspectives: Studies of History and Tradition in the Four Gospels* I, Sheffield 1980, 101-136.

FREEDMAN, H. – SIMON, M., ed., *Midrash Rabbah, Genesis*, London 1961.

FREYNE, S., *The Twelve: Disciples and Apostles. A Study in the Theology of the First Three Gospels*, London 1968.

FRIEDRICH, B., «κῆρυξ», *TDNT* III, 683-696.

FRIEDRICH, G., «Beobachtungen zur messianischen Hohepriestererwartung in den Synoptikern», *ZTK* 53 (1956) 265-311.

————, «Die beiden Erzählungen von der Speisung in Mark 6,31-44; 8,1-9», *TZ* 20 (1964)10-22.

FULLER, R.H., *The Formation of the Resurrection Narratives*, Philadelphia 1980.

FUSCO, V., «Dalla missione di Galilea alla missione universale. La tradizione del discorso missionario (Mt 9,35-10, 42; Mc 6,7-13; Lc 9,1-6; 10,1-16)», in G. GHIBERTI, ed., *La missione nel mondo antico e nella Bibbia*, RSB 1, Bologna 1990, 101-125.

GAMBA, G.G., «Considerazioni in margine alla redazione di Mc 2,13-17» *DivThom* 72 (1969) 201-226.

GARNET, P., «The Baptism of Jesus and the Son of Man Idea» *JSNT* 9 (1980) 46-65.

GARRETT, S.R., *The Demise of the Devil: Magic and the Demonic in Luke's Writings*, Minneapolis 1989.

GERO, S., «The Spirit as Dove at the Baptism of Jesus», *NTS* 18/1 (1976) 17-35.

GNILKA, J., *Jesus von Nazareth. Botschaft und Geschichte*, Freiburg im Breisgau 1993; English trans., *Jesus of Nazareth. Message and History*, tr. S.S. Schatzmann, Peabody 1997.

GOGUEL, M., *Au Seuil de l'évangile Jean-Baptiste*, Paris 1928.

GREEVEN, H., «περιστερά», *TDNT* VI, 63-72.

GRINDEL, J., «Matthew 12. 18-21», *CBQ* 29 (1967) 110-115.

GRUNDMANN, W., «δεξιός», *TDNT* II, 37-40.

————, «The Christ-Statements of the New Testament», *TDNT* IX, 527-580.

GUILLEMETTE, P., «Un enseignement nouveau, plein d'autorité», *NT* 22/3 (1980) 222-247.

GUNDRY, R.H., *The Use of the Old Testament in St. Matthew's Gospel with Special Reference to the Messianic Hope*, NTS 18, Leiden 1967.

HAHN, F., *Christologische Hoheitstitel. Ihre Geschichte im frühen Christentum*, Göttingen 1964².

————, *Das Verständnis der Mission im neuen Testament*, Neukirchen – Vlyun 1963; English trans., *Mission in the New Testament*, tr. F. Clarke, SBT 1/47, London 1965.

HAREN, M.J., «The Naked Young Man: a Historian's Hypothesis on Mark 14,51-52», *Bib* 79 (1998) 525-531.

HARRISON, E.F., «The Son of God among the Sons of Men. II. Jesus and Andrew», *BS* 102 (1945) 170-178.

HAUCK, F., «παραβολή», *TDNT* V, 744 - 761.

HAWKINS, J.C., *Horae Synopticae, Contributions to the Study of the Synoptic Problem*, Oxford 1909².

HECKEL, T.K., *Vom Evangelium des Markus zum viergestaltigen Evangelium*, Tübingen 1999.

HEDRICK, C.W., «The Role of "Summary Statements" in the Composition of the Gospel of Mark: A Dialogue with Karl Schmidt and Norman Perrin» *NT* 26/4 (1984) 289-311.

HEIL, J.P., *Jesus' Walking on the Sea. Meaning and Gospel Functions of Matt. 14,22-33, Mark 6, 45-52 and John 6,15b-21*, AnBib 87, Rome 1981.

HEISING, A., «Das Kerygma der wunderbaren Fischvermehrung (Mk 6,34-44 parr)», *BiLe* 10 (1969) 52-57.

————, *Die Botschaft der Brotvermehrung*, SBS 15, Stuttgart 1966.

HENGEL, M., *Nachfolge und Charisma. Eine exegetisch-religionsgeschichtliche Studie zu Mt 8,21f. und Jesu Ruf in die Nachfolge*, BZNW 34, Berlin 1968; English trans., *The Charismatic Leader and His Followers*, tr. J.C.G. Greig, Edinburgh 1981.

HERGENRÖDER, C., *Wir schauten seine Herrlichkeit. Das johanneishe Sprechen vom Sehen im Horizont von Selbsterchließung Jesu und Antwort des Menschen*, FB 80, Würzburg 1996.

HILLS, J.V., «Luke 10. 18 – Who Saw Satan Fall?», *JSNT* 46 (1992) 25-40.

HIRSCH, S., *Taufe, Versuchung und Verklärung Jesu*, Berlin 1932.

HUNZINGER, H., «σίναπι», *TDNT* VII , 287-291.

IERSEL, B.M.F. VAN, «Die wunderbare Speisung und das Abendmahl in der synoptischen Tradition (Mk vi 35-44 par., viii 1-20 par)», *NT* 7 (1964) 167-194.

IWE, J.C., *Jesus in the Synagogue of Capernaum: The Pericope and its Programmatic Character for the Gospel of Mark. An Exegetico-Theological Study of Mk 1:21-28*, TG.T 57, Roma 1999.

JACKSON, H., «The death of Jesus in Mark and the Miracle from the Cross», *NTS* 33 (1987) 16-37.

JEREMIAS, J., «γραμματεύς», *TDNT* I, 740-742.

————, *Die Gleichnisse Jesu*, Göttingen 1970[8]; English trans., *The Parables of Jesus*, tr. S.H. Hooke, London 1972[3].

————, *New Testament Theology*, London 1971.

————, «Paarweise Sendung im Neuen Testament», in ID., *Abba: Studien zur neutestamentlichen Theologie und Zeitgeschichte*, Göttingen 1966, 132-139.

————, «παῖς θεοῦ in the New Testament», *TDNT* V, 700-717.

————, «ποιμήν», *TDNT* VI, 485-502.

————, *The Central Message of the New Testament*, London 1965.

JOHNSON, E.S., «Mark 15,39 and the so-called Confession of the Roman Centurion», *Bib* 81 (2000) 406-413.

————, «Mark VIII. 22-26: The Blind Man from Bethsaida», *NTS* 25 (1978-79) 370-383.

JOHNSON, L., «Who was the Beloved Disciple», *ExpTim* 77 (1965-66) 157-158.380.

JOHNSON, L.T., *The Writings of the New Testament. An Interpretation*, Minneapolis 1999.

JOHNSON, S.R., «The Identity and Significance of the Neaniskos in Mark», *Forum* 8 (1992) 123-139.

JONGE, M.D., «Christian Influence in the Testaments of Twelve Patriarchs», *NT* 4 (1960) 182-235.

JUEL, D.H., *A Master of Surprise. Mark Interpreted*, Minneapolis 1994.

KARNETSKI, M., «Die Galiläische Redaktion im Markusevangelium», *ZNW* 52 (1961) 238-272.

KATO, Z., *Die Völkermission im Markusevangelium. Eine Redaktions-geschichtliche Untersuchung*, EHST 23/252, Bern – Frankfurt 1986.

KAZMIERSKI, C.R., *Jesus, the Son of God. A Study of the Markan Tradition and its Redaction by the Evangelist*, FB 33, Würzburg 1979.

KECK, L.E., «The Introduction to Mark's Gospel», *NTS* 12 (1965-66) 352-370.

————, «The Spirit and the Dove», *NTS* 17 (1970-1971) 41-67

KELBER, W.H., *The Kingdom in Mark*, Philadelphia 1974.

KERMODE, F., *The Genesis of Secrecy. On the Interpretation of Narrative*, Cambridge 1980.

KERTELGE, K., *Die Wunder Jesu im Markusevangelium. Eine redaktionsgeschichtliche Untersuchung*, SANT 23, München 1970.

KESSLER, M., «Narrative Technique in 1 Sm 16,1-13», *CBQ* 32 (1970) 543-554.

KIILUNEN, J., *Die Vollmacht im Widerstreit. Untersuchung zum Werdegang von Mk 2,1-3,6*, AASFDHL 40, Helsinki 1985.

KILPATRICK, G.D., «Jesus, His Family and His Disciples», *JSNT* 15 (1982) 3-19.

————, «The Gentile Mission in Mark and Mark 13: 9-11», in D.E. NINEHAM, ed., *Studies in the Gospels*, Fs. R.H. Lightfoot, Oxford 1957, 145-158.

————, «Verbs of Seeing», in J.K. ELLIOTT, ed., *The Language and Style of the Gospel of Mark*, Leiden 1993, 179-180.

KINGSBURY, J.D, *The Christology of Mark's Gospel*, Philadelphia 1983.

————, «The Religious Authorities in the Gospel of Mark», *NTS* 36 (1990) 42-65.

KITTEL, G., «ἀκολουθέω», *TDNT* I, 210-216.

KLAUCK, H.J., *Vorspiel im Himmel, Erzähltechnik und Theologie im Markusprolog*, Neukirchen – Vluyn 1997.

KOCH, D.A., *Die Bedeutung der Wundererzählungen für die Christologie des Markusevangeliums*, BZNW 42, Berlin 1975.

KÖSTER, H., «σπλαγχνίζομαι», *TDNT* VII, 548-559.

KREMER, J., «"ὁράω", see», *EDNT* II, 526-529.

KÜSTER, V., *Jesus und das Volk im Markusevangelium. Ein Beitrag zum interkulturellen Gespräch in der Exegese*, BTS 28, Neukirchen – Vluyn 1996.

KUTHIRAKKATTEL, S., *The Beginning of Jesus' Ministry According to Mark's Gospel (1,14-3,6). A Redaction Critical Study*, AnBib 123, Roma 1990.

LAMPE, G.W.H., *The Seal of the Spirit*, London 1951[4].

LEANEY, A.R.C., «The Gospels as Evidence for First-Century Judaism», in D.E. NINEHAM – *al.*, ed., *Historicity and Chronology in the New Testament*, London 1965, 28-45.

LEGRAND, L., «The Good Shepherd in the Gospel of Mark», *ITS* 29/3 (1992) 234-255.

LENTZEN-DEIS, F., «Das Motive der "Himmelsöffnung" in verschiedenen Gattungen der Umweltliteratur des Neuen Testaments», *Bib* 50 (1969) 301-327.

———, *Die Taufe Jesu nach den Synoptikern. Literarkritische und gattungsgeschichtliche Untersuchungen*, FThSt 4, Frankfurt 1970.

LEWIS, A.S., ed., *The Old Syriac Gospels or Evangelion da-Mepharreshe*, London 1906.

LIGHTFOOT, R.H., *Locality and Doctrine in the Gospels*, London 1938.

———, *The Gospel Message of St. Mark*, Oxford 1950.

LINDARS, B., «Matthew, Levi, Lebbaeus and the Value of the Western Text», *NTS* 4 (1958) 220-222.

LOHMEYER, E., *Galiläa und Jerusalem*, Göttingen 1936.

LÜHRMANN, D., «Die Pharisäer und die Schriftgelehrten im Markusevangelium», *ZNW* 78 (1987) 169-185.

MADDEN, P.J., *Jesus' Walking on the Sea. An Investigation of the Origin of the Narrative Account*, BZNW 81, Berlin – New York 1997.

MALBON, E.S., «Disciples/Crowds/Whoever: Markan Characters and Readers», *NT* 28/2 (1986) 104-130.

———, «Galilee and Jerusalem. History and Literature in Marcan Interpretation», *CBQ* 44 (1982) 242-255.

———, «τῇ οἰκίᾳ αὐτοῦ: Mark 2. 15 in Context», *NTS* 31 (1985) 282-292.

———, «The Jesus of Mark and the Sea of Galilee», *JBL* 103/3 (1984) 363-377.

MALONEY, E.C., *Semitic Interference in Marcan Syntax*, SBLDS 51, Chico 1981.

MÁNEK, J., «Fishers of Men», *NT* 2 (1957) 138-141.

MANNS, F., *Essais sur le Judéo-Christianisme*, SBFA 12, Jerusalem 1977.

MARCUS, J., «Jesus' Baptismal Vision», *NTS* 41(1995) 512-521.

———, *The Mystery of the Kingdom of God* , SBLDS 90, Atlanta 1986.

MARSHALL, C.D., *Faith as a Theme in Mark's Narrative*, SNTSMS 64, Cambridge 1989.

MARSHALL, I.H., «Son of God or Servant of Yahweh? – A Reconsideration of Mark 1. 11», *NTS* 15 (1968-1969) 326-336.

MARXSEN, W., *Mark the Evangelist. Studies on the Redaction History of the Gospel*, Nashville 1969.

MASUDA, S., «The Good News of the Miracle of the Bread. The Tradition and its Markan Redaction», *NTS* 28 (1982) 191-219.

MATERA, F.J., «The Incomprehension of the Disciples and Peter's Confession (Mark 6,14-8, 30)», *Bib* 70 (1989) 153-172.

MATJAŽ, M., *Furcht und Gotteserfahrung. Die Bedeutung des Furchtmotivs für die Christologie des Markus*, FB 91, Würzburg 1999.

MAUER, C., «Knecht Gottes und Sohn Gottes im Passionsbericht des Markusevangeliums», *ZTK* 50 (1953) 1-38.

MAUSER, U., *Christ in the Wilderness. The Wilderness Theme in the Second Gospel and its Basis in the Biblical Tradition*, SBT 39, London 1963.

MAY, D.M., «Mark 2.15: The Home of Jesus or Levi?», *NTS* 39 (1993) 147-149.

MCARTHUR, H.K., «The Parable of the Mustard Seed», *CBQ* 33 (1971) 198-210.

MEIER, J.P., *A Marginal Jew. Rethinking the Historical Jesus* 2, New York 1994.

MENKEN, M.J.J., «The Matthew-Luke Agreements in Mt 14,13-14 / Lk 9,10-11 (PAR. MK 6,30-34). The Two-Source Theory Beyond the Impasse», *ETL* 60 (1984) 25-44.

MEYE, R.P., *Jesus and the Twelve. Discipleship and Revelation in Mark's Gospel*, Grand Rapids 1968.

MEYER, B.F., *The Aims of Jesus*, London 1979.

MEYER, R., «ὄχλος», *TDNT* V, 582-584.586-590.

MICHAELIS, W., «ὁράω», *TDNT* V, 315-382.

MICHEL, O., «τελώνης», *TDNT* VIII, 88-105.

MIDDENDORF, H., *Gott sieht. Eine terminologische Studie über das Schauen Gottes im AT*, Breslau 1935.

MINEAR, P.S., «Audience Criticism and Markan Ecclesiology», in H. BALTENSWEILER – B. REICKE, ed., *Neues Testament und Geschichte. Historisches Geschehen und Deutung im Neuen Testament*, Fs. O. Cullmann, Zürich 1972, 79-89.

MOLONEY, F.J., *A Body Broken for a Broken People. Eucharist in the New Testament*, Massachusetts 1997.

MOLONEY, F.J., *Disciples and Prophets. A Biblical Model for the Religious Life*, London 1980.

———, «The Vocation of the Disciples in the Gospel of Mark», *Salesianum* 43 (1981) 487-516.

MONTEFIORE, H., «Revolt in the Desert?», *NTS* 8 (1961-62) 135-141.

MOTYER, S., «The Rending of the Veil: A Markan Pentecost?», *NTS* 33 (1987) 155-157.

MOULTON, J.H., *A Grammar of New Testament Greek*. III. *Syntax*, Edinburgh 1963.

MÜLLER, P.-G., «βλέπω», *EDNT* I, 221-222.

NARDONI, E., «A Redactional Interpretation of Mark 9: 1», *CBQ* 43 (1981) 365-384.

NEIRYNCK, F., *Duality in Mark. Contributions to the Study of Markan Redaction* BETL 31, Leuven 1988.

NESTLE, E., «Zur Taube als Symbol des Geistes», *ZNW* 7 (1906) 358-59.

NEUGEBAUER, F., «Die wunderbare Speisung (Mk 6,30-44 parr.) und Jesu Identität», *KD* 32 (1986) 254-277.

NIELSEN, H.K., *Heilung und Verkündigung*, ATD 22, Leiden 1987.

NÖTSCHER, F., *«Das Angesicht Gottes Sehen» nach biblischer und babylonischer Auffassung*, Würzburg 1924.

PAINTER, J., «When is a House not a Home?. Disciples and Family in Mark 3.13-35», *NTS* 45 (1999) 498-513.

PATSCH, H., «Abendmahlsterminologie außerhalb der Einsetzungsberichte. Erwägungen zur Traditionsgeschichte der Abendmahlsworte», *ZNW* 62 (1971) 210-231.

PERRIN, N., *The New Testament: An Introduction*, New York 1974.

———, «Towards an Interpretation of the Gospel of Mark», in H.D. BETZ, ed., *Christology and a Modern Pilgrimage. A Discussion with Norman Perrin*, Claremont 1971, 1-78.

PESCH, R., «Berufung und Sendung, Nachfolge und Mission. Eine Studie zu Mk 1,16-20», *ZTK* 91 (1969) 1-31.

———, *Der reiche Fischfang*, Düsseldorf 1969.

———, «"Eine neue Lehre aus Macht". Eine Studie zu Mk 1,21-28», in J.B. BAUER, ed., *Evangelienforschung. Ausgewählte Aufsätze deutscher Exegeten*, Graz 1968, 241-276.

———, «Ein Tag vollmächtigen Wirkens Jesu in Kapharnaum (Mk 1,21-34. 35-39)», *BiLe* 9 (1968) 114-128.

PESCH, R., «Levi-Matthäus (Mc 2,14/mat 9,9; 10,3) Ein Beitrag zur Lösung eines alten Problems», *ZNW* 59 (1968) 40-56.

———, *Simon Petrus. Päpste und Papsttum*, Stuttgart 1980.

PETERSON, P.M., *Andrew, Brother of Simon Peter. His History and His Legends*, NTS 1, Leiden 1958.

PHILO, «*Quis Rerum Divinarum Heres*», in *The Works of Philo*, tr. C.D. Yonge, Peabody 1993, 276-303.

———, «*Quaestiones et Solutiones in Genesin, III*», in *The Works of Philo*, tr. C.D. Yonge, Peabody 1993, 841-863.

POPPI, A., *L'inizio del Vangelo. Predicazione del Battista, Battesimo e Tentazione di Gesù*, Padova 1976.

PORTER, S.E., *Idioms of the Greek New Testament*, Sheffield 1994^2.

———, *Verbal Aspect in the Greek of the New Testament, with Reference to Tense and Mood*, New York 1989.

POTTERIE, I. DE LA, «Le sens primitif de la multiplication des Pains», in J. DUPONT, ed., *Jésus aux origines de la Christologie*, Gembloux 1975, 303-329.

PREUSS, H.D., «אוֹי», *TDOT* VI, 225-250.

PRYKE, E.J., *Redactional Style in the Marcan Gospel. A Study of Syntax and Vocabulary as Guides to Redaction in Mark*, SNTSMS, 33 Cambridge 1978.

QUESNELL, Q., *The Mind of Mark. Interpretation and Method through an Exegesis of Mark 6,52*, AnBib 38, Rome 1969.

RÄISÄNEN, H., *Das Messiasgeheimnis im Markusevangelium. Ein redaktionskritischer Versuch*, SFEG 28, Helsinki 1976.

REISER, M., *Syntax und Stil des Markusevangeliums*, WUNT 2/11, Tübingen 1984.

RENGSTORF, H.K., «ἀπόστολος», *TDNT* 1, 398-447.

———, «μαθητής», *TDNT* IV, 390-461.

REPLOH, K.-G., *Markus – Lehrer der Gemeinde. Eine redaktionsgeschichtliche Studie zu den Jüngerperikopen des Markus-Evangeliums*, SBM 9, Stuttgart 1969.

RHOADS, D. – DEWEY, J. – MICHIE, D., *Mark as Story. An Introduction to the Narrative of a Gospel*, Minneapolis 1999^2.

RICHARDSON, A., *An Introduction to the Theology of the New Testament*, New York 1958.

———, «The Feeding of the Five Thousand. Mark 6: 34-44» *Int* 9 (1955) 144-149.

RICHTER, G., «Zu den Tauferzählungen Mk 1,9-11 und Joh 1,32-34», *ZNW* 65 (1974) 43-56.

ROBERT, P. DE, *Le Berger d'Israël. Essai sur le thème pastoral dans l'Ancien Testament*, Neuchâtel 1968.

ROLOFF, J., *Apostolat – Verkündigung – Kirche. Ursprung, Inhalt und Funktion des kirchlichen Apostolamtes nach Paulus, Lukas und den Pastoralbriefen*, Gütersloh 1965.

————, *Das Kerygma und der irdische Jesus. Historische Motive in den Jesus-Erzählungen der Evangelien*, Göttingen 1970.

RUCKSTUHL, E., «Jesus als Gottessohn im Spiegel des markinischen Taufberichts», in U. LUZ – H. WEDER, ed., *Die Mitte des Neuen Testaments*, Fs. E. Schweizer, Göttingen 1983, 193-220.

RUMAINEK, R., *Dio pastore d'Israele secondo Ezechiele 34 e l'applicazione messianica nel vangelo di Matteo*, Excerpta ex dissertatione ad Doctoratum in Facultate Theologiae, PUG, Roma 1979.

SAMUEL, M., *The Lord is my Shepherd. The Theology of a Caring God*, New Jersey 1996.

SAND, A., *Das Gesetz und die Propheten*, BU 11, Regensburg 1974.

SCHELKLE, K.H., *Discipleship and Priesthood. A Biblical Interpretation*, New York 1965.

SCHENKE, L., *Die Wundererzählungen des Markusevangeliums*, SBB, Stuttgart 1974.

————, *Studien zur Passionsgeschichte des Markus. Tradition und Redaktion in Markus 14, 1-42*, Würzburg 1971.

SCHILLE, G., *Die urchristliche Kollegialmission*, ATANT 48, Zürich 1967.

SCHMAHL, G, *Die Zwölf im Markusevangelium. Eine redaktionsgeschichtliche Untersuchung*, TTS 30, Trier 1974.

SCHMIDT, J., *Das Gewand der Engel. Der historische Hintergrund von Mk 16,1-8 par und dessen Einfluß auf die Thematik und literarische Form der Apostlegeschichte*, Bonn 1999.

SCHMIDT, K.L., *Der Rahmen der Geschichte Jesu.* Darmstadt 1964.

SCHMIDT, W.H., *Die Schöpfungsgeschichte der Priesterschrift*, Neukirchen – Vluyn 1964.

SCHNEEMELCHER, W., ed., *Neutestamentaliche Apokryphen*, Tübingen 1990; English trans., *New Testament Apocrypha I. Gospels and Related Writings*, tr. R. McL. Wilson, Cambridge 1991.

SCHOLTISSEK, K., *Die Vollmacht Jesu. Traditions und Redaktionsgeschichtliche Analysen zu einem Leitmotiv Markinischer Christologie*, NTAbh 25, Aschendorff 1992.

SCHREIBER, J., *Theologie des Vertrauens. Eine redaktionsgeschichtliche Untersuchung des Markusevangeliums*, Hamburg 1967

SCHRENK, G., «εὐδοκέω», *TDNT* II, 738-751.

SCHULZ, A., *Nachfolgen und Nachahmen: Studien über das Verhältnis der neutestamentlichen Jüngerschaft zur urchristlichen Vorbildethik*, SANT 6, München 1962.

SCHWEIZER, E., «"υἱός", D. New Testament», *TDNT* VIII, 363-392.

SCOBIE, C.H.H., *John the Baptist*, London 1964.

SEETHALER, A., «Die Brotvermehrung – ein Kirchenspiegel?», *BZ* 34 (1990) 108-112.

SEITZ, O.J.F., «*Preparatio Evangelica* in the Marcan Prologue», *JBL* 82 (1963) 201-206.

SELLIN, G., «Das Leben des Gottessohnes. Taufe und Verklärung Jesu als Bestandteile eines vormarkinischen "Evangeliums"», *Kairos* 25 (1983) 237-253.

SENIOR, C.P., «The Struggle to be Universal: Mission as Vantage Point for New Testament Investigation», *CBQ* 46 (1984) 63-81.

SENIOR, D. – STUHLMUELLER, C., *The Biblical Foundations for Mission*, New York 1983.

SHEPHERD, T., «The Narrative Function of Markan Intercalation», *NTS* 41 (1995) 522-540.

SHINER, W.T., *Follow Me! Disciples in Markan Rhetoric*, SBLDS 145, Atlanta 1995.

SMITH, C.R., «Errant Aorist Interpreters», *GTJ* 2 (1981) 205-226.

SMITH, C.W.F., «Fishers of Men: Footnotes on a Gospel Figure», *HTR* 52 (1959) 187-203.

SMITH, R.H., *Easter Gospels. The Resurrection of Jesus according to the Four Evangelists*, Minneapolis 1983.

SMITH, T.V., *Petrine Controversies in Early Christianity*, WUNT 2/15, Tübingen 1985.

SOGGIN, J.A., «רעה», *TLOT* 3, 1246-1248.

SPICQ, C., «σπλαγχνίζομαι», *TLNT* 3, 273-275.

STAGG, F., «The Abused Aorist», *JBL* 91 (1972) 222-231.

STEGEMANN, E.W., «Zur Rolle von Petrus, Jakobus und Johannes im Markus-evangelium», *TZ* 42 (1986) 366-374.

STEICHELE, H.-J., *Der Leidende Sohn Gottes*, Regensburg 1980.

STEIN, R.H., «A Short Note on Mark XIV.28 and XVI.7», *NTS* 20 (1973-1974) 445-452.

STEINHAUSER, M.G., «The Form of the Bartimaeus Narrative (Mark 10,46-52)», *NTS* 32 (1986) 583-595.

STOCK, A., *Call to Discipleship. A Literary Study of Mark's Gospel*, Wilmington 1982.

STOCK, K., *Boten aus dem Mit-Ihm-Sein*, AnBib 70, Rome 1975.

————, «Das Bekenntnis des Centurio. Mk 15,39 im Rahmen des Markusevangeliums», *ZKT* 100 (1978) 289-301.

————, «Die Machttaten Jesu. Ihr Zeugnis in den synoptischen Evangelien», *Communio* 18/3 (1989) 195-206.

————, «Gliederung und Zusammenhang in Mk 11-12», *Bib* 59 (1978) 481-515.

————, «I discepoli nel vangelo di san Marco», in L. CILIA, ed., *Marco e il suo vangelo*. Atti del convegno internazionale di studi «Il vangelo di Marco», Venezia, 30-31 Maggio 1995, Milano 1997, 17-32.

————, «Il discepolo di Gesù nei vangeli sinottici», in S.A. PANIMOLLE, ed., *Dizionario di Spiritualità Biblico-Patristica* 4. Apostolato – Discepolo – Missione, Roma 1992, 88-104.

————, «La conoscenza dei demoni (Mc 1,34)», *PSV* 18 (1988) 93-112.

————, «Theologie der Mission bei Markus», in K. KERTELGE, ed., *Mission im Neuen Testament*, Freiburg – Basel – Wien 1982, 130-144.

STRAUSS, D.F., *Das Leben Jesu. Kritisch bearbeitet*, Tübingen 1840; English trans., *The Life of Jesus Critically Examined*, tr. G. ELIOT, Philadelphia 1972.

SWETNAM, J., «On the Identity of Jesus», *Bib* 65 (1984) 412-416.

TANNEHILL, R.C., «The Disciples in Mark: The Function of a Narrative Role», *JR* 57 (1977) 386-405.

TELFER, W., «The Form of a Dove», *JTS* 29 (1928) 238-242.

TELFORD, W.R., *The Theology of the Gospel of Mark*, Cambridge 1999.

THEISSEN, G., *Urchristliche Wundergeschichten. Ein Beitrag zur Form-geschichtlichen Erforschung der Synoptischen Evangelien*, Gütersloh 1974; English trans., *The Miracle Stories of the Early Christian Tradition*, tr. F. McDonagh, Edinburgh 1983.

TOLBERT, M.A., *Sowing the Gospel*, Minneapolis 1989.

TOOLEY, W., «The Shepherd and Sheep Image in the Teaching of Jesus», *NT* 7 (1964) 15-25.

TURNER, C.H., «ὁ υἱος μου ὁ ἀγαπητός», *JTS* 27 (1925/26) 113-129.

————, «Marcan Usage: Notes, Critical and Exegetical, on the Second Gospel», *JTS* 26 (1925) 12-20, 225-240.

TURNER, N., *Grammatical Insights into the New Testament*, Edinburgh 1966.

ULANSEY, D., «The Heavenly Veil Torn: Mark's Cosmic Inclusio», *JBL* 110 (1991) 123-125.

VANCIL, J.W., «Sheep, Shepherd», *ABD* 5, 1187-1190.

VANHOYE, A., «La fuite du jeune homme nu (Mc 14,51-52)», *Bib* 52 (1971) 401-406.

VERMES, G., *Scripture and Tradition in Judaism*, Leiden 1961.

VIA, D.O., *The Ethics of Mark's Gospel - in the Middle of Time*, Philadelphia 1985.

VIELHAUER, P., «Erwägungen zur Christologie des Markusevangeliums», in ID., *Aufsätze zum Neuen Testament*, München 1965, 199-214.

VIGNOLO, R., «Cercare Gesù: tema e forma del vangelo di Marco», in L. CILIA, ed., *Marco e il suo vangelo*. Atti del convegno internazionale di studi «Il vangelo di Marco», Venezia, 30-31 Maggio 1995, Milano 1997, 77-114.

————, «Una finale reticente. Interpretazione narrativa di Mc 16,8», *RBI* 38 (1990) 129-189.

VÖGTLE, A., *Offenbarungsgeschehen und Wirkungsgeschichte*, Freiburg 1985.

VOLLENWEIDER, S., «"Ich sah den Satan wie einen Blitz vom Himmel fallen" (Lk 10 18)», *ZNW* 79 (1988) 187-203.

VORSTER, W.S., «Characterisation of Peter in the Gospel of Mark», *Neot* 21 (1987) 57-76.

VOUGA, F., *Jésus et la loi selon la tradition synoptique*, Genève 1988.

WEBB, R.L., «John the Baptist and His Relationship to Jesus» in B. CHILTON – C.A. EVANS, ed., *Studying the Historical Jesus: Evaluations of the State of Current Research*, Leiden 1994, 179-229.

WEEDEN, T.J., *Mark – Traditions in Conflict*, Philadelphia 1971.

————, «The Heresy that Necessitated Mark's Gospel», *ZNW* 59 (1968) 145-158.

WEISS, J., *Earliest Christianity. A History of the Period A. D. 30–150* I, New York 1959.

WENDLING, E., *Die Entstehung des Marcus-Evangeliums*, Tübingen 1908.

WIARDA, T., «Peter as Peter in the Gospel of Mark», *NTS* 45 (1999) 19-37.

WILCOX, M., «The Denial-Sequence in Mark XIV. 26-31, 66-72», *NTS* 17 (1970-71) 426-436.

WILLIAMS, J.F., «Mission in Mark», in W.J. LARKIN – J.F. WILLIAMS, ed., *Mission in the New Testament. An Evangelical Approach*, Maryknoll 1998, 137-151.

WINK, W., *John the Baptist in the Gospel Tradition*, SNTSMS 51, Cambridge 1968.

WREDE, W., *The Messianic Secret*, Cambridge 1971.

WUELLNER, W.H., *The Meaning of «Fishers of Men»*, Philadelphia 1967.

WYNNE, G.R., «Mending their Nets», *ExpTim* 7/8 (1909) 282-285.

YATES, J.E., «The Form of Mk 1. 8B "I Baptised you with Water; he will Baptise you with the Holy Spirit"», *NTS* 4 (1958) 334-338.

ZERWICK, M. – GROSVENOR, M., *A Grammatical Analysis of the Greek New Testament*, Roma 1993[4].

ZERWICK, M., *Biblical Greek*, Rome 1963.

————, *Untersuchungen zum Markus-Stil. Ein Beitrag zur stilistischen Durcharbeitung des Neuen Testaments*, Roma 1937.

ZIENER, G., «Die Brotwunder im Markusevangelium», *BZ* 4 (1960) 282-285.

INDEX OF AUTHORS

TABLE OF CONTENTS

TESI GREGORIANA

Since 1995, the series «Tesi Gregoriana» has made available to the general public some of the best doctoral theses done at the Pontifical Gregorian University. The typesetting is done by the authors themselves following norms established and controlled by the University.

Published Volumes [Series: Theology]

1. NELLO FIGA, Antonio, *Teorema de la opción fundamental. Bases para su adecuada utilización en teología moral*, 1995, pp. 380.

2. BENTOGLIO, Gabriele, *Apertura e disponibilità. L'accoglienza nell'epistolario paolino*, 1995, pp. 376.

3. PISO, Alfeu, *Igreja e sacramentos. Renovação da Teologia Sacramentária na América Latina*, 1995, pp. 260.

4. PALAKEEL, Joseph, *The Use of Analogy in Theological Discourse. An Investigation in Ecumenical Perspective*, 1995, pp. 392.

5. KIZHAKKEPARAMPIL, Isaac, *The Invocation of the Holy Spirit as Constitutive of the Sacraments according to Cardinal Yves Congar*, 1995, pp. 200.

6. MROSO, Agapit J., *The Church in Africa and the New Evangelisation. A Theologico-Pastoral Study of the Orientations of John Paul II*, 1995, pp. 456.

7. NANGELIMALIL, Jacob, *The Relationship between the Eucharistic Liturgy, the Interior Life and the Social Witness of the Church according to Joseph Cardinal Parecattil*, 1996, pp. 224.

8. GIBBS, Philip, *The Word in the Third World. Divine Revelation in the Theology of Jen-Marc Éla, Aloysius Pieris and Gustavo Gutiérrez*, 1996, pp. 448.

9. DELL'ORO, Roberto, *Esperienza morale e persona. Per una reinterpretazione dell'etica fenomenologica di Dietrich von Hildebrand*, 1996, pp. 240.

10. BELLANDI, Andrea, *Fede cristiana come «stare e comprendere». La giustificazione dei fondamenti della fede in Joseph Ratzinger*, 1996, pp. 416.

11. BEDRIÑAN, Claudio, *La dimensión socio-política del mensaje teológico del Apocalipsis*, 1996, pp. 364.

12. GWYNNE, Paul, *Special Divine Action. Key Issues in the Contemporary Debate (1965-1995)*, 1996, pp. 376.

13. NIÑO, Francisco, *La Iglesia en la ciudad. El fenómeno de las grandes ciudades en América Latina, como problema teológico y como desafío pastoral*, 1996, pp. 492.

14. BRODEUR, Scott, *The Holy Spirit's Agency in the Resurrection of the Dead. An Exegetico-Theological Study of 1 Corinthians 15,44b-49 and Romans 8,9-13*, 1996, pp. 300.

15. ZAMBON, Gaudenzio, *Laicato e tipologie ecclesiali. Ricerca storica sulla «Teologia del laicato» in Italia alla luce del Concilio Vaticano II (1950-1980)*, 1996, pp. 548.

16. ALVES DE MELO, Antonio, *A Evangelização no Brasil. Dimensões teológicas e desafios pastorais. O debate teológico e eclesial (1952-1995)*, 1996, pp. 428.

17. APARICIO VALLS, María del Carmen, *La plenitud del ser humano en Cristo. La Revelación en la «Gaudium et Spes»*, 1997, pp. 308.

18. MARTIN, Seán Charles, *«Pauli Testamentum». 2 Timothy and the Last Words of Moses*, 1997, pp. 312.

19. RUSH, Ormond, *The Reception of Doctrine. An Appropriation of Hans Robert Jauss' Reception Aesthetics and Literary Hermeneutics*, 1997, pp. 424.

20. MIMEAULT, Jules, *La sotériologie de François-Xavier Durrwell. Exposé et réflexions critiques*, 1997, pp. 476.

21. CAPIZZI, Nunzio, *L'uso di Fil 2,6-11 nella cristologia contemporanea (1965-1993)*, 1997, pp. 528.

22. NANDKISORE, Robert, *Hoffnung auf Erlösung. Die Eschatologie im Werk Hans Urs von Balthasars*, 1997, pp. 304.

23. PERKOVIĆ, Marinko, *«Il cammino a Dio» e «La direzione alla vita»: L'ordine morale nelle opere di Jordan Kuničić, O.P. (1908-1974)*, 1997, pp. 336.

24. DOMERGUE, Benoît, *La réincarnation et la divinisation de l'homme dans les religions. Approche phénomenologique et théologique*, 1997, pp. 300.

25. FARKAŠ, Pavol, *La «donna» di Apocalisse 12. Storia, bilancio, nuove prospettive*, 1997, pp. 276.

26. OLIVER, Robert W., *The Vocation of the Laity to Evangelization. An Ecclesiological Inquiry into the Synod on the Laity (1987)*, Christifideles laici *(1989) and Documents of the NCCB (1987-1996)*, 1997, pp. 364.

27. SPATAFORA, Andrea, *From the «Temple of God» to God as the Temple. A Biblical Theological Study of the Temple in the Book of Revelation*, 1997, pp. 340.

28. IACOBONE, Pasquale, *Mysterium Trinitatis. Dogma e Iconografia nell'Italia medievale*, 1997, pp. 512.

29. CASTAÑO FONSECA, Adolfo M., *Δικαιοσύνη en Mateo. Una interpretación teológica a partir de 3,15 y 21,32*, 1997, pp. 344.

30. CABRIA ORTEGA, José Luis, *Relación teología-filosofía en el pensamiento de Xavier Zubiri*, 1997, pp. 580.

31. SCHERRER, Thierry, *La gloire de Dieu dans l'oeuvre de saint Irénée*, 1997, pp. 328.

32. PASCUZZI, Maria, *Ethics, Ecclesiology and Church Discipline. A Rhetorical Analysis of 1Cor 5,1-13*, 1997, pp. 240.

33. LOPES GONÇALVES, Paulo Sérgio, *Liberationis mysterium. O projeto sistemático da teologia da libertação. Um estudo teológico na perspectiva da regula fidei*, 1997, pp. 464.

34. KOLACINSKI, Mariusz, *Dio fonte del diritto naturale*, 1997, pp. 296.

35. LIMA CORRÊA, Maria de Lourdes, *Salvação entre juízo, conversão e graça. A perspectiva escatológica de Os 14,2-9*, 1998, pp. 360.

36. MEIATTINI, Giulio, *«Sentire cum Christo». La teologia dell'esperienza cristiana nell'opera di H.U. von Balthasar*, 1998, pp. 432.

37. KESSLER, Thomas W., *Peter as the First Witness of the Risen Lord. An Historical and Theological Investigation*, 1998, pp. 240.

38. BIORD CASTILLO Raúl, *La Resurrección de Cristo como Revelación. Análisis del tema en la teología fundamental a partir de la* Dei Verbum, 1998, pp. 308.

39. LÓPEZ, Javier, *La figura de la bestia entre historia y profecía. Investigación teológico-bíblica de Apocalipsis 13,1-8*, 1998, pp. 308.

40. SCARAFONI, Paolo, *Amore salvifico. Una lettura del mistero della salvezza. Uno studio comparativo di alcune soteriologie cattoliche postconciliari*, 1998, pp. 240.

41. BARRIOS PRIETO, Manuel Enrique, *Antropologia teologica. Temi principali di antropologia teologica usando un metodo di «correlazione» a partire dalle opere di John Macquarrie*, 1998, pp. 416.

42. LEWIS, Scott M., *«So That God May Be All in All». The Apocalyptic Message of 1 Corinthians 15,12-34*, 1998, pp. 252.

43. ROSSETTI, Carlo Lorenzo, *«Sei diventato Tempio di Dio». Il mistero del Tempio e dell'abitazione divina negli scritti di Origene*, 1998, pp. 232.

44. CERVERA BARRANCO, Pablo, *La incorporación en la Iglesia mediante el bautismo y la profesión de la fe según el Concilio Vaticano II*, 1998, pp. 372.

45. NETO, Laudelino, *Fé cristã e cultura latino-americana. Uma análise a partir das Conferências de Puebla e Santo Domingo*, 1998, pp. 340.

46. BRITO GUIMARÃES, Pedro, *Os sacramentos como atos eclesiais e proféticos. Um contributo ao conceito dogmático de sacramento à luz da exegese contemporânea*, 1998, pp. 448.

47. CALABRETTA, Rose B., *Baptism and Confirmation. The Vocation and Mission of the Laity in the Writings of Virgil Michel, O.S.B.*, 1998, pp. 320.

48. OTERO LÁZARO, Tomás, *Col 1,15-20 en el contexto de la carta*, 1999, pp.312.

49. KOWALCZYK, Dariusz, *La personalità in Dio. Dal metodo trascendentale di Karl Rahner verso un orientamento dialogico in Heinrich Ott*, 1999, pp. 484.

50. PRIOR, Joseph G., *The Historical-Critical Method in Catholic Exegesis*, 1999, pp. 352.

51. CAHILL, Brendan J, *The Renewal of Revelation Theology (1960-1962). The Development and Responses to the Fourth Chapter of the Preparatory Schema* De deposito Fidei, 1999, pp. 348.

52. TIEZZI, Ida, *Il rapporto tra la pneumatologia e l'ecclesiologia nella teologia italiana post-conciliare*, 1999, pp. 364.

53. HOLC, Paweł, *Un ampio consenso sulla dottrina della giustificazione. Studio sul dialogo teologico cattolico luterano*, 1999, pp. 452.

54. GAINO, Andrea, *Esistenza cristiana. Il pensiero teologico di J. Alfaro e la sua rilevanza morale*, 1999, pp. 344.

55. NERI, Francesco, *«Cur Verbum capax hominis». Le ragioni dell'incarnazione della seconda Persona della Trinità fra teologia scolastica e teologia contemporanea*, 1999, pp. 404.

56. MUÑOZ CÁRDABA, Luis-Miguel, *Principios eclesiológicos de la «Pastor Bonus»*, 1999, pp. 344.

57. IWE, John Chijioke, *Jesus in the Synagogue of Capernaum: the Pericope and Its Programmatic Character for the Gospel of Mark. An Exegetico-Theological Study of Mk 1:21-28*, 1999, pp. 364.

58. BARRIOCANAL GÓMEZ, José Luis, *La relectura de la tradición del éxodo en l libro de Amós*, 2000, pp. 332.

59. DE LOS SANTOS GARCÍA, Edmundo, *La novedad de la metáfora κεφαλή – σῶμα en la carta a los Efesios*, 2000, pp. 432.

60. RESTREPO SIERRA, Argiro, *La revelación según R. Latourelle*, 2000, pp. 442.

61. DI GIOVAMBATTISTA, Fulvio, *Il giorno dell'espiazione nella Lettera agli Ebrei*, 2000, pp. 232.

62. GIUSTOZZO, Massimo, *Il nesso tra il culto e la grazia eucaristica nella recente lettura teologica del pensiero agostiniano*, 2000, pp. 456.

63. PESARCHICK, Robert A., *The Trinitarian Foundation of Human Sexuality as Revealed by Christ according to Hans Urs von Balthasar. The Revelatory Significance of the Male Christ and the Male Ministerial Priesthood*, 2000, pp. 328.

64. SIMON, László T., *Identity and Identification. An Exegetical Study of 2Sam 21–24*, 2000. pp. 386.

65. TAKAYAMA, Sadami, *Shinran's Conversion in the Light of Paul's Conversion*, 2000, pp. 256.

66. JUAN MORADO, Guillermo, *«También nosotros creemos porque amamos». Tres concepciones del acto de fe: Newman, Blondel, Garrigou-Lagrange. Estudio comparativo desde la perspectiva teológico-fundamental*, 2000, pp. 444.

67. MAREČEK, Petr, *La preghiera di Gesù nel vangelo di Matteo. Uno studio esegetico-teologico*, 2000, pp. 246.

68. WODKA, Andrzej, *Una teologia biblica del dare nel contesto della colletta paolina (2Cor 8–9)*, 2000, pp. 356.

69. LANGELLA, Maria Rigel, *Salvezza come illuminazione. Uno studio comparato di S. Bulgakov, V. Lossky, P. Evdokimov*, 2000, pp. 292.

70. RUDELLI, Paolo, *Matrimonio come scelta di vita: opzione – vocazione – sacramento*, 2000, pp. 424.

71. GAŠPAR, Veronika, *Cristologia pneumatologica in alcuni autori cattolici postconciliari. Status quaestionis e prospettive*, 2000, pp. 440.

72. GJORGJEVSKI, Gjoko, *Enigma degli enigmi. Un contributo allo studio della composizione della raccolta salomonica (Pr 10,1–22,16)*, 2001, pp. 304.

73. LINGAD, Celestino G., Jr., *The Problems of Jewish Christians in the Johannine Community*, 2001, pp. 492.

74. MASALLES, Victor, *La profecía en la asamblea cristiana. Análisis retórico-literario de 1Cor 14,1-25*, 2001, pp. 416.

75. FIGUEIREDO, Anthony J., *The Magisterium-Theology Relationship. Contemporary Theological Conceptions in the Light of Universal Church Teaching since 1835 and the Pronouncements of the Bishops of the United States*, 2001, pp. 536.

76. PARDO IZAL, José Javier, *Pasión por un futuro imposible. Estudio literario-teológico de Jeremías 32*, 2001, pp. 412.

77. HANNA, Kamal Fahim Awad, *La passione di Cristo nell'Apocalisse*, 2001, pp. 480.

78. ALBANESI, Nicola, *«Cur Deus Homo»: la logica della redenzione. Studio sulla teoria della soddisfazione di S. Anselmo arcivescovo di Canterbury*, 2001, pp. 244.

79. ADE, Edouard, *Le temps de l'Eglise. Esquisse d'une théologie de l'histoire selon Hans Urs von Balthasar*, 2002, pp. 368.

80. MENÉNDEZ MARTÍNEZ, Valentín, *La misión de la Iglesia. Un estdio sobre el debate teológico y eclesial en América Latina (1955-1992), con atención al aporte de algunos teólogos de la Compañía de Jesús*, 2002, pp. 344.

81. COSTA, Paulo Cezar, *«Salvatoris Disciplina». Dionísio de Roma e a Regula fidei no debate teológico do terceiro século*, 2002, pp. 272

82. PUTHUSSERY, Johnson, *Days of Man and God's Day. An Exegetico-Theological Study of ἡμέρα in the Book of Revelation*, 2002, pp. 332.

83. BARROS, Paulo César, *«Commendatur vobis in isto pane quomodo unitatem amare debeatis». A eclesiologia eucarística nos* Sermones ad populum *de Agostinho de Hipona e o movimento ecumênico*, 2002, pp. 344.

84. PALACHUVATTIL, Joy, *«He Saw». The Significance of Jesus' Seeing Denoted by the Verb* εἶδεν *in the Gospel of Mark*, 2002, pp. 312.

Finito di stampare
il 19 marzo 2002

presso la tipografia
"Giovanni Olivieri" di E. Montefoschi
00187 Roma - Via dell'Archetto, 10,11,12